'The grim reality of today's crises could not be more alerting of the need to expedite implementation of the responsibility to protect. This book invites reflection and provides practical suggestions on moving beyond rhetorical and reiterated commitments to developing practical agendas for action; not only by international actors in inter-governmental fora, but also by regional and national actors at the domestic level, where the most significant potential for strengthening atrocity prevention resides. Ultimately, effective prevention requires informed, coordinated, and timely action by all those in a position to turn this noble aspiration into a solid and sustained reality.'

Adama Dieng, *Under-Secretary-General, Special Adviser of the Secretary-General on the Prevention of Genocide*

'This book is an important and useful resource for all actors that are committed to applying atrocity prevention in practice. As we witness unimaginable atrocities in various parts of the world, policy makers have to take practical steps to implement their responsibility to protect populations from mass atrocities. Jacob and Mennecke provide much needed input to this process through a set of highly instructive essays.'

Christian Leffler, *R2P Focal Point of the European Union, Deputy-Secretary General of the EU's European External Action Service*

'This multi-disciplinary collection speaks to both critics and supporters of R2P. For the former, it provides evidence that R2P has in fact translated "words into deeds". For the latter, it demonstrates that R2P can – and must – extend beyond the United Nations to regions and national contexts, but also beyond governments to key domestic stakeholders. The book usefully points to new avenues through which R2P's objectives can be realised, given the more challenging geopolitical context in which the norm will be debated and the increasing fragmentation of conflicts and societies that heighten the risk of atrocity crimes.'

Jennifer Welsh, *Canada 150 Research Chair in Global Governance and Security at McGill University, and former Special Adviser to the UN Secretary General on the Responsibility to Protect*

'An impressive and timely contribution to the ongoing reflection on how to translate norms and political commitments into effective actions to prevent atrocities in our changing world.'

Judge Silvia Fernandez de Gurmendi, *former President of the International Criminal Court and incoming Chair of the Global Action against Mass Atrocity Crimes (GAAMAC)*

'The timeliness of Jacob and Mennecke's book is all to stark. For those who today face bombardment in Syria, or persecution in Myanmar, the Responsibility to Protect is not an academic enterprise. Rather, it is a life-saving emerging norm, the implementation of which needs to be accelerated. Thus, the political debates and at times political theater outlined in the book will provide them with little solace. But for practitioners, this book is a necessary resource in the process of translating norms and theory into live-saving practice. Only by undertaking a frank assessment of efforts thus far, the arguments for and against R2P, and the outlining of real-world examples of how to implement R2P will be able to collectively turn rhetoric into reality and narrow the gap between expectation and the lived realities of those who face a daily risk of atrocities.'

Naomi Kikoler, *Acting Director, Simon-Skjodt Center for the Prevention of Genocide, United States Holocaust Memorial Museum*

'The Responsibility to Protect (R2P) is the organising principle for the international community to respond to mass atrocities inside sovereign borders. For over a decade, the United Nations has emphasized the importance of moving from the words endorsed unanimously in 2005 to deeds. This timely, important and international collection of essays addresses the protection and prevention record to date, and how the remaining implementation gaps might be filled by relevant actors and institutions.'

Professor Emeritus Ramesh Thakur, *The Australian National University*

'This book by Jacob and Mennecke focuses on the uneven and imperfect reality of the implementation of the norm of the Responsibility to Protect (R2P) over the past decade. At a time when 68.5 million people are displaced by persecution, conflict, and atrocities, this book examines the gap between the rapid advance of R2P as a mobilizing principle of international diplomacy, and the harsh reality of the failure to halt atrocities in Syria, Yemen, Myanmar, and elsewhere. This book offers unique and practical perspectives on how we can work together to ensure that the failures of the past are not endlessly repeated. It is a book that is committed to enhancing the policy and practice of atrocity prevention.'

Dr Simon Adams, *Executive Director, Global Centre for the Responsibility to Protect*

'This book is a very useful tool for policymakers and practitioners; it demystifies R2P, and unpacks and situates it within our everyday life.'

Ms Felistas Mushi, *Chairperson of Tanzania's National Committee on the Prevention and Punishment of Genocide, Crimes against Humanity, War Crimes and all Forms of Discrimination*

IMPLEMENTING THE RESPONSIBILITY TO PROTECT

This book examines core thematic approaches to the Responsibility to Protect (R2P) and analyzes case studies regarding the implementation of this important global norm.

The volume analyzes this process at international, regional and local levels, and identifies an urgent need to progress from conceptual debates toward implementation in practice, in order to understand how to operationalize the preventive dimension of the R2P. It argues that R2P implementation necessarily entails the efforts of actors across governance levels, and that it is more effective when integrated into existing sites of practice aimed at strengthening human rights and accountability for populations in atrocity risk situations. The book addresses R2P implementation in the context of agendas such as resilience, gender, development cooperation, human rights, transitional justice, peacekeeping, and civil–military relations. It details progress and challenges for implementation in the United Nations, regionally in Africa, Europe and Southeast Asia, and through national atrocity prevention architectures. The volume provides readers with a breadth of understanding in terms of both the development and current status of the R2P norm, and practical tools for advancing its implementation.

This book will be of much interest to students of the Responsibility to Protect, Human Rights, Peace Studies, and International Relations in general.

Cecilia Jacob is a fellow in the Department of International Relations, the Australian National University, Canberra.

Martin Mennecke is associate professor of international law at the University of Southern Denmark and adviser to the R2P Focal Point in the Danish Foreign Ministry.

Global Politics and the Responsibility to Protect
Series Editors
Alex J. Bellamy *University of Queensland,*
Sara E. Davies, *Griffith University* and Monica Serrano *The City University of New York*

The aim of this book series is to gather the best new thinking about the Responsibility to Protect into a core set of volumes that provides a definitive account of the principle, its implementation, and its role in crises, that reflects a plurality of views and regional perspectives.

Evaluating the Responsibility to Protect
Mass Atrocity Prevention as a Consolidating Norm in International Society
Noële Crossley

International Organizations and the Rise of ISIL
Global Responses to Human Security Threats
Edited by Daniel Silander, Don Wallace and John Janzekovic

Reviewing the Responsibility to Protect
Origins, Implementation and Controversies
Ramesh Thakur

Ethics, Obligation, and the Responsibility to Protect
Contesting the Global Power Relations of Accountability
Mark Busser

Implementing the Responsibility to Protect
A Future Agenda
Edited by Cecilia Jacob and Martin Mennecke

For more information about this series, please visit: www.routledge.com/Global-Politics-and-the-Responsibility-to-Protect/book-series/GPRP

IMPLEMENTING THE RESPONSIBILITY TO PROTECT

A Future Agenda

Edited by Cecilia Jacob and Martin Mennecke

LONDON AND NEW YORK

First published 2020
by Routledge
2 Park Square, Milton Park, Abingdon, Oxon OX14 4RN

and by Routledge
52 Vanderbilt Avenue, New York, NY 10017

Routledge is an imprint of the Taylor & Francis Group, an informa business

© 2020 selection and editorial matter, Cecilia Jacob and Martin Mennecke; individual chapters, the contributors

The right of Cecilia Jacob and Martin Mennecke to be identified as the authors of the editorial material, and of the authors for their individual chapters, has been asserted in accordance with sections 77 and 78 of the Copyright, Designs and Patents Act 1988.

All rights reserved. No part of this book may be reprinted or reproduced or utilised in any form or by any electronic, mechanical, or other means, now known or hereafter invented, including photocopying and recording, or in any information storage or retrieval system, without permission in writing from the publishers.

Trademark notice: Product or corporate names may be trademarks or registered trademarks, and are used only for identification and explanation without intent to infringe.

British Library Cataloguing-in-Publication Data
A catalogue record for this book is available from the British Library

Library of Congress Cataloging-in-Publication Data
Names: Jacob, Cecilia, editor. | Mennecke, Martin, editor.
Title: Implementing the responsibility to protect : a future agenda / edited by Cecilia Jacob and Martin Mennecke.
Description: Abingdon, Oxon ; New York, NY : Routledge, 2020. | Series: Global politics and the responsibility to protect | Includes bibliographical references and index.
Identifiers: LCCN 2019018261 | ISBN 9780367265533 (hardback) | ISBN 9780367265526 (paperback) | ISBN 9780429293795 (ebook)
Subjects: LCSH: Responsibility to protect (International law)
Classification: LCC KZ4082 .I47 2020 | DDC 341.4/8—dc23
LC record available at https://lccn.loc.gov/2019018261

ISBN: 978-0-367-26553-3 (hbk)
ISBN: 978-0-367-26552-6 (pbk)
ISBN: 978-0-429-29379-5 (ebk)

Typeset in Bembo
by Apex CoVantage, LLC

Printed in the United Kingdom by Henry Ling Limited

CONTENTS

List of tables x
Preface xi
Notes on contributors xiii
List of abbreviations xv
Foreword xviii
Gareth Evans

    Introduction: the challenges of implementing the R2P norm 1
    Cecilia Jacob and Martin Mennecke

1 R2P as an atrocity-prevention framework: concepts and institutionalization at the global level 16
   Cecilia Jacob

PART I
National implementation mechanisms 35

2 Denmark and the implementation of R2P 37
   Martin Mennecke

3 Atrocity prevention under the Obama administration 61
   Stephen Pomper

PART II
Regional implementation mechanisms   87

4 ASEAN regionalism and capacity-building for atrocities prevention: challenges and prospects   89
Noel M. Morada

5 African experiences of R2P implementation   109
Frank O. Okyere

6 Europe's engagement with R2P in a transitional international order   124
Edward Newman and Cristina G. Stefan

PART III
Atrocity prevention   139

7 Atrocity prevention, national resilience, and implementation   141
Stephen McLoughlin

8 Atrocity prevention in practice: studying the role of Southeast Asian women in atrocity prevention   156
Sara E. Davies

PART IV
International legal accountability   177

9 Linking human rights accountability and compliance with R2P implementation   179
Ekkehard Strauss

10 Linking the past and the present: the contribution of transitional justice to security after complex conflicts   197
Susanne Karstedt and Michael Koch

PART V
Peacekeeping, civil–military assistance, and stabilization   213

11 Implementing R2P through United Nations peacekeeping operations: opportunities and challenges   215
Charles T. Hunt and Lisa Sharland

12 Civil–military relations and R2P: the Afghan experience   236
    William Maley

    Conclusion: R2P at a crossroads: implementation or
    marginalization   251
    Ivan Šimonović

Index   268

TABLES

4.1	ASEAN human rights protection principles in key documents	91
4.2	The ASEAN Human Rights Declaration: universal vs. relative principles	93
10.1	Transitional justice processes and post-conflict violence five years after the end of conflict	204
10.2	Start of transitional justice during and post-conflict: violence 1–5 and 6–10 years after the end of conflict	205
10.3	Amnesties for state and non-state agents: post-conflict violence (1–5 years)	207

PREFACE

The motivation for this book was a desire to advance the scholarly literature on the Responsibility to Protect (R2P) toward a more practical agenda, and to inform implementation on the ground. Currently, R2P is often described as a "UN norm," but it is high time that it starts to count most for the many people around the world caught up in situations of conflict and fragility. Therefore, the next generation of R2P scholarship needs to focus on practical solutions to strengthen the capacity of states and other actors to prevent mass atrocities. We hope that this volume will contribute to steering the literature into new and productive directions grounded in practice while providing R2P practitioners with useful input for their important work.

Many of the chapters in this volume were first presented as invited papers from leading experts at a two-day conference "Implementing the Responsibility to Protect: Domestic Processes and Foreign Assistance," hosted at The Australian National University in Canberra on October 26–27, 2016 (see Jacob 2017). Professor the Hon. Gareth Evans and the former UN Special Advisor to the Secretary-General on the Responsibility to Protect (2016–2018), Dr Ivan Šimonović, delivered keynote addresses, and contributed both to this volume. The conference sought to cut across academic and policy divides to foster coherent thinking around effective implementation in a number of related sectors and levels of governance, and to draw out lessons from case studies in the field. The conference prompted lively discussion and new conversations that we have sought to capture in this volume. We invited additional authors to contribute to the volume to expand the geographic and thematic dimensions of the book.

This project would not have been possible without the support of the Coral Bell School of Asia Pacific Affairs and the Department of International Relations in the College of Asia and the Pacific at The Australian National University, the Asia Pacific Centre for the Responsibility to Protect based at the University of

Queensland, and the Australian Department of Foreign Affairs and Trade (DFAT). Special thanks go to Professor Michael Wesley for embracing and supporting the concept of the project from its very first iteration, and also to Professor Alex Bellamy and Dr Mathew Davies for much valued support. We would also like to thank Patrick Lawless, Lara Nassau, and Sue Moore from DFAT in particular for their contributions. We also would like to appreciate the support provided by the Law Department of the University of Southern Denmark.

We also want to thank the participants of the conference who represented a wide cross-section of government agencies, diplomatic missions, think-tanks, civil society organizations, and academic experts who enriched the discussion and challenged the authors to move their arguments forward in their chapters. The contributions also confirmed the importance of turning academic attention to implementation, and the need for cross-fertilization of academic–practitioner ideas.

This edited volume taps into the rich and diverse expertise of scholars and practitioners from various fields and disciplines. Not all the contributors would identify themselves as R2P experts per se; rather they bring their expertise from fields such as law, criminology, political science, and international relations to weigh in on key dimensions of the R2P implementation agenda to delve deeper into these issues. We would like to thank the contributors for supporting the concept and vision of the project, and for being so patient in seeing the publication through with us.

We would like to thank the editorial team at Routledge, particularly Andrew Humphreys, for such professional and courteous management of the publication process, and to the three anonymous reviewers for providing very helpful comments on the manuscript. Our deep appreciation goes to Mary-Louise Hickey at The Australian National University for her meticulous editing of the full manuscript and her astounding patience and good humor. Finally, our strongest and ongoing support has come from our families; thank you to Chris Jacob and Alana Samson for your love and patience. This book is dedicated to our children for whom we continually strive for a better future – Yohann, Immanuel, Jude, and Lily.

Cecilia Jacob
Canberra

Martin Mennecke
Copenhagen

Reference

Jacob, Cecilia, 2017. "Implementing the Responsibility to Protect: Domestic Processes and Foreign Assistance," Conference Report (Canberra: Department of International Relations, ANU, July).

CONTRIBUTORS

Sara E. Davies is Associate Professor and Australian Research Council Future Fellow at the Centre for Governance and Public Policy, School of Government and International Relations, Griffith University.

Gareth Evans, AC QC FASSA FAIIA, is Chancellor and Honorary Professorial Fellow at The Australian National University, and Chair of the International Advisory Board of the Global Centre for the Responsibility to Protect. Former Australian Foreign Minister and President Emeritus of the International Crisis Group, he co-chaired the International Commission on Intervention and State Sovereignty.

Charles T. Hunt is a Vice Chancellor's Senior Research Fellow and ARC DECRA fellow in the Social and Global Studies Centre at RMIT University, and an honorary Senior Research Fellow at the Asia Pacific Centre for the Responsibility to Protect.

Cecilia Jacob is Fellow in the Department of International Relations, Coral Bell School of Asia Pacific Affairs, The Australian National University.

Susanne Karstedt is Professor in the School of Criminology and Criminal Justice, Griffith University.

Michael Koch is Head of Social Planning in the Department of Social Affairs of Detmold, Germany.

William Maley is Professor of Diplomacy at the Asia-Pacific College of Diplomacy, Coral Bell School of Asia Pacific Affairs, The Australian National University.

Stephen McLoughlin is Lecturer in International Relations at Liverpool Hope University.

Martin Mennecke is Associate Professor, Department of Law, University of Southern Denmark, and Academic Adviser on Responsibility to Protect to the Danish Ministry of Foreign Affairs.

Noel M. Morada is Director, Regional Diplomacy and Capacity Building, at the University of Queensland.

Edward Newman is Professor of International Security at the School of Politics and International Studies, University of Leeds.

Frank O. Okyere is Research Associate and Training Facilitator at the Faculty of Academic Affairs and Research, Kofi Annan International Peacekeeping Training Centre, Ghana.

Stephen Pomper was Special Assistant to President and Senior Director for Multilateral Affairs and Human Rights at the US National Security Council during President Barack Obama's second term.

Lisa Sharland is the Head of International Program at the Australian Strategic Policy Institute (ASPI) and a non-resident fellow in the Protecting Civilians in Conflict Program at the Stimson Center in Washington, DC.

Ivan Šimonović is Professor of Law at the University of Zagreb, Croatia. He has served as the UN Special Advisor to the Secretary-General on the Responsibility to Protect (2016–2018). Prior to this, Dr. Šimonović was Assistant Secretary-General for Human Rights and Head of the Office of the High Commissioner for Human Rights in New York. Before joining the United Nations in 2010, Dr. Šimonović held the position of Minister for Justice of Croatia. He was previously Deputy Minister for Foreign Affairs and Permanent Representative to the United Nations in New York, where he served as President of the Economic and Social Council.

Cristina G. Stefan is Associate Professor of International Relations at the School of Politics and International Studies, University of Leeds, and a Founding Director of the European Centre for the Responsibility to Protect (ECR2P).

Ekkehard Strauss served in different functions with the OSCE and the UN in Geneva, New York, and the field, most recently as Representative of the UN High Commissioner for Human Rights in Mauritania (2013–2018).

ABBREVIATIONS

ACWC	ASEAN Commission on the Promotion and Protection of the Rights of Women and Children
AHRD	ASEAN Human Rights Declaration
AICHR	ASEAN Inter-Governmental Commission on Human Rights
AIPR	ASEAN Institute for Peace and Reconciliation
APB	Atrocities Prevention Board
APCR2P	Asia Pacific Centre for the Responsibility to Protect
ARSA	Arakan Rohingya Salvation Army
ASEAN	Association of Southeast Asian Nations
ASEAN–ERAT	ASEAN–Emergency Rapid Assessment Team
AU	African Union
BRICS	Brazil, Russia, India, China, and South Africa
CAR	Central African Republic
CEDAW	Convention on the Elimination of All Forms of Discrimination Against Women
CONUN	United Nations Working Party
DDR	disarmament, demobilization, and reintegration
DPKO/DFS	Department of Peacekeeping Operations and Department of Field Support
DPPA	Department of Political and Peacebuilding Affairs
DRC	Democratic Republic of the Congo
ECCAS	Economic Community of Central African States
ECOMOG	Economic Community of West African States Monitoring Group
ECOWAS	Economic Community of West African States
EU	European Union
FARDC	Forces Armées de la République Démocratique du Congo

FIB	Force Intervention Brigade
GAAMAC	Global Action Against Mass Atrocity Crimes
GDP	gross domestic product
GEN	Gender Equality Network
HRC	Human Rights Council
HRuF	Human Rights up Front
ICC	International Criminal Court
ICGLR	International Conference on the Great Lakes Region
ICISS	International Commission on Intervention and State Sovereignty
IGAD	Intergovernmental Authority on Development
IPC	interagency policy committee
ISAF	International Security Assistance Force
ISI	Inter-Services Intelligence
ISIS	Islamic State of Iraq and Syria
LGBT	lesbian, gay, bisexual, and transgender
M23	*Mouvement du 23 Mars*
MINUSCA	United Nations Multidimensional Integrated Stabilization Mission in the Central African Republic
MONUC	United Nations Organization Mission in the Democratic Republic of the Congo
MONUSCO	United Nations Organization Stabilization Mission in the Democratic Republic of the Congo
NAP	National Action Plan
NATO	North Atlantic Treaty Organization
NGO	non-governmental organization
NIE	National Intelligence Estimate
NLD	National League for Democracy
NSC	National Security Council
OHCHR	Office of the United Nations High Commissioner for Human Rights
OIC	Organisation of Islamic Cooperation
ONUC	Opération des Nations Unies au Congo
P5	Permanent Five
POC	protection of civilians
PRIO	Peace Research Institute Oslo
PRT	Provincial Reconstruction Team
PSD10	Presidential Study Directive 10
PTS	Political Terror Scale
R2P	Responsibility to Protect
REC	Regional Economic Community
RFJ	Rewards for Justice
SADC	Southern African Development Community
SDG	Sustainable Development Goal
START	Study of Terrorism and Responses to Terrorism

T/PCCs	troop and police contributing countries
TANU	Tanganyika African National Union
TRC	truth (and reconciliation) commission
UN	United Nations
UNAMID	African Union–United Nations Mission in Darfur
UNAMSIL	United Nations Mission in Sierra Leone
UNGA	United Nations General Assembly
UNMIS	United Nations Mission in Sudan
UNMISS	United Nations Mission in South Sudan
UNOCI	United Nations Operation in Côte d'Ivoire
UNSC	United Nations Security Council
UNSG	United Nations Secretary-General
UPR	Universal Periodic Review
USAID	United States Agency for International Development
USUN	US Mission to the United Nations
VSI	Violent Societies Index
WPS	Women, Peace and Security

FOREWORD

In a world as full of cynicism, double standards, crude assertions of national interest, and realpolitik as ours continues to be, it is very easy to believe that ideas do not matter very much. Achieving fundamental change in the way states and their leaders think and behave is as hard as international relations gets. But that is exactly the task that those of us involved in the creation of the Responsibility to Protect (R2P) concept set out to achieve two decades ago.

With the horror of Cambodia in the 1970s repeated in a new explosion of genocidal violence in the Balkans and Central Africa in the 1990s, it had become apparent that, even after the horrors of the Holocaust and all the many developments in international human rights law and international humanitarian law that followed the Second World War, the international community was still a completely consensus-free zone when it came to the "right to intervene" to halt or avert mass atrocity crimes. As United Nations (UN) Secretary-General Kofi Annan lamented to the General Assembly in 2000: "If humanitarian intervention is, indeed, an unacceptable assault on sovereignty, how *should* we respond to a Rwanda, to a Srebrenica – to gross and systematic violations of human rights that offend every precept of our common humanity?" (Annan 2000, 34, emphasis in original).

That challenge was answered, and the beginnings of a new consensus forged, in the report in 2001 of the Canadian-sponsored International Commission on Intervention and State Sovereignty, which I had the pleasure and privilege of co-chairing. This initiated the breakthrough concept of the "responsibility to protect," which – by emphasizing "responsibility" rather than "right," "protection" rather than "intervention," and prevention as well as reaction – made it politically possible for the first time for the Global North and South to find common ground. Eventually, after a long and fraught diplomatic process, the UN General Assembly, sitting at head of state and government level at the 2005 World Summit, unanimously endorsed the principle of R2P, with its three distinctive pillars (although these pillars were not articulated quite so clearly as such until the Secretary-General's report to the Assembly four years later): the responsibility of a state to its own people not to either commit such mass atrocity crimes or allow them to occur (Pillar One); the responsibility of other states to assist those lacking the capacity to so protect (Pillar Two); and the responsibility of the international community to respond with "timely and decisive action" – including ultimately with coercive military force if that is authorized by the Security Council – if a state is "manifestly failing" to meet its protection responsibilities (Pillar Three).

The initiators of the R2P concept were trying neither to create new international legal rules nor undermine old ones. Our intended contribution was not to international relations theory, but political practice. We knew that in the real world, it was going to be hard to get perfect results, but we wanted to change the way that the world's policymakers, and those who influence them, thought and above all acted in response to emerging, imminent, and actually occurring mass atrocity crimes behind sovereign state walls. The bottom line was to change the habits of centuries by generating a reflex international response, not only in words but also in deeds, that genocide, other crimes against humanity, and major war crimes were everybody's business, not nobody's.

Looking at the catastrophic series of events in Syria, where R2P has gained no traction at all, largely because of negative reaction by the BRICS states (Brazil, Russia, India, China, and South Africa) to the initially successful – but then divisive and ultimately failed – military intervention in Libya in 2011, it would be easy to say that nothing has changed for the better. The continuing ugly situation in the Congo, the disastrous war in Yemen, and the terrible ethnic cleansing of Rohingya people in Myanmar have all further reinforced the cynics who say that this whole norm-building enterprise has been a waste of time – or worse. But measuring R2P against the four benchmarks we had in mind from the beginning – its role as a normative force, a catalyst for institutional change, and a framework for both prevention and effective reaction – my own assessment is more positive, albeit not remotely complacent.

Normatively, R2P has achieved a global take-up unimaginable for the earlier concept of "humanitarian intervention" which R2P has now rightly, and almost completely, displaced (a certain lingering US academic nostalgia for that language notwithstanding). True, many states are still clearly more comfortable with the first two pillars of R2P (the responsibility of all states to protect their own peoples and that of others to assist them) than they are with the third (the world's responsibility to react effectively, by measures extending from persuasion to coercion, when that protection fails). But there is no longer any serious dissent evident in relation to any of the elements of the 2005 Resolution. The best evidence lies in the General Assembly's annual interactive debates since 2009, which have shown ever stronger and more clearly articulated support for what is now widely accepted as a new political (if not legal) norm, and in the literally scores of resolutions specifically referencing R2P, in whole or part, that have continued to be passed by the Security Council.

Institutionally, more than fifty states and intergovernmental organizations have now established R2P "Focal Points" – designated high-level officials whose job is to analyze atrocity risk and mobilize appropriate responses. Civilian response capability is receiving much more organized attention, as is the need for militaries to rethink their force configuration, doctrine, rules of engagement, and training to deal better with mass atrocity response operations.

Preventively, R2P-driven strategies have had a number of notable successes, particularly in stopping the recurrence of strife in Kenya after 2008; in the West African cases of Sierra Leone, Liberia, Guinea, and Côte d'Ivoire over the last decade; and Kyrgyzstan after 2010. Volatile situations such as Burundi get the kind of continuing Security Council attention unknown to Rwanda in the 1990s. Strong civilian protection mandates are now the norm in peacekeeping operations. And the whole preventive toolkit, long and short term, structural and operational, is much better understood, albeit with action still often lagging behind rhetoric.

Reactively, however, where it matters most that R2P make a difference, it must be acknowledged that the record has been at best mixed. On the positive side are the success stories in Kenya in 2008, Côte d'Ivoire in 2011, and at least initially in Libya in 2011, and the partial success that can be claimed for UN operations in Congo, South Sudan, and the Central African Republic. But against this must be weighed serious failures in Sri Lanka, Sudan, above all in Syria, and most recently now Myanmar. Re-establishing Security Council consensus in these hardest of cases is not impossible, but it will take time. Brazil's "Responsibility While Protecting" proposal remains the most constructive of all the suggested ways forward, requiring as it would all Council members to debate more comprehensively the criteria that need to be met before any use of force is authorized and to accept close monitoring and review of any coercive military mandate throughout its lifetime.

By any historical standard, the speed and extent of the evolution of R2P, in the few short years since the idea was conceived, has been remarkable. My own strong instinct is that no policymakers anywhere in the world really want to see a return to the bad old days of Cambodia, Rwanda, and the Balkans. We sometimes forget just how bad those days were: for example, then US Secretary of State Henry Kissinger reportedly felt able to say to Thai Foreign Minister Chatichai Choonhavan in November 1975, seven months after the Khmer Rouge had commenced their genocidal reign of terror: "Tell the Cambodians that we will be friends with them. They are murderous thugs, but we won't let that stand in our way." As cynical as so many of our political leaders continue so often to be, I suspect the time really has gone when any of them could now feel able to talk like that.

All that said, achieving the complete *implementation* of R2P in all its necessary dimensions – the effective prevention of the occurrence, continuation, and recurrence of mass atrocity crimes – is still manifestly a work in progress. The task of the next generation of policymakers, and those who seek to influence them, is above all to turn largely accepted principles into consistently applied practice. This book will make a major contribution to achieving just that.

Gareth Evans

Reference

Annan, Kofi, 2000. "We the Peoples: The Role of the United Nations in the Twenty-First Century: Report of the Secretary-General," A/54/2000, March 27.

INTRODUCTION

The challenges of implementing the R2P norm

Cecilia Jacob and Martin Mennecke

Introduction

The international community has made significant progress in defining and consolidating the international Responsibility to Protect (R2P) norm since it was first introduced to the global political lexicon in 2001 (ICISS 2001). Importantly, strong international support for the responsibility of states to protect populations within borders from mass atrocities has been achieved. For example, the United Nations (UN) Security Council and other UN bodies have passed dozens of resolutions and presidential statements referencing R2P,[1] evidence that R2P has been acknowledged at the highest levels of international decision-making. In addition, in 2017 and 2018, the UN General Assembly voted with resounding majorities to make R2P a formal item of its agenda.

Yet, despite an ever-growing body of international rules, norms, and institutions dedicated to preventing, regulating, and ending violent conflict, untold human suffering continues around the world. In Syria, Yemen, the Congo, and Myanmar, to name a few, populations are subjected to systematic and targeted violence, forced to bear witness to horrendous suffering,[2] and propelled into deprivation through forced displacement and destroyed livelihoods. As the number of UN resolutions with references to R2P has increased, so too have trends in violent conflict and atrocities against civilians demonstrated an upward trajectory, with the year 2015 marking the return to the highest levels of violent conflict and fatalities since the end of the Cold War (Melander, Pettersson, and Themnér 2016).

This is the paradox of R2P implementation. The international community is struggling to translate normative commitments on human protection into tangible delivery on its core responsibilities to uphold human rights and protect civilians from mass atrocities. Mobilizing preventive or protection responses *during* contexts of heightened conflict has historically proven severely inadequate, and even counterproductive. Today, this coincides with a lack of understanding of what a "successful" R2P intervention might look like, and a marked return of major power competition, which in recent years, through shifting geopolitical dynamics, has moved the momentum and commitment on R2P objectives to the background.

Scholars have argued that a significant transformation of the post-Second World War international liberal order – characterized by open global markets, international institutionalism, and the promotion of democratic governance – is occurring (Slaughter 2004). Challenges to this international liberal order include first, a redistribution of global power away from the United States to a multipolar world that includes rising powers, such as China. These power reconfigurations may fundamentally alter the workings of multilateral organizations whose legitimacy and capacity to govern are contingent on the global political context (Thakur 2017). The second is the fragmentation of global conflicts at the regional and local level, a reality for which the United Nations was not designed (Weiss et al. 2014). Third is the growing populism and re-embracing of traditional sovereignty in populations and by leaders of countries that used to be key actors in the international liberal order.

In the context of waning global support for multilateralism, there is a need for a fundamental revaluation of, first, the context in which R2P is to be operationalized, and second, the avenues envisaged to achieve the broader objectives of the norm. On the first point, the 2001 International Commission on Intervention and State Sovereignty report on R2P was published in a specific historical moment; it was informed by the tragic failure of the international community to protect populations from genocide and ethnic cleansing in Rwanda and Bosnia, and uncertainty about the legitimacy of using military force for human protection purposes, as witnessed in Kosovo in 1999. The historical context in which R2P was birthed has steered the process of conceptual refinement of R2P toward a specific understanding of what mass atrocities look like without ever solving the dilemma of humanitarian intervention – i.e., the legal, ethical, political, and security implications of external military intervention into complex dynamics of violence within states, and in particular for situations when the UN Security Council cannot agree on authorizing a forceful response.

Today, many atrocities occur on a lower intensity than those of the genocides of the 1990s, or indeed those of the Cold War era, enduring over much more prolonged periods of conflict. Some of these conflicts have been sustained by interference by major powers and political solutions to these extended conflicts are yet to be forthcoming. Unique, therefore, is the conflation between two distinct trends of ongoing fragmentation and the prevalence of state-based armed conflict, with resurgent geopolitical and populist dynamics without the restraints of bipolarity and deterrence of the Cold War period. The confluence of these trends has ushered in a new paralysis in global decision-making and undermined the trust in international cooperative solutions to threats of mass atrocities and violent conflict.

From R2P as normative concept to R2P as preventive policy

The arrival of R2P at the United Nations in 2005 also made an impression on the scholarly literature. For example, the shift in emphasis from the special crime of genocide to the wider set of atrocity crimes encompassed by R2P unencumbered scholars from the narrow legal definition of "genocide" that had locked many researchers into contestation over defining incidents of mass atrocities as actual genocides. This shift allowed for the building up of a systematic analysis of the causes, dynamics, and effective tools for preventing a wider spectrum of massive human rights violations. Much of the early R2P literature centered on the concept's relation to the older idea of "humanitarian intervention" and the status of state sovereignty under the new R2P norm. This type of conceptual discussion was further facilitated by the 2009 report of the UN Secretary-General on R2P which introduced a three-pillar approach to the R2P concept, giving rise to writings on the content of the different pillars and their relationship to each other (Ban 2009). In 2011, another cluster of academic interest emerged as many articles were written on the NATO (North Atlantic Treaty Organization) intervention in Libya, its meaning for R2P, and whether it violated international law.

In response to shifting global political dynamics, international policymakers, scholars, and advocates of R2P have in recent years consciously redirected the focus of the debate on R2P toward the preventive and practical dimensions of the concept. There were a number of reasons for this strategic shift in the discussions on R2P.

First and most importantly, following the controversies surrounding the R2P-inspired intervention in Libya in 2011, there was an overriding political imperative among R2P proponents to rebuild the consensus on R2P in order to ensure its longevity and long-term acceptance. Sharp resistance among some states to the alleged misuse of R2P in Libya – namely, violations of the principles of sovereign integrity and non-interference – caused advocates of R2P to re-establish common ground on the less politically divisive framing of R2P as preventive norm. Indeed, R2P-critical states frequently assert that there is no disagreement on the fundamental imperative to prevent mass atrocity crimes, but rather point to a fear of abuse or misuse of the principle through an interventionist practice. This meant that beyond the specific context of the discussions on the Libya intervention, it seemed more promising to generate momentum for R2P by focusing on its role in atrocity *prevention*.

The second reason behind the fundamental reconsideration of the avenues envisaged to accomplish the objectives of R2P has been an overall strategic move within the UN system to prioritize prevention and political solutions to crises (Guterres 2017; see also United Nations Political Affairs 2015). The impetus for this broader organizational reform had its founding in the "Human Rights up Front" initiative to mainstream human rights and change the culture from one of reaction to prevention across the UN organization (Gilmour 2014; Kurtz 2015). This was a response by the UN to findings of "systemic failure" to prevent atrocity crimes in Sri Lanka in the final phases of the civil conflict in 2008–2009 (United Nations 2012). In 2015, three major reviews of UN peace operations, the implementation of the Women Peace and Security agenda, and the UN's peacebuilding architecture called for improved preventive capacity of the UN system, and prioritization of political solutions to violent conflict (United Nations 2015a, 2015b; UN Women 2015). Similarly, the new UN Secretary-General António Guterres made prevention one of his priorities.

Third, as the political salience of R2P has spread, there has been a greater interest and recognition among a widening cohort of intergovernmental organizations, member states, and non-state actors of their respective contributions to atrocity prevention. As the chapters in this volume attest, awareness increased both within various UN organs, such as the Human Rights Council, but also among other actors such as foreign affairs ministries of member states and civil society groups, of the importance of their work to strengthening the resilience of societies and redressing risk factors for atrocity. This means that practitioners have begun to consider new opportunities for implementing R2P objectives within their work in a wide variety of areas – foreign policy, development cooperation, civil–military assistance, human rights promotion, and transitional justice.[3]

Fourth and finally, the widening gap between R2P and other human rights norms, on the one hand, and the increasing number of situations in which populations are subjected to atrocity crimes, on the other hand, forced R2P proponents to turn R2P discussions from conceptual issues toward preventive policy and actual implementation. This need for "operationalization" has been stressed in numerous calls by the UN Secretary-General, the UN Special Advisor for R2P, and civil society, and has become a new mantra among R2P actors.

The motif behind this book

Notably, these newer trends have only partially been analyzed in the scholarly literature on R2P. For example, new mechanisms such as the establishment and work of national Focal Points to advance the national implementation of R2P or their Global Network have only received cursory attention in academic writing. The same applies to the cross-regional "Groups of Friends" that over fifty states have founded in both Geneva and New York to advance the role of R2P at the United Nations. Very little has been written on how states can unfold the preventive potential of R2P across government. By and large, the emerging R2P practice of states and other actors has been overlooked.

The aim of this book is therefore twofold. First, to advance the current R2P literature by adding multiple scholarly perspectives on what is meant by implementing and "operationalizing" R2P and to reflect critically on how such efforts differ from and go beyond regular human rights work and traditional conflict prevention.

Importantly, what does implementation mean for different actors situated in diverse national, institutional or political contexts, given their own vantage points and sets of unique challenges? Second, to provide policymakers and practitioners with analytical insights into the current state of affairs of R2P in practice. The book aims to push the R2P debate into new fields and an increasingly operational direction by looking at relevant examples and providing analysis that can help R2P Focal Points and others to carry out their mandates.

This book does not attempt to create a "one-size-fits-all" formula for R2P implementation. Rather, it lays out a conceptual and practical framework for understanding the nature of mass atrocities and atrocity prevention, and examines the implications of R2P for actors across the spectrum of political, legal, and security sectors for domestic and foreign policy agendas by looking at examples from different national and regional contexts.

The underlying assumption in this book is that R2P is much more effective in preventing atrocities if it shapes policy *prior* to the escalation of an atrocity risk, and where it serves to strengthen the resilience of societies to manage an atrocity risk *before* it occurs. A second assumption inherent in the book is that R2P is a universal responsibility shared by domestic stakeholders within and *beyond* the foreign ministries and national R2P Focal Points. While much of the theoretical work on R2P has established the responsibility of and discussed implications for the international community through the United Nations and forceful intervention, much less attention has been paid to how R2P may guide domestic institutions, foreign policy outside the United Nations, development, and security cooperation to where the potential for mitigating atrocity risk and strengthening resilience is optimal.

This book serves to broaden and deepen the scope of the R2P literature by emphasizing institutional sites and thematic agendas that have a strong bearing on the prevention of atrocities in practice. The approach diverges from the standard literature on R2P prevention that employs and stays limited to the "three-pillar" framework. The three pillars of R2P are the state's primary responsibility to prevent and protect populations, an international responsibility to assist with atrocity prevention and, in the case of state failure, to protect through international interventions, including the use of force as a last resort and if authorized by the UN Security Council. However, analyses generated by this framework tend to focus on the actions of the state as a monolithic whole, rather than unpacking the specific implications of R2P prevention for its constituent institutions, and stovepipes academic literature toward the international community's "third pillar" capacity for forceful intervention, constraining the scope of the debate and its practical applicability. By transcending these debates that structure the existing R2P literature, this volume introduces nuance and analysis into what the state and other actors can actually do at the domestic and regional levels to operationalize R2P to fulfill international responsibilities, and points to practical strategies that states can use to leverage their foreign engagements to enhance the atrocity-prevention agenda among partner states.

Key themes in the book

The approach of the edited volume is multidisciplinary, drawing on cutting-edge research in the fields of atrocity prevention, international relations, international law, criminology, governance and regulatory studies, and peace and conflict studies. Thematically, the book examines atrocity prevention, human rights, accountability, peacekeeping and civil–military operations, peacebuilding, transitional justice, and the rule of law in relation to R2P. Importantly, several chapters of this book build on the experience of key practitioners who have worked with the implementation of R2P in practice, both in national agencies and at the United Nations. The book thus provides firsthand insights into the challenges and prospects of turning R2P into an operational norm. Across the various chapters, the book investigates a number of cross-cutting themes that run through the volume, including the following.

The implementation of the international R2P norm through states, regional organizations, and non-state actors

The implementation of abstract international principles such as R2P into tangible policy agendas requires a deliberate translation and articulation of policy implications in varied institutional contexts. The contributors to the volume illustrate the salience of the R2P agenda to specific institutional domains such as the judiciary, policing, the military, and peacekeeping, and to specific thematic agendas such as atrocity prevention, human rights, peacebuilding, transitional justice, development cooperation, and the rule of law. In doing so, they not only expand the implementation agenda to practical domains that have close proximity to the social and political contexts where the risk of atrocity crimes are addressed, but they also provide substance to the broader international norms debates around explaining where, how, and to what degree international norms affect actors' behavior. These insights contribute to meta-level theoretical approaches that emphasize the role of international norms in shaping the preferences and behavior of actors (state and non-state) that is prominent in international relations, and that carve out appropriate mechanisms for compliance and refinement of the rules in areas regulated by international law. This cross-cutting theme also deals with the question of the appropriate lexicon and programmatic challenges when one moves from meta-level normative debates and the United Nations to technical and practical details in the national, regional, and local implementation agenda.

Social and political contexts of mass atrocities as key to R2P implementation strategies

This volume engages with the question of how mass atrocities are conceptualized to inform the implementation agenda. Drawing on empirical insights at the local, regional, and global levels, a connecting theme in this volume is how to bridge the global–local gap that exists between the dynamics of mass atrocities in their specific historical, social, and political contexts, with the need for international, regional, and state-level resourcing and policy frameworks. In particular, the book emphasizes the importance of contextual knowledge and expertise on local conflict situations in formulating appropriate atrocity-prevention strategies and the importance of leadership by local- and regional-level stakeholders. Chapters by Sara E. Davies, Noel M. Morada, Frank O. Okyere, and Stephen McLoughlin, for example, demonstrate various challenges and corresponding strategies by local actors for implementing R2P that corresponds with the historical and political contingencies of each atrocity situation, with illustrations drawn from the regions of Africa and Southeast Asia.

Decision-making processes and institutional architectures of R2P implementation

Institutional responses that build capacity and strengthen resilience to atrocity crimes must be diversified. This includes vertically from international to regional, state and sub-state levels, and horizontally across sectors. Embedded in this volume, therefore, is the objective of identifying how existing processes and architectures may be fruitfully leveraged, or new institutional mechanisms designed, to respond to the challenges of implementation. What are the contingencies that need to be accounted for, and how can institutional designs meet the challenge of being both contextually relevant and consistent in principled commitment to the R2P objectives of atrocity prevention and population protection? While the case studies presented in the book are by no means exhaustive, they illustrate a variety of creative solutions and lessons learned that show how a number of agencies and actors have chosen to grapple with the implications of R2P for their own work. Ekkehard Strauss's chapter on human rights accountability, for example, shows how a group of actors within the Human Rights Council considered how the Council and the international human rights instruments might be mobilized to advance the preventive aspect of the R2P agenda. Martin Mennecke's chapter further demonstrates how Denmark as an advocate of R2P has contributed to expanding the conceptualization and implementation of R2P into new domains of governance and practice such as development, human rights, and civil society engagement. These examples should prompt a wider range of actors to consider R2P from a more creative lens and to leverage existing relationships and avenues of influence where atrocity prevention could be advanced.

Accountability as an integral part of R2P implementation

One of the central themes of the project that connects the varied theoretical, thematic, and institutional foci of the chapters is the question of accountability. As the counterpart to responsibility, accountability that is credible, legitimate, and consistent from the highest to the lowest levels of governance is an imperative that brings coherence to the R2P implementation agenda. Accountability is discussed in this volume in terms of dealing with past injustices that may increase the likelihood of future atrocity crimes, holding responsible actors to account for taking appropriate measures to prevent atrocities and protect populations, and outlining the need for accountability measures as an effective deterrent to the prevention of future mass atrocities. Themes that feature in a number of contributions to the project include how the principle of accountability could/should be conceptually consistent across the sites for implementation, and what kinds of mechanisms could protect accountability in the context of R2P. The chapters by Susanne Karstedt and Michael Koch, and Strauss, are dedicated to the relationship between a variety of accountability mechanisms and atrocity prevention. This theme is treated empirically in chapters such as those by Stephen Pomper and William Maley, where the recourse to accountability mechanisms – or failure, as in the latter case of Afghanistan – had significant implications for the outcomes of atrocity-prevention efforts.

The added value of atrocity prevention and responsibility to protect

The book focuses on the necessary turn from normative discussions to implementation. One of the key issues in this regard is what difference R2P makes in practice – compared to policies focusing on conflict prevention or human rights. As Ivan Šimonović writes in his concluding essay, R2P's "added value should not be presumed, but demonstrated." If R2P changes the equation, it will be accepted by practitioners as a meaningful addition to the toolkit. The question of R2P's added value is discussed in several chapters – including the question of whether it is necessary or helpful to use explicit R2P language or to avoid it, for example, for fear of R2P's political and politicized status. We see in the case of Europe that R2P holds a normative significance for policymakers and is effective in galvanizing political support for atrocity prevention, discussed in the chapters by Mennecke, and Edward Newman and Cristina Stefan. The United States, however, has steered clear of incorporating the language of R2P in domestic policy, but this has not prevented it from developing a unique institutional architecture that has effectively implemented R2P in numerous country situations, as described in Pomper's chapter.

Challenges of implementation

While the book agrees that implementation has to be at the heart of the academic and political discussion on R2P, it explores how this new focus, if taken seriously, can give rise to new challenges. Several chapters examine what these potential obstacles are, which (perhaps) can be overcome, and how. Lessons learned will be shared and ideas for future strategies outlined. Maley's chapter on civil–military cooperation in Afghanistan, for example, brings home the significance of getting implementation right. He shows how the external intervention into Afghanistan ultimately failed to prevent the continuation of "killings in 'slow motion'" (see Chapter 12) despite a commitment by the International Security Assistance Force to rebuild, therefore missing a crucial opportunity to prevent numerous atrocities since 2001. Likewise, Pomper's chapter on the US Atrocities Prevention Board, and Charles T. Hunt and Lisa Sharland's chapter on peacekeeping, point to the difficult political decisions that need to be taken when dealing with armed groups and life-or-death scenarios where compromise on normative commitments might be necessary.

Overview of the book

In the following, we briefly introduce the chapters in this volume in addition to this introduction and the foreword by Gareth Evans. In Chapter 1, Cecilia Jacob introduces the field of atrocity prevention as a way to ground the R2P implementation agenda in the existing research and policy frameworks. It describes developments in the institutionalization of R2P across the UN system where global efforts have focused to date. It shows how the institutional positioning of R2P within the UN has structured the primary understandings of the relationship between R2P and atrocity prevention that have been formative of early initiatives to implement R2P at the domestic and regional levels. These demonstrate both the extent and limitations of existing implementation efforts and provide context for the chapters that follow to show where greater creativity and opportunities exist to strengthen current implementation efforts. The remainder of the book is divided into five parts.

Part I examines national implementation mechanisms by presenting in-depth case studies from Denmark and the United States. Denmark is one of the key international proponents of R2P and its operationalization, and Mennecke's Chapter 2 traces a series of initiatives taken by the government to implement R2P at both global and national levels. For example, Denmark is one of the co-founders of the Global Network of R2P Focal Points and a member of the steering group of the Global Action Against Mass Atrocity Crimes (GAAMAC). This chapter examines Denmark's relationship to R2P, how atrocity prevention can make a difference to Danish foreign policy, and how Denmark through its human rights work and in the field of development cooperation can turn R2P into practice. In this context, the chapter identifies potential challenges such as political opposition to the use of explicit references to R2P and outlines concrete suggestions for how these obstacles can be overcome to advance atrocity prevention as an operational part of Danish foreign policy.

Chapter 3 turns to the experiences of the United States in implementing atrocity-prevention policy in a number of international atrocity-risk situations. Pomper provides an insider's view on where the Barack Obama administration's efforts to prevent mass atrocities succeeded, where they did not, and where future policymakers might find useful lessons, both positive and negative. It focuses in particular on situations in which policy changes and innovations appear to have had a positive effect, however modest, and on efforts to develop new capabilities under the policy. It offers an "after action" assessment of the administration's atrocity-prevention policy, drawing from interviews with former senior officials and others to identify both the strengths and contributions of the policy and its most pronounced shortcomings. The chapter also draws on the author's reflections on his tenure as senior director for African Affairs, Multilateral Affairs and Human Rights on the staff of the Obama administration's National Security Council, as well as his experience as chairperson of the US Atrocities Prevention Board.

Part II presents three case studies of regional implementation from Southeast Asia, Africa, and Europe. Chapter 4 by Morada looks at the Association of Southeast Asian Nations (ASEAN) regionalism and capacity-building for atrocities prevention. ASEAN has consciously re-oriented its brand of regionalism toward a more people-centered and people-oriented direction since the adoption of the Bali Concord II in 2003. This has paved the way for the organization's shared aspiration for building a community that upholds good governance, democracy, and human rights protection, which are all anchored in the comprehensive notion of security that also includes human security. A number of declarations and agreements, including the ASEAN Charter, recognize international norms and universal principles that not only uphold the rights and responsibilities of states but also those that protect the fundamental rights of people, including the vulnerable and marginal communities in the region. This chapter examines the dynamics of atrocity prevention in ASEAN by identifying the key domestic and regional factors that influence its member states' position and policies on R2P in general, and the importance of atrocity prevention in particular. Specifically, it examines relevant cases of Cambodia, Indonesia, Myanmar, and the Philippines to demonstrate the challenges and prospects for atrocity prevention in the region.

In Chapter 5, Okyere discusses African experiences of R2P implementation. In spite of the adoption of R2P at the 2005 United Nations World Summit, millions of innocent civilians across the African continent have been murdered, raising serious concerns about the effectiveness of its implementation. Although there have been some successes, the state has been the most obvious culprit in all the cases of failure to protect populations in Africa. This is not helped by persisting political contestations at the regional (African Union) level fueling further discontent toward R2P's application. Whereas it is widely accepted that state-level implementation presents the greatest potential for atrocity prevention, the state capacity and posture required for effective prevention has largely not been articulated. This chapter demonstrates why it has been generally difficult to implement R2P in Africa. It argues that effective implementation of R2P in Africa requires a reformulation of the state to accommodate the hybrid forms of governance and local sources of resilience which, historically, have been the harbingers of peace, justice, and social protection on the continent.

Turning to Europe, Newman and Stefan's Chapter 6 explores the European Union's (EU) engagement with the R2P principle and considers its potential international normative role. In the first section, the theoretical context of global normative contestation around issues such as R2P is introduced. This is done against the background of the "normative power Europe" debate in order to assess the EU's role in promoting R2P globally, at a time when many argue that the EU's normative authority is in decline and rising powers are increasingly resisting aspects of the liberal international order. The second section focuses on internal normative contestation processes taking place within the EU. Despite support for R2P among key European states, the collective internalization of R2P in Europe has been slow. The third section explores the EU's potential to take a meaningful leadership role on R2P, despite the challenges identified within each of the two layers of contestation. As a test, the response of the EU to the contemporary refugee "crisis" does not augur well both for European collective action around R2P, or in terms of normative credibility in global perspective.

Part III is the first of three thematic sections on the book and focuses on atrocity prevention. In Chapter 7, McLoughlin argues that the recent convergence of policy and scholarly interest in how atrocities are avoided raises strong possibilities for implementation. The chapter first charts the conceptual development of R2P's first pillar – the state's responsibility to protect its populations. While R2P emerged out of the debate in the 1990s about how the international community should respond to humanitarian emergencies such as Rwanda, Kosovo, and Srebrenica, the concept has broadened to consider the question of how national actors can avoid such emergencies in the first place. Second, the chapter assesses the growing scholarly interest in the question of why genocide and other mass atrocities do not occur, despite the presence of risk. Understanding what local and national actors do to mitigate risk is of central importance to R2P's first pillar, yet a clear picture of such dynamics has only recently emerged. Finally, the chapter considers how national resilience contributes to implementation. It argues that the knowledge of existing practices of risk mitigation is slowly being utilized to develop an atrocity-prevention lens, which then facilitates the dissemination of knowledge and insights related to national resilience.

In Chapter 8, Davies opens up the significant but too often neglected gender dimension of atrocity prevention through a case study on the role of women in advancing atrocity prevention in Southeast Asia. It is widely recognized that R2P is best implemented in ways that build upon existing sources of national resilience and empower populations at risk. Acts of sexual and gender-based violence in conflict and non-conflict situations that are widespread and systematic are international crimes that fall under the R2P principle. Women and girls remain most at risk of being targeted for these crimes. The targeting of women and girls, as well as men and boys, is attributable to the particular forms of gender discrimination and gender inequality that are pervasive in politically unstable and conflicted situations. To promote a gendered approach to R2P that addresses these sources of risk, this chapter argues that prevention work must focus on the elimination of discrimination, and the strengthening of women's participation in the sectors necessary to deliver sustainable peace and conflict prevention. This chapter then explores the role of the ASEAN Commission on the Promotion and Protection of the Rights of Women and Children to examine to what extent its work has been concerned with gender inequality and gender discrimination with a view to enhancing the participation of women in protection roles, and also preventing gender-based violence in conflict.

Part IV of the book examines complex questions of international accountability, compliance, and justice that transpire from the practical implications of operationalizing R2P. In Chapter 9, Strauss takes up the question of accountability and compliance with international human rights with specific reference to R2P implementation. His chapter begins with a short introduction about the general link between human rights obligations and R2P on the basis of the most recent discussion on the need for further clarification of challenges to the implementation of R2P. This is followed by a section on the relationship between R2P and human rights obligations of states under international law. The following two sections outline a general concept of human rights accountability and compliance for the application of R2P and implementation mechanisms regarding this concept. Conclusions are then drawn in relation to the present political environment of the R2P discussion, and practical and measured recommendations are suggested as a way of moving forward.

Karstedt and Koch's Chapter 10 looks at the relationship between transitional justice and security after complex conflicts, and argues that accountability for past atrocity crimes and violations of human rights are an important dimension of the R2P implementation agenda. As such, transitional justice mechanisms forge a link between the past, the present, and the future by deterring future violations, developing institutions that are legitimate, and strengthening the rule of law in general. However, the potential of transitional justice mechanisms and in particular trials has been widely contested. Contemporary transitional justice operates in the aftermath of "multipolar" and "horizontal" violence, where both state and non-state actors are involved. Such complex conflicts pose major challenges to transitional justice procedures, and to the implementation of R2P processes. Based on a data set of sixty-three (post)conflict societies from 1976 to 2012, the impact of transitional justice mechanisms on security in terms of levels of different types of violence, rule of law, and general institutional capacity is analyzed for a period of up to ten years. Even in the wake of complex conflicts, transitional justice mechanisms in general do not have counterproductive or adverse outcomes. Improvement of security in terms of a reduction of violence is the most likely and consistent impact of transitional justice mechanisms. In conclusion, it is suggested where resources and efforts in transitional justice should be focused in order to contribute to state resilience.

Finally, Part V brings the discussions of R2P implementation into the domain of the security sector, where national and international security providers seeking to prevent atrocities face physical challenges of direct confrontation plus broader political and strategic considerations associated with maintaining peace that often complicate efforts to prevent atrocities and protect civilians. In Chapter 11, Hunt and Sharland assess opportunities and challenges for implementing R2P through UN peacekeeping operations. Efforts to implement R2P in practice, they argue, have consistently pointed to peace operations as one possible avenue. For example, the Secretary-General has identified UN peacekeeping missions as an appropriate instrument for operationalizing R2P. The emergence of the protection of civilians (POC) as a center of gravity for modern UN peacekeeping has led many to identify synergies and add further weight to the case. However, implementing

R2P through UN peacekeeping presents a number of principled, political, and practical challenges. This chapter explores these issues. The first section traces the broadening and deepening of POC in recent years and analyzes its significance for implementing R2P, as well as for the current consensus on UN peacekeeping. The second section draws on empirical examples from the field, including the POC sites in South Sudan and the Force Intervention Brigade in the Democratic Republic of the Congo, to identify a range of opportunities as well as challenges associated with emergent POC strategies and practices in the field. The final section lays out a series of recommendations highlighting where more work is required to enhance the implementation of R2P through the UN's peace operations going forward.

In Chapter 12, Maley looks at the role of civil–military assistance as another type of external security intervention with the potential to strengthen national resilience and prevent atrocities. This is done through a detailed case study of Afghanistan from which many lessons can be drawn. Since the communist coup of April 1978, Afghanistan has had more than its experience of mass atrocity crime, and as a result, one might have expected the post-2001 international intervention in Afghanistan to have paid a considerable amount of attention to protecting the Afghan population against recurrences of this phenomenon. The picture, however, has been much more complex, even where civil–military cooperation has been brought to the center of operational planning, notably with the deployment of mixed civil and military Provincial Reconstruction Teams (PRTs). This chapter examines the Afghanistan experience in order to identify ways in which the threat of mass atrocity crime in international operations can receive the attention it deserves. Key factors that emerge from the case include a strong US commitment to using kinetic means to address the threat posed by perceived enemies, an unwillingness to confront diplomatically the challenge posed by sanctuaries in neighboring countries for forces willing to attack civilians as part of this strategy, the value to opponents of the new Afghan state of random attacks on civilians as a means of symbolizing the state's weakness, and the preoccupation of PRT actors with a diverse range of challenges, distracting attention from mass atrocity crime as a routine danger. The chapter identifies how the lessons could inform future civil–military assistance operations to strengthen the atrocity-prevention capacity of such missions.

The book concludes with a reflective essay by former Special Advisor to the UN Secretary-General on R2P Šimonović on the current state of R2P implementation from a global vantage point. The central proposition in this concluding chapter is that the value of R2P depends on how far it serves its aim to prevent atrocity crimes. Analyzing the impact of R2P to date, this chapter argues that R2P is at a crossroads: its future lies in implementation or marginalization. The states and institutions that have committed themselves to R2P will lose their credibility unless they take steps to ensure its effective implementation. The chapter proceeds in three parts. First, it assesses key areas of progress and challenges to the implementation of R2P within the UN system. Second, it presents an argument as to why R2P should be revived and fully implemented rather than marginalized. And third, it details the proposals advanced for a new agenda to realize this goal.

Thus, the book underscores the overall call to turn the narrative of implementation into a practice of implementation. This is necessary to sustain R2P as a norm and to realize its key objective of protecting populations from new atrocity crimes.

Notes

1 This includes, at the time of writing, seventy-seven Security Council resolutions and twenty-one presidential statements, as well as thirteen UN General Assembly resolutions and thirty-nine UN Human Rights Council resolutions. See Global Centre for the Responsibility to Protect (2018a, 2018b, 2018c).
2 Human Rights Watch, for example, has documented the traumatic experiences of women forced to watch the rape and massacre of their children before being subjected to torture themselves. The human cost of such brutal violence during the military campaigns against the Rohingya cannot be measured in numbers alone Bouckaert (2017).
3 For an analysis of the efforts among UN officials, diplomats, and experts to conceptualize the relationship of R2P to the work of the Human Rights Council grounded in a legal context, and setting discussions of implementation on a unique path in Geneva compared to the politically oriented discussions among UN agencies in New York, see Jacob (2018).

References

Ban Ki-moon, 2009. "Implementing the Responsibility to Protect: Report of the Secretary-General," A/63/677, January 12.
Bouckaert, Peter, 2017. *Massacre by the River: Burmese Army Crimes Against Humanity in Tula Toli* (New York: Human Rights Watch).
Gilmour, Andrew, 2014. "The Future of Human Rights: A View from the United Nations," *Ethics and International Affairs* 28, no. 2: 239–50.
Global Centre for the Responsibility to Protect, 2018a. "R2P References in United Nations General Assembly Resolutions," July 31, www.globalr2p.org/media/files/unga-resolutions-with-r2p-language-31-july-2018.pdf.
Global Centre for the Responsibility to Protect, 2018b. "R2P References in United Nations Human Rights Council Resolutions," December 3, www.globalr2p.org/media/files/hrc-resolutions-r2p-3-december-2018.pdf.
Global Centre for the Responsibility to Protect, 2018c. "R2P References in United Nations Security Council Resolutions and Presidential Statements," November 27, www.globalr2p.org/media/files/unsc-resolutions-and-statements-with-r2p-table-as-of-27-november-2018-1.pdf.
Guterres, António, 2017. "Secretary-General's Remarks to the Security Council Open Debate on 'Maintenance of International Peace and Security: Conflict Prevention and Sustaining Peace'," New York, January 10.
ICISS (International Commission on Intervention and State Sovereignty), 2001. *The Responsibility to Protect: Report of the International Commission on Intervention and State Sovereignty* (Ottawa: International Development Research Centre).
Jacob, Cecilia, 2018. "From Norm Contestation to Norm Implementation: Recursivity and the Responsibility to Protect," *Global Governance* 24, no. 3: 391–409.
Kurtz, Gerritt, 2015. "With Courage and Coherence: The Human Rights Up Front Initiative of the United Nations," Policy Paper (Berlin: Global Public Policy Institute).
Melander, Erik, Therése Pettersson, and Lotta Themnér, 2016. "Organized Violence, 1989–2015," *Journal of Peace Research* 53, no. 5: 727–42.
Slaughter, Anne-Marie, 2004. *A New World Order* (Princeton, NJ: Princeton University Press).

Thakur, Ramesh, 2017. *The United Nations, Peace and Security: From Collective Security to the Responsibility to Protect*, 2nd edn (Cambridge: Cambridge University Press).

UN Women, 2015. *Preventing Conflict; Transforming Justice; Securing the Peace: A Global Study on the Implementation of United Nations Security Council Resolution 1325* (New York: United Nations).

United Nations, 2012. *Report of the Secretary-General's Internal Review Panel on United Nations Action in Sri Lanka* (New York: United Nations).

United Nations, 2015a. *The Challenge of Sustaining Peace: Report of the Advisory Group of Experts for the 2015 Review of the United Nations Peacebuilding Architecture* (New York: United Nations, June 29).

United Nations, 2015b. "The Future of United Nations Peace Operations: Implementation of the High-Level Independent Panel on Peace Operations," A/70/357–S/2015/682, September 2.

United Nations Political Affairs, 2015. *Strategic Plan 2016–2019* (New York: Department of Political Affairs, November 20).

Weiss, Thomas G., David P. Forsythe, Roger A. Coate, and Kelly-Kate Pease, 2014. *The United Nations and Changing World Politics* (Boulder, CO: Westview Press).

1
R2P AS AN ATROCITY-PREVENTION FRAMEWORK

Concepts and institutionalization at the global level

Cecilia Jacob

Prevention is politically salient and normatively powerful as a rallying cry for those Responsibility to Protect (R2P) advocates seeking to advance the implementation of R2P. Not only is there consensus that prevention needs to be prioritized in global policymaking, but since 2017, the United Nations (UN) reform agenda has been geared around the strengthening of prevention and sustaining peace, which should – theoretically – offer a conducive context for R2P implementation to be strengthened. Atrocity prevention, however, is a specific agenda that responds to four manifestations of violence – genocide, war crimes, crimes against humanity, and ethnic cleansing. The UN Secretary-General has articulated a very broad definition of prevention in the reform agenda that includes conflict prevention, development, and human rights promotion. Each of these agendas complement atrocity-prevention efforts; however, there is also a need to acknowledge the specific risk factors and dynamics of atrocity crimes when formulating context-specific responses to potential or actual atrocities on the ground.

The 2001 International Commission on Intervention and State Sovereignty's (ICISS) report on R2P linked R2P directly to the field of atrocity prevention, arguing that the "responsibility to prevent" constitutes the first priority of R2P. Importantly, the responsibility to prevent not only resides within the UN, but is also present across and within UN member states, and at the regional level (ICISS 2001, 26). This initial call was incorporated into paragraphs 138 and 139 in the 2005 World Summit Outcome document relating to the responsibility of states and the international community to prevent and protect, and prevention has been front and center in the conceptual development of R2P since the UN Secretary-General's first annual report on R2P (United Nations General Assembly 2005; Ban 2009). R2P is the first and only international framework on atrocity prevention; it therefore serves as the "touchstone" for atrocity prevention in global norm-building processes and policy frameworks.

This chapter introduces the field of atrocity prevention as a way to ground the R2P implementation agenda in existing research and policy frameworks. To date, global efforts have focused on the institutionalization of R2P across the UN system; this chapter describes developments in that institutionalization. It shows how the institutional positioning of R2P within the UN has structured primary understandings of the relationship between R2P and atrocity prevention, which have influenced early initiatives to implement R2P at the domestic and regional levels. These demonstrate both the extent and limitations of existing implementation efforts, and provide context for the chapters in this volume to show where greater creativity and opportunities exist to strengthen current implementation efforts.

The chapter proceeds in three parts. First, it provides an account of the development of the field of atrocity prevention and introduces key policy approaches that have been developed in this broader literature. Second, it explains the two primary ways in which R2P has been conceptualized as an atrocity-prevention framework within the UN. The first is the crimes-based approach, advanced most notably under the intellectual leadership of Special Advisor to the UN Secretary-General on R2P, Jennifer Welsh. The second is the human rights-based approach that links the objectives of R2P implementation with stronger accountability for human rights, and for strengthening state capacity in the areas of governance and the rule of law. Both approaches conceptualize the nature and dynamics of mass atrocity crimes, and legal accountability frameworks for regulating these.

Third, the chapter examines how R2P is being institutionalized within the UN system. It argues that R2P increasingly performs a regulatory role in guiding member states and UN actors to respond to the threat or instances of gross violations of human rights. Yet, as a norm, R2P operates in varied ways, and is shaped by the organizational logic and specific social context of implementation. Variation in the interpretation and implementation of the R2P norm in practice serves to expand the parameters of the international community's understanding of mass atrocities and strategies for preventing them, prods open new avenues for creativity in interpreting and expanding existing mandates, and, from the perspective of global governance, illustrates limitations for achieving justice and security for populations in local contexts of violence.

Defining mass atrocities and thinking strategically about atrocity prevention

One of the key insights that has catalyzed the development of the field of atrocity prevention has been the recognition that the concept of mass atrocities is much broader than the concept of genocide. The International Criminal Court's Rome Statute (1998) defined the crimes of genocide, crimes against humanity, and war crimes, providing an international lexicon of "atrocity law" (Scheffer 2002) for identifying and defining the widespread and systematic targeting of civilians during periods of armed conflict and peacetime. Whereas episodes of mass violence that meet the legal criteria of genocide are rare (Straus 2012), atrocities are much more common, usually manifesting in smaller reiterated patterns of political violence that peak and trough over time, and often in non-linear trajectories (Karstedt 2013).

Mass atrocities have been under-studied in the literature on armed conflict and security for most of the twentieth century. Prior to the end of the Cold War, scholars focused their research on identifying the causes of interstate war as a strategy for the prevention of future conflicts (Valentino 2014). Mass civilian casualties were not absent during the Cold War period, however. Indeed, many of the most significant episodes of mass violence took place during this time, including in Nigeria, Burundi, East Pakistan, Cambodia, Indonesia, and Guatemala. Yet these twentieth-century mass atrocities were seen through a Cold War lens, in which mass civilian suffering was taken for granted as an unfortunate consequence of armed conflict rather than as a social context of violence worth studying in its own right. Viewed as domestic sovereignty concerns – not the remit of the international community – international political, legal, and scholarly attention to mass atrocities remained confined to a narrow conceptualization of genocide during the Cold War period (Harff 2017). Early twentieth-century genocides in Armenia and the Holocaust set a high bar for identification of genocides given the uniqueness of the phenomenon of one-sided, targeted mass killings on the basis of ethnicity/race/religion, as defined in the Convention on the Prevention and Punishment of the Crime of Genocide.[1]

Over the past twenty years, changing trends in armed conflict toward primarily internal conflicts with very high civilian casualty rates have prompted the emergence of a political science research community focused on dynamics of violence. Genocides and ethnic cleansing in the 1990s, notably in Rwanda and the Balkans, were turning points both in the establishment of international criminal law,[2] and in the systematic study of the risk factors, triggers, and escalatory pathways of atrocity events, which then led to the development of more accurate and reliable atrocity-prevention frameworks (Straus 2016). Researchers started to ask why mass killings occur in some conflicts yet not in others, what motivates states and rebel groups to engage in mass killings of civilians, and what are the actual dynamics of violence and strategic logics of civilian killings during armed conflict (Smeulers and Hoex 2010; Klusemann 2012; Lemarchand 2009). There is no agreed upon "science" of atrocity prevention; however, a number of atrocity risk assessment frameworks (United Nations 2014) and atrocity risk lists[3] have been established to encourage more systematic tracking of potential atrocity situations, and detailed prevention "toolkits" have been developed to help guide policymakers respond to evidence of escalating atrocity situations. Despite these developments, as Scott Straus (2016, 23) has noted, we still have a very limited understanding of what tools work, when, and in which combination.

Key findings that have emerged in this growing scholarly literature on mass violence include a better understanding of the social contexts in which violence occurs. At the end of the Cold War, mass targeted civilian killings were formerly understood to be the indiscriminate and unavoidable consequence of war (collateral damage), or driven by primordial "ethnic hatreds" that were largely beyond the realm of external influence (Kaplan 1993). There is now strong empirical evidence to show that targeted civilian killings follow strategic logics for garnering support or exercising control over civilian populations (Cohen 2016; Kalyvas 2006; Weinstein 2007). These strategic logics are primarily, if not exclusively, instrumental and coordinated by powerful actors seeking to achieve tangible political or military objectives (Valentino 2014, 94). Further, large-scale quantitative studies have identified structural factors in societies that have been prone to mass killings.[4] These tend to focus on indicators of governance, security, accountability for legacies of mass violence, the presence of minority identity groups that face discriminatory or exclusionary state policy and practices, and the presence of armed conflict. Both internal structural dynamics and external factors, such as interfering powers, enhance the likelihood that a state will face mass atrocity violence. Structural factors may increase the risk that a society will be vulnerable to mass atrocity violence, including the presence of organized military or militia with the capacity to orchestrate, mobilize, and carry out a widespread and systematic campaign of violence. The confluence of these structural factors with specific triggers – crisis events such as deeply contested elections, political assassinations, or external political or economic shocks – in the context of heightened vulnerability (Straus 2015) leads a society or nation down the path of mass atrocity violence escalation.

Atrocity-prevention frameworks therefore address both the structural and the direct, or operational, dimensions that generate the potential and likelihood that mass atrocities will occur. Structural prevention refers to interventions that are directed toward changing long-term underlying conditions that foster risk of potential atrocity crimes. These may include targeting unaccountable governance structures, reforming a security apparatus that supports a repressive regime and acts with impunity, rectifying patterns of discrimination against particular population groups through political and legal reform, and supporting transitional justice mechanisms where there has been a lack of recourse to redress for past injustices, atrocity crimes, and systematic human rights violations. Structural prevention is therefore targeted at measures that enhance political representation and the rule of law, social justice, and human rights accountability. The idea behind structural prevention is that early intervention to strengthen social resilience and mitigate structural vulnerabilities within a society provides the most cost-effective and efficient form of prevention (discussed further by Stephen McLoughlin, Chapter 7 in this volume).

Direct, or operational, prevention is employed once violence has been triggered to either dissuade or incapacitate perpetrators from carrying out targeted violence against a civilian population. These measures are intended to halt the escalation of violence and protect civilian populations, and are more coercive in nature. Patterns of violence in early-onset mass atrocity situations include a disproportionate civilian death toll in a conflict that would indicate direct targeting of populations, attacks on civilian infrastructure, and systematic patterns of violence across territory and time (Straus 2016). Direct prevention includes a range of non-military measures, such as economic sanctions, travel bans, asset freezes, and targeted military measures such as airstrikes and intervention to halt an imminent or ongoing atrocity.

Atrocity prevention can be differentiated from broader conflict prevention agendas, therefore, by an assessment of the dynamic of violence in which widespread and systematic civilian targeting becomes a strategy for attaining political or military objectives. Patterns of violent conflict that inflict mass indiscriminate violence against civilians are also deemed war crimes or crimes against humanity. Therefore, while broader conflict prevention strategies may complement and advance atrocity prevention, scholars and practitioners have advocated that atrocity prevention be understood as a distinct area of policy and strategic intervention so that preventive measures can be put in place to counter the specific dynamics driving mass atrocity violence.

The United States has operationalized the language of atrocity prevention in its own foreign policy and strategic planning by associating the commission of mass atrocity crimes abroad with its own national interest. In 2008, the Genocide Prevention Taskforce, led by former Secretary of State Madeleine K. Albright and former Secretary of Defense William S. Cohen, produced a flagship report guiding US policy on atrocity prevention:

> We conclude in this report that preventing genocide is an achievable goal. Genocide is not the inevitable result of "ancient hatreds" or irrational leaders. It requires planning and is carried out systematically. There are ways to recognize its signs and symptoms, and viable options to prevent it at every turn if we are committed and prepared. Preventing genocide is a goal that can be achieved with the right organizational structures, strategies, and partnerships – in short, with the right blueprint.
>
> *(Albright and Cohen 2008, xv–xvi)*

The authors of the report articulated a definition of "genocide" that reflected the dynamics of mass atrocities described in the preceding paragraphs – namely, that understanding the political utility and strategic logic of targeted mass civilian killings could inform a policy agenda aimed at preventing it. In doing so, it brought atrocity prevention into the central domain of political and strategic decision-making of the US administration. The authors also linked genocide and mass atrocity prevention as a "threat" to "American values and interests" (Albright and Cohen 2008, xv), a position that was upheld by US President Barack Obama in the 2011 Presidential Study Directive 10 (PSD10). PSD10 states that the prevention of genocide and mass atrocities are a "core national security interest and core moral responsibility of the United States" (Obama 2011) and established the Atrocities Prevention Board (see Stephen Pomper, Chapter 5 in this volume).

This policy and operational framework on atrocity prevention is unique to the United States.[5] There is no comparable global framework on atrocity prevention to date that is able to bring together such a coordinated approach to policymaking, integrated analysis on potential or unfolding crises, and clear strategic planning to prepare for timely preventive action. In the following sections, I consider the implementation of R2P as the only international framework available to date to guide atrocity-prevention efforts at the global level. While the United Nations tends not to use the language of atrocity prevention, with the exception of the Office on Genocide Prevention and the Responsibility to Protect, R2P provides the normative and political tools for mobilizing preventive responses to atrocity situations. In this sense, the UN employs a rather distinct, principle-based approach to atrocity prevention that informs member states' own understanding and policy formation in this area. Whether or not the policy objectives of atrocity prevention need to be framed in terms of R2P, given its often fraught political association with interventionism that certain member states routinely assert, or whether it should serve as a stand-alone atrocity-prevention lens, is a highly salient question. Arguably, the political "baggage" that R2P brings with it could be dispensed with in pursuit of a more neutral and technical atrocity-prevention framework that could achieve similar ends. There is merit in ensuring that an atrocity-prevention lens be incorporated across UN peace operations, and that field programming be instituted in areas such as human rights, development, and peacebuilding to ensure systematic monitoring of early-warning signs. The UN's Framework of Analysis for Atrocity Crimes is now used across these operational areas (United Nations 2014). While some observers question the capacity of staff to conduct this analysis effectively, given their current skillset and training,[6] it signals a move to integrate atrocity prevention more systematically into UN field operations in order to strengthen its early-warning and early-action capacity.

Yet R2P remains an important reference point to mark international consensus on its normative and principled grounding within the context of sovereign responsibility and collective action in the face of mass atrocity situations, and scoped within the authority of UN Security Council authorization for the use of military force to halt mass atrocities. These dimensions elevate the core policy objectives of an atrocity-prevention policy framework, particularly one framed in reference to the national interest of the intervening state, to a global consensus over the shared norms and values that provide the moral backing for political action. This richer normative positioning of atrocity prevention within the R2P framework has encouraged a broader discussion of how to pursue accountability for state and international responsibility on atrocity prevention and population protection. Two approaches that link R2P and atrocity prevention at the UN, grounded in international criminal accountability and human rights accountability, respectively, are discussed briefly ahead. I then assess the diverse areas of institutionalization where R2P has been implemented within the UN, and where efforts could be strengthened to enhance the institution's preventive capacity in the specific area of atrocity crimes.

Conceptualizing R2P and atrocity prevention at the United Nations

The conceptualization of mass atrocities as international crimes has enabled key advocates of R2P to make a distinction between the tools and objectives of atrocity prevention from the more general category of conflict prevention that drives much of the UN's institutional approach to preventive work.

A crimes-based approach

From 2014 to 2016, Special Advisor Welsh spearheaded research on a crimes-based approach to atrocity prevention that generated clarity around this distinct approach. Welsh and her colleagues contended that "preventive strategies associated with R2P should be aimed at *attacks directed at any population, committed in a widespread or systematic manner, in furtherance of a state or organizational policy, irrespective of the existence of discriminatory intent or an armed conflict*" (Reike, Sharma, and Welsh 2015, 24, emphasis in original). They argued for an emphasis on crimes against humanity, as not only do these encompass genocide, war crimes, and ethnic cleansing, but they also cast a broader scope to capture widespread and systematic violence (not just killing) by state and non-state actors that occur in situations of either war or peace. In doing so, this approach distinguishes between the tools and policy objectives of atrocity prevention and conflict prevention in two distinct agendas. It develops a criminological model that focuses on perpetrators, victims, and situations, and identifies specific stages of regression toward atrocity crimes. This model systematizes how policy tools might mitigate the risk factors and/or change the escalatory dynamics in each of these specific stages that lead to atrocity crimes, distinguishing between "targeted" and "systemic" prevention.

The crimes-based approach to atrocity prevention emphasizes individual accountability through international criminal law, and offers a different lens through which to consider accountability for atrocity crimes (Reike 2016). Within this overarching crimes-based approach, a long-term "social crime prevention" lens pursues the strengthening of justice and the rule of law to mitigating structural risk factors for atrocity crimes within domestic settings, and is pertinent in the context of structural prevention strategies. "Direct" crime prevention strategies are relevant in the context of immediate situational responses to international crimes – for example, through the International Criminal Court, and the use of coercive measures such as sanctions and military airstrikes (Reike 2014, 461). The crimes-based approach endorses the legality of using military force short of war for preventive purposes when mass atrocities are imminent, and therefore associates international accountability for international crimes with Security Council authorization to operationalize this coercive preventive action. In doing so, it responds to critiques of R2P as a guise for Western interventionism and regime change by shifting the focus away from military intervention to one of prevention, and by considering limited and targeted non-military and military coercive tools that could dissuade or incapacitate perpetrators from committing atrocity crimes without resorting to full-scale military intervention. The focus on individual criminal accountability for key perpetrators of atrocity crimes, and addressing impunity at the domestic level, serves to enlarge the debate around the accountability of different actors for their responsibilities in accordance with existing international legal frameworks.

A human rights-based approach

By their very nature, atrocity crimes are widespread human rights violations, and scholars and practitioners have been paying increasingly closer attention to the idea that the mechanisms to monitor and prosecute human rights also serve as valuable mechanisms for strengthening atrocity prevention. Atrocity risk lists have proven effective in identifying country situations where the risk of mass atrocity violence is high; however, still missing in the analysis is an identification of which situations will deteriorate into mass atrocity violence, and when. Many country situations may sit on risk lists for years. While this helps policymakers identify those countries that need to be regularly monitored, additional early warning and analysis tools are required to translate these indicators into an effective catalyst for early action.

Human rights establishments offer an important institutional mechanism for tracking patterns of widespread and systematic violations of human rights that are strong indicators of atrocity violence. They are attuned to human rights violations that foster discrimination and political suppression to which other agencies within the UN, such as development, are not geared. The international human rights system, and in some cases, regional and national-level human rights institutions, have developed a capacity to provide systematic reporting on human rights indicators, and therefore could potentially help fill the accountability gaps between international human rights standards and implementation by state actors at the domestic level. The potential ways in which the UN Human Rights Council has been envisaged to implement R2P to prevent atrocity crimes, particularly in relation to the first and second pillars of state responsibility and international assistance, are discussed by Ekkehard Strauss in Chapter 9 in this volume. However, important here are functions that the Human Rights Council could and does fulfill. First, there is a potential early-warning role that the Council could play in detecting risk and an early onset of atrocity crimes by monitoring trends and patterns in violence escalation. Second, the Human Rights Council provides a strong mechanism for information flows that connect state-level human rights situations to global decision-making bodies to facilitate early action to prevent atrocities. Third, the accountability function of the Human Rights Council requires transparency and consistency in reporting by member states, with functions for special investigations and inquiries into situations of concern. This final function helps overcome, to some degree, the predicament of atrocity prevention, namely that effective international action to prevent atrocity crimes requires external interference in the domestic affairs of the state in question. Human rights bodies' actions that follow through on their mandates for monitoring and capacity-building could help depoliticize key aspects of atrocity-prevention efforts by playing a role that would otherwise be seen as deeply interventionist if carried out by other political bodies in the UN or between member states.

Prioritizing prevention in a fragmented institutional context

In 2009, around 33,000 civilians were killed in a military campaign led by the Sri Lankan armed forces that ended the three-decade-long civil conflict between the Liberation Tigers of Tamil Eelam and the state. Despite having a field presence and sufficient warning, the UN failed to prevent what were later deemed to be war crimes and crimes against humanity committed by both parties to the conflict during the final phase of hostilities (United Nations Human Rights Council 2015). The Internal Review Panel on United Nations Action in Sri Lanka (2012, paragraph 80) concluded that "systemic failure" was to blame for UN inaction. Situated in the normative context of R2P, Secretary-General Ban Ki-moon responded to the evidence of a systemic lack of coordination and response mechanisms by implementing the Human Rights up Front (HRuF) initiative to mainstream human rights protection and atrocity prevention across the UN system (Kurtz 2015). Further momentum to incorporate prevention into UN reform came in 2015 with the release of three major reviews into UN peacekeeping, peacebuilding, and women, peace, and security that emphasized the need to strengthen prevention and political solutions to ending conflict (United Nations 2015a, 2015b; UN Women 2015).

These reviews culminated in Security Council Resolution 2282 (2016) and General Assembly Resolution 70/262 (2016) that articulated a "new organizational approach to the maintenance of international peace and security, through the concept of 'sustaining peace'" (Thomson 2017). These developments have moved the thrust of political capital expended on R2P and the prevention agenda from its preoccupation with conceptual refinement and consensus building toward concrete implementation (Jacob 2018). Upon taking office, Secretary-General António Guterres embarked immediately on mapping out the UN's prevention capacities and restructuring field offices to commence the extensive coordination and streamlining of the highly segregated operations of key agencies. This included a merger between the Department of Political Affairs and the Peacebuilding Support Office into a new Department of Political and Peacebuilding Affairs (DPPA), and the reorganization of the former Department of Peacekeeping Operations into the new Department of Peace Operations that now manages all large field missions, including special political missions.

As Guterres (2017a) advances UN reforms to centralize and coordinate prevention in the UN, questions are emerging about the capacity of the UN to formalize atrocity-prevention responsibilities of states and to ensure compliance. The issues are not just about technocratic operationalization, but are seen as pressing political and legal concerns. While R2P has been formally institutionalized in the UN (Welsh 2013), R2P language has been increasingly included in numerous Security Council, General Assembly, and Human Rights Council resolutions,[7] and several success stories can be identified (Streitfeld-Hall 2015), consistent and effective implementation of atrocity prevention and response remains an elusive goal.

The implications of carving out new global governance responsibilities for preventing and halting mass atrocities requires the political will among UN member states to harness the institutional capabilities of the Security Council and the General Assembly. This may potentially include developing new capabilities that challenge the default framing of mass atrocities within the contexts of threats to international peace and security, or conflict prevention, that remains current practice (Strauss 2015). Further, an effective governance framework would need to align the work of the Security Council and the General Assembly with legal interpretations of atrocity prevention within the Human Rights Council and other relevant bodies where there is a tendency for independent assessment of the same crisis scenarios without transparent information sharing or coordination. The creation of formal mechanisms for implementation and compliance with R2P has been resisted by states to date (Serrano 2015), and although the idea of the Human Rights Council establishing a monitoring and compliance mechanism for R2P was floated in the past (Arbour 2008), the Human Rights Council has consistently distanced itself from such suggestions, due to fears of internal meddling by certain states (Strauss 2016).

Political will among member states to prioritize prevention at the UN has waxed and waned in the years since Boutros Boutros-Ghali's (1992) landmark report "An Agenda for Peace." The new agenda is distinct in its sustained political move within the UN toward prevention that has been integral to the rationale and design of the structural and bureaucratic reforms being implemented. The current reforms to institutionalize prevention correspond with a tangible need to redress institutional fragmentation, mandates, and response mechanisms (Cliffe 2017).

The original HRuF concept note was an internal document intended to redress the institutional deficits within the system that led to the situation in Sri Lanka. By linking mass human rights violations with contexts of mass atrocity crimes, HRuF was the first purposive document to develop a joint understanding of the coordinated procedures that a response to imminent atrocities would entail (Ban 2013). Yet to date, the inability of UN bodies to "move along a continuum of ... increasingly coercive measures and to review their effectiveness vis-à-vis mass atrocities without time-consuming negotiations of new decisions or resolutions" (Strauss 2015, 56) has stymied the development of a coherent institutional strategy for responding to imminent or ongoing mass atrocities. The next section considers in more detail the formal and non-formal efforts to respond to inconsistencies in the implementation of R2P within the Security Council, the Secretariat, and the General Assembly to illustrate the ways in which various conceptions of atrocity prevention have informed the institutionalization of R2P in these bodies.

Institutionalizing prevention

The prevention of large-scale loss of life and human suffering is the normative foundation on which the UN Charter was developed, and in pragmatic terms, prevention of violent conflict is much less costly and more effective than response. In 2015, the High-Level Independent Panel on UN Peace Operations made the following assessment of the UN's conflict prevention capacity:

> In contrast to mediation and peacekeeping, where decades of international experience have delivered a number of core lessons and basic principles, the prevention of armed conflicts is approached in an *ad hoc* manner with many disparate and disconnected perspectives – diplomatic, political, developmental,

and economic among others. . . . Put simply, the international community is failing at preventing conflict.

(United Nations 2015c, paragraph 64)

While referring to conflict prevention, the recommendations of the High-Level Independent Panel included references to mass atrocities and targeted civilian attacks (United Nations 2015c, 2, 24, 26–27). The overall findings point to the general difficulties that the UN faces in preventing human protection crises and in finding political solutions to resolve them. The challenge is not the absence of institutional mechanisms and capacities within the UN, but rather the absence of a strategic way of thinking about how existing capacities should be leveraged to build a coherent prevention capability across the system (Luck 2018).

The decision by member states not to identify an institutional "home" for R2P responsibilities in the 2005 World Summit Outcome document created the potential for R2P to fall by the wayside of international politics. Scholars were concerned that without significant persuasion and advocacy, R2P would fail to gain adequate traction to become formalized in UN structures and state practice. Jutta Brunnée and Stephen Toope (2005, 134) were particularly concerned with locating institutional responsibilities for R2P, arguing that "one cannot consider norms separately from the institutions that shape, interpret, and apply the norms." In the context of the 2005 World Summit Outcome document, the newly created bodies that seemed most salient to mandate the prevention aspects of R2P were the Peacebuilding Commission and the Human Rights Council. The decision to restrict the scope of the Peacebuilding Commission to post-conflict situations only, and indecision over the details of the Human Rights Council, excluded the formal integration of R2P into these bodies. The Security Council was the only UN body referred to in the 2005 World Summit Outcome document (United Nations General Assembly 2005), with the use of force to be legitimated through Chapter VII mandates only. In the absence of reform to the composition and working methods of the Security Council, the potential that Council politics could suffocate R2P was also considered problematic (Brunnée and Toope 2005).

In hindsight, the exclusion of specific institutional responsibilities for R2P has allowed for the development of a stronger conceptual foundation for R2P over the years. As detailed ahead, the lingering ideological resistance to mainstreaming R2P into the workings of the Human Rights Council indicates that early institutionalization may have been premature and lacking in a fundamental purpose to which member states could agree. The recent departure from a "post-conflict peacebuilding" framework toward a new paradigm of "sustaining peace" along the full spectrum of the conflict continuum is emblematic of a conceptual evolution within the UN in response to notable human protection crises – and failures. As was the case with the institutionalization of HRuF after the failure to prevent mass civilian killings in Sri Lanka, specific experiences have generated a unique institutional environment for advancing a more integrated approach to prevention and response than that envisaged in either the ICISS report or the 2005 World Summit Outcome document.

Importantly, the graduated conceptual development of R2P has been commensurate with the expanding interpretation of existing mandates underway by UN bodies where R2P-related responsibilities are recognized to be within their remit. The most interesting aspects of normative progress, therefore, has not been contestation over the meaning of the norm itself. Rather, the unfolding institutional reform has stemmed from the implementation of the norm in practice, and in lieu of formal or radical institutional restructuring. Diplomats, officials, and non-state advocates have in this case managed to navigate between formal politics and institutional constraints to regulate behavior and promote a greater level of accountability among international organizations and state actors (Jacob 2018). As individual states, organizations, and UN agencies reflect internally on the implications of the new norm for their own practices, these agents have contributed to expanding the parameters of the norm into new areas of operationalization that feed back into international norm-making processes (Jacob 2018).

Within the UN, the Security Council, the Secretariat, and the General Assembly are the political bodies through which R2P has been advanced and operationalized, and increased focus on the role of the Human Rights Council has grown over recent years. The remainder of this section discusses each in turn.

The Security Council

The legitimacy of international collective action on R2P is premised on the authority of the Security Council. It provides the enforcement capacity that serves as both deterrent for offending behavior and incentive to expand non-coercive options. Without a tough enforcement mechanism available to the international community, the rationale to promote R2P to a broader base of regional, state, and sub-state levels is undermined. In practice, caution among UN member states toward R2P rests in large part on the potential abuse of R2P by powerful states to intervene within the domestic affairs of states, and the ineffectiveness of the Security Council in crises such as Syria and Yemen challenges the legitimacy of R2P as a core international principle. According to Alex Bellamy, the strengthening of the R2P norm among states was facilitated by the clarification "that the principle was essentially *political* and normative, that it conformed to the UN Charter and did not aspire to amend international law" (Bellamy 2016, 259, emphasis in original). In doing so, the Council confirmed to states the commitment that was made at the 2005 World Summit and alleviated concerns among states that R2P was a façade for humanitarian intervention or a threat to state sovereignty.

Despite these guarantees, the Security Council seems unable to find an equilibrium between excessive interventionism and inaction in its strategic responses to human protection crises. Not only do the restraints of geopolitics and national interest hamper effective cooperation among Council members, but a number of factors have been identified as trends within Council institutional practice that decreases its efficiency and effectiveness for preventive action. These include the rising number of crises with which the Council is faced, a lack of coordination and information sharing across the UN system, and poor time-management that detracts from time spent developing preventive responses to escalating crises (Security Council Report 2017). Nonetheless, the Council is a vital institution to build a broader-based regulatory regime for strengthening R2P objectives of atrocity prevention and civilian protection.

Beyond the deterrent function that the Security Council fulfills through its capacity to enforce Chapter VII resolutions, the embrace of R2P language and reasoning within Council decision-making and formal texts has generated new opportunities and networks to reform the working methods of the Council. In the absence of progress on formal institutional reform of the Council, several state-led initiatives emerged to address the accountability deficit within it, and to promote more consistent protection responses to crises.

In 2011, R2P-wary members of the UN accused the NATO-led intervention in Libya of misusing the R2P justification included in Security Council Resolution 1973 (2011) to overreach its mandate. The resolution permitted NATO to impose a no-fly zone over Libya to halt attacks by Muammar Gaddafi's regime on the Libyan population; NATO's use of airstrikes, however, assisted the rebels, altered the balance of power on the ground, and facilitated regime change in the country. In response to the political fallout from the intervention among UN member states that objected to NATO's actions, the Brazilian Permanent Representative to the UN, Antonio Patriota, distributed a memo to the members of the General Assembly to advocate for clearer accountability measures of Council-mandated use of force. Brazil's diplomatic leadership eventually waned in advocating for its "Responsibility While Protecting" initiative after Patriota's term. Yet the bold memo – while initially controversial – galvanized political sentiments among a majority constituency within the UN membership (Kenkel and Stefan 2016), and currently two noteworthy initiatives are underway to advocate for much stronger accountability of the Council's working methods and decision-making.

The first is the "Code of Conduct Regarding Security Council Action Against Genocide, Crimes Against Humanity or War Crimes," launched in 2015 by the Accountability, Coherence, and Transparency group of twenty-four UN member states. The code commits all permanent and elected members of the Council not to vote against any credible resolution aimed at preventing or halting mass atrocity crimes. By October 2018, 118 states supported the code (Permanent Mission of the Principality of Liechtenstein to the United Nations New York 2018). The second is a French/Mexican initiative that calls on the Permanent Five (P5) members of the Security Council to never veto or block a draft resolution aimed at preventing or ending atrocities unless able to propose an alternative plan, in accordance with international law, that can achieve similar goals. As of June 27, 2017, ninety-six states (Global Centre for the Responsibility to Protect n.d.) support the "Political Statement on the Suspension of the Veto in Case of Mass Atrocities" (2015) launched by France in 2015. Whereas France and the United Kingdom are the only members of the P5 committed to the initiatives, the political momentum is illustrative of the functioning of R2P in effecting a change in institutional expectations and logics over time.

The Secretariat

The Secretariat has been instrumental in channeling information to the Security Council, and coordinating meetings including the former Horizon-Scanning Briefings (2010–2013) and the newly instigated Situational Awareness Briefings (since 2016) to bring situations of concern for preventive action to the attention of the Council. Secretary-General Ban set up new committees in the Office of the Deputy Secretary-General and the Executive Office of the Secretary-General that serve as a fulcrum for early-warning and high-level decision-making. The Executive Committee, comprised of director-level leadership across key agencies, funds, and departments, meets on a monthly basis to review situations of concern and determine areas of key UN policy. These regional monthly reviews, and appraisals of these reviews conducted by the Deputies Committee at the Assistant and Under-Secretary-General level, are currently the main preventive mechanism within the UN system to provide joint analysis of potential and ongoing crises.

The DPPA within the Secretariat has also played a more prominent role in coordinating and aligning the preventive diplomacy and mediation function of the department with broader UN conflict-management operations (United Nations Department of Political Affairs 2015). One of the key conclusions of the High-Level Independent Panel on UN Peace Operations report was the need to support and invest further in political resolutions to conflict situations; a recommendation endorsed by Secretary-General Ban in his report on the future of peace operations. The call by Guterres (2016) for a "surge in peace diplomacy" in his 2016 vision statement has been a reiterated theme throughout his tenure to date to continue raising the priority of prevention of mass atrocities and armed conflict as central to ongoing reform (see also Guterres 2017b).

Through the Special Advisors to the Secretary-General on the Prevention of Genocide and R2P, the Secretariat has fostered the conceptual development of R2P norms among member states. This includes the Secretary-General's annual reports on R2P, hosting the annual informal dialogues on R2P, and participation in annual ministerial meetings on R2P hosted by the Global Centre for the Responsibility to Protect. The annual dialogues serve as a platform upon which to develop R2P norms and generate consensus on the core areas of international agreement, and have therefore contributed to a substantive move from debate over the validity of R2P itself toward debates over implementation (Schmidt 2016). The office has also played a crucial role in providing early warning and engaging in preventive diplomacy to contribute to behind-the-scenes prevention.

The General Assembly

The General Assembly serves as a crucial consensus building and decision-making body at the UN. It has yet to develop dedicated mechanisms for dealing with mass atrocities, however, and has yet to use its emergency session procedure Uniting for Peace (United Nations General Assembly 1950) to exercise a specific role in mass atrocity prevention and response that was envisaged in the 2001 ICISS report. To date, General Assembly Uniting for Peace resolutions have framed crises in the context of international peace and security, or the prevention of armed conflict, and have consequently evaded a specific responsibility to address situations of mass atrocities (Strauss 2015). There is latent capacity within the Assembly to institutionalize R2P deeper in the UN. This includes through formal dialogues on R2P, budgetary facilitation by the fifth committee to fund the joint office of the Special Advisors to the Secretary-General on the Prevention of Genocide and R2P which is needed to extend their work to mainstream R2P in the UN, and the agreement over working procedures on R2P implementation. Such developments could strengthen the governance of international atrocity-prevention norms without creating overly burdensome compliance mechanisms that many states have long resisted (International Coalition for the Responsibility to Protect 2009; Wolter 2007).

The General Assembly has held annual dialogues on R2P since 2009 that coincide with the release of the Secretary-General's report on R2P. With the exceptions of 2009 and 2018, these talks have been informal, evidence of the difficulty that advocate states have had in getting R2P formalized within the Assembly. According to Megan Schmidt, the Assembly dialogues have generated five core themes that have changed the tone of the debate among states and shaped common perceptions within the Security Council over the applicability of R2P in its response to mass atrocities and civilian protection crises (see Schmidt 2016). Progressive dialogues in the Assembly through an open platform for states to raise and mitigate inhibitions over the potential implications for R2P have facilitated consensus building among member states, as well as strengthened expectations that the Council should adhere to international R2P norms (Bellamy 2016). Substantively, these dialogues have served to identify the role of peacekeeping, peacebuilding, and human rights capabilities within the UN for supporting R2P objectives, but also emphasized the governance, security, and socioeconomic dimensions of state and civil society levels of responsibility that have supported a layering of responsibility and accountability for R2P.

Conclusion

To sum up this brief survey, the institutionalization of R2P in the UN through the 2005 World Summit Outcome document fell short of establishing institutional mandates and mechanisms dedicated to the implementation of R2P – with the caveat that the legitimacy of international collective action on R2P ultimately rests on Security Council authority. In the decade that followed the World Summit, institutional focus turned to conceptual development and consensus building within the UN and among member states and civil society, rather than through formal institutional reform. With the conceptual widening of R2P, notable institutional reform has unfolded in a graduated manner through a process of revisiting, challenging, and reinterpreting mandates of UN bodies with functions commensurate with various aspects of R2P such as atrocity prevention, state capacity-building, human rights promotion, peacebuilding, and peace enforcement. These conceptual and institutional developments have been integral to the development of domestic and regional R2P implementation efforts examined throughout this book.

Notes

1. The Convention on the Prevention and Punishment of the Crime of Genocide was adopted by the United Nations General Assembly on December 9, 1948 as General Assembly Resolution 260. The Convention entered into force on January 12, 1951.
2. The International Criminal Tribunals of Rwanda and Yugoslavia served as precedents to the International Criminal Court, including the development of substantial jurisprudence in international criminal law.
3. Examples include the Political Instability Task Force early warning datasets developed by Barbara Harff and Ted Gurr, now maintained by the Center for Systemic Peace, www.systemicpeace.org/; the Center for Preventive Action at the Council on Foreign Relations' annual "Preventive Priorities Surveys"; the Minority Rights Group International's "Peoples Under Threat" reports; and the Atrocity Forecasting Project, School of Politics and International Relations, The Australian National University, http://politicsir.cass.anu.edu.au/research/projects/atrocity-forecasting.
4. See the work of the Political Instability Task Force; the Center for Preventive Action at the Council on Foreign Relations; Minority Rights Group International; and the Atrocity Forecasting Project.
5. Although it has received less support under the administration of US President Donald J. Trump, the Board continues its work, and provides an example of how national policymakers can bring together a coordinated strategic approach to the prevention of mass atrocities.
6. Interview with human rights expert and former UN field staff, Washington, DC, April 26, 2018.
7. At the time of writing, this included seventy-seven references in Security Council resolutions, twenty-one references in Security Council presidential statements, thirty-nine references in Human Rights Council resolutions, and thirteen references in General Assembly resolutions. See Global Centre for the Responsibility to Protect (2018a, 2018b, 2018c).

References

Albright, Madeleine K., and William S. Cohen, Co-Chairs, 2008. *Preventing Genocide: A Blueprint for US Policymakers* (Washington, DC: United States Holocaust Memorial Museum, American Academy of Diplomacy, and the Endowment of the United States Institute of Peace).

Arbour, Louise, 2008. "The Responsibility to Protect as a Duty of Care in International Law and Practice," *Review of International Studies* 34, no. 3: 445–58.

Ban Ki-moon, 2009. "Implementing the Responsibility to Protect: Report of the Secretary-General," A/63/677, January 12.

Ban Ki-moon, 2013. "Rights Up Front: A Plan of Action to Strengthen the UN's Role in Protecting People in Crises. Follow-Up to the Report of the Secretary-General's Internal Review Panel on UN Action in Sri Lanka," July 9, http://innercitypress.com/sriban1rightsupfronticp.pdf.

Bellamy, Alex J., 2016. "UN Security Council," in Alex J. Bellamy and Tim Dunne, eds, *The Oxford Handbook of the Responsibility to Protect* (Oxford: Oxford University Press), 249–268.

Boutros-Ghali, Boutros, 1992. "An Agenda for Peace: Preventive Diplomacy, Peacemaking and Peace-keeping," A/47/277–S/24111, June 17.

Brunnée, Jutta, and Stephen J. Toope, 2005. "Norms, Institutions and UN Reform: The Responsibility to Protect," *Journal of International Law and International Relations* 2, no. 1: 121–37.

Cliffe, Sarah, 2017. *UN Peace and Security Reform: Cautious Steps in the Right Direction* (New York: Center on International Cooperation, New York University).

Cohen, Dara Kay, 2016. *Rape During Civil War* (Ithaca, NY: Cornell University Press).

Global Centre for the Responsibility to Protect, 2018a. "R2P References in United Nations Human Rights Council Resolutions," December 3, www.globalr2p.org/media/files/hrc-resolutions-r2p-3-december-2018.pdf.

Global Centre for the Responsibility to Protect, 2018b. "R2P References in United Nations General Assembly Resolutions," July 31, www.globalr2p.org/media/files/unga-resolutions-with-r2p-language-31-july-2018.pdf.

Global Centre for the Responsibility to Protect, 2018c. "R2P References in United Nations Security Council Resolutions and Presidential Statements," November 27, www.globalr2p.org/media/files/unsc-resolutions-and-statements-with-r2p-table-as-of-27-november-2018-1.pdf.

Global Centre for the Responsibility to Protect, n.d. "UN Security Council Code of Conduct," www.globalr2p.org/our_work/un_security_council_code_of_conduct.

Guterres, António, 2016. *Challenges and Opportunities for the United Nations* (Lisbon, Portugal: Secretary-General Vision Statement, April 4).

Guterres, António, 2017a. "Enhancing Performance in the Peace and Security Pillar," Inter-Office Memorandum, January 3, https://peaceoperationsreview.org/wp-content/uploads/2017/01/enhancing_performance_in_the_peace_and_security_pillar.pdf.

Guterres, António, 2017b. "Secretary-General's Remarks to the Security Council Open Debate on 'Maintenance of International Peace and Security: Conflict Prevention and Sustaining Peace'," January 10.

Harff, Barbara, 2017. "Genocide and Political Mass Murder: Definitions, Theories, Analyses," in Michael Stohl, Mark I. Lichbach, and Peter Nils Grabosky, eds, *States and Peoples in Conflict: Transformations of Conflict Studies* (Abingdon: Routledge), 208–30.

ICISS (International Commission on Intervention and State Sovereignty), 2001. *The Responsibility to Protect: Report of the International Commission on Intervention and State Sovereignty* (Ottawa: International Development Research Centre, 2001).

Internal Review Panel on United Nations Action in Sri Lanka, 2012. *Report of the Secretary-General's Internal Review Panel on United Nations Action in Sri Lanka* (New York: United Nations, November).

International Coalition for the Responsibility to Protect, 2009. "State-by-State Positions on the Responsibility to Protect," August 11, www.responsibilitytoprotect.org/files/Chart_R2P_11August.pdf.

Jacob, Cecilia, 2018. "From Norm Contestation to Norm Implementation: Recursivity and the Responsibility to Protect," *Global Governance* 24, no. 3: 391–409.

Kalyvas, Stathis N., 2006. *The Logic of Violence in Civil War* (Cambridge: Cambridge University Press).

Kaplan, Robert D., 1993. *Balkan Ghosts: A Journey Through History* (New York: St. Martin's Press).

Karstedt, Susanne, 2013. "Contextualizing Mass Atrocity Crimes: Moving toward a Relational Approach," *Annual Review of Law and Social Science* 9: 383–404.

Kenkel, Kai Michael, and Cristina G. Stefan, 2016. "Brazil and the Responsibility While Protecting Initiative: Norms and the Timing of Diplomatic Support," *Global Governance* 22, no. 1: 41–58.

Klusemann, Stefan, 2012. "Massacres as Process: A Micro-Sociological Theory of Internal Patterns of Mass Atrocities," *European Journal of Criminology* 9, no. 5: 468–80.

Kurtz, Gerrit, 2015. "With Courage and Coherence: The Human Rights Up Front Initiative of the United Nations," Policy Paper (Berlin: Global Public Policy Institute, July).

Lemarchand, René, 2009. *The Dynamics of Violence in Central Africa* (Philadelphia: University of Pennsylvania Press).

Luck, Edward C., 2018. "Why the United Nations Underperforms at Preventing Mass Atrocities," *Genocide Studies and Prevention: An International Journal* 11, no. 3: 32–47.

Obama, Barack, 2011. "Presidential Study Directive 10: Directive on Creation of an Interagency Atrocities Prevention Board and Corresponding Interagency Review," August 4.

Permanent Mission of the Principality of Liechtenstein to the United Nations New York, 2018. "List of Supporters of the Code of Conduct Regarding Security Council Action Against Genocide, Crimes Against Humanity or War Crimes, as Elaborated by ACT," October 4, www.regierung.li/media/medienarchiv/2018-10-04_CoC_List_of_supporters.pdf.

"Political Statement on the Suspension of the Veto in Case of Mass Atrocities," 2015. August 1, http://responsibilitytoprotect.org/ACT%20English.pdf.

Reike, Ruben, 2014. "The 'Responsibility to Prevent': An International Crimes Approach to the Prevention of Mass Atrocities," *Ethics & International Affairs* 28, no. 4: 451–76.

Reike, Ruben, 2016. "The Struggle for Individual Criminal Accountability in a World of States: From 'New' to 'Credible' to 'Rough' Justice," *Journal of Intervention and Statebuilding* 10, no. 3: 446–51.

Reike, Reuben, Serena K. Sharma, and Jennifer M. Welsh, 2015. "Conceptualizing the Responsibility to Prevent," in Serena K. Sharma and Jennifer M. Welsh, eds, *The Responsibility to Prevent: Overcoming the Challenges of Atrocity Prevention* (Oxford: Oxford University Press), 21–37.

Scheffer, David J., 2002. "The Future of Atrocity Law," *Suffolk Transnational Law Review* 25, no. 3: 389–432.

Schmidt, Megan, 2016. "UN General Assembly," in Alex J. Bellamy and Tim Dunne, eds, *The Oxford Handbook of the Responsibility to Protect* (Oxford: Oxford University Press), 269–87.

Security Council Report, 2017. "Can the Security Council Prevent Conflict?" Research Report No. 1 (New York: Security Council Report, February 9).

Serrano, Mónica, 2015. "National Focal Points for R2P: Institutionalizing the Responsibility to Prevent," in Serena K. Sharma and Jennifer M. Welsh, eds, *The Responsibility to Prevent: Overcoming the Challenges of Atrocity Prevention* (Oxford: Oxford University Press), 83–100.

Smeulers, Alette, and Lotte Hoex, 2010. "Studying the Microdynamics of the Rwandan Genocide," *British Journal of Criminology* 50, no. 3: 435–54.

Straus, Scott, 2012. "Retreating from the Brink: Theorizing Mass Violence and the Dynamics of Restraint," *Perspectives on Politics* 10, no. 2: 343–62.

Straus, Scott, 2015. "Triggers of Mass Atrocities," *Politics and Governance* 3, no. 3: 5–15.

Straus, Scott, 2016. *Fundamentals of Genocide and Mass Atrocity Prevention* (Washington, DC: United States Holocaust Memorial Museum).

Strauss, Ekkehard, 2015. "Institutional Capacities of the United Nations to Prevent and Halt Atrocity Crimes," in Serena K. Sharma and Jennifer M. Welsh, eds, *The Responsibility to Prevent: Overcoming the Challenges of Atrocity Prevention* (Oxford: Oxford University Press), 38–82.

Strauss, Ekkehard, 2016. "UN Human Rights Council and High Commissioner for Human Rights," in Alex J. Bellamy and Tim Dunne, eds, *The Oxford Handbook of the Responsibility to Protect* (Oxford: Oxford University Press), 315–34.

Streitfeld-Hall, Jaclyn D., 2015. "Preventing Mass Atrocities in West Africa," Occasional Papers No. 6 (New York: Global Centre for the Responsibility to Protect, September).

Thomson, Peter, 2017. "Building Sustainable Peace for All," President of the General Assembly Briefing, January 20, www.un.org/pga/71/2017/01/20/building-sustainable-peace-for-all/.

UN Women, 2015. *Preventing Conflict, Transforming Justice, Securing the Peace: A Global Study on the Implementation of United Nations Security Council Resolution 1325* (New York: United Nations).

United Nations, 2014. *Framework of Analysis for Atrocity Crimes: A Tool for Prevention* (New York: Joint Office of the Special Advisors to the Secretary-General on the Prevention of Genocide and the Responsibility to Protect).

United Nations, 2015a. "The Future of United Nations Peace Operations: Implementation of the Recommendations of the High-Level Independent Panel on Peace Operations," A/70/357–S/2015/682, September 2.

United Nations, 2015b. *The Challenge of Sustaining Peace: Report of the Advisory Group of Experts for the 2015 Review of the United Nations Peacebuilding Architecture* (New York: United Nations, June 29).

United Nations, 2015c. *Uniting our Strengths for Peace: Politics, Partnership and People: Report of the High-Level Independent Panel on United Nations Peace Operations* (New York: United Nations, June 16).

United Nations Department of Political Affairs, 2015. *Strategic Plan 2016–2019* (New York: Department of Political Affairs, November 20).

United Nations General Assembly, 1950. "Uniting for Peace," A/RES/377(V), November 3.

United Nations General Assembly, 2005. "2005 World Summit Outcome," A/RES/60/1, October 24.

United Nations Human Rights Council, 2015. "Report of the OHCHR Investigation on Sri Lanka (OISL)," A/HRC/30/CRP.2, September 16.

Valentino, Benjamin, 2014. "Why We Kill: The Political Science of Political Violence Against Civilians," *Annual Review of Political Science* 17: 89–103.

Weinstein, Jeremy M., 2007. *Inside Rebellion: The Politics of Insurgent Violence* (Cambridge: Cambridge University Press).

Welsh, Jennifer M., 2013. "Norm Contestation and the Responsibility to Protect," *Global Responsibility to Protect* 5, no. 4: 365–96.

Wolter, Detlev, 2007. *A United Nations for the 21st Century: From Reaction to Prevention* (Baden-Baden: Nomos).

PART I
National implementation mechanisms

PART 1
National implementation mechanisms

2
DENMARK AND THE IMPLEMENTATION OF R2P

Martin Mennecke

All but a few detractors support, in principle, the United Nations (UN) norm "Responsibility to Protect" (R2P). But what does R2P mean in practice? How can support for R2P be operationalized beyond speeches at the UN? This chapter seeks to spell out how Denmark, a strong supporter of R2P, could integrate atrocity prevention more efficiently into its foreign policy.

Denmark is an interesting case. It currently ranks last on the list of 162 countries on the watch list of the Early Warning Project of the US Holocaust Memorial Museum (2019), and, indeed, genocide or crimes against humanity seem a very unlikely possibility in Denmark. Other issues dominate the Danish political landscape: immigration, Brexit, and terrorism, to name just a few. The recent government strategy on Danish foreign policy and security issues does not once refer to atrocity prevention (Ministry of Foreign Affairs of Denmark 2017).

And yet, the prevention of atrocity crimes is a task in which Danish policymakers should take an interest, as it relates directly to other Danish foreign policy priorities. Atrocity crimes destabilize countries and entire regions, they impact trade and development, they cause millions of people to flee, they traumatize societies and ignite a cycle of revenge and conflict, and they represent a breakdown of the international rule of law – all developments which are diametrically opposed to what Danish foreign policy seeks to achieve.

As a small European country, Denmark strives for a world based on the international rule of law, the prevention of conflict and gross human rights violations, and fewer refugees in the world (Permanent Mission of Denmark to the United Nations 2016, 3–6; see also the founding document of the previous Danish government coalition, Danish Government 2016, 41–43). Atrocity crimes violate, very starkly, the basic dignity of humanity as well as the values on which Danish foreign policy is based. The prevention of atrocity crimes should therefore also be seen as a foreign policy priority which echoes and reinforces other Danish foreign policy priorities.[1] This would be in line with what has been recognized, for example, by the European Union (EU) and the United States. Thus, in 2016, the EU "Global Strategy" stated that "without global norms and the means to enforce them, peace and security, prosperity and democracy—our vital interests—are at risk"; "the EU will also promote the responsibility to protect" (European External Action Service 2016, 39, 42). US President Barack Obama's "Presidential Study Directive 10" stated already in 2011 that "preventing mass atrocities and genocide is a core national security and a core moral responsibility of the United States. Our security is affected when masses of civilians are slaughtered, refugees flow across borders, and murderers wreak havoc on regional stability and livelihoods" (Obama 2011; for a similar discussion regarding Australia, see Bellamy 2010, 441–443).

This chapter examines how atrocity prevention can be effectively integrated into Danish foreign policy and focuses in particular on Danish efforts regarding human rights and development cooperation (for an earlier study, see Kendal 2013). Denmark has been an instrumental actor regarding the creation of international cooperation on R2P, and this contribution has been key to advancing and implementing R2P internationally. This dimension of Danish R2P efforts is particularly important as R2P continues to be (comparatively speaking) a new norm worthy of support as, for example, through affirmative resolutions and statements. This chapter focuses, however, on what Denmark can do to practice R2P in its *own* foreign policy, what challenges exist, and how they could be addressed. The focus is on *practicing* R2P, through concrete measures that seek to prevent atrocity crimes.

The following section briefly introduces Denmark's role in international cooperation on R2P. I then examine Danish efforts regarding human rights and development cooperation, as they both represent key priorities of Danish foreign policy and could underscore the preventive character of R2P. These sections include an analysis of existing challenges and issues that remain to be addressed, before the chapter concludes with a set of practical recommendations for the future.

Denmark and R2P

For a number of years, Denmark has been one of the leading supporters of R2P and its implementation (for recognition of Denmark's role in the UN context, see Ban 2013, paragraph 57).[2] In order to advance and strengthen the norm, as well as its operationalization, the Danish government has chosen a three-pronged approach: to strengthen R2P cooperation with other governments, with international organizations, and with civil society.

National governments are the primary bearer of R2P. It therefore makes sense for Denmark to collaborate with other countries in order to learn from their work with the implementation of R2P. Denmark does so in a number of fora, including a small informal group of like-minded countries that seeks to apply R2P to their own policies and practice. This group, the International Atrocity Prevention Working Group, meets twice yearly and is composed of Australia, Canada, Denmark, Germany, the Netherlands, the United Kingdom, and the United States. The group has proven instrumental for strategizing about how to advance atrocity prevention at the national and international levels. It has also generated concrete inputs concerning R2P processes at the UN and produced outcomes such as bilateral cooperation on thematic R2P projects and in-country situations. Denmark hosted a meeting of this group in April 2015 in Copenhagen, and continues to participate in shaping its ongoing work.

In another key development, Denmark in 2010 co-founded the international network of R2P Focal Points – a global forum where senior R2P practitioners from national governments can exchange experiences, share good practices, and build a community of commitment (on the role of the Danish R2P Focal Point, see Kendal 2013, 14ff; on the global Focal Point network, see Global Centre for the Responsibility to Protect n.d.). Denmark plays an active role in the leadership of this network, and is a member of its newly founded steering group.

In 2013, Denmark and Ghana organized the first international meeting of R2P Focal Points outside New York in order to underscore that R2P is first and foremost about what happens at the national level rather than what is proclaimed in speeches at the UN. As a follow-up, in 2014, Denmark cooperated with the Kofi Annan International Peacekeeping Training Centre and the Global Centre for the Responsibility to Protect and organized the first R2P practitioner training for African military personnel, government officials, and civil society. The course has since been offered on an annual basis, and may also become part of the curriculum at other peacekeeping training schools (see Kofi Annan International Peacekeeping Training Centre n.d.).

International organizations play an important role in implementing Pillars One and Two of R2P: cooperation to prevent and stop atrocity crimes will often be linked to the framework of the UN or that of a regional organization. Denmark works at the UN toward the operationalization of R2P inside and across the UN system, as well as among member states. Denmark is an active member of the Groups of Friends of R2P, both in Geneva and New York (currently as the group's co-chair), and also supports the work of the Joint Office of the two UN Special Advisers in the field of atrocity prevention.

In addition, Denmark has engaged strongly with the EU to initiate a cross-institutional discussion on how the EU could integrate R2P into its work. As a resourceful and influential regional organization, the EU has many entry points for atrocity prevention. For example, the EU has representations in more than 130 countries around the world, enabling it to learn often firsthand about relevant risk factors on the ground and to initiate preventive measures.

Lasting Danish efforts, together with those of the Netherlands and other like-minded EU member states, have helped to facilitate the appointment of an EU Focal Point for R2P inside the European External Action Service. This Focal Point is meant to catalyze the internal process to work with atrocity-prevention issues across the EU system. There are already concrete outcomes of this internal work with atrocity prevention such as the explicit inclusion of R2P into the EU's "Global Strategy" (European External Action Service 2016) and the European

Commission's newest proposal for a new development policy paper (European Commission 2016, paragraph 52). Denmark has also co-organized several expert-level meetings of R2P desk officers from all EU member states in the United Nations Working Party (CONUN) which develops common EU policies on UN issues. This initiative led to the adoption in 2015 of a set of recommendations on how the EU should work with R2P which is now being reviewed annually and, as necessary, revised by the CONUN expert group. Finally, Denmark has engaged the European External Action Service on how to integrate atrocity-prevention issues into the EU's new early-warning system and how to continuously share this information with member states.

In regard to civil society, Denmark has established strong relationships with key players including the Global Centre for the Responsibility to Protect, the International Coalition for the Responsibility to Protect, and the Simon Skjodt Centre for the Prevention of Genocide at the US Holocaust Memorial Museum. Denmark works closely with these international civil society groups, as well as with local partners, to ensure that non-state expertise and experience is included in the process of atrocity prevention. This cooperation also acknowledges the fact that civil society can make its own contribution to atrocity prevention and is needed to keep governments committed to the new and complex agenda of atrocity prevention. Against this background, Denmark partnered in 2014 with the aforementioned civil society groups and a number of other governments (including Australia, Costa Rica, Switzerland, and Tanzania) to organize the first meeting of a new international initiative called Global Action Against Mass Atrocity Crimes (GAAMAC).[3] This informal network convenes governments, international organizations, civil society, and relevant professionals to create an open forum for exchanging best practices.

Through these various initiatives, Denmark has established itself as one of the key players in the international R2P community. The next two sections examine how Danish foreign policy can integrate R2P as a means of effective atrocity prevention – starting with Danish human rights efforts.

Denmark, human rights, and R2P

In much of the academic literature on R2P, surprisingly little is made of the relationship between R2P and human rights, particularly given the overlap between the protection of a population against atrocity crimes and the protection of the human rights of that population. The crime of genocide, for example, protects existential human rights of certain groups within the population. Similarly, crimes against humanity capture the widespread or systematic abuse of basic human rights of any civilian population. Thus, the effective implementation of R2P will contribute to the protection of essential human rights just as the effective protection of human rights will help the successful implementation of R2P (see Ban 2009, paragraphs 7, 16, 17, 22, 33, 35, 44, 47, 67, and 68). In light of this relationship, the question for the practitioner then becomes whether all work done on human rights issues can also be seen as work toward the implementation of R2P – making the two indistinguishable and as one. In other words: is everything eventually R2P?

Human rights and R2P: more of the same, or is there an added value?

This overlap between R2P and human rights is a key concern for the implementation agenda, as to add R2P to the busy schedule of a ministry official only makes sense (and can only succeed) if R2P entails an added value compared to the human rights work already done by a foreign ministry. This question also applies to R2P and development cooperation and to all efforts to operationalize R2P – be it in the Foreign Ministry, the Ministry of Justice, or the Ministry of Defence.

This is a key question which all too often is neglected in the academic literature and by civil society efforts in the field. Especially in times of austerity and competing and other cross-cutting agendas, it is essential to spell out why a certain issue such as R2P requires special attention. It is not enough to rely on normative arguments that merely stipulate that "never again" should atrocity crimes be committed. Such an approach helps to generate speeches, but not action. This is more so when the key objective is to see atrocity prevention in practice, and not just stated as a reference point in wordy resolutions. The question, therefore, is whether R2P, beyond adding a label and a normative dimension, changes anything in practice when it comes to human rights.

The overwhelming answer is positive; R2P and atrocity prevention can lead to, and may require, distinct measures to be taken. The added value of R2P is related to the specific focus of R2P on the four atrocity crimes. At its core, R2P is not about creating a democratic, rule-of-law-based, free society, but is specifically about protecting populations from mass atrocities. This means that not all human rights work is closely linked to the implementation of R2P. Evidently, the risk of atrocity crimes being committed is significantly lower in democratic, rule-of-law-based free societies, but their creation can only be a long-term goal and relates to questions of structural prevention. For the immediate future, in order to prevent atrocity crimes, the focus has to be on those human rights that are key when it comes to warning signs for the immediate commission of atrocity crimes. Thus the UN Framework of Analysis for Atrocity Crimes refers, with regard to the prevention of atrocity crimes, to the importance of protecting and promoting specific human rights (Joint UN Office for the Prevention of Genocide and Responsibility to Protect 2014, 3, 11).

This means that the effective implementation of R2P requires, as appropriate, the focus on certain human rights issues, as these have a particular potential in leading up to atrocity crimes – rather than just to address general human rights violations. This is more pertinent in countries that have been identified as also facing other significant risks regarding the commission of atrocity crimes. It makes much more sense for human rights officers in such countries to pay particular attention to R2P issues in order to prevent atrocity crimes, as their commission equals the total negation of essential human rights. In the words of former UN High Commissioner for Human Rights, Zeid Ra'ad al Hussein (2015), R2P "is emphatically not 'just another agenda item'," but "must guide" the work on human rights.

In scenarios with significant risks for atrocity crimes, R2P awareness is thus not just a matter of labeling, but is a step toward identifying those human rights measures which can specifically address R2P-related risks and help to prioritize them accordingly. In turn, R2P thus assists human rights efforts and helps to identify and address issues that otherwise might not receive timely or sufficient attention.

For Denmark, advancing and strengthening human rights is an explicit government priority (see, for example, Rasmussen 2015; Danish Government 2011, 32). In order to realize this goal and to prevent the total negation of essential human rights through atrocity crimes, it is necessary to continuously consider the practical linkages between R2P and Danish work on human rights issues. As a member of all major human rights instruments, Denmark has numerous options about where to reinforce its human rights efforts by integrating R2P into the work on human rights issues. One of the key international fora that works on the promotion and protection of human rights is the UN Human Rights Council in Geneva. It has not shed all the weaknesses of its predecessor and does not have the same enforcement powers as the UN Security Council, but it has been equipped with some meaningful innovations, including the Universal Periodic Review (UPR) process. The Human Rights Council is currently of particular interest for Danish foreign policy, as Denmark for the first time since its establishment in 2006 is a member of the Council for the period 2019–2021 (see Jensen 2016).

As a result, the following analysis of how Denmark can best integrate R2P into its human rights efforts focuses on what Denmark can do in regard to the Human Rights Council. This is not to diminish the potential role of other human rights bodies in advancing the implementation of R2P, but merely serves to highlight one forum in which R2P and Danish human rights efforts can overlap and reinforce one another, and which additional measures atrocity prevention requires from existing human rights policies.[4]

Integrating R2P into Danish work at the UN Human Rights Council

The Human Rights Council provides a number of different opportunities for operationalizing atrocity prevention. At the general level, one can again distinguish between promoting R2P as a key norm and promoting R2P as an operational matter. Especially in Geneva, for many states, R2P is still a relatively new matter – and therefore, outreach on the significance of R2P in the human rights system remains important. A Group of Friends for R2P was only established in Geneva in 2015 (its counterpart in New York has existed since 2008) and, unlike New York, Geneva does not have annual dialogues on the role and meaning of R2P. Thus Denmark and others should continuously engage in R2P outreach activities in Geneva, through the Group of Friends, inside the EU, and together with other like-minded governments such as those active in the GAAMAC initiative or the Latin American Network for Genocide and Mass Atrocity Prevention (for further information on the Latin American Network, see Auschwitz Institute for Peace and Reconciliation n.d.). Such efforts will help to strengthen R2P as a norm and increase its acceptance, and may gradually enable a more focused approach and better results in atrocity prevention in Geneva.

On the operational side, each of the three R2P pillars entails concrete policy options for how Danish foreign policy can integrate R2P into its human rights efforts. Under Pillar One, Denmark has the responsibility to protect its own population from atrocity crimes. While there is no Danish legislation that explicitly refers to R2P or atrocity prevention, there are a host of different measures that help to achieve this very result inside Denmark. This includes, for example, Danish efforts to prosecute hate crimes, initiatives to learn from past atrocity crimes on Denmark's national commemoration day (Auschwitz Day), and Danish teaching material against Holocaust denial.

In order to strengthen R2P as a norm and to give practical meaning to Pillar One in a European context, Denmark could report on these measures in its own UPR to the Human Rights Council. Denmark could also more generally report on how Danish institutions provide relevant protection. Such a step would reaffirm the universal importance of Pillar One and strengthen the R2P norm by its explicit application in practice. It would also send a signal to other countries to consider the same practical approach to R2P and to do so outside the context of mere references to the importance of R2P during the annual UN dialogues or discussions on armed intervention in the UN Security Council, where, more often than not, prevention is no longer an option.

In Denmark's most recent UPR report on the national human rights situation, the Danish government for the first time stated that it "continuously aims to exercise its responsibility to protect" (United Nations Human Rights Council 2015a, paragraph 22). This was an important first signal for the relevance and importance of R2P, but also a step that should be elaborated further in the future. Because Denmark currently faces no substantial risks for atrocity crimes, it should seek to explain what is being done in terms of human rights at the national level to sustain this situation. R2P does not require a separate chapter in the national report, but should be interwoven into relevant parts of the submission.

Under Pillar Two, the focus shifts to international assistance and to the encouragement of other states to exercise their responsibility to protect their populations against atrocity crimes. Also in this context, the UPR process in the Human Rights Council could play an important role. As part of the UPR, countries can pose questions to the state under review, as well as make concrete recommendations. From an R2P perspective, the UPR can be used to highlight and commend good practices, as well as to pinpoint immediate or structural R2P risks and make recommendations in that regard. All this would again highlight the preventive nature of R2P and help to make it evident that R2P is primarily not about armed interventions. Indeed, R2P could help to identify priorities that are particularly important for the human rights situation in a given country.

For the practitioner, however, a number of challenges could arise from such an application of R2P, and these issues need to be addressed to ensure the successful integration of atrocity prevention into human rights efforts. As with the inclusion of R2P into the national UPR report, the first obstacle for the inclusion of R2P into the review of other states will be the very limited time available for each state to ask questions (for more information on the procedure of a UPR session, see United Nations Human Rights Council n.d.a). Potential R2P concerns will compete with other issues raised in this short period. Moreover, Denmark traditionally only questions countries where it has embassy representation, allowing for a priori input and subsequent follow-up. This means there would be no Danish UPR questions to a number of states, even though they face concrete R2P issues. This challenge could potentially be addressed by collaborating with other states which share an interest in advancing the preventive R2P agenda through the UPR.

At a more general level, these considerations underscore that R2P has to be carefully integrated into existing human rights efforts, rather than superimposed. There may be occasions when a new awareness of atrocity prevention leads to the inclusion of a question inspired by R2P concerns, but there will also be occasions when other issues are considered more pressing and need to be prioritized within the respective UPR session.

In this context, another important question to consider is whether it is necessary or useful to invoke R2P, as such, in the UPR process, or whether these matters should be addressed in a more implicit manner. With a view to reaffirming and strengthening the norm, it may seem preferable to use explicit R2P language in relevant statements, questions, and resolutions. An explicit R2P reference about a certain country's responsibility to protect its people may also help to clarify the nature of the concern and to solicit an appropriate response.

If we focus on the substance of atrocity prevention, however, one could on the other hand question whether the insistence on R2P language indeed advances the prospects of implementing R2P measures. It is well known that today, regardless of R2P's origin in the unanimously adopted World Summit Outcome document in 2005, there exists a small, but vocal, number of UN member states who are clearly opposed to R2P and its operationalization. Some dismiss it with reference to NATO's intervention in Libya, others question it because of an alleged Western bias; it is a fact that some states would not respond positively to R2P being introduced as the framework of their UPR. In such a situation, it seems questionable whether the inclusion of R2P language into the UPR really can contribute to the effective implementation of R2P. In other words, a case-by-case approach is necessary. While in general, R2P language should be used to highlight its meaning and significance, sometimes a less explicit approach to R2P may result in more R2P. Political discussions on R2P and its scope, as well as R2P outreach attempts to skeptical or critical states, may be better placed in the context of other, less operational fora such as the annual R2P dialogue in the UN General Assembly rather than in result-oriented procedures such as the UPR.

All this suggests that the application of R2P throughout the UPR process is possible and can be meaningful, but it also underscores that it has to be prepared carefully and designed after a contextual analysis in order to calibrate the R2P input and gain support from the human rights experts within a ministry. R2P has to be considered as part of the UPR preparations. On that basis, atrocity prevention can be integrated into the UPR and can strengthen both the UPR and R2P.

In addition to the UPR, there are other opportunities for identifying and addressing R2P issues in the Human Rights Council. For example, a number of the special rapporteurs under the Human Rights Council work on topics or with actors that are very relevant to the prevention of atrocity crimes. This is true both for some rapporteurs with a thematic mandate – for example, the one concerned with minority issues; the one working on the rights of indigenous peoples; and the one focused on transitional justice (i.e., the promotion of truth, justice, reparation, and guarantees of non-recurrence) – as well as those who focus on a country with significant R2P issues such as North Korea and Myanmar.[5] In regard to these special procedures, Denmark and like-minded countries could explore how R2P issues can be integrated into the mandates or meetings and dialogues with the special rapporteurs.

Pillar Three, which often mistakenly is seen as the prerogative of the UN Security Council, can be implemented through measures taken at the Human Rights Council. Here, the international community steps up and guards the responsibility to protect the relevant population from atrocity crimes, as the given country is not able or willing to do so. This applies, for example, when the Human Rights Council establishes commissions of inquiry, as these often have mandates that look into R2P issues such as the documentation of atrocity crimes and entail a discussion of potential avenues for accountability – without the consent of the concerned government. An illustration of this can be seen in the respective reports by the Human Rights Council's commissions on North Korea and Syria (cf. United Nations Human Rights Council 2014, 2016b).

Another opportunity to apply Pillar Three is to call a special session of the Human Rights Council. There have been twenty-eight such sessions; several of those dealt directly with R2P risks and discussed necessary R2P measures, including sessions regarding the situations in South Sudan, Burundi, and Myanmar, respectively.[6] Special sessions can gather regional and international attention to urgent R2P risks; they can encourage or pressure the relevant government to live up to its responsibility under Pillar One; and they can operationalize it and, by invoking and concretizing R2P, strengthen the norm and the universal recognition of R2P. This can also find its expression in resolutions adopted at a special session and result in the call for specific measures inspired by R2P to address specific atrocity risks.[7]

It is clear that there are numerous options on how Denmark's foreign policy could advance both human rights and R2P during its membership of the Human Rights Council. The relationship between R2P and Geneva is still underdeveloped and additional steps, as outlined previously, should be taken. The same applies to human rights initiatives outside the Human Rights Council; for example, those on which Denmark works in regional groupings such as the Nordic human rights dialogue or through the EU. At the Human Rights Council, the establishment of a Group of Friends of R2P provides Geneva with a new forum to take this topic further and to cooperate with like-minded governments and civil society in this regard. Such implementation of R2P would help the Council fulfill its mandate of preventing human rights violations as well as help states to realize the preventive nature of R2P. This could in the long run also make R2P less controversial among those states that remain somewhat ambivalent about it.

Denmark, development cooperation, and R2P

Similar to the linkages between human rights and R2P, the field of development cooperation has so far not been adequately covered in academic research on atrocity prevention.[8] While capacity-building is frequently listed as a measure relevant to long-term prevention, there has been little analysis and few practical examples for connecting the dots.

One important exception is the work done by the US development agency USAID, which published a field guide entitled "Helping Prevent Mass Atrocities" (USAID 2015). This document is a unique attempt to introduce practitioners to how to link their efforts in practice with the field of atrocity prevention. The guide builds on the premise that atrocity crimes represent the opposite of development – they destroy lives, societies, trust, and institutions. By way of illustration, it was noted that the Rwandan genocide caused its national gross domestic product (GDP) to fall by more than 60 percent (see USAID 2015, 11, for additional examples illustrating the impact of mass atrocities on development figures from a number of countries).

In the following section, I briefly examine how the relationship between atrocity prevention and development cooperation could look in a Danish context. Denmark is still one of the few countries that annually gives more than the UN-recommended 0.7 percent of its national GDP to development assistance; thus, development cooperation continues to be an important instrument of Danish foreign policy (see Ministry of Foreign Affairs of Denmark 2016, 3). The link to atrocity prevention should be self-evident; development cooperation aims to create conditions which allow everyone to live in just, peaceful, and inclusive societies (see UN Sustainable Development Goals 2016).[9] However, as in the earlier discussion on human rights, the first question to be addressed is whether the integration of atrocity prevention would add something to ongoing efforts of development cooperation.

Development cooperation and R2P: more of the same, or is there added value?

The added value of R2P lies again in the specific focus on atrocity crimes and protecting populations from mass atrocities. In practice, not all development cooperation efforts are directly linked to the implementation of R2P. While there may be a contribution toward lowering the overall risk for atrocity crimes, regular and unspecified development cooperation only relates to structural prevention. For a more targeted or short-term impact on the prevention of atrocity crimes, the focus has to be on identifying development efforts that relate directly to warning signs for atrocity crimes. One concrete example could be support of a national forum or mechanism to deal with identity-based tensions. Yet again, the UN "Framework of Analysis" can provide helpful pointers for the prevention of atrocity crimes, as can the USAID field guide (see, for example, Joint UN Office for the Prevention of Genocide and Responsibility to Protect 2014, paragraphs 3.7, 9.6; USAID 2015, 12–13).

This means that in regard to development cooperation, similarly to human rights, the implementation of R2P requires a focus on certain issues, as those have particular potential in leading up to atrocity crimes. This is true in countries that have been identified as also facing other significant risks regarding the commission of atrocity crimes. In such countries, it is very helpful for development cooperation officials to pay particular attention to R2P issues in order to prevent atrocity crimes which would endanger the very basis of the work they are doing. Identifying and addressing R2P-related risks will assist and strengthen development efforts in such situations. This process of integrating R2P risks and R2P measures could also be described as applying an atrocity-prevention lens or R2P lens to development cooperation.

There are various areas of development cooperation where Denmark could integrate atrocity prevention to take these issues forward. For example, R2P can be consulted when drafting a new concept note outlining development cooperation with a partner country. An R2P-informed analysis will not always lead to specific or new measures, but an appropriate R2P can serve several purposes. This includes considering R2P risk factors and the drawing up of scenarios that include the potential commission of atrocity crimes, as well as designing relevant countermeasures. This could, for example, take form in specific capacity-building measures in relevant sectors or contributions to establishing a national early-warning system. As discussed earlier, the benchmark for successfully integrating an R2P lens is not the adoption of R2P language across all future country papers, but the conscious consideration of atrocity risks where relevant.

By way of example, as mentioned earlier, Denmark has, since 2013, collaborated with Ghana on training officials from Ghana and other African nations from within the security sector (both police and military), civil society, and relevant ministries on both R2P and its implementation.[10] Other actors have partnered with Ghana on building national institutions that can assist in preventing atrocity crimes and function as part of a national early-warning system. This resulted in the establishment of Ghana's National Peace Council, which has played a very important role in the prevention of election violence through facilitating dialogue among relevant actors across the country, as well as identifying risk issues such as the use of inflammatory language (on the Peace Council and its role, see Awinador-Kanyirige 2014). Denmark has cooperated with the National Peace Council, as one of its senior officials served as Ghana's national Focal Point for R2P. Similarly, Denmark has supported the West Africa Network for Peacebuilding in authoring an assessment of Ghana's institutional awareness of R2P and capacity to address R2P issues (see West Africa Network for Peacebuilding 2016).

Integrating R2P into development cooperation

In this section, I detail the linkages between atrocity prevention and development cooperation and how they can be operationalized. This information is based on a workshop held in Kampala, Uganda – "The Role of Atrocity Prevention and Responsibility to Protect in Development Cooperation" – that was organized by the Danish Ministry of Foreign Affairs and USAID in March 2016, and assisted by a civil society partner, the International Coalition for the Responsibility to Protect.[11] The workshop brought together development practitioners, government representatives, and civil society actors from throughout East Africa, working in a range of sectors including human rights, development, and atrocity prevention.[12]

The workshop was the first of its kind to focus on the operational relationship between development cooperation and atrocity prevention. It was convened to increase the understanding of R2P and atrocity prevention among the development community, to identify the conceptual and practical links between development cooperation and atrocity prevention, to introduce tools for early warning regarding R2P/atrocity prevention and highlight their relevance for development cooperation, to discuss if/how development practitioners can further embed an "R2P/atrocity prevention lens" within their existing work, and to identify and strategize on practical examples of how development cooperation policies and projects can help to address risk factors relevant for atrocity crimes. Participants shared their knowledge and experiences, as well as challenges, opportunities, and concrete actions that can be undertaken by development practitioners to contribute toward atrocity prevention and response.

The workshop introduced participants to the four R2P crimes and early-warning frameworks that can help development practitioners to identify risk factors and indicators for atrocity crimes, the underlying processes, and relevant actors.[13] In the discussion, participants used practical examples/scenarios in applying the frameworks to identify key issues facing individual countries in the region. It was noted that, when conducting the documentation and assessment necessary for identifying the risk for atrocity crimes, one must consider factors such as the motives and drivers that influence perpetrators; what means are available to commit atrocity crimes; who the targeted victim groups are; what third-party actors may influence the commission or prevention of crimes; what societal, institutional, and other resiliencies may be in place; and what triggering events may increase risk. Following the completion of an assessment, it was critical to ensure that the assessment reaches those who are best placed to analyze the gathered information, develop and operationalize relevant policy, and monitor implementation.

While each country is complex and unique, there are common issues that affect states throughout East Africa. These include, but are not limited to, youth bulge, with the majority of citizens below the age of thirty years; high unemployment, particularly among youth; the presence of militant groups; the high number of accessible small arms and light weapons; past histories of conflict and/or atrocity crimes; cycles of discrimination and favoritism based on ethnic, political, or other identities; and the violation of the rights of women and girls, including through the commission of atrocity crimes toward these populations.

Within the R2P community, the links between atrocity prevention/R2P and development cooperation are often declared commonplace – but as we already noted, little has been done to elaborate or to translate them into practice. The workshop looked at the prevention of atrocity crimes, the potential development cooperation means to respond to atrocity crimes, and the role of development actors after R2P crimes have been committed ("prevent – respond – recover").

At the outset, participants agreed that the commission of atrocity crimes is the antithesis of development, making such efforts impossible and setting a country back economically, socially, and politically. Moreover, upon examination of the risk factors and indicators for atrocity crimes, it is evident that there is a clear link between the work being undertaken by development practitioners and the building of state resilience for the prevention of such crimes. This shows in various areas of development cooperation such as good governance, rule of law, security sector reform, and sustainable growth.

In regard to the concept underlying R2P, development programs are highly relevant when considering Pillars One and Two, i.e., the primary responsibility of the state to protect its population and the role of the international community to provide assistance to uphold those obligations, respectively. State initiatives to strengthen national architecture for atrocity prevention, as well as external support to enhance capacity to protect civilians against atrocity crimes, are therefore entry points for development actors to contribute toward the implementation of R2P.

Development practitioners working in the field can serve as key actors in monitoring emerging risks through their own documentation, as well as through engaging with local actors. By sharing such information with relevant stakeholders, and if trained on atrocity-prevention risk factors, development practitioners and their counterparts can contribute toward raising awareness needed to take early, preventive, and specific action.

In the field, practitioners can meet a range of challenges when seeking to realize the links between atrocity prevention and development cooperation. The workshop participants identified and discussed a number of these including financial and other resource constraints, the technical and political divide, the challenge of safely collecting and sharing relevant information, the hesitance to label potential issues as "atrocity crimes," and the question of whether adding an R2P lens indeed changes the outcome of development cooperation compared to working under a conflict prevention framework.

Participants agreed that any attempt to integrate R2P into development cooperation has to be mindful of existing resources and requires a case-based as well as context-specific approach. In addition, atrocity-prevention efforts do not always need to refer to R2P, as such, if in the given scenario the label only creates or adds political controversy. In regard to conflict prevention, there is a considerable overlap with atrocity prevention, but in certain scenarios, the R2P lens can provide important pointers to deciding which issues to prioritize and to address. This is the more so, as R2P includes atrocity crimes committed outside conflict and also entails a specific focus on particularly vulnerable groups within the population.

In addition, participants stated that it was necessary to integrate atrocity prevention into development programming in capitals and in the field. This includes being able to identify relevant information in the field and to respond in capitals efficiently to the potential risks that have been identified. Participants recalled the importance of learning from experience where atrocities could have been avoided if the identified potential risks were responded to in a timely fashion.

Looking ahead, participants articulated a range of recommendations that can be taken forward as stakeholders seek to further embed an "atrocity-prevention lens" within development policies and programming while heeding the "do not harm" approach.

Consider and act on the implications of atrocity prevention for existing and future development cooperation programming

R2P has been agreed by all UN member states, and atrocity crimes can occur anywhere. If an atrocity risk analysis indicates that a given country faces significant issues, development actors should examine their existing programming and reflect on future initiatives in light of this assessment to assess whether they sufficiently address atrocity-prevention needs.

Increase programming that focuses on addressing root causes of future atrocity crimes

While the typical goal of development programming is to implement long-term initiatives that contribute to the general betterment of society, atrocity prevention requires one to think about atrocity crimes together with root causes – this means to explore the underlying causes of conflict and tension in a given society, in particular after a war or other humanitarian emergency. This will contribute toward the development of sustainable peace and thus support societal and government capacity for atrocity prevention. This also means that efforts to integrate R2P into development cooperation have to reach beyond human rights and rule-of-law programs, and include sectors such as growth, health, and agriculture.

Adjust development cooperation processes to allow for timely and flexible responses to atrocity risks

As development actors may find themselves supporting or directly implementing programs in situations that can become unstable and potentially ripe for atrocity crimes, it is critical that policies and programming provide the flexibility that is needed to address the changing needs of populations. This may include altering programs themselves, or reallocating or dedicating funds to address emerging R2P needs.

Integrate an "atrocity-prevention lens" within programming assessments and evaluations

Many development actors use "checklists" in order to assess how a program considers and affects/contributes toward key issues such as human rights protection and gender inclusivity. For the future, development actors should integrate atrocity-prevention risk factors into these assessment processes to ensure that their programming does not increase atrocity risks in the country and contributes toward building state resilience for the prevention of atrocity crimes.

Support human rights mechanisms and documentation processes as avenues for atrocity risk assessment

Development actors should consider projects that contribute toward the establishment or strengthening of local, national, and regional human rights mechanisms that can document and monitor human rights issues which serve as early warning signs of potential R2P crimes. Additionally, supporting civil society and other actors documenting human rights violations, including protection of activists and security for witnesses involved in legal proceedings, will enable such actors to make atrocity risk assessments and contribute toward accountability.

Support and facilitate dialogue, mediation, and reconciliation processes, where possible and appropriate

In some settings, particularly those where all or most actors involved have grievances or an interest at stake, development actors may be able to assist in the facilitation or support of processes to promote dialogue and peaceful settlement of disputes. Development actors could also assist in convening stakeholders to consider and address an issue impacting their locality – for example, the spread of illicit arms – that may be overly sensitive to the parties involved and thus require external support.

Localize development programming, including through direct partnerships with local organizations and actors

Through increasing local engagements and partnerships, development actors will be able to enhance their understanding of key R2P issues and indicators of risk for atrocity crimes, establish holistic programming priorities that take into account the immediate as well as long-term needs of affected populations, and establish more sustainable projects that – through cooperation with local actors – will empower country-based partners and strengthen the early-warning capacities of development cooperation.

Cooperate locally with international partners on atrocity prevention

R2P has been agreed by all UN member states, and Pillar Two concerning the international responsibility to assist with national atrocity prevention applies to all member states. Joint efforts by development partners will help to strengthen the national resilience against atrocity crimes. Such efforts should also engage as appropriate the relevant UN agencies in the given country, as the UN's Human Rights up Front initiative pursues a similar agenda of preventing massive human rights violations (see Inter-Agency Standing Committee 2015).

The report from the Kampala workshop makes it clear that important links exist between the role of atrocity prevention in development cooperation. At the conceptual level, this seems straightforward and logical, but to realize these links, practical steps need to be taken. Workshop participants agreed that development practitioners can have a role in preventing the commission of atrocity crimes, but can also play a role in responding to their actual commission or in their aftermath.

The Kampala meeting highlighted the important pioneering work done by USAID and underscored the interest of local development stakeholders to engage with these issues – even if the R2P agenda and its specific language may be new and not that well known or understood. Indeed, in cooperation with local partners, development practitioners can play a key role in assessing in-country risk factors and in designing tailored, as well as appropriate, responses.

The findings of the Kampala workshop were confirmed in a second workshop on atrocity prevention for development practitioners held in Phnom Penh, Cambodia, in August 2017. This meeting was organized by USAID, the Australian Foreign Ministry, the Danish government, and local partners from civil society. Discussions with over fifty participants from Southeast Asia underscored the relevance of R2P in the region and the value that R2P can add to development work.

Denmark can partner in this area with USAID and the EU, as well as international and local civil society. It will help to include R2P language in relevant policy documents and country papers, but the real progress will be measured in the actual inclusion of atrocity prevention into relevant development cooperation initiatives on the ground.

Denmark and the implementation of R2P: lessons learned and future recommendations

This chapter has explored how R2P can be implemented as part of Danish foreign policy in the areas of human rights and development cooperation. As with all preventive efforts, it will ultimately remain difficult to assess to what extent the integration of R2P indeed will help to prevent atrocity crimes. At the same time, cases such as South Sudan, where massive atrocity crimes were committed and atrocity prevention had not been integrated into initial development cooperation efforts, strongly suggest that the effective integration of R2P and its implementation are relevant to all prevention work (for an analysis of the positive impact of implementing R2P, see Halakhe 2013, 18–19). The following recommendations for concrete steps could help better integrate R2P within Danish foreign policy.

Announce specific R2P priorities and countries

R2P is a cross-cutting agenda that has to impact all policy areas to achieve effective and timely atrocity prevention. It must be thought of and implemented across departments but will face competition from other, similar agendas (for example, climate and gender) for attention and resources. Any internal R2P implementation strategy has to heed these conditions, and should prioritize specific R2P integration efforts.

While being mindful of resource restraints, one concrete step to operationalize R2P would be to establish an annual internal list of three "R2P priority countries" based on an atrocity risk assessment that draws on relevant actors inside the Ministry, embassies, and the early-warning system of the EU and its partners. For a period of time, the Danish R2P work could prioritize atrocity-prevention efforts in these countries (without precluding the potential need to respond to other R2P needs or crises in third countries). Such an approach would allow an increase and focus of R2P awareness across the system while working toward concrete results in a small number of cases, thus strengthening the overall recognition of R2P as a relevant and practical framework, as well as creating focus and accountability.

R2P is not a panacea, and the work on how to operationalize atrocity prevention is only beginning. R2P should not be pushed as a broad, *conceptual* agenda; rather, its integration should be driven by a results-focused approach. Fewer, specific, and targeted R2P initiatives will gradually result in more R2P implementation and sustainable atrocity prevention. In regard to the policy areas under review here, such initiatives could include the integration of R2P into relevant UPRs and country programming.

Make R2P more meaningful and visible within internal processes

More than ten years after its inception, R2P is still a new concept when it comes to operational matters. It is little known among practitioners on the ground, there are persistent misconceptions, and there is little help for how to apply it in practice. The Danish integration of R2P should therefore support the development of practical guidance, including the production of short "how to do R2P" notes addressing R2P and specific areas of foreign policy (human rights, development cooperation, and so on) and R2P in regard to the aforementioned three "R2P priority countries"; this will also help to make atrocity prevention more sustainable in regard to the frequent rotation of relevant staff on key positions throughout the system.

R2P overlaps partially with the general work done on human rights and in the field of development cooperation and conflict prevention, but partially it is distinct. Any effort to integrate atrocity prevention into these fields should spell out how R2P will add something to already existing measures. This will motivate those tasked to implement R2P and highlight the necessity for mainstreaming atrocity prevention.

R2P has introduced a new and specific language about responsibilities, atrocity crimes, pillars, and more. When moving toward implementing atrocity prevention, a balance needs to be struck between adhering to this R2P language in speeches and program documents in order to strengthen the norm and raise awareness for the specific issues, avoiding the "purist trap." In some instances, to insist on R2P language may make it more difficult to work on atrocity prevention, as the terminology of R2P or atrocity prevention locally may be considered inappropriate or too political. Ultimately, it is the R2P content of a proposed policy that matters.

Strengthen the Danish R2P Focal Point

R2P and its implementation depend on having an anchor inside the system who functions as a catalyst, convener, and driver of the process. The appointment of a senior official as central R2P Focal Point has proven essential for the Danish experience with operationalizing R2P. Only if there is such high-level attention to the matter can the topic make progress throughout the system. It is key that the Focal Point and his/her role are known throughout the Ministry and embassies – this also facilitates regular sharing of relevant information with the Focal Point and his/her team.

Given the Focal Point's senior status, it is key to provide him/her with the necessary support. Currently this is achieved, part-time, through an adviser within the Human Rights and International Law department of the Foreign Ministry. The novelty and complexity of practicing R2P – as well as the multi-actor processes of implementing it, both domestically and internationally – make it essential to maintain, and preferably increase, this support to the Focal Point. This will enhance the efficiency of preventive work and help to strengthen R2P's implementation throughout relevant networks. R2P is too novel and, at first sight, abstract for its implementation to function without a designated R2P desk officer. The example of other countries shows that the mere appointment of an R2P Focal Point alone does not generate any concrete efforts to implement atrocity prevention within and across the national system.

Since the first appointment of an R2P Focal Point in the Danish Ministry of Foreign Affairs, the Danish Focal Point has been placed within the legal department, in the person of the Undersecretary of Legal Affairs. This approach has worked well, as it ensures conceptual clarity (i.e., R2P is *not* the same as every other policy already run by the Foreign Ministry) and allows for R2P implementation across different policy areas, geographical regions, and the three pillars of R2P.

Do more R2P outreach inside and outside the Ministry of Foreign Affairs

The implementation of R2P depends on staff beyond the R2P Focal Point and his/her direct support team. Only a broader R2P awareness and knowledge, as well as financial resources, will allow for meaningful and effective work on R2P issues. This means that key officials inside the Ministry and at relevant embassies upon appointment will need to receive brief introductions to the relevance of R2P to their portfolio. This needs to happen on a regular basis to reach beyond the rotation cycles of relevant staff. In addition, operational R2P knowledge should be integrated into country-specific pre-deployment briefings and other training opportunities for relevant staff. The R2P Focal Point should, on his/her travels, as appropriate, carry out outreach and support the integration of R2P into relevant programs.

The Danish Focal Point and his/her support team should finalize the draft version of a national Danish R2P report which seeks to outline R2P activities across the Danish government, including all three pillars and relevant work done outside the Foreign Ministry. This will strengthen the public and interagency awareness of atrocity prevention, how it relates to Danish policies, and what specific challenges it raises. At the international level, this national R2P report will be a welcome and much needed example of how a government can work in practice with R2P as a whole. In particular, an honest assessment of the difficulties of operationalizing atrocity prevention may help to generate improved outcomes and a better understanding of R2P across international R2P networks.

In recognition of atrocity prevention being inherently interlinked with key goals of Danish foreign policy, the first Danish R2P report should be endorsed and presented by the Danish Foreign Minister. Such acknowledgment would send a strong signal internationally and throughout the Danish system which could reinforce the awareness and willingness to integrate R2P.

Further strengthen R2P mainstreaming outside Denmark

Denmark should continue to work with the EU Focal Point on R2P and the Joint Office of the UN Special Advisers on the Prevention of Genocide and the Responsibility to Protect in order to advance and strengthen atrocity prevention done by member states and throughout the EU and UN systems. Denmark should, in particular, work with the European External Action Service to make use of the EU's early-warning system to identify and respond to risks for atrocity crimes.

R2P is an international norm with its origins in the United Nations and relevance for national authorities, regional organizations, and the UN. Denmark should continue its leadership on strengthening R2P as a norm and operational policy tool by engaging in relevant international fora including the EU, the UN (in Geneva and New York, including the annual R2P dialogue in the UN General Assembly), the Global Network of R2P Focal Points, the two Groups of Friends of R2P, GAAMAC, and in smaller, informal settings such as the International Atrocity

Prevention Working Group. The focus should be on those fora that allow work on the application of R2P in practice.

Sometimes, R2P is seen as a contentious norm, even by Danish officials, especially after the NATO intervention in Libya. Some therefore believe that to integrate R2P would negatively impact other Danish foreign policy efforts. In reality, however, the support for R2P as a preventive norm remains strong and cross-regional. While remaining mindful of the issues, Denmark should continue to champion R2P through statements and actions as the norm remains a key catalyzer of international efforts to prevent atrocity crimes. R2P has a strong basis in the unanimously agreed-upon World Summit Outcome document, and provides for a helpful division of labor.

Denmark should, in all its work on atrocity prevention, maintain the view that all three pillars of R2P are essential, mutually supportive, and non-sequential. Due to its specific focus on the prevention of and protection against four atrocity crimes, R2P is distinct from other efforts and requires special Danish and international attention and knowledge to be implemented effectively.

The implementation of R2P and its integration into regular foreign policymaking remains a work in progress. This is true for Denmark, as well as internationally. There is much talk about operationalizing R2P, but only the US government has attempted to institutionalize atrocity prevention and established, under the Obama administration, the interagency Atrocity Prevention Board (see Finkel 2014). Many other states with a positive approach toward R2P have only translated their commitment into a statement at the annual R2P dialogue in the UN General Assembly, or have focused on the normative side and seek to advance the incorporation of R2P language into UN resolutions. Other states have appointed an R2P Focal Point in their government, but only a few have provided that official with a clear mandate or resources to implement R2P across the respective government.

The Danish focus has rightly shifted toward *doing* R2P rather than talking R2P. Denmark has successfully partnered with like-minded states such as Ghana, the Netherlands, and the United States to unpack and advance the operational R2P agenda, and to do so also outside the UN in New York. Denmark should continue to work toward increasing the number of governments and other actors that focus on questions of implementation, including through the Global R2P Focal Point network.

Over the last few years, Danish work on atrocity prevention has, with relatively few resources, led to a number of concrete, tangible outcomes. This leadership has generated recognition within the UN system, by other governments, and across civil society. With atrocity crimes continuing to be committed on a daily basis, and with countless refugees fleeing from the horrors of crimes against humanity, Danish work on R2P is not a normative project, but a matter of national interest.

Acknowledgments

This chapter is an abridged version of a study that builds on interviews, observations, and analysis carried out in Denmark and at Danish embassies, including those in Accra, Brussels, Geneva, Kampala, and New York. For the original study, see http://um.dk/da/udenrigspolitik/folkeretten/folkeretten-a/responsibility-to-protect/. The author would like to thank all Danish officials for their time and contributions, in particular the former Danish Focal Point on R2P, Undersecretary for Legal Affairs, Tobias Rehfeldt, and the R2P expert inside the Foreign Ministry, Senior Advisor Tomas Kønigsfeldt. In addition, thanks go to the author's two research assistants Juliette Paauwe and Max Schiel at the University of Southern Denmark. The conclusions and recommendations made in this chapter are the author's alone and do not necessarily represent the official position of the Danish government.

Notes

1 See Danish Government (2016, 43), pointing to the need to protect Christian minorities that suffer from persecution. See also the founding document of the previous government coalition which referred explicitly to R2P as a key principle and to the task of operationalizing R2P. Danish Government (2011, 39).
2 See also the remarks by Ambassador Alfonso Lenhardt (2016), Deputy Head of the United States Agency for International Development (USAID). "Many of you in this room have been critical partners to the museum and to the US government in these efforts and I thank you all for that. I would especially like to recognize our friends in the Danish government . . . and I look forward to our continued collaboration." See also Kendal (2013, 14ff).
3 Denmark continues to serve, together with other governments and civil society representatives, on the steering group of GAAMAC. For more information, see Global Action Against Mass Atrocity Crimes (n.d.).
4 Other agencies and institutions relevant to the implementation of R2P in Geneva include, for example, the Office of the High Commissioner for Human Rights and the Office of the UN High Commissioner on Refugees.
5 As of August 2017, there were forty-four thematic and twelve country mandates. Cf. United Nations Human Rights Office of the High Commission (n.d.).
6 For an overview of the special sessions of the Human Rights Council, see United Nations Human Rights Council (n.d.b). The examples referred to are the United Nations Human Rights Council (2017, 2016a, 2015b).
7 See, for example, the special session on the situation in South Sudan in December 2016 and Resolution S-26/1 (2016), preambular paragraph 13. See also the statements by Slovakia (on behalf of the European Union), the Netherlands and Rwanda (on behalf of the Group of Friends of R2P), and Australia. United Nations Human Rights Council (2016c).
8 Since the leading journal on atrocity prevention, *Global Responsibility to Protect*, was launched in 2009, there has not been one article devoted to this topic. Civil society has organized a few exchanges between the development cooperation community and R2P advocates. See, for example, Budapest Centre for Mass Atrocities Prevention (n.d.).
9 Specific goals under Goal 16 include the reduction of all forms of violence, the strengthening of national institutions to prevent all violence, and the promotion of non-discriminatory laws and policies.
10 These R2P training courses continue to be organized and hosted by the Kofi Annan International Peacekeeping and Training Centre in Accra, Ghana. For more information, see Global Centre for the Responsibility to Protect (2014).
11 This section builds on the workshop report compiled by the author.
12 Workshop participants worked in Burundi, Ethiopia, Kenya, Rwanda, Somalia, South Sudan, Tanzania, and Uganda. In addition, the organizers welcomed participants from Australia, Germany, Ghana, and the United Nations Development Programme. The meeting was held under Chatham House rules; nothing in the report can or should be attributed to individual participants.

13 The workshop used the Joint UN Office for the Prevention of Genocide and Responsibility to Protect (2014), and the "Mass Atrocities Assessment Framework" developed by the US government (on file with the author).

References

al Hussein, Zeid Ra'ad, 2015. "High Commissioner's Statement to High-Level Panel on Implementing R2P in the Geneva Context," November 19, www.ohchr.org/EN/News-Events/Pages/DisplayNews.aspx?NewsID=16776&LangID=E.

Auschwitz Institute for Peace and Reconciliation, n.d. "Latin American Program," www.auschwitzinstitute.org/what-we-do/latin-america-programs/.

Awinador-Kanyirige, William A., 2014. "Ghana's National Peace Council," Global Centre for the Responsibility to Protect Policy Brief, August, www.globalr2p.org/media/files/2014-august-policy-brief-ghana-national-peace-council.pdf.

Ban Ki-moon, 2009. "Implementing the Responsibility to Protect: Report of the Secretary-General," A/63/677, January 12.

Ban Ki-moon, 2013. "Responsibility to Protect: State Responsibility and Prevention: Report of the Secretary General," A/67/929–S/2013/399, July 9.

Bellamy, Alex J., 2010. "The Responsibility to Protect and Australian Foreign Policy," *Australian Journal of International Affairs* 64, no. 4: 432–48.

Budapest Centre for Mass Atrocities Prevention, n.d. "Mass Atrocities Prevention and Development," www.genocideprevention.eu/development/.

Danish Government, 2011. "Et Danmark der står sammen," October, www.stm.dk/publikationer/Et_Danmark_der_staar_sammen_11/Regeringsgrundlag_okt_2011.pdf.

Danish Government, 2016. "For et friere, rigere og mere trygt Danmark," www.stm.dk/multimedia/Regeringsgrundlag2016.pdf.

Early Warning Project of the US Holocaust Memorial Museum, 2019. "Denmark," in "Ranking of All Countries: Statistical Risk Assessment 2018–19," https://earlywarningproject.ushmm.org/ranking-of-all-countries.

European Commission, 2016. "Proposal for a New European Consensus on Development: Our World, Our Dignity, Our Future," Communication from the Commission to the European Parliament, the Council, the European Economic and Social Committee and the Committee of the Regions, COM(2016) 740 final, Strasbourg: European Commission, November 22.

European External Action Service, 2016. "Shared Vision, Common Action: A Stronger Europe – A Global Strategy for the European Union's Foreign and Security Policy," June, http://eeas.europa.eu/archives/docs/top_stories/pdf/eugs_review_web.pdf.

Finkel, James P., 2014. "Atrocity Prevention at Crossroads: Assessing the President's Atrocity Prevention Board After Two Years," Center for the Prevention of Genocide Occasional Paper No. 2, September, www.ushmm.org/m/pdfs/20140904-finkel-atrocity-prevention-report.pdf.

Global Action Against Mass Atrocity Crimes, n.d. "About GAAMAC," www.gaamac.org.

Global Centre for the Responsibility to Protect, 2014. "KAIPTC R2P Course," www.globalr2p.org/our_work/kaiptc_r2p_course.

Global Centre for the Responsibility to Protect, n.d. "Our Work," www.globalr2p.org/our_work/global_network_of_r2p_focal_points.

Halakhe, Abdullahi Boru, 2013. "'R2P in Practice': Ethnic Violence, Elections and Atrocity Prevention in Kenya," Global Centre for the Responsibility to Protect Occasional Paper No. 4, December, www.globalr2p.org/media/files/kenya_occasionalpaper_web.pdf.

Inter-Agency Standing Committee, 2015. "Human Rights Up Front: An Overview," https://interagencystandingcommittee.org/system/files/overview_of_human_rights_up_front_july_2015.pdf.

Jensen, Kristian, 2016. "Launch of Denmark's Candidature for Membership of the Human Rights Council in 2019–2021," Permanent Mission of Denmark to UN Geneva, March 1, http://fngeneve.um.dk/en/News/newsdisplaypage/?newsID=E4F61D5B-3CC6-4E78-BDF7-2F32AC8CF6F5.

Joint UN Office for the Prevention of Genocide and Responsibility to Protect, 2014. *Framework of Analysis for Atrocity Crimes: A Tool for Prevention* (New York: United Nations), www.un.org/en/preventgenocide/adviser/pdf/framework%20of%20analysis%20for%20atrocity%20crimes_en.pdf.

Kendal, David, 2013. "Denmark and the Responsibility to Protect (R2P): How Denmark Can Further Contribute to the Prevention of Mass Atrocities," Policy Research Paper (Copenhagen: Kendal Human Rights Consulting, September), http://um.dk/en/danida-en/partners/research/other//~/media/UM/English-site/Documents/Danida/Partners/Research-Org/Research-studies/Denmark%20and%20the%20Responsibility%20to%20Protect%202013.pdf.

Kofi Annan International Peacekeeping Training Centre, n.d. "Responsibility to Protect Course (R2P)," www.kaiptc.org/kaiptc-course/responsibilty-to-protect-course/.

Lenhardt, Alfonso, 2016. "The Future of the US Government's Efforts on Atrocity Prevention," United States Holocaust Memorial Museum, May 23, www.youtube.com/watch?v=xu1_9oGYfNI&feature=youtu.be.

Ministry of Foreign Affairs of Denmark, 2016. *The Government's Priorities for Danish Development Cooperation 2017: Overview of the Development Cooperation Budget 2017–2020* (Copenhagen: Ministry of Foreign Affairs of Denmark, August).

Ministry of Foreign Affairs of Denmark, 2017. *Udenrigs- og Sikkerhedspolitisk Strategi 2017–2018* (Copenhagen: Ministry of Foreign Affairs of Denmark, June), http://um.dk/da/udenrigspolitik/aktuelle-emner/udenrigs-og-sikkerhedspolitisk-strategi-2017-18/.

Obama, Barack, 2011. "Presidential Study Directive 10: Directive on Creation of an Interagency Atrocities Prevention Board and Corresponding Interagency Review," August 4.

Permanent Mission of Denmark to the United Nations, 2016. "Statement by Denmark," 71st Session of the General Assembly of the United Nations, September 26, https://gadebate.un.org/sites/default/files/gastatements/71/71_DK_en.pdf.

Rasmussen, Lars Løkke, 2015. "Prime Minister Lars Løkke Rasmussen's Statement at the Opening of the 70th United Nations General Assembly on 28 September 2015," www.stm.dk/_p_14244.html.

UN Sustainable Development Goals, 2016. "Goal 16: Promote Just, Peaceful and Inclusive Societies," www.un.org/sustainabledevelopment/peace-justice/.

United Nations Human Rights Council, 2014. "Report of the Commission of Inquiry on Human Rights in the Democratic People's Republic of Korea," A/HRC/25/63, February 7.

United Nations Human Rights Council, 2015a. "National Report Submitted in Accordance with Paragraph 5 of the Annex to Human Rights Council Resolution 16/21: Denmark," A/HRC/WG.6/24/DNK/1, November 9.

United Nations Human Rights Council, 2015b. "Preventing the Further Deterioration of the Human Rights Situation in Burundi," 24th Special Session, December 17.

United Nations Human Rights Council, 2016a. "The Human Rights Situations in South Sudan," 26th Special Session, December 14.

United Nations Human Rights Council, 2016b. "Report of the Commission of Inquiry on Human Rights on the Syrian Arab Republic," A/HRC/33/35, August 11.

United Nations Human Rights Council, 2016c. "26th Special Session of the Human Rights Council on the Human Rights Situation in South Sudan, December 14," www.ohchr.org/EN/HRBodies/HRC/SpecialSessions/Session26/Pages/26thSpecialSession.aspx.

United Nations Human Rights Council, 2017. "The Human Rights Situation of the Minority Rohingya Muslim Population and Other Minorities in the Rakhine State of Myanmar," 27th Special Session, December 5.

United Nations Human Rights Council, n.d.a. "Basic Facts About the UPR," www.ohchr.org/EN/HRBodies/UPR/Pages/BasicFacts.aspx.

United Nations Human Rights Council, n.d.b. "Sessions," www.ohchr.org/EN/HRBodies/HRC/Pages/Sessions.aspx.

United Nations Human Rights Office of the High Commission, n.d. "Special Procedures of the Human Rights Council," www.ohchr.org/EN/HRBodies/SP/Pages/Welcomepage.aspx.

USAID, 2015. "Field Guide: Helping Prevent Mass Atrocities," April, www.usaid.gov/sites/default/files/documents/1866/Field%20Guide%20Mass%20Atrocities.pdf.

West Africa Network for Peacebuilding, 2016. "Institutional Capacities for the Implementation of R2P in West Africa: A Case Study of Ghana" (Accra: West Africa Network for Peacebuilding, February), http://um.dk/~/media/UM/English-site/Documents/Danida/Partners/Research-Org/Research-studies/R2P%20research%20project%202016.pdf?la=en.

3

ATROCITY PREVENTION UNDER THE OBAMA ADMINISTRATION

Stephen Pomper

Introduction

This chapter provides an insider's view on where the efforts of the administration of former US President Barack Obama to prevent mass atrocities succeeded, where they did not, and where future policymakers might find useful lessons, both positive and negative.[1] It focuses in particular on situations in which policy changes and innovations appear to have had a positive effect, however modest, and on efforts to develop new capabilities under the policy. It offers an "after action" assessment of the administration's atrocity-prevention policy, drawing from interviews with former senior officials and others to identify both the strengths and contributions of the policy and its most pronounced shortcomings.[2]

Bringing the blueprint to life: 2012–2016

On April 23, 2012, President Obama placed his personal imprimatur on the administration's approach to atrocity prevention with a speech at the United States Holocaust Memorial Museum. It was a time when those individuals who worked on prevention issues in the administration saw evidence that the prevention community's blueprint was working, notwithstanding uncertainty about Libya and deep concerns about Syria. Assertive US leadership on the global stage – channeled where possible through the United Nations (UN) and guided by support in the upper reaches of the US government – appeared in many cases to be yielding positive outcomes. Next, the team turned its focus to creating the institutional structures that the Genocide Prevention Task Force had imagined might take prevention efforts to the next level (see Genocide Prevention Task Force 2008).

Although those structures were formally rolled out in President Obama's April 2012 speech, they were the outgrowth of a process that had been ongoing for the better part of a year. Eight months earlier, on August 4, 2011, the president had issued a mass atrocities directive, Presidential Study Directive 10, which traced its lineage back to the Task Force report and Samantha Power's *A Problem from Hell* (Genocide Prevention Task Force 2008; Power 2002). The echoes were striking. In its first sentence, the directive made clear that atrocity prevention would now be a mainstream priority for US foreign policy, deeming the prevention of genocide and mass atrocities to be a "core national security interest and a core moral responsibility of the United States" (Obama 2011a). The new language would later engender some criticism when commentators observed that the Obama administration did not, in practice, put atrocity prevention on the same level as other top national security priorities, such as the proliferation of weapons of mass destruction, counter-terrorism, and energy security (Alleblas et al. 2017, 4). When asked about the use of the term "core interest," two former senior officials suggested that, in hindsight, "strong" or "important" interest might have been better calibrated to the administration's actual approach.[3]

In a further echo of Power's work and the Task Force report, the directive noted that in the face of a potential mass atrocity, "our options are never limited to either sending in the military or standing by and doing nothing" (Obama 2011a). Finally, the directive ordered the establishment of an Atrocities Prevention Board (APB) very much like the committee that the Task Force had recommended. The board would comprise representatives from all national security departments and agencies, and be chaired by the National Security Council's (NSC's) senior director for multilateral affairs and human rights. To inform the board's work, the directive set in motion a 100-day review of the US government's prevention and response capabilities, which would then produce gap-filling recommendations to the president.

The NSC team leading the review pushed hard to make best use of that moment by building consensus around worthy proposals that, under different circumstances, might languish either for lack of momentum or because they ran afoul of one or more agencies' perceived institutional interests. The biggest breakthroughs that approach yielded were with the intelligence community, which agreed to commit the resources necessary to produce the first National Intelligence Estimate (NIE) on the global risk of mass atrocities and also to be more flexible about providing surging capabilities to get more accurate ground truth during crisis situations. The interagency review also generated commitments from agencies and departments to focus greater energy on developing training, lessons learned analysis, capacity to deploy civilian technical experts to crisis areas, performance incentives to encourage atrocity reporting and preventive actions, alert channels to ensure that early warnings and dissenting views on atrocity situations would be heard by senior officials, and new partnerships with other governments, regional organizations, the UN, and the private sector. Implementation proved to be uneven, but giving the board a presidential mandate and creating the expectation that departments and agencies would be accountable to it for progress on presidentially approved commitments created motivation and opportunities for departments and agencies to allocate staff and resources to atrocity prevention.

At the same time, the review group struggled to make progress on two prominent potential policy innovations. First, the Treasury Department would not commit to supporting the development of a new executive order that would have permitted the US government to designate perpetrators of atrocities for financial sanctions wherever they might be. Proponents argued that a standing authority would allow the United States to apply pressure to atrocities perpetrators, regardless of whether they hailed from a country where the United States had a sanctions program in place. The Treasury Department, however, believed that the traditional country-specific approach was sufficient; its officials also feared that creating a new global authority would crank expectations unrealistically high for a constant stream of high-impact designations and place an unsustainable burden on scarce Treasury Department personnel.

Second, for its part, the Defense Department expressed concern about recommending new legislation that would permit the prosecution of perpetrators of crimes against humanity or war crimes on the basis of their presence in the United States. Defense Department lawyers were particularly concerned that such legislation could become the pretext for other states to engage in politicized prosecutions of US service members and officials.

A final report summarizing review-generated recommendations wound up hedging on both items, leaving the Atrocities Prevention Board to work on them further, and made its way to the Oval Office as a mixture of normative findings, proposed protocols to govern the operations of the Atrocities Prevention Board, and recommendations of both a broad and a specific character on developing and strengthening atrocity-prevention capabilities. President Obama approved the recommendations in March 2012, roughly a month before his April 23 rollout speech at the United States Holocaust Memorial Museum.

Setting up the Atrocities Prevention Board

One question with which the 100-day review had to wrestle was what bureaucratic form the board would take. It was unrealistic to expect that either the national security cabinet, with officials at the level of Secretary of State Hillary Clinton and Secretary of Defense Robert Gates, or their deputies, would function as the board, so clearly the board would have to be an interagency policy committee (IPC) composed of senior directors and assistant secretaries. As was typical for IPCs, a working-level body chaired by the NSC director for war crimes and atrocity prevention (the sub-APB) would meet more frequently – generally on a weekly basis – to keep tabs on emerging crises, develop policy papers, and prepare matters for consideration by the board.

That configuration did not make everyone happy. David Pressman suggests that casting the board as "just another" IPC subordinate to the deputies and principals robbed it of what could have been its highest function: visibly pushing senior policymakers to make tough choices on thwarting atrocities and raising the political costs for them if they did not.[4] NSC leadership did look at the board as a mechanism for making sure that future Rwandas would not slip through the cracks, but they expected it to do so within the conventional hierarchy of NSC-led policymaking bodies. That approach was consistent with the Task Force report recommendations, which focused on the creation of a policy-coordinating committee at the assistant-secretary level (Genocide Prevention Task Force 2008).

That said, a concerted effort was made to give the IPC a strong institutional presence, including by developing a public constituency for it and its work. Principals were requested to appoint their departmental representatives "by name," which was intended to invite reflection on the specific qualifications of the individuals appointed, and the presidentially approved recommendations in the 100-day report called for one principals and two deputies committee meetings a year to review the board's track record. In practice, the NSC worked closely with agencies to identify strong candidates with a relevant background, and the first generation of the board included several members with ranks above the assistant-secretary level.

The rollout for both a Comprehensive Strategy for Atrocity Prevention (see White House 2012) and the board was intended to give some lift to both the board's work and the broader atrocity-prevention agenda. As commentators have noted, the April 23 rollout – during which the board attended Obama's speech at the United States Holocaust Memorial Museum and then joined a White House-hosted event at the Eisenhower Executive Office Building – gave the board a far higher public profile than the average IPC. That, of course, created some political risks because of the way in which it raised expectations, but it also reflected an understanding that generating and maintaining strong public support was critically important for the sustainability of the atrocity-prevention agenda.

In seeking to develop that agenda, the board operated within certain parameters. Under its protocols, it would meet every month to make sure that it was constantly reviewing the landscape for emergent atrocity threats. At the same time, however, the board would generally steer clear of matters already being covered by other processes operating at an equivalent or higher level – such as South Sudan, Sudan, or Syria – unless the board had particular insight or value to bring to the ongoing discussion. For example, if a country-specific IPC needed support in developing models for an accountability mechanism, it might turn to the board for policy guidance and expertise.

By default, that approach meant that the bulk of the board's focus would be on countries in which the United States did not have strategic interests, as traditionally conceived, and where violence had not yet escalated to the point at which a whole region was destabilized. The sub-APB would work with the intelligence community to develop a calendar of countries to work through, but the board's agenda would also be flexible so that if a pop-up crisis required it to pivot, it could do so. To be effective at driving policy for any of those countries, however, the board needed to develop mechanisms for identifying the places most needing attention, secure the help of regional bureaus at the State Department in teeing up points for decision, and engage ambassadors in the field to help ensure that the decisions would be implemented.

That was not something that the board was instantly equipped to do. Getting into a working rhythm and building confidence with the relevant players would take time and involve some trial and error. In the meantime, the board would become familiar with the atrocity risk landscape through the intelligence community's monthly early-warning briefings and focus heavily on building the atrocity-prevention toolkit.

Before turning to look at how the board and the new atrocity-prevention policy influenced US decision-making – and may have helped shape outcomes – during the period since 2012, a few caveats are necessary. First, the heavy focus on internal process here is for the sake of creating a historical record from which to learn, not to suggest that process is a surrogate for achieving actual results. Moreover, although the chapter offers a subjective view of where the board and the administration's atrocity-prevention policy seem to have been most effective, those judgments are inherently fraught. It is impossible to know for certain whether or not actions that the US government took at the board's direction, or with the policy in mind, might have been taken in the absence of either. And it is even more difficult to know whether results in the field are better understood as attributable in whole or in part to US engagement, or to other factors. Finally, the situations that the board worked on and to which the policy applied often were protracted crises that might well remain desperate situations even after the immediate threat of mass killing was addressed, so deeming US engagement a "success" would be difficult even if it achieved its immediate objectives. The conclusions offered in the following sections should be understood through this lens.

Building a *modus operandi*: the Rakhine State crisis

The first few months of board meetings involved a certain amount of casting about while the group came to grips with its mandate. One country discussion in particular helped sharpen the NSC's sense of how the board could most usefully operate. The country in question was Myanmar, and the issue related to violence against the minority Rohingya population in Myanmar's Rakhine State. In early summer 2012, allegations that three Rohingya men had raped and killed an ethnic Rakhine woman spiked a cycle of reprisal violence that killed hundreds of Rohingya civilians. Advocacy groups flagged the uptick in anti-Rohingya violence for the NSC multilateral affairs directorate and began reaching out to contacts across the government, suggesting that this was the sort of situation that the Atrocities Prevention Board was created to address. Some State Department regional experts voiced skepticism internally about how much US engagement would be able to affect the situation, but the board nevertheless took it up. A July meeting that covered Rakhine along with other ethnic conflicts in Myanmar helped the board get up to speed on the plight of the Rohingya; the board would return to the topic that October when violence in Rakhine spiked again.

The October 2012 meeting included newly installed Ambassador Derek Mitchell, as well as representatives of both regional and functional bureaus from the board's member agencies. President Obama's plans to make a landmark trip to Yangon in November created a helpful backdrop. Not only would there be a political urgency within both the US and Myanmar governments to address the escalation of violence that would mar the trip, but the trip created leverage that the US government could use to draw attention to its concerns. The embassy reported on senior diplomatic engagement with both the Myanmar government and like-minded partners on the ground, which Mitchell had brought together in a diplomatic coalition to advance the atrocity-prevention and protection agenda in Rakhine. Together, they would deliver the message to Myanmarese President Thein Sein's government that the plight of the Rohingya needed to be addressed.

Perhaps the most important outcome of the meeting was that it helped establish a common understanding among senior policymakers – both in Washington and in the field – that the United States needed to prioritize protection of the Rohingya as a bilateral issue. Members of the board who also served on the deputies committee brought that perspective into the deputies' planning discussions for the president's upcoming trip, and Power could draw on it when she traveled to Burma to help prepare for the president's November visit. Moreover, the president himself addressed the violence when he traveled to Yangon in November. Obama spoke about the violence in his historic address to the people of Myanmar and referred to the Rohingya people by their preferred name rather than the "Bengali" term of disparagement. He said:

> Today, we look at the recent violence in Rakhine State that has caused so much suffering, and we see the danger of continued tensions there. For too long, the people of this state, including ethnic Rakhine, have faced crushing poverty and persecution. But there is no excuse for violence against innocent people. And the Rohingya hold themselves – hold within themselves the same dignity as you do, and I do.
>
> *(Obama 2012)*

The US government continued to press for protection of the Rohingya after the 2012 visit, with the board and sub-APB periodically checking in on progress, but it was never able to persuade its Myanmarese counterparts to make the kind of major reforms that might have eased tensions over the longer term. The government would make general commitments that were sufficient to give the impression of progress, but show weak or even counterproductive follow-through. For example, in 2014, it took the positive step of creating a pilot mechanism to verify Rohingya citizenship, which was fatally undercut when it required Rohingya seeking to use the mechanism to identify as "Bengali." US officials hoped that the 2015 election that installed Aung San Suu Kyi at the top of the civilian government would be helpful, although they were under no illusions that she would be a champion for the Rohingya. Indeed, the military's heavy-handed response to attacks by Rohingya radicals in 2016 presaged a devastating pulse of violence in 2017, when more than 600,000 Rohingya would be driven out of Rakhine in what UN Human Rights

Commissioner Zeid Ra'ad al Hussein credibly characterized as a "textbook example of ethnic cleansing" (Keaten 2017).

Looking back at the Obama administration's focus on Rakhine, a former senior official suggests that the US government's engagement likely made a difference for a time but did not generate enough political will in Myanmar to set in motion meaningful progress on issues such as citizenship for the Rohingya.[5] In this way, Rakhine demonstrated both the potential and the limitations of the administration's Atrocities Prevention Board and its atrocity-prevention policy. Both could help drive engagement and make certain that the United States did not look away from atrocities as they happened. They could focus the attention of senior leadership. But the tools for implementing the policy were highly imperfect, the effect of US efforts were difficult to measure, and the crises in question would often be of a nature that might be temporarily slowed or frozen but would be very difficult to fix.

Developing atrocity-prevention and response efforts in Burundi, the Central African Republic, and beyond

A survey of other atrocity-prevention efforts finds the board sometimes playing a central role driving early attention to emerging crises, and in other cases, finding itself more on the periphery of policymaking. In Burundi, by way of example, the board worked to help the US government get ahead of a crisis centered around the extension of President Pierre Nkurunziza's term in office and may have helped stave off the worst of the violence. In the Central African Republic (CAR), the board was less at the center of activity, and it was a broader range of officials implementing the administration's new prevention policy who, at a critical moment, catalyzed the provision of tens of millions of dollars to support the efforts of French and regional troops in staunching escalating violence. Beyond specific country situations, other atrocity-prevention and response tools were developed.

Burundi

The board first discussed Burundi in 2012, when there were already strong indications that the country's 2015 presidential elections could be a flashpoint for violence. President Nkurunziza was approaching the end of his second term, but it was increasingly clear that he would seek to remain in power despite a widely held understanding that he was required to step down under the 2005 Arusha Accords, which had ended a long and bloody civil war. The legal provision that related to seeking a third term unfortunately left room for interpretation, and there was little doubt that Burundi's courts, which were less than independent, would tilt any decision in favor of Nkurunziza. Burundi watchers and atrocity-prevention experts inside the US government worried that Nkurunziza's move to cement his rule could undo the fragile peace that the country had built since 2005. Perhaps even more worrisome were the measures that Nkurunziza, his allies, and his opponents were taking in anticipation of unrest. Armed youth militias – the *imbonerakure* – were increasingly active, and politically motivated killings were on the rise (Alleblas et al. 2017).

The board's involvement on Burundi was, to some extent, a function of the limited bandwidth of the relevant regional offices. The African-focused regional offices at the NSC and the State Department had nearly fifty countries in their portfolio and a seemingly endless stream of major crises to manage. They were not well positioned to focus significant attention on upstream prevention efforts in a tiny country where the United States had limited strategic interests. At the same time, however, Embassy Bujumbura – under the leadership of Ambassador Dawn Liberi – was increasingly concerned about the gathering atrocity threat. To help jumpstart US atrocity-prevention efforts, the board stepped in. It commissioned an interagency team to travel to Burundi and to prepare a report that would both analyze the risks and offer recommendations about how to manage them. Within the framework of that exercise, the United States Agency for International Development (USAID) and the State Department found additional resources to bolster violence-prevention programming. Importantly, the exercise had the strong support of both the embassy and regional offices, which participated in the board's deliberations.

The board also helped establish atrocity prevention in Burundi as a priority for US senior officials. Ambassador Power – by then the US permanent representative to the UN – arranged to be the most senior US official ever to travel to Burundi when she visited the country in 2014, to underscore in person that the United States was watching the situation closely. Following that trip, the US Mission to the United Nations (USUN) fought furiously against canceling the mandate for the UN special political mission at the end of 2014, finally conceding only because of the impossibility of imposing such a mission on a non-consenting country. Because of the multiyear focus, when the situation began to escalate in 2015, a knowledgeable corps of officers at every level of the government was already prepared to respond.

As reports filtered in that neighboring Rwanda (which wanted to see Nkurunziza step down) was instigating opposition violence, senior officials in the administration quietly reached out to President Paul Kagame and others to insist that such interference must stop. Deputies met twice to discuss the imposition of targeted sanctions to send a message to perpetrators of violence in Burundi and would-be imitators, ultimately blessing the imposition of even-handed sanctions against both government and opposition figures associated with fomenting violence (*Guardian* 2015). Days before the Treasury Department announced the sanctions, the White House released a video message from President Obama urging political leaders to "put aside the language of hate and division" (Obama 2015). Although Washington made clear its disapproval of both Nkurunziza's decision to seek a third term and the conduct of elections in July of that year, as the risk of widespread violence increased, US diplomacy focused on de-escalation and a negotiated settlement rather than an insistence that the current government must go. In January 2016, when the UN Security Council traveled to Burundi, Power used her second visit in just a year and a half to warn against escalation.

As with the US response to the anti-Rohingya violence in 2012, it is hard to know just how much effect US government efforts spurred by the board had on the ground. Even making generous assumptions, it is still more difficult to describe the outcome of this several-year effort as a "success." The outcome, after all, was not a secure, rights-respecting Burundi or even a Burundi that could credibly be described as on its way out of the woods. Without regional leadership or a strong UN negotiator to help craft a political solution, the country entered a state of protracted crisis. And yet the core objective – which Power described during the Security Council's 2016 trip as "trying to prevent a small fire from becoming a large one" (Hackel and Sokan 2016) – was arguably achieved. Burundi suffered too much violence and too much chaos, to be sure, but it did not return to the mass slaughter of innocents that had wracked both Burundi and neighboring Rwanda in past decades.

Central African Republic

The administration's efforts in CAR are less an illustration of the board's effect than of the effect of the broader atrocity-prevention policy. The immediate history of the CAR crisis started in 2012, when the Séléka – a predominantly Muslim rebel group from the northern part of the country – began an offensive that would culminate, in March 2013, in the capture of the country's capital city, Bangui, and President Francois Bozize being driven from power. Bolstered by foreign fighters from Chad and Sudan, the Séléka waged a brutal campaign marked by burning villages and wanton attacks on civilians. The violence escalated further in mid-2013 when Christian and animist fighters coalesced into an "anti-balaka" ("anti-machete") armed movement to oppose the Séléka. The anti-balaka began its own campaign of ethnically targeted violence against Muslim and Peuhl communities. As the situation edged closer to all-out ethnic violence, the region relied on a local peacekeeping force to contain it. That force – which began under the auspices of the Economic Community of Central African States (ECCAS) and then merged into an African Union mission in fall 2012 – was not up to the task. By October 2012, UN officials were warning of a risk of genocide.

In early December of that year, whatever was left of the dam seemed to burst. According to reports from the field, violence was spreading through the neighborhoods of Bangui; neighbors were turning on neighbors. Early on a Saturday morning, Power forwarded one particularly vivid email to Susan Rice at the NSC, who agreed that the picture was grim, and shared the report with Deputy National Security Advisor Tony Blinken. Blinken put a deputies meeting on the calendar for later that morning. There was broad consensus at the start of the meeting: all agreed that there was a need to prevent the situation from becoming another Rwanda, and all agreed that the United States had be part of the solution. There were no questions about whether CAR was properly the United States' problem and no suggestion that, as a Francophone country, it should be left to the French.

As Blinken went around the room seeking recommendations for what could be done, ideas popped up quickly: the Defense Department could airlift African troops to support the French "Sangaris" contingent that would be the core of the response; the United States might be able to equip the troops with excess defense supplies. The State Department would look into whether a group of religious leaders could travel to the region to try to calm some of the intercommunal tensions. The USUN would work with colleagues on the UN Security Council to generate an "all necessary measures" mandate under which the French could comfortably use force to stabilize the situation. By the beginning of the following week, the United States had a multi-pronged strategy for calming the situation in Bangui that included up to $60 million in defense support to the French and local peacekeeping forces and $40 million in peacekeeping operations funding (White House 2013). It also included a recorded message from President Obama to the people of CAR urging calm. Obama was en route to Nelson Mandela's funeral, but agreed to use part of his stopover time in Senegal to make the recording (Brown 2013).

It was a significant package to push out the door so quickly, but it had a long backstory. For months, staffers from the NSC's Africa directorate, Power's team at the USUN, and allies across the departments and agencies had been working in both formal and informal groups to develop a viable plan to address the deteriorating situation on the ground. The situation had come before the board on several occasions, but the outcome was inconclusive; the conversations had proven more useful for informing participants about the situation than formulating an actual policy. Although, pinpointing precisely why that was the case is difficult, the board struggled to identify leverage that the United States might have exercised over a set of actors that seemed far removed from its influence, or to formulate meaningful policy options.

In practice, then, policy was formulated and driven by regional experts at the NSC and the State Department, working within the framework of the broader atrocity-prevention policy. Behind the scenes, those officials were traveling to Paris to coordinate and explore a potential French intervention, working with the Defense Department and USAID to develop ways in which the United States might furnish support, and – to ensure that a senior US official was invested in the issue and would track it beyond the immediate crisis – working to schedule a trip by Ambassador Power to the region in December. As soon as Blinken put the deputies meeting on the Saturday morning schedule, NSC's Africa directorate rushed to catalog the wish list that had been developed at the working level. That was the unseen script that would drive the deputies meeting. Forty-eight hours later, every item on the list was under way.[6]

As with Myanmar and Burundi, it is impossible to sound a triumphalist note about CAR. On the one hand, the violence could have been more severe, and important progress has been made in knitting the state back together. In early 2016, the country was able to hold general elections, which saw former prime minister and mathematics professor Faustin Touadera elected to the presidency. On the other hand, high levels of violence persist in parts of the country, with Séléka and anti-balaka forces continuing to square off and the UN peacekeeping force struggling to maintain order. Moreover, reviews of the US government's performance have been mixed. One account suggested that the US government moved too haltingly to arrest the crisis during the first ten months of 2013, when Séléka's rampage took many innocent lives, and specifically faulted the board for failing to generate earlier action.

A former official close to the CAR response agrees that the 2013 response was hardly perfect, and suggests in particular that the United States should have been more active during the first part of 2013, when the Séléka were on the march across the country – perhaps by appointing a senior US diplomat to do shuttle diplomacy among relevant conflict parties before the most acute violence began later in the year.[7] Because all embassy personnel had been evacuated in December 2012 and the US government did not have an ambassador on the ground, there was no go-to person to do such shuttle diplomacy in the region. Instead, the US government relied on ECCAS to do what it could to manage the crisis. The same former official, however, argues that this critique somewhat misses the forest for the trees, noting that the US government was working intensively throughout the year to ready a strong crisis response for the moment when it would be most needed.[8] By making clear that atrocity prevention was a presidential priority, the mass atrocities directive (Presidential Study Directive 10) lent a sense of urgency to that work and set the stage for the deputies to put in motion a robust response in November.

New capacity-tool development

Beyond its effect on US posture toward specific countries, the Obama administration's atrocity-prevention policy also created an impetus for the development of certain new capabilities, although the final inventory of new tools attributable to the policy was perhaps smaller than might have been anticipated or hoped for at the time of the 100-day review. The most meaningful new additions to the toolkit included the following.

Suspension of entry

Presidential Proclamation 8697, launched alongside Presidential Study Directive 10 on August 4, 2011, created a new tool intended to deter perpetrators of serious human rights and humanitarian law violations and abuses by suspending their ability to enter the United States (Obama 2011b). Denial of entry to the United States can be a powerful motivator for perpetrators who have family or friends in the country (e.g., children studying at college). One State Department expert who had worked on the Côte d'Ivoire crisis in 2010 and 2011 recalled that a US travel ban announced at the end of 2010 under different authority had been a particularly useful tool for pressuring President Laurent Gbagbo, who had a daughter in Atlanta (Reuters 2010).

That said, the proclamation was probably not used to full advantage in the Obama administration. The document contains a loophole that effectively nullifies the operative provisions of the proclamation when the entry of the person in question "would not harm the foreign relations interests of the United States" (Obama 2011b, 1). The document contains no requirement that this "would not harm" determination be made at senior levels of the State Department, and in practice it was unclear how broadly that provision was applied. Although subsequent legislation seemed to give the State Department greater authority both to designate perpetrators before they applied for visas and to disclose those designations publicly, divisions within the department about how and when to exercise that authority meant that it was effectively not on the table during interagency discussions.

Notwithstanding those challenges, evidence suggests that visa sanctions can be a useful tool for encouraging positive human rights behavior. For example, the administration relied in part on the proclamation to beneficial effect in devising consequences for Uganda's passage of anti-LGBT (lesbian, gay, bisexual, and transgender) legislation in 2014 (Harris and Pomper 2014). There is room for further work to consider how the proclamation and legislative visa ban authorities might be most effectively used in other prevention-related contexts given constraints.

National Intelligence Estimate

The first-ever NIE on the global risk of mass atrocities was a useful tool for scanning the horizon and identifying the countries at greatest risk of mass-scale civilian casualties, as well as seeing the connections between mass atrocities and other security threats. A version of the text was made available to certain foreign partners, and the intelligence community offered briefings to members of Congress and staff. A May 2016 executive order formalizing the atrocity-prevention strategy, as well as the structure and protocols of the board, calls for the intelligence community to update its judgments in the NIE to inform the board's ongoing work (Obama 2016). Properly framed, those updated judgments should be able to assist the board in developing its long-term agenda and help departments and agencies engage in long-term planning and resource allocation to address future atrocity-prevention needs.

Rewards for Justice legislation and other International Criminal Court assistance

The administration worked closely with Congress to pass bipartisan legislation in 2013 that expanded the Rewards for Justice (RFJ) Program to allow an unprecedented level of US government support for International Criminal Court (ICC) efforts (US Department of State n.d.). Previous RFJ legislation had permitted the State Department to offer cash rewards of up to $5 million for information leading to the arrest or conviction of foreign nationals accused of war crimes, crimes against humanity, or genocide by certain international tribunals. Consistent with long-standing congressional concerns that the ICC might someday seek to prosecute

US service members, the previous RFJ legislation purposefully excluded the ICC from those tribunals. The desire to facilitate the apprehension of Lord's Resistance Army leader Joseph Kony helped overcome those concerns, however, and in January 2013, the RFJ expansion legislation eliminated the restriction that barred awards for information leading to the arrest or conviction of ICC indictees.

As political acceptance of the court expanded, the executive branch deepened its cooperation in other ways. Two operations of particular note included assisting the Office of the Prosecutor to transfer to The Hague former Congolese warlord Bosco Ntaganda (who turned himself in at the US embassy in Kigali in March 2013) (York 2013) and senior Lord's Resistance Army commander Dominic Ongwen (who surrendered in the Central African Republic in January 2015) (BBC News 2015a). Toward the end of the administration, however, growing signs that the prosecutor was preparing to move toward a formal investigation of US conduct in and relating to Afghanistan raised serious questions about whether the United States would sustain that level of cooperation (Pomper 2017).

Peacekeeping expansion and reform

The administration invested considerable effort in strengthening and reforming multilateral peacekeeping, and making it a more flexible and effective instrument for civilian protection. Although President Obama met with leading troop contributors on the margins of his first trip to the UN General Assembly in 2009, the big push on peacekeeping came during the second term. Following up on a summit led by Vice President Joe Biden in September 2014, Obama headlined a 2015 leaders' summit that required governments to make certain commitments if they wanted to participate. The event yielded commitments for more than 40,000 new troops (including police) together with more than forty helicopters, twenty-two engineering companies, eleven naval and riverine units, and thirteen field hospitals (United Nations Peacekeeping 2015). For its part, during the last three years of the Obama administration, the US government sponsored a new program to upgrade rapid response capabilities in a select group of African partners (White House 2014); upgraded its own peacekeeping policy for the first time in more than twenty years (White House 2015); championed reforms to improve mission leadership and demand accountability for UN troops that engage in human rights abuses (Power 2015); promoted the "Kigali Principles on the Protection of Civilians," a set of guidelines intended to promote more proactive and effective engagement by UN troops operating under civilian protection mandates (Lederer 2016); and pressed for the UN Security Council to develop a new mechanism (which was not completed) by which assessed UN contributions could be used to support a portion of the costs of authorized African Union missions (United Nations 2016).

Unfinished work

In addition to noting the tools that the administration developed and strengthened, important also to note are the ones that failed to emerge from interagency discussions. In the area of financial tools, the board prepared a draft executive order on atrocities that would have created a global authority to designate for sanctions large-scale violators of human rights, as had been discussed during the 2011–2012 review process. The majority view within departments and agencies was that this executive order would streamline the imposition of targeted sanctions – or credible threats of sanctions – in the context of crises arising in countries where the US government had not already created a sanctions program and where the process of creating one might either be slow or cause unwanted bilateral friction (BBC News 2015b). Even if some of the designees had few assets in the United States (often the case with, for example, African warlords accused of atrocities), the thought was that many potential perpetrators would want to avoid inclusion on what would come to be seen as the "US atrocities list."

The Treasury Department strongly opposed the issuance of the new order, however, arguing that it would create unmeetable expectations within the advocacy community and create undue burdens on the department's small staff. The Treasury Department also voiced concerns about the overuse of sanctions in general and the potential effect on the dollar as a reserve currency, although outside experts convened by the NSC to discuss US sanctions policy suggested that neither of those was an especially great concern for a targeted sanctions program of the nature contemplated. Still, despite a principals meeting that sought to bridge gaps, the Treasury Department's concerns carried the day, and the order was never issued. A year and a half after principals deliberated over the order, however, Congress enacted legislation – the Global Magnitsky Human Rights Accountability Act – that created a global designation authority for individuals who have engaged in gross corruption or the abuse of human rights defenders (UAWire 2016). While the Global Magnitsky legislation achieved some of the objectives of the global order that the Obama administration had discussed, the Donald J. Trump administration took a very significant further step in issuing Executive Order 13818, which permits the designation of any foreign person determined "to be responsible for or complicit in, or to have directly or indirectly engaged in, serious human rights abuse" (Berschinski 2018).

Another major tool that failed to emerge from the interagency process during the Obama administration was a draft proposal that would have made crimes against humanity an offense under US law. The term "crimes against humanity" is generally understood to refer to widespread or systematic attacks against civilians (United Nations Office on Genocide Prevention and the Responsibility to Protect n.d.), with "attacks against civilians" referring to a range of law of war or human rights violations, such as murder, sexual assault, and torture. The notion that crimes against humanity are of international concern dates to the Nuremberg trials (Robert H. Jackson Center n.d.) and is one that the United States has long supported, including in the drafting of the International Criminal Court Rome Statute. Indeed, as noted previously, recent legislation permits the State Department to offer a multi-million-dollar cash award for information that leads to the prosecution or conviction of a foreign person accused of crimes against humanity in a mixed, hybrid, or international tribunal, such as the ICC. Consensus within the US government broke down, however, around the question of whether domestic courts should be able to assert jurisdiction over a foreign national accused of crimes against humanity purely because that person is present in the state. The Defense Department, in particular, has longstanding concerns that the assertion by the United States of "present in" jurisdiction puts US service members and other officials in jeopardy of prosecution abroad. The concern is that other countries might reciprocally assert such jurisdiction to arrest and prosecute US officials present in their countries on trumped-up or political charges. Noting that the United States already has multiple criminal statutes that create "present in" jurisdiction – including for torture, genocide, child soldier recruitment, and piracy – the Departments of Justice and State took the view that the statute did not create additional legal risk for US personnel, particularly because the proposal included certain safeguards (e.g., providing for pre-charge consultation among the Justice Department and other key departments) to ensure careful consideration of any reciprocal or other policy implications before bringing charges under the statute. Those assurances were not sufficient to overcome Defense Department concerns, however, and the proposal never made it past the deputies committee.

Some commentators have also suggested that the development of military doctrine for the protection of civilians is an area that remains underdeveloped. The board embraced the addition of an appendix on mass atrocity response operations to the Department of Defense's Joint Publication 3–07.3 (see US Department of Defense 2012). The appendix is drawn largely from the 2010 Mass Atrocities Response Operations handbook by the Harvard Kennedy School's Carr Center for Human Rights Policy and the US Army Peacekeeping and Stability Operations Institute. Commentators have subsequently suggested, however, that the board should have looked more closely into whether that addition represented sufficient progress. One recent review of the military's literature on civilian protection described the US Army's translation of joint doctrine into its own training and doctrine publications as a "halfhearted effort" and argues that "the minimal ... doctrinal treatment that exists does not provide the military planner with a comprehensive guide to preventing and responding to atrocity crimes during the course of armed conflict" (Atkins 2016).[9] A former senior administration official argued, however, that although any doctrine could likely be improved, there is no such thing as a "right" doctrine that would by itself change the military's reluctance to embrace humanitarian intervention.[10]

Blueprint as policy: did atrocity-prevention efforts make a difference?

Asked whether the Obama administration's prevention policy was ultimately worthwhile, former senior officials were on the whole positive and underscored benefits that flowed from placing a conscious emphasis on atrocity prevention. At the same time, however, there was a general sense that redefining bureaucratic processes and lending a stronger sense of mission to the US government's prevention efforts would not by themselves be sufficient to avoid future Libyas and Syrias.

The affirmative case

Former officials who praised the policy and its implementation tended to group their comments as follows.

Focusing senior-level attention and guiding policy on below-the-radar situations, officials expressed near-uniform agreement that the policy was important for generating focus on situations that could otherwise slide beneath the notice of senior policymakers until a full-blown crisis had developed, and the range of options for staving off horrific violence had significantly narrowed. That kind of upstream work was important for moral and humanitarian reasons, but it was also important for avoiding regional destabilization that could have negative national security implications. Former Deputy National Security Advisor Ben Rhodes said that, because of the strategy,

> I found the atrocity-prevention focus and early warning signs to be more a driver of policy. I saw them elevating the profile of issues not otherwise on the agenda. As a result, these issues were in the White House in a different way. I remember the president being involved on Côte d'Ivoire. On the Central African Republic. On South Sudan.[11]

Echoing those sentiments, former National Security Advisor to Vice President Biden, Jake Sullivan, notes, "Let's remember that we sort of take a case like CAR for granted because it seems a bit soft – not that big a lift. But compare it to what another administration would do in a similar situation without this policy. Nothing."[12]

Surge capacity and backstopping

A number of former officials spoke about the additional capacity created by bringing together functional experts from across the government to bear down on a problem that might not otherwise be fully staffed. Former Atrocities Prevention Board member Jeremy Weinstein spoke of "empowering people who care about these issues and are more powerful than they would be from within their silos – and also benefit from the White House access they gain through the NSC chair."[13]

In another variation on the theme of surge capacity, board members knew that they could be called to meet at pretty much any time if a crisis arose, and the board was sometimes more nimble than were regional processes at coming together quickly. On multiple occasions, the board convened for pop-up weekend conversations to fill a planning gap. The announcement of a board meeting would occasionally prompt the regional group to convene in advance so they could be the first to occupy the relevant policy space. The NSC multilateral affairs directorate dubbed that the "APB effect."

Options, expertise, and intelligence

Former officials who ran deputy-level processes expressed particular appreciation for the way in which the board marshaled intelligence and cultivated options so that deputies could usefully weigh in on atrocity-related issues. Former Deputy National Security Advisor Avril Haines saw value in "having informed views at the table regarding the various ways in which you might mitigate the chances of violent incidents erupting into mass atrocities, particularly when animated by hatred or prejudice."[14] Haines noted that,

> For example, recognizing the value of, and recommending the use of, public messaging in some circumstances from certain credible voices on tolerance and peace was important. Experts in this area generally knew what the content of such a message would be and had the networks and tools to deploy it intelligently. Through the conversation they'd also be educating high-level policy makers to the idea that there are special issues relating to this category of crimes and special tools that ought to be deployed.[15]

A framework for developing tools

The strategy writ large provided a rolling impetus to develop and deploy new capabilities that otherwise would not have seen the light of day, argues Weinstein: "You need a concerted effort to develop the toolkit.... Who cares about these things in the absence of a specific policy and structure? If you have the policy and the structure, then you get a foothold, and allow outside groups to hold you accountable."[16]

Shortcomings, challenges, and possible solutions

Although most former officials interviewed were solidly supportive of the board and atrocity-prevention strategy for the noted reasons, they also identified serious challenges that surfaced as the administration sought to move from the Task Force report to an actual policy.

Overcoming challenges to multilateral action

One of the major gaps in the Task Force report, and in the policy that flowed from it, was a failure to grapple fully with scenarios in which a veto-wielding member of the UN Security Council blocks authorization of collective measures that are required to address an atrocity situation. That always had the potential to be a substantial obstacle to US prevention efforts, because working within a multilateral framework – to optimize burden sharing, effectiveness, and legitimacy – was a key emphasis of *A Problem from Hell*, the Task Force report, and the administration's strategy. In practice, however, it was unclear how big a problem it would be. During the first few years of the administration, it seemed that Russia and China could generally be pressured into joining the United States and its partners even when their instincts might have led them in a different direction – as was the case in Côte d'Ivoire (where the Russians reluctantly joined the Security Council in affirming the legitimacy of Alassane Ouattara's election as president and pressuring Gbagbo to step down) and Libya. In Syria, however, a combination of factors – Vladimir Putin's replacement of Dmitry Medvedev as president of Russia in May 2012, the messiness of the Libyan intervention, and Russia's perceived strategic interests – brought this trend to a crashing halt. Recalling how Secretary of State Madeleine Albright had spurred the Security Council to action in the Balkans in 1995 by producing aerial photographs of mass graves around Srebrenica (Crossette 1995), the United States sought to raise the costs of intransigence by declassifying and posting information about regime atrocities and packaging the information in ways that would be easily digested. Russia, however, was prepared to absorb those costs, and over time a numbing could be observed not just in the Security Council and the broader public (which the Russians sought to exacerbate through an active disinformation campaign) but even within the US government. "People were overwhelmed by the sheer scope and variety of the horror inflicted," says one former senior official.[17]

The question, then, may be whether the United States can devise tools that will either apply more effective pressure on Russia to work constructively in the Security Council or afford a viable alternative to Security Council-sanctioned action. As Harold Koh has suggested, one area for focused work could be an effort to develop a considered legal framework, with appropriate limiting principles, that would make it clear to Moscow that the United States considers itself to have the legal right of forcible intervention to address extreme humanitarian emergencies. At least in 2013, Russia's concerns about the threat of force outside a Security Council-sanctioned framework helped bring it to the table in New York. Any effort to develop a legal framework would have to be approached with eyes open to the challenges. That humanitarian intervention is prohibited by the UN Charter is by far the dominant (although not the exclusive) perspective within international legal circles, and any shift away from that view by the US government will be intensively scrutinized for fealty to the Charter's text and history. An approach that is not well supported and subject to robust limiting principles will be criticized as illegitimate and damaging to the rules-based international order. As a policy matter, any legal justification would have to be framed such that the United States could abide its reciprocal application by other countries (Pompper 2018b).

With respect to other coercive measures, the relatively successful US collaboration with the European Union (EU) in the context of the Democratic Republic of the Congo (DRC) targeted sanctions offers one possible model to emulate. "Taking joint action with the EU on sanctions is not common or easy," says one veteran of the DRC sanctions effort. "The fact that we went the extra mile was impactful. That should be the norm."[18] Additionally, although proceeding multilaterally may be strongly preferred when it comes to financial sanctions, the United States also has a significant range of options for proceeding unilaterally, including potential new tools. For example, a 2017 Enough Project publication urged new strategies, such as targeting perpetrator networks (as the Treasury Department did on a modest scale when it simultaneously so designated DRC General Francois Olenga and one of his business concerns), using anti-money laundering tools, and potentially broadening the use of secondary-type sanctions – that is, sanctions that impose restrictions on foreign (as opposed to US) entities that do business with regimes or actors that the United States is seeking to pressure (Brooks-Rubin 2017). The Center for Global Development has also promoted the notion of preemptive contract sanctions, which would "put creditors and investors on notice that any future contracts to a regime would not be considered binding on successor governments" (Center for Global Development n.d.).

Although those new tools, as well as the new global designation authority created by Executive Order 13818, may be helpful in creating useful leverage – even where multilateral pressure is unavailable – like all sanctions, they are most likely to be effective if employed as part of a political strategy, with off-ramps that allow lifting when parties meet demands. Collateral effects – including damage to the local economy (which can have negative humanitarian consequences) and impacts on US businesses with interests there – should also be carefully weighed when considering the application of new sanctions and should be minimized to the extent possible.

Finally, the multilateral institutions with a role in driving international criminal justice – most importantly, the UN Security Council and the ICC – have not yet been able to deliver fully on their promise for deterring, punishing, or restraining perpetrators of atrocity crimes. As one former official noted, norm and institutional development have proceeded apace in recent decades, but the apprehension and sentencing of perpetrators has not. Whether or not the ICC can overcome extraordinary political and practical challenges to become an effective forum for the prosecution of atrocity crimes is not yet clear. One lesson of the ICC period, however, is the critical importance of local and regional cooperation to the apprehension of alleged perpetrators. The concerted efforts of the European community to bring war criminals to justice from the Balkans conflicts of the 1990s stand in stark contrast to efforts to bring to justice Sudanese President Omar Bashir, who has been able to travel relatively widely, particularly in Africa, including to ICC states parties (France24 [wires] 2017). Moreover, the Security Council has done virtually nothing to back up the court, even in situations (such as the Darfur cases) that arose out of a Security Council referral. That leads some former officials to emphasize the importance of leaning more heavily on regional mechanisms and developing the local support that will give those mechanisms sufficient strength so that their decisions are enforced.

Greater space for pragmatism

While recognizing that the topic is somewhat amorphous, a number of former senior officials suggested that the Obama administration sometimes boxed itself in by seeking to serve multiple values-linked goals at the same time, and that future administrations would do better to preserve greater flexibility. The comments had echoes of the longstanding "peace-versus-justice" debate about the tensions that can arise when seeking to forge diplomatic compromise with individuals alleged to have committed mass atrocities, who may resist peace absent guarantees that they will not face justice. One former official notes that steps to advance accountability for atrocity crimes, such as an ICC referral, can make a leader like Syrian President Bashar al-Assad feel as though he is in an existential battle, making him less likely to strike a deal that would protect civilians. "What happens to the Assads of the world?" asks the former official. "If it were up to me, I'd put them on a resort island with lifetime protection."[19] Still another former official underscores that, "We have got to get a lot more comfortable cutting deals with really bad guys."[20] At the same time, that official acknowledges the enormous downsides of seeming to reward perpetrators of the most serious international crimes with impunity: "We don't want to create incentives to commit atrocities."[21]

Although drawing sharp lessons from these reflections was difficult, what emerged was a sense that the United States should force itself to be realistic about how much leverage it has and the extent to which it can effectively pursue civilian protection, accountability, and democratic governance simultaneously in future crises. That is not to say that the United States should ever abandon any of those objectives, or pursue peace at any cost, but to recognize that sometimes being nuanced about how to pursue accountability and governance objectives may be helpful during periods when officials have acute concerns about civilian protection. In some situations, the course change may simply be a matter of sequencing – for example, prioritizing de-escalation and civilian protection over calls for transition and immediate accountability when the situation requires it but preserving as much latitude as possible to pursue both in the long term.

Communications: striking the right tone

Shaping expectations and communicating the prevention agenda to Congress and the public will be essential to political and financial support for prevention-related projects. During the Obama administration, those efforts suffered at certain points for several reasons.

First, the 2008 Task Force report helped set expectations sky high for the atrocity-prevention agenda by simultaneously broadening the scope of "genocide" to include a far wider range of atrocities and declaring that ending genocide was an achievable goal. The administration, if anything, augmented those expectations with the high-profile rollout of the Atrocities Prevention Board – and indeed, with the very name of the board. Notwithstanding early efforts to manage expectations by explaining that the board was not a panacea and would not in fact be dealing with matters already receiving high-level attention, bridging the gap between the aspirational rhetoric of the Task Force report and the reality of the board's mission was difficult – particularly while Syria burned.

Second, much as the board and its members welcomed and sought input from civil society, the advocacy community persistently suggested that it lacked sufficient access to the board and its work. In hindsight, one reason for the disconnect may be that the board was focused on its role as an IPC, which dealt in classified and other non-public information, and generally kept its deliberations internal to the US government. By contrast, the advocacy community may have had expectations that the board would be more active in trying to raise public awareness around atrocity issues and also in visibly pushing more senior officials to develop the political will to take certain risks in the service of the atrocity-prevention agenda.

For similar reasons (i.e., because the board was conceived of as an IPC and therefore a quintessentially executive-branch entity), early efforts to cultivate a congressional constituency for its work were thin. Although some already sympathetic staffers took an interest in its agenda, understood its focus, and sought to educate others, the effort was not fully successful. One concern that quickly emerged was the difficulty of securing regional bureau cooperation on board-endorsed efforts unless the functional components most closely tied to the board could offer some resources by way of support. The State Department's "J Bureau" (which had responsibility for civilian security, democracy, and human rights) pressed for funding and was able to secure a modest earmark to support prevention-related work, but congressional support remained tenuous.

Looking ahead: a fork in the road?

Just past the eleventh anniversary of the Task Force report, the world looks very different from the way it did when the report launched. Although the Task Force report informed the creation of a policy and a process that former officials generally believe has added some value, those tools have not necessarily had the full real-world effect that was hoped for or intended. The promise that ending genocide and other mass atrocities is an achievable goal does not necessarily seem more realistic today than it did in 2008, and in some ways, it seems more aspirational. Great power tensions have strained the international order that, it was hoped, would provide the framework and tools for addressing those crises. A UN-authorized intervention in Libya ended in chaos. A revanchist Russia has put itself beyond shaming in the Syria crisis and made clear its open hostility to the protection of human rights around the world. Against that backdrop, the atrocity-prevention movement needs to decide where to go next.

One option would be to focus mainly on expanding and perfecting the niche that the board carved out for itself. Under that approach, the US government would focus on further institutionalizing the board so that its work becomes yet better integrated with the mainstream of US foreign policy. Work could also continue on developing new tools – for example, a crimes-against-humanity statute – and to bring along other international partners to help bolster US efforts.

Although many of those suggestions are worthy (and, indeed, consistent with recommendations made herein), this chapter suggests that cleaving strictly to that path will cause a missed opportunity to learn from the past and to fill in some holes that must be addressed for the atrocity-prevention project to be more successful in the future. Although room for improvement remains, the US government has now learned how to configure itself in a way that addresses the structural issues raised by *A Problem from Hell* and the Task Force report. Much as appreciating and preserving those gains is important, also important is recognizing the magnitude of what those formal and structural changes failed to do in Libya and Syria. The very substantial damage caused by the failure of the system to bring to heel the Syria crisis is particularly important. That damage accrued primarily to the innocents caught up in the horrific violence and secondarily to political stability in the Middle East and Europe, but it also had an incidental effect on the credibility of the atrocity-prevention agenda writ large.

To further advance the US government's effectiveness at preventing atrocities, it will need both to consolidate the progress it has made in implementing the core recommendations from the Task Force report and look beyond to compensate for gaps in capabilities and for obstacles to multilateral action at the United Nations that affected its ability to shape positive outcomes in Libya and Syria. Further internal steps will have to be taken by the executive branch to strengthen prevention capacities while expanding interaction with Congress and civil society on atrocity-prevention matters (for a more detailed list of recommendations, see Pomper 2018a).

Acknowledgments

This chapter is an abridged version of Pomper (2018a). It draws from the author's reflections on his tenure as senior director for African Affairs, Multilateral Affairs and Human Rights on the staff of the Obama administration's National Security Council, as well as his experience as chairperson of the US Atrocities Prevention Board.

Notes

1 The report on which this chapter is based (see Acknowledgments) also includes an inquiry into the historical and intellectual background of the Obama administration's efforts in this area and a discussion of the Obama administration's approach to the atrocity crimes crises in Libya and Syria.
2 Interviewees who agreed to be identified are (in alphabetical order) Salman Ahmed, Alex Bick, Tony Blinken, Todd Buchwald, Anna Cave, Andrew Gilmour, Avril Haines, Grant Harris, Naomi Kikoler, Tom Malinowski, Rob Malley, Gideon Maltz, Derek Mitchell, David Mortlock, Charlotte Oldham-Moore, Samantha Power, David Pressman, Ben Rhodes, Susan Rice, Adam Smith, Donald Steinberg, Jacob Sullivan, Beth Van Schaack, Colin Thomas-Jensen, Mona Yacoubian, Howard Wachtel, Jeremy Weinstein,

Anne Witkowsky, and Lawrence Woocher. In some cases, interviewees preferred that their quotes not be attributed to them by name.
3 Author interviews with former senior administration officials, May 2017.
4 Author interview with David Pressman, April 25, 2017.
5 Author interview with former senior administration official, January 2018.
6 Author interview with Anna Cave, May 31, 2017.
7 Ibid.
8 Ibid.
9 Atkins (2016) argues that to remedy shortcomings, it may be helpful, among other efforts, to consider the application of prevention and response doctrine beyond the context of peacekeeping and stability operations (where they are currently cabined) and explore more granular recommendations that have emerged, such as adding atrocity prevention and response tasks to the military's Universal Joint Task List.
10 Email to author from former senior administration official, August 2017.
11 Author interview with Ben Rhodes, May 3, 2017.
12 Author interview with Jacob Sullivan, May 19, 2017.
13 Author interview with Jeremy Weinstein, April 24, 2017.
14 Email to author from Avril Haines, August 12, 2017.
15 Ibid.
16 Author interview with Weinstein.
17 Email to author from former senior administration official, August 2017.
18 Author interview with administration official, April 24, 2017.
19 Author interview with former senior administration official, May 2017.
20 Ibid.
21 Ibid.

References

Alleblas, Tessa, Eamon Aloyo, Sarah Brockmeier, Philipp Rotmann, and Jon Western, 2017. *In the Shadow of Syria: Assessing the Obama Administration's Efforts on Mass Atrocity Prevention* (The Hague: The Hague Institute for Global Justice).

Atkins, Alison F., 2016. "Atrocity Prevention and Response During Armed Conflict: Closing the Capability Gap," *Army Press Online Journal*, January 1, www.armyupress.army.mil/Portals/7/Army-Press-Online-Journal/documents/Atkins-1Jan16.pdf.

BBC News, 2015a. "LRA Rebel Dominic Ongwen Surrenders to US Forces in CAR," January 7, www.bbc.com/news/world-africa-30705649.

BBC News, 2015b. "Venezuelan Leader Maduro Condemns New US Sanctions," March 10, www.bbc.com/news/world-latin-america-31813127.

Berschinski, Rob, 2018. "Trump Administration Notches a Serious Human Rights Win. No, Really," *Just Security*, January 10, www.justsecurity.org/50846/trump-administration-notches-human-rights-win-no-really/.

Brooks-Rubin, Brad, 2017. "Yes, We Have Leverage: A Playbook for Immediate and Long-Term Financial Pressures to Address Violent Kleptocracies in East and Central Africa," Enough Project Policy Brief, June, https://enoughproject.org/wp-content/uploads/2017/06/YesWeHaveLeverage_June2017_Enough.pdf.

Brown, Hayes, 2013. "The Inside Story of how the US Acted to Prevent Another Rwanda," *ThinkProgress*, December 20, https://thinkprogress.org/the-inside-story-of-how-the-u-s-acted-to-prevent-another-rwanda-e91beac73aca.

Center for Global Development, n.d. "Preemptive Contract Sanctions," www.cgdev.org/topics/preemptive-contract-sanctions.

Crossette, Barbara, 1995. "US Seeks to Prove Mass Killings," *New York Times*, August 11.

France24 (wires), 2017. "South Africa Tells ICC It Didn't Break Rules by Failing to Arrest Sudan's Bashir," April 8, www.france24.com/en/20170408-south-africa-tells-icc-break-rules-failing-arrest-sudan-bashir-war-crimes.

Genocide Prevention Task Force, 2008. *Preventing Genocide: A Blueprint for US Policymakers* (Washington, DC: United States Holocaust Memorial Museum, American Academy of Diplomacy, and the United States Institute of Peace).

Guardian, 2015. "Obama Hits Burundi Security Officials with Sanctions Over Continuing Violence," November 23.

Hackel, Joyce, and Kenny Sokan, 2016. "US Ambassador Samantha Power: 'The Match Could Be Laid' to Ignite Burundi Conflict," *Public Radio International*, February 1, www.pri.org/stories/2016-02-01/us-ambassador-power-warns-match-could-be-laid-down-ignite-burundi.

Harris, Grant, and Stephen Pomper, 2014. "Further US Efforts to Protect Human Rights in Uganda," *White House Blog*, June 19, https://obamawhitehouse.archives.gov/blog/2014/06/19/further-us-efforts-protect-human-rights-uganda.

Keaten, Jamey, 2017. "UN Rights Chief: Rohingya Seemingly Face 'Ethnic Cleansing'," *APNews*, September 11, www.apnews.com/693bc5d24ca44213b5ab11c4755dd8e1.

Lederer, Esther M., 2016. "US Approves UN Use of Force to Protect Civilians in Conflict," *Washington Times*, May 11.

Obama, Barack, 2011a. "Presidential Study Directive on Mass Atrocities," *White House*, August 4, https://obamawhitehouse.archives.gov/the-press-office/2011/08/04/presidential-study-directive-mass-atrocities.

Obama, Barack, 2011b. "Proclamation 8697 – Suspension of Entry as Immigrants and Non-immigrants of Persons Who Participate in Serious Human Rights and Humanitarian Law Violations and Other Abuses," August 4, www.gpo.gov/fdsys/pkg/DCPD-201100548/pdf/DCPD-201100548.pdf.

Obama, Barack, 2012. "Remarks by President Obama at the University of Yangon," November 19, https://obamawhitehouse. archives.gov/the-press-office/2012/11/19/remarks-president-obama-university-yangon.

Obama, Barack, 2015. "Message from President Obama to the People of Burundi," November 13, www.youtube.com/watch?v=FToWhIRAM34.

Obama, Barack, 2016. "Comprehensive Approach to Atrocity Prevention and Response," Executive Order, May 18, https://obamawhitehouse.archives.gov/the-press-office/2016/05/18/executive-order-comprehensive-approach-atrocity-prevention-and-response.

Pomper, Stephen, 2017. "USG Statement on Int'l Criminal Court Probe into Alleged US War Crimes Is Missing Some Things," *Just Security*, December 14, www.justsecurity.org/49360/usg-statement-intl-criminal-court-probe-alleged-u-s-war-crimes-missing-2/.

Pomper, Stephen, 2018a. *Atrocity Prevention under the Obama Administration: What We Learned and the Path Ahead* (Washington, DC: Simon-Skjodt Center, United States Holocaust Memorial Museum, February).

Pomper, Stephen, 2018b. "Trump vs. International Law: The Challenge of Articulating a Legal Framework for Humanitarian Intervention," *OpinioJuris*, October 5, http://opiniojuris.org/2018/10/05/trump-vs-international-law-the-challenge-of-articulating-a-legal-framework-for-humanitarian-intervention/.

Power, Samantha, 2002. *A Problem from Hell: America and the Age of Genocide* (New York: Basic Books).

Power, Samantha, 2015. "The Future of United Nations Peacekeeping," Testimony Before the Senate Foreign Relations Committee, December 9, www.foreign.senate.gov/imo/media/doc/120915_ Power_Testimony.pdf.

Reuters, 2010. "US Slaps Travel Ban on Ivory Coast's Gbagbo," December 22, www.reuters.com/article/us-ivorycoast-usa-idUSTRE6BK5VQ20101221.

Robert H. Jackson Center, n.d. "The Influence of the Nuremberg Trial on International Criminal Law," Tove Rosen, ed., www.roberthjackson.org/speech-and-writing/the-influence-of-the-nuremberg-trial-on-international-criminal-law/.

UAWire, 2016. "Obama Expands Magnitsky Act Globally," December 25, www.uawire.org/news/obama-expands-magnitsky-act-globally.

United Nations, 2016. "Stronger United Nations Partnership with African Union Possible Due to Revamped Regional Arrangements, Security Council Presidential Statement Says," Meetings Coverage and Press Releases, May 24, www.un.org/press/en/2016/sc12370.doc.htm.

United Nations Office on Genocide Prevention and the Responsibility to Protect, n.d. "Definitions: Crimes Against Humanity," www.un.org/en/genocideprevention/crimes-against-humanity.html.

United Nations Peacekeeping, 2015. "Leaders' Summit on Peacekeeping," September 28, http://peacekeeping.un.org/en/leaders-summit-peaceekeeping.

US Department of Defense, 2012. "Joint Publication 3–07.3: Peace Operations," August 1, https://fas.org/irp/doddir/dod/jp3-07-3.pdf.

US Department of State, n.d. "War Crimes Rewards Program," www.state.gov/j/gcj/wcrp/index.htm.

White House, 2012. "Fact Sheet: A Comprehensive Strategy and New Tools to Fight Atrocities," April 23, https://obamawhitehouse.archives.gov/the-press-office/2012/04/23/fact-sheet-comprehensive-strategy-and-new-tools-prevent-and-respond-atro.

White House, 2013. "Fact Sheet: US Assistance to the Central African Republic," December 19, https://obamawhitehouse.archives.gov/the-press-office/2013/12/19/fact-sheet-us-assistance-central-african-republic.

White House, 2014. "Fact Sheet: US Support for Peacekeeping in Africa," August 6, https://obamawhitehouse.archives.gov/the-press-office/2014/08/06/fact-sheet-us-support-peacekeeping-africa.

White House, 2015. "Fact Sheet: US Support to Peace Operations 2015 Leaders' Summit on UN Peacekeeping," September 28, https://obamawhitehouse.archives.gov/the-press-office/2015/09/28/fact-sheet-us-support-peace-operations-2015-leaders-summit-un.

York, Geoffrey, 2013. "Warlord Bosco Ntaganda Surrenders to US Embassy in Rwanda," *The Globe and Mail*, March 18.

PART II
Regional implementation mechanisms

4
ASEAN REGIONALISM AND CAPACITY-BUILDING FOR ATROCITIES PREVENTION

Challenges and prospects

Noel M. Morada

Introduction

Atrocities prevention has become a major concern of the Association of Southeast Asian Nations (ASEAN), given the continuing spill-over effects in the region of the humanitarian crisis in Myanmar since communal violence erupted in Rakhine State in 2012. Although Myanmar's human rights problem has been a serious issue for ASEAN since 2007, the persecution of the Muslim Rohingya amidst growing Buddhist nationalism in the country highlighted the constraints faced by the organization in responding to human protection issues. The crisis has undoubtedly forced ASEAN to rethink the practicality of strictly adhering to its non-interference principle, especially in dealing with an errant member who fails to fulfill its primary Responsibility to Protect (R2P) vulnerable populations within its territory.

This chapter examines the challenges and prospects for ASEAN's capability for atrocities prevention by analyzing the relevant human protection principles adopted by the organization and the factors that influence member states' responses to human rights protection issues in the region. Specifically, it identifies the relevant constraints faced by the organization in implementing R2P in the context of Myanmar's communal conflicts, as well as the achievements and emerging challenges in atrocities prevention in other member states of ASEAN. This chapter argues that it is critically important for ASEAN to seriously rethink its non-interference and consensus decision-making principles if the organization wants to become more effective in responding to humanitarian protection issues. There is no question that these norms have rendered the organization incapable of meaningfully advancing human rights protection and of implementing human protection principles that it has adopted since the ratification of the ASEAN Charter in 2008.

The chapter proceeds in two parts. First, I provide an overview of the human protection principles adopted by ASEAN, followed by a discussion of the challenges and prospects for advancing atrocities prevention in the region. Second, the dynamics of ASEAN's dealings with human rights and human protection issues in

Myanmar are examined, along with the achievements and emerging challenges in the region in implementing R2P in other member states.

ASEAN's principles on human protection: an overview

Although ASEAN has not formally adopted the language of R2P, human protection principles have been incorporated in its formal documents and agreements since the Bali Concord II in 2003. Specifically, the ASEAN Charter; the blueprints of the ASEAN Community pillars related to Political-Security and Socio-Cultural communities; and the terms of reference of various ASEAN mechanisms have highlighted the importance of human protection norms in the vision, objectives, and long-term goals of the organization. This includes human rights protection, tolerance of and respect for diversity, protection of women and children, and protection of migrant workers, among others. In the ASEAN Charter, for example, good governance, the rule of law, and human rights protection were recognized as fundamental principles in promoting the group's shared values and objectives. It also included a provision for the creation of a regional human rights body, which paved the way for the establishment of the ASEAN Inter-Governmental Commission on Human Rights (AICHR). Table 4.1 shows the important elements of human protection principles that have been adopted by ASEAN in various relevant documents since 2008.

Table 4.1 suggests that human rights protection is a key component of ASEAN's community-building vision; both the *rights* and *responsibilities* of member states are acknowledged, and the values of tolerance and respect for diversity are also recognized. Based on the total number of mentions across these documents, human rights protection scored the highest (eighteen), followed by peace, conflict management, and conflict resolution (sixteen); then rule of law (ten), and democracy and democratic values (ten) (Morada 2016, 122). In the ASEAN Charter and the blueprints of the ASEAN Political-Security Community and the ASEAN Socio-Cultural Community, the primary responsibility of member states in implementing the people-oriented principles were underscored. Thus, one can argue that the concept of state responsibility in relation to human protection, respect for diversity, and adherence to international norms is not alien to ASEAN, and has been part of the community-building efforts of the organization and in promoting ASEAN regionalism (Morada 2016). Meanwhile, the three mechanisms – the AICHR, the ASEAN Commission on the Promotion and Protection of the Rights of Women and Children (ACWC), and the ASEAN Institute for Peace and Reconciliation (AIPR) – were tasked to give priority to promoting awareness and building capacity for protection of human rights, protection of women and children, and peace and reconciliation in their respective terms of reference (Morada 2016).

While ASEAN has adopted the human rights protection principles, traditional norms are still deeply embedded in the organization's diplomatic culture, which values respect for territorial integrity, sovereignty, and non-interference in the domestic affairs of member states. More importantly, the "ASEAN Way" of

TABLE 4.1 ASEAN human rights protection principles in key documents

Key Terms	ASEAN Charter	Political-Security Community	Socio-Cultural Community	AICHR Terms of Reference	ACWC Terms of Reference	AIPR Terms of Reference	Total Mentions
Human rights protection	4	5	4	4	1	-	18
Peace, conflict management/resolution	1	6	-	-	1	8	16
Democracy/democratic values/respect for fundamental freedoms	3	3	-	3	1	-	10
Rule of law/rules-based community	3	6	-	1	-	-	10
Good governance	3	4	-	1	-	-	8
Promote awareness/capacity-building on human rights protection/peace, reconciliation, and conflict prevention	1	1	1	2	1	2	8
Rights and responsibilities of member states/shared responsibilities	2	1	1	1	1	1	7
Respect for rights of women and children/protection of women and children	-	1	3	-	3	-	7
Tolerance/respect for diversity/inter-communal/interfaith dialogue	1	2	1	1	1	1	7
Adherence to international laws on humanitarian, human rights, protection of women and children	1	1	1	2	1	-	6
Peace and stability	2	4	-	-	-	-	6
Humanitarian assistance/refugees/displaced persons	-	6	-	-	-	-	6
People-oriented ASEAN	2	1	2	-	-	-	5
Gender mainstreaming/elimination of violence against women	-	1	3	-	-	1	5
Culture of peace/peace-oriented values	1	4	-	-	-	-	5
Peacebuilding/peace process	-	3	-	-	-	2	5
Comprehensive security/human security/human development	1	2	1	-	-	-	4
Protection of migrant workers/against human trafficking/people smuggling	-	3	1	-	-	-	4
Social protection	-	-	2	-	-	-	2

Key
ACWC: ASEAN Commission on the Promotion and Protection of the Rights of Women and Children
AICHR: ASEAN Inter-Governmental Commission on Human Rights
AIPR: ASEAN Institute for Peace and Reconciliation
Source: Morada (2016, 120).

decision-making anchored on consultation and consensus is still the operative principle when it comes to dealing with regional issues, such as human rights, refugees, trafficking of persons, migrants, and so on. Although this process ensures the group's cohesion in its collective decisions, it also means that the effectiveness of ASEAN's response to certain regional issues are constrained by consensus that is based on the "least common denominator" and avoidance of opposition by any member which may invoke its right to veto any decision, especially if its sovereignty is affected. Indeed, the cohesion of ASEAN has been tested especially on issues related to several political and humanitarian crises in Myanmar, the problem in southern Thailand,[1] and the South China Sea dispute.[2] Particularly in the case of Myanmar following the eruption of communal violence in Rakhine since July 2012, some member states, former ASEAN officials, and civil society groups have called on the relaxation of the non-interference principle when it comes to internal conflicts and humanitarian crisis issues that spill over into other member states. As discussed ahead, ASEAN's engagement with Myanmar since it became a member in 1997 has been primarily concerned about human rights protection – the house arrest of Aung San Suu Kyi (2003–2010), the military's violent crackdown against Buddhist-led protests (2007), the humanitarian crisis in the aftermath of Cyclone Nargis (2008), and the protection of stateless people like the Rohingya. Notwithstanding the newly elected government under the National League for Democracy (NLD) that took over in 2016, the communal conflict in Rakhine remains unresolved and ASEAN appears to have "relaxed" the non-interference principle in dealing with Myanmar on the Rohingya issue. This has been especially so following reported attacks by a militant group sympathetic to the Rohingya in Rakhine in October 2016 and August 2017, which again spurred another wave of refugees into neighboring Bangladesh as the military conducted clearing operations in the area. Accordingly, given the regional impact of continuing communal conflict in Rakhine as well as other ethnic conflicts in Myanmar, ASEAN has been under scrutiny regarding the commitment of its members to implement the human protection principles that it has adopted since 2008.

It is significant to point out that while the ASEAN Charter and other relevant ASEAN documents recognize the importance of promoting human rights protection as a key component of ASEAN community-building, there remains an ideological divide among member states on the universality of this norm (Morada 2016, 126). In 2012, ASEAN leaders signed the ASEAN Human Rights Declaration (AHRD) during a summit meeting in Phnom Penh. The AHRD was criticized by human rights advocates in the region as adhering to a relativist view of human rights norms and failing to uphold the Universal Declaration of Human Rights. This prompted the ASEAN leaders to issue a statement reaffirming their commitment to the Universal Declaration (see ASEAN 2012a). Table 4.2 summarizes the relevant sections of the AHRD by placing universal and relative principles side by side.

It is evident that while the AHRD contains certain universal principles on human rights protection, it also recognizes the importance of national contexts and diversity of legal systems or cultures of member states. For example, although Paragraph 8 recognizes the importance of upholding human rights and fundamental freedoms of every person, it also qualifies this universal principle as subject to domestic laws of member states and must "meet the just requirements" of national security and public order. On the issue of the death penalty, the AHRD qualifies the universal principle that recognizes the "inherent right to life which shall be protected by law" with "save in accordance with law" (Paragraph 11). This implies that ASEAN member states are under no obligation to conform to the universal principle of abolishing the death penalty at home, and instead allows upholding national laws on capital punishment. These limiting clauses underscore the primacy of national laws and domestic contexts of member states in interpreting international norms and how they are to be implemented. The AHRD neither aims to have member states uniformly adhere to international human rights standards, nor to develop its own regional norms, at least for now. Instead, the diversity of political contexts is acknowledged, and domestic legal norms are privileged.

Notwithstanding the creation of the AICHR in 2009, only five members of ASEAN thus far have their own national human rights institutions. The AICHR itself cannot force member states to set up national human rights institutions; its existing mandate is limited only to promoting awareness about human rights protection. The regional mechanism cannot monitor or hear complaints of human rights violations committed in member states; neither can it impose sanctions

TABLE 4.2 The ASEAN Human Rights Declaration: universal vs. relative principles

Universal Principles	Relative Principles
1. [a] All persons are born free and equal in dignity and rights. They are endowed with reason and conscience and should act towards one another in a spirit of humanity. 2. Every person is entitled to the rights and freedoms set forth herein, without distinction of any kind, such as race, gender, age, language, religion, political or other opinion, national or social origin, economic status, birth, disability or other status. 7. All human rights are universal, indivisible, interdependent, and interrelated.	6. The enjoyment of human rights and fundamental freedoms must be balanced with the performance of corresponding duties as every person has responsibilities to all other individuals, the community and the society where one lives. It is ultimately the primary responsibility of all ASEAN Member States to promote and protect all human rights and fundamental freedoms. 7. At the same time, the realization of human rights must be considered in the regional and national context bearing in mind different political, economic, legal, social, cultural, historical and religious backgrounds.

(Continued)

TABLE 4.2 (Continued)

Universal Principles	Relative Principles
8. The human rights and fundamental freedoms of every person shall be exercised with due regard to the human rights and fundamental freedoms of others.	8. The exercise of rights and fundamental freedoms shall be subject only to such limitations as are determined by law solely for the purpose of securing due recognition for the human rights and fundamental freedoms of others, and to meet the just requirements of national security, public order, public health, public safety, public morality, as well as the general welfare of the peoples in a democratic society.
11. Every person has inherent right to life which shall be protected by law.	11. No person shall be deprived of life save in accordance with law.
16. Every person has the right to seek and receive asylum in another State …	16. … in accordance with laws of such State and applicable international agreements.
18. Every person has the right to a nationality …	18. … as prescribed by law.
26. ASEAN Member States affirm all the economic, social and cultural rights in the Universal Declaration of Human Rights.	34. ASEAN Member States may determine the extent to which they should guarantee the economic and social rights found in this Declaration to non-nationals, with due regard to human rights and the organization and resources of their respective national economies.

Source: ASEAN Human Rights Declaration 2012, adapted from Morada (2016, 125–26).
[a] Numbers correspond to the numbered paragraphs in the AHRD.

against them. Even for those ASEAN members that already have national human rights institutions, there is significant variation in their adherence to the Status of National Institutions (the Paris Principles), particularly in relation to autonomy or independence. Currently, only five members of ASEAN – Indonesia, Malaysia, the Philippines, Thailand, and Vietnam (which does not have a national human rights commission) – have been alternately elected to the United Nations (UN) Human Rights Council since its creation in 2006, and have participated in its Universal Periodic Review. Although Myanmar has also participated in the review process, it has not accepted all the recommendations for improving human rights protection in that country (Morada 2016).

While acknowledging the current limitations to ASEAN's existing mechanisms for human rights protection and the principles enunciated in the AHRD, Vitit Muntarbhorn suggests that the following are important stepping stones for the development of human rights law in ASEAN. First, all member states should accede to all international human rights law as binding law both at the national and regional levels, and should include "comprehensive measures premised on civil, political, economic, social and cultural rights indivisibly (such as responsive laws, policies and practices)." Second, the group should establish "national systems to protect people's human rights" and member states should "open the door to regional mechanisms if there are no national remedies." Third, member states should commit themselves to ensuring that "there is no retrogression when ASEAN instruments are drafted and adopted" and that "there should be value added to strengthen and not undermine international standards on human rights and democracy" (Muntarbhorn 2017).

Overall, the gap between the principles adopted by ASEAN on human rights and its implementation by member states raises the question of whether norms on human rights protection in general remain aspirations for now rather than strictly shared values to which ASEAN members are deeply committed. ASEAN is still in the process of developing its regional identity where the transformation of its aspirations into shared values is still very much constrained by the diversity of its members' political and cultural contexts. Given that member states in general remain protective of their sovereignty, the regional organization's capacity to prevent and respond to systematic human rights violations and atrocities will be limited. Even so, it must be recognized that ASEAN has also responded to human rights violations and humanitarian crisis situations involving member states, especially in the case of Myanmar since 2007.

ASEAN atrocities prevention: challenges and prospects

Myanmar: relaxing ASEAN's non-interference principle for human protection?

Since its admission to ASEAN, Myanmar has put to the test ASEAN's traditional norm of non-interference and its resolve in dealing with human rights protection in the region. Its acceptance into the group has been premised on the willingness of the military junta to move the democratization process in the country forward based on a promised roadmap. Three important events in Myanmar served as major turning points in ASEAN's regional diplomacy as far as promoting human rights protection and responding to humanitarian crises are concerned: the Buddhist-led protests in 2007, Cyclone Nargis in 2008, and the communal conflict in Rakhine that erupted in mid-2012.

The Buddhist-led protests

The Myanmar government's decision to lift subsidies on fuel in August 2007 caused swift and unannounced increases in the prices of basic commodities, and triggered widespread protests throughout the country against the military junta. Initially, the government attempted to contain the situation by arresting those who participated in the demonstrations. The demonstrations spread to Yangon, Mandalay, Sittwe, and more than twenty other cities throughout the country by September, with an estimated 50,000–100,000 people participating in Yangon alone. Some 15,000 monks and 150 nuns took part on the sixth day of protests in Yangon even as an alliance of Buddhist monks threatened to continue the protests until the military junta was deposed. Former ASEAN Secretary-General Ong Keng Yong expressed hope that the government would not take strong action that would lead to a confrontation (BBC News 2007). However, on September 26, the military began its violent crackdown on protesters by attacking them with batons and tear gas, arresting civilians and Buddhist monks, and sealing off the Shwedagon Pagoda, which is a major site of demonstrations in Yangon. The total number of casualties in the military suppression remains contested. The government claimed that only ten to fifteen people were killed, while a Special Rapporteur to the UN Human Rights Council said that at least an additional sixteen people died during the forceful clampdown, seventy-four people went missing, and up to 1,000 were detained in connection with the protests (Hoge 2007).

The international community, led by ASEAN's Western dialogue partners, denounced the military junta's forceful crackdown against the protesters and announced sanctions against the regime. ASEAN, however, did not support these sanctions against Myanmar, as such policies would have exacerbated further the suffering of the ordinary people. Even so, given intense international pressure, a proposal was made for the inclusion of Myanmar's violent crackdown against protesting civilians on the agenda of the ASEAN Summit in November of the same year, which was chaired by Singapore. Singapore invited the UN special envoy to Myanmar, Ibrahim Gambari, to brief the ASEAN leaders about his fact-finding visit to the country in the aftermath of the political crisis. However, Myanmar used its veto power and invoked the non-interference principle to block the inclusion of the country's political crisis on the summit's agenda, a move supported by Laos and Vietnam (Arnold 2007).

During the ASEAN Summit in 2007, leaders signed the ASEAN Charter, which marked an important milestone capping the association's fortieth founding anniversary. Despite the adoption of the Charter, however, Philippines President Gloria Macapagal-Arroyo stated that its ratification would face some difficulties in her country's legislature if Myanmar failed to release Suu Kyi from house arrest and return to its promised path to democratization (Arnold 2007). It was an attempt on the part of the Philippines to persuade other members of ASEAN to seriously examine the implications of the military junta's continuing intransigence for the group's cohesion and credibility vis-à-vis its dialogue partners and the international community. Indeed, without the Charter provisions for sanctions against errant members, Myanmar would remain a burden to ASEAN's community-building efforts and to its promotion of international norms and principles such as good governance, the rule of law, and human rights protection in the region. The period of ratification of the ASEAN Charter could have been a good opportunity for the members to exert concerted pressure on Myanmar's government to abide by these principles and to fulfill its primary responsibility to protect the human rights of its people. Unfortunately, however, such an opportunity was missed as ASEAN remained divided between those who still adhered to the traditional norms of the organization and those who believed in balancing those norms with universal and people-centered principles. Indeed, the ASEAN Charter upholds both state-centered (sovereignty and non-interference) and people-centered (universal human rights and international humanitarian law) principles. It also recognizes the primary responsibility of states to protect human rights and reaffirms the concept of comprehensive security, which includes human security.

Cyclone Nargis

Less than a year after the widespread protests in September 2007, tropical Cyclone Nargis hit the southern part of Myanmar on May 2, 2008, which resulted in a massive humanitarian crisis. Official figures indicate that 84,500 people were killed and more than 53,000 were missing after the two-day disaster that devastated the Ayeyarwady Delta region (International Federation of Red Cross and Red Crescent Societies 2011).[3] While the government initially accepted relief assistance from neighboring countries immediately after the cyclone hit, the military junta on May 9 blocked international humanitarian assistance – especially from Western countries – as it feared that relief operations involving foreign aid workers and some military troops could be a pretext for intervention. This drew strong condemnation from the international community, including some permanent members of the UN Security Council. The French ambassador to the UN condemned the military junta's refusal to accept international aid, suggesting that this could lead to "a true crime against humanity." He denied allegations made by Myanmar's ambassador to the UN that Paris had sent a warship, instead asserting that the ship carried 1,500 tons of food and medicine for survivors (BBC News 2008). French Foreign Minister Bernard Kouchner called on the UN to invoke R2P as the basis for a resolution to force the military junta to allow international assistance into the country even without the consent of the Myanmar government (Mydans 2008). Some UN officials, however, resisted such calls, as they expressed hope that the junta would eventually be persuaded to allow international relief assistance and foreign aid workers to enter the country (Mydans 2008).

Eventually, the impasse over international humanitarian assistance was resolved after ASEAN used its influence over Myanmar through "backdoor diplomacy." Former ASEAN Secretary-General Surin Pitsuwan led a delegation of officials from the region to Yangon and convinced the military junta to allow international humanitarian assistance to enter using ASEAN as the main conduit. One week after the disaster, the ASEAN–Emergency Rapid Assessment Team (ASEAN–ERAT) was set up and, in coordination with the ASEAN Committee on Disaster Management, was dispatched to Myanmar to make an initial assessment of the critical needs in the aftermath of the cyclone. ASEAN–ERAT, which was also tasked to complement the work of the United Nations Disaster Assessment and Coordination team and those of the Myanmar government, recommended the creation of the "Humanitarian Coalition for the Victims of Cyclone Nargis" that would act as "a coordinating platform for relief and recovery" (ASEAN Secretariat 2009, 10).

The Rakhine crisis and Rohingya issue

Prior to 2012, the Rohingya issue in Myanmar was not a major concern for ASEAN, except for their outflow as "illegal migrants" in the Indian Ocean. As chair of the fourteenth ASEAN Summit in 2009, Thailand called for "cooperation among countries of origin, transit and destination" even as it also underscored the importance of addressing the issue "in a larger context, such as the contact group of affected countries" and through the Bali process. The ASEAN Secretary-General was also tasked to coordinate with the Myanmar government to "obtain the relevant statistics" related to illegal immigrants in the Indian Ocean (ASEAN 2009). Since 2007, Thailand has been criticized by various human rights groups for failing to protect the Rohingya who were fleeing from Bangladesh and Myanmar, some of whom were allegedly abused and detained as illegal migrants by military authorities after their boats landed on Thai territory and were towed back to sea, adrift for several days with barely enough food and water (MacKinnon and Sturcke 2009). An increased outflow of Rohingya refugees in 2009 was precipitated by a crackdown in Bangladesh against undocumented asylum seekers in an effort to stem the exodus of more than 8,000 Rohingya before the Myanmar elections in 2010. Reports in the Bangladesh media in late December 2009 that Myanmar had agreed to repatriate some 9,000 refugees caused widespread panic among undocumented Rohingya (Lewa 2010).

However, ASEAN was forced to respond to this humanitarian crisis in Myanmar following the eruption of communal violence in Rakhine in May and June 2012 between Muslim and Buddhist communities, which further aggravated the outflow of Rohingya refugees. Former ASEAN Secretary-General Surin took a "personal interest" regarding the Rohingya situation during the annual ASEAN ministerial meeting in Phnom Penh in July that year and sought the cooperation of both Myanmar and Bangladesh during his meeting with their respective foreign ministers (Radio Free Asia 2012). In their special meeting in August 2012, ASEAN foreign ministers issued a statement that expressed continuing concerns about the situation in Rakhine. On the one hand, they encouraged the government of Myanmar to continue to enhance the steps it had taken with the help of UN agencies and non-governmental organizations in responding to the humanitarian crisis, and they expressed readiness to assist Myanmar in addressing the crisis in Rakhine, with the consent of the government. On the other hand, the ministers also underscored that "the promotion of national solidarity and harmony among various communities in Myanmar constitute an integral part of Myanmar's ongoing democratization and reform process," even as they also expected that it would "continue to remain consistent with its commitment on the irreversibility of democratization and reform process in the country" (ASEAN 2012b).

The plight of the Rohingya and its impact in the region have raised the issue of whether ASEAN should begin relaxing its non-interference principle to allow the organization to effectively respond to humanitarian crisis situations. Some former ASEAN officials and parliamentarians have argued that it is time to re-examine the application of this principle, which to some extent has constrained ASEAN from responding more effectively to internal problems that spill over to other member states. For example, in April 2015, former Malaysian Foreign Minister Syed Hamid Albar called for a review of the non-interference principle during his speech at the ASEAN Civil Society Conference in Kuala Lumpur, arguing that it was imperative if ASEAN is "to build a tolerant society and address human rights abuses and regional security" even as the region cannot be "bogged down with problems that are prolonged or intensified by the blanket application of non-interference" (Channel News Asia 2015). Albar, together with former Malaysian Prime Minister Ahmad Badawi, former ASEAN Secretary-General Surin, and former Thai Foreign Minister Kasit Promiya, also sent a letter to the ASEAN chair in April 2015 during the summit in Malaysia calling for stepped-up engagement to address the issue of intolerance in Myanmar, including discriminatory laws. They pointed out that "the rising intolerance against religious and ethnic minorities in Myanmar will undermine the country's reform process, and may affect regional community-building, including ASEAN economic integration" (Humaniti 2015). For its part, the ASEAN Parliamentarians for Human Rights called on the leaders of ASEAN to urgently respond to the escalating humanitarian crisis and the growing atrocities risks affecting the Rohingya and other vulnerable minorities in Myanmar. For them, the problem represented a "direct threat to ASEAN nations" as it posed security risks and economic strains to the region even as it undermined the shared commitment of member states to "protecting all people from persecution and violence" (ASEAN Parliamentarians for Human Rights 2015).

In October 2016, another outbreak of violence occurred in Rakhine following an attack by some 200 militants (allegedly sympathetic to the Rohingya) against the Myanmar border police at Maungdaw and Bittadaung townships. Military clearing operations against the militants resulted in another outflow of Rohingya refugees to Bangladesh even as allegations were made that Myanmarese troops committed atrocities against them. In response to mounting international pressure on her government, Suu Kyi called a special informal meeting of the ASEAN foreign ministers in Yangon in December following demonstrations in Kuala Lumpur (led by Malaysian Prime Minister Najib Razak), Bangkok, and Jakarta against the persecution of the Rohingya. The Yangon meeting focused on the resumption of humanitarian assistance to affected communities and asked the Myanmar government to provide continual updates to ASEAN members about the evolving situation in Rakhine. ASEAN members expressed their commitment to help Myanmar to rebuild and restore peace and stability in Rakhine. The Malaysian foreign minister proposed that ASEAN should set up an independent body of experts and other eminent persons to investigate and corroborate official accounts of the Myanmar government on the situation in Rakhine (Mon and Naing 2016). During a meeting of the Organisation of Islamic Cooperation (OIC) in Kuala Lumpur in January 2017, Malaysian Prime Minister Najib called on Naypidaw: "the killing must stop, the burning of houses must stop, the violation of women and girls must stop" even as he accused the government of committing "genocide" against the Rohingya community (Roughneen 2017). OIC Special Envoy to Myanmar, Syed Hamid Albar, sought UN intervention to prevent "genocide" against the Rohingya (Sipalan and Harris 2017). In February, Malaysia sent a humanitarian aid ship to Yangon and later to Bangladesh to deliver food and emergency supplies to affected Muslim communities in Rakhine. The Myanmar government did not allow the ship to dock in Rakhine's capital and insisted that the aid be equally distributed to both Muslim and Buddhist communities (Latiff 2017). Meanwhile, during the ASEAN Summit in Manila in April 2017, Indonesian President Joko Widodo met with Suu Kyi and offered capacity-building assistance to train the Myanmar police, and to facilitate health, education, and livelihood programs (Sheany 2017).

As expected, Myanmar's Foreign Ministry denied allegations of genocide against the Rohingya and criticized the OIC for ignoring the October attacks and the government's "genuine efforts" to address the crisis in Rakhine. It also accused the Malaysian government of exploiting the crisis "to promote a certain political agenda" to divert attention from corruption allegations against the ruling party (Roughneen 2017). A commission set up by the Myanmar government and headed by a former military general in its interim report in January 2017 said that it had "so far found no evidence of genocide against Rohingya Muslims" and "not enough evidence to support widespread rape allegations" (BBC News 2017). However, it softened its position and promised to investigate the allegations of abuse even as it also sought more information from the UN following the release of the report by the Office of the UN Human Rights Commissioner in February 2017 that alleged sexual violence against some Rohingya women (Roughneen 2017). Expressing deep concern over the allegations of widespread human rights violations in Rakhine, Suu Kyi assured the UN High Commissioner for Human Rights that the government would take the necessary measures if "there is clear evidence of abuses or violations" (Glauert 2017).

Meanwhile, the Advisory Commission on Rakhine State that was created by the NLD government in September 2016 and headed by former UN Secretary-General Kofi Annan released its interim report in March 2017. Although it was not mandated to investigate specific allegations of human rights violations in that state, it identified a set of recommendations to address the structural and institutional causes of conflict in the area, including the humanitarian crisis brought about by the October 2016 attacks by militants. It called on the central and state governments to allow full and unimpeded humanitarian access to all areas affected by the violence, including adequate assistance to all communities in cooperation with international partners; to allow full, regular, local, and foreign media access in Rakhine; and to ensure that the perpetrators of the violence are held accountable based on the conduct of an independent and impartial investigation (Advisory

Commission on Rakhine State 2017, 7–8). The commission also recommended that both the central and state governments give priority to addressing socioeconomic development issues in Rakhine; to training security forces, including human rights protection and respect for diversity of communities; to ensuring freedom of movement of people who are citizens and ensuring that the government establishes a clear strategy and timeline for citizenship verification process; to preparing a comprehensive strategy toward the eventual closure of all internally displaced peoples camps in Rakhine; to encouraging interfaith dialogue among communities; and to ensuring representation and participation in public life especially for the Muslim communities, and for the Myanmar government to continue with its initiative to brief ASEAN members on a regular basis about the broader dimensions and regional implications of the situation in Rakhine, including maintaining a special envoy to engage with its neighbors (Advisory Commission on Rakhine State 2017, 9–15).

A day after the Rakhine Advisory Commission submitted its final report to Suu Kyi, a militant group calling itself the Arakan Rohingya Salvation Army (ARSA) staged another attack on August 25, 2017 against border police, which was met with lethal force by the Myanmar military in clearing operations for several weeks. It was initially estimated following the militant attacks that more than 1,000 people were killed (including militants and civilians) and over 40,000 were internally displaced in Rakhine. However, the non-governmental organization Médicins Sans Frontières (Doctors Without Borders) claimed that more than 6,700 Rohingyas were killed in the first month of the violence in Rakhine, including some 730 children below the age of 5 (McPherson 2007).[4] Over 600,000 Rohingyas had fled to Bangladesh by the end of November 2017, even after the Tatmadaw claimed that it ended its clearing operations in the first week of September. It also denied that its security forces committed atrocities against fleeing Rohingyas, including the rape of women and violence against children. Amidst strong international condemnation from some members of the UN over the high-handed response to the violence in Rakhine, Myanmar's government and the military highlighted the threat posed by the Rohingya militants to the stability of the country and denied that "ethnic cleansing" or "genocide" against the Rohingyas were taking place. As well, Suu Kyi tried to assure the international community that those who violated human rights in Rakhine would be prosecuted. For its part, ASEAN issued a statement on September 24, 2017, condemning the ARSA attacks and welcomed the commitment of the Myanmar government to end the violence in Rakhine, among others. Malaysia, however, distanced itself from ASEAN's statement, as it did not use the term Rohingya and failed to condemn the alleged atrocities committed against them by security forces. To date, Myanmar has refused an independent fact-finding mission set up by the UN Human Rights Council to visit the country to investigate the human rights violations in Rakhine. It also terminated cooperation with the UN by not allowing Yang-hee Lee, the Special Rapporteur on Human Rights in Myanmar, to visit Myanmar in early 2018 to conduct her own investigation before the end of her term. Although Suu Kyi expressed her government's commitment to fully implement the recommendations made by the Rakhine Advisory Commission, it remains uncertain whether the military and the state government in Rakhine would support her position.

The continuing communal conflict in Rakhine has created serious tensions between the civilian NLD government and the military, with the latter being egged on by more conservative elements in the military and Buddhist nationalist groups to intervene and ensure the protection of the country's national security. Mounting pressure from ASEAN and the international community for Myanmar to do more to protect the Rohingya has placed Suu Kyi in a very tight spot, especially in balancing external criticisms of her government vis-à-vis rising nationalist sentiments at home against foreign intervention in the country's domestic affairs. On the one hand, Suu Kyi's NLD government needs help from the international community to prevent future violence in Rakhine and to implement the Advisory Commission's recommendations. On the other hand, her ability to do so will depend very much on the support and cooperation of the military to effectively implement these recommendations, such as revising certain discriminatory laws (the citizenship law of 1982, or the law on the protection of race and religion passed in 2014). For now, the military adamantly resists international calls to amend the country's citizenship law, which does not recognize the Rohingya even as an ethnic group in Myanmar. Under the existing 2008 constitution, the military could also effectively block any attempt by the NLD to amend these laws (including the constitution itself), as it controls 25 percent of the seats in the national parliament. As well, the military effectively controls key cabinet positions related to home affairs, defense, and border security, and dominates the eleven-member National Defence and Security Council, which is an advisory group to the country's president.

Overall, the democratic transition in Myanmar remains fragile amidst continuing communal tensions in Rakhine and the unresolved ethnic armed rebellion in other states. It is likely that the risks of atrocities will also continue in other conflict areas of the country, as the military and the civilian NLD government are not in agreement on the framework and strategy for negotiating peace with seventeen armed ethnic organizations. While the NLD believes that peace negotiations with armed ethnic organizations should be based on the 1947 Panglong Agreement which allows them autonomy, the military insists that these ethnic groups should adhere to the 2008 constitution, should uphold Myanmar's unitary government, and should sign the national ceasefire agreement before any peace talks can proceed.

Achievements and emerging challenges to implementing R2P

The focus on Myanmar's Rohingya issue and human rights violations in that country seem to have overshadowed some important achievements in ASEAN as far as atrocities prevention is concerned. It is important to recognize that there have been positive developments in some member states since the adoption of the R2P principle in the UN General Assembly in 2005. For example, Cambodia and the Philippines have become parties to the Rome Statute of the International

Criminal Court. A hybrid tribunal – the Extraordinary Chambers of the Courts of Cambodia – which was set up in 2006, convicted Kang Kek Iew in 2010 and top Khmer Rouge leaders Nuon Chea and Kheiu Samphan in 2014 of crimes against humanity. All three are now serving life sentences in Cambodia. In 2013, Cambodia passed a law against the denial of Khmer Rouge atrocities after an opposition politician allegedly claimed that the notorious Tuol Sleng prison[5] was run by Vietnamese troops after the ouster of the Khmer Rouge regime. In September 2016, the Cambodian foreign minister announced the appointment of a national R2P Focal Point, making Cambodia the first ASEAN member to do so. Meanwhile, prior to signing the Rome Statute in 2011, the Philippines in 2009 passed its domestic law against genocide and crimes against humanity. It was signed by President Macapagal-Arroyo a few weeks after election-related violence saw the massacre of over fifty local journalists and civilians in Maguindanao, which was staged by a warlord clan against a political rival in Mindanao. Charges were filed against over 150 perpetrators of the crime and a special court was created to expedite the hearing of these cases.

Notwithstanding strong adherence to the group's traditional norms on sovereignty and non-interference, eight ASEAN member states have thus far contributed to UN peace support missions abroad (see Thayer 2014).[6] Within the region, some members voluntarily sent troops to Cambodia during the period 1993–1997 under the United Nations Transitional Authority in Cambodia, and to Timor-Leste in 1999–2000 under the United Nations Transitional Administration in East Timor. It must be noted, however, that these individual country peacekeeping contributions were not undertaken under the banner of ASEAN (indeed, at the time, Cambodia was not yet a member of ASEAN). In the case of Timor-Leste, the consent of Indonesia was secured before the deployment of peacekeeping troops from ASEAN members was allowed. In 2003, Indonesia permitted unarmed military monitors from five ASEAN members to observe the ceasefire in Aceh, and in 2004, the Philippines invited Malaysian military personnel to observe the peace talks between the government and the Moro Islamic Liberation Front, which was brokered by Kuala Lumpur (Thayer 2014).

The importance of peacekeeping operations was recognized in the ASEAN Political-Security Community blueprint in 2009 with the creation of a regional network of national peacekeeping centers. The ASEAN Defence Ministers' Meeting in 2011 later adopted the idea that led to the establishment of the ASEAN Peacekeeping Centres Network. It is unlikely, however, that ASEAN members would agree to either UN peacekeeping operations within the region, or to the creation of an ASEAN standby force, given the sensitivity of member states to non-intervention and their preference for peacebuilding through existing ASEAN mechanisms (Thayer 2014).

Despite the mentioned achievements, some emerging challenges to implementing R2P in the region remain. These include some setbacks in the promotion of human rights protection in some ASEAN member states as governments crack down on fundamental liberties and the culture of impunity by law enforcers is tolerated. The rise of religious extremism is also an emerging problem. In the Philippines, for example, the risk of atrocities increased significantly over 2016 in relation to the government's anti-drug war campaign after President Rodrigo Duterte came to power. Since July 2016, over 9,000 people have been killed in the country, most of whom were alleged victims of extra-judicial or vigilante killings in relation to the drug war. While the Philippine National Police has acknowledged that about one-third of those were killed during legitimate police anti-drug operations, investigations into the other fatalities have not been resolved satisfactorily. Although the Duterte administration has categorically denied that it sanctions extra-judicial killings, it has refused to allow the UN Special Rapporteur on Extrajudicial, Summary or Arbitrary Executions to conduct an independent and unconditional investigation. In Cambodia, the ruling party has resorted to harassment and intimidation of the political opposition in the run-up to the 2018 general elections, raising concerns about an increased risk of political violence in the country. The situation has been exacerbated by questions about the neutrality of the Cambodian army amidst warnings from Prime Minister Hun Sen that an opposition victory could lead to chaos of a "Syrian proportion" (Sokhean 2017). This suggests that the ruling party will not easily give up power in the face of unfavorable election results.

In Indonesia, the risk of atrocities against religious minorities and ethnic Chinese may increase if the government fails to contain the rise of extremist groups who have been attacking these communities since 2012 through hate speech and violence. For example, local elections in Jakarta in 2017 took on racial and religious undertones as fundamentalist Muslim groups filed a case against the former Jakarta governor, a Christian ethnic Chinese, for blasphemy against Islam during the campaign period. He was found guilty and sentenced to two years in prison. In Thailand, the military government has been in power for four years since the coup of May 2014, with no clear indication of when it intends to hold general elections to give way to a civilian government. It has cracked down on fundamental liberties – such as freedoms of the press, speech, and assembly – and has not outlined a clear policy to end the conflict in southern Thailand. Although there were initiatives for peace talks in 2016, the prospects for a formal peace dialogue remain dim, given that the military appears unprepared to respond to demands by rebels for autonomy or devolution of power (Parameswaran 2016). In the meantime, intermittent violence in the southern provinces of Thailand are likely to continue, some of which have been perpetrated by rebel groups and have targeted civilians.

These challenges to implementing R2P in the region stem from certain institutional weaknesses of ASEAN member states, especially in promoting good governance, the rule of law, and human rights protection. For ASEAN members still facing internal armed rebellion – Indonesia, Myanmar, the Philippines, and Thailand – the legitimacy of the state is still contested mainly due to poverty, historical grievances, inadequate basic services, and lack of access to justice, especially in conflict areas. Improving the capacity of states in ASEAN to respond to the root causes of these identity-based conflicts is therefore key to preventing atrocities in the region. While some ASEAN members like the Philippines may have been more open to international assistance in dealing with internal conflicts, some (Myanmar and Thailand) are more reluctant to do so as the militaries in both states remain dominant in determining policies related to internal security. Thus, it is quite important for ASEAN members to give priority to security sector reform, specifically in enhancing the non-traditional role of the military through peacebuilding, interfaith dialogue, and conflict prevention. Indeed, given that the majority of ASEAN's members have contributed to UN peace missions abroad, they could utilize this experience and knowledge gained from peacekeeping operations at home, especially in the protection of civilians and conflict prevention. It is also important that education and training in human rights protection and atrocities prevention should be incorporated in the curriculum of police and military academies, as well as mainstreaming these in the state's national security framework and policies. At the regional level, the security sector through the ASEAN Defence Ministers' Meeting should consider engaging in a regular dialogue with the AICHR, the ACWC, and the AIPR on human rights, atrocities prevention, the protection of civilians, and conflict prevention. The international community can also mainstream atrocities prevention in ASEAN by supporting activities such as UN–ASEAN and cross-regional dialogue between ASEAN and the African Union, for example, and focus on the exchange of learning experiences and best practices, capacity-building assistance, and education and training.

Conclusion

Atrocities prevention has become a major concern in ASEAN, given the continuing spill-over effects in the region of the humanitarian crisis in Myanmar since the eruption of communal violence in Rakhine in 2012. Although Myanmar's human rights problem has been a serious issue for ASEAN since 2007, the persecution of the Muslim Rohingya amidst growing Buddhist nationalism in the country has highlighted the constraints faced by the organization in responding to human protection issues in member states. The crisis forced ASEAN to rethink the practicality of strictly adhering to the non-interference principle in dealing with an errant member who fails to fulfill its primary responsibility to protect vulnerable populations within its territory. Indeed, there have been increasing calls made by critical stakeholders from various sectors – including some former heads of government, diplomats, and ex-ASEAN officials – to seriously consider relaxing this principle, especially in the context of responding to humanitarian crisis situations that impact the region.

ASEAN will remain ineffective if errant member states insist on using their veto power and scuttle collective efforts to prevent and respond to atrocities. Thus, it is critically important for ASEAN members to seriously rethink its non-interference and consensus decision-making principles as it embarks on reviewing the ASEAN Charter and the terms of reference of the AICHR, the ACWC, and the AIPR. There is no question that these norms have rendered the organization incapable of meaningfully advancing human rights protection and implementing the human protection principles that it has adopted since the ratification of the ASEAN Charter in 2008. As well, ASEAN leaders should consider enhancing the protection mandate of the AICHR and the ACWC, which should include monitoring and accepting complaints of human rights violations among its members. The enhanced mandate should also include mainstreaming R2P in the agenda of these mechanisms, as well as an action plan that sets specific targets such as signing and ratifying international treaties and conventions related to atrocities prevention and creating and/or enhancing national human rights institutions for *all* member states. Overall, without an enhanced protection mandate for the AICHR and the ACWC, the group will not be able to manage the risk factors faced by many ASEAN member states, particularly those that remain institutionally weak in addressing the root causes of internal conflicts.

Notes

1   For example, during the 2005 ASEAN Summit chaired by Malaysia, former Thai Prime Minister Thaksin Shinawatra threatened to walk out of the meeting of leaders if the question of human rights in southern Thailand was raised on ASEAN's agenda.
2   For example, ASEAN foreign ministers for the first time failed to issue a joint communiqué at the end of their meeting in Cambodia in July 2012 over the issue of crafting a collective statement on the South China Sea dispute. As chair of ASEAN at the time, Cambodia refused to accommodate input from the Philippines and Vietnam that criticized China's aggressive behavior in the area.
3   The military junta stopped updating the death toll past 138,000, apparently due to fears of political fallout even as some reports from the UN, aid organizations, and media sources claimed that the government underestimated the number of people killed in the worst natural disaster that hit the country.
4   Accordingly, some 69 percent died of gunshot wounds, 9 percent were burned alive inside houses, and 5 percent died of beatings.
5   Tuol Sleng or Security Prison 21 (S-21) in Phnom Penh, served as a facility in which suspected enemies of the Khmer Rouge were tortured. It has since been converted into a genocide museum.
6   At the end of January 2014, total Southeast Asian contributions to UN peace missions (including police, military experts, and troops) stood at: Brunei (26), Cambodia (342), Indonesia (1,697), Malaysia (909), the Philippines (703), and Thailand (33). Singapore contributed twenty-two personnel in 2013. Although Vietnam has not sent peacekeeping troops, it contributes $1 million annually for UN peace missions and is in the process of amending its constitution to allow for deployment of troops under the auspices of the UN.

References

Advisory Commission on Rakhine State, 2017. "Interim Report and Recommendations," March, www.rakhinecommission.org/app/uploads/2017/03/Advisory-Commission-Interim-Report.pdf.
Arnold, Wayne, 2007. "Rift Over Myanmar Emerges at ASEAN Summit," *New York Times*, November 19.
ASEAN, 2009. "Chairman's Statement of the 14th ASEAN Summit, 'ASEAN Charter for ASEAN Peoples'," Cha-am, February 28–March 1, http://asean.org/chairman-s-statement-of-the-14th-asean-summit-asean-charter-for-asean-peoples-cha-am-28-february-1-march-2009/.
ASEAN, 2012a. "Phnom Penh Statement on the Adoption of the ASEAN Human Rights Declaration (AHRD)," November 19, http://asean.org/phnom-penh-statement-on-the-adoption-of-the-asean-human-rights-declaration-ahrd/.

ASEAN, 2012b. "Statement of ASEAN Foreign Ministers on the Recent Developments in the Rakhine State, Myanmar," Phnom Penh, August 17, www.asean.org/wp-content/uploads/images/archive/documents/Statement%20of%20ASEAN%20FM%20on%20Recent%20Developments%20in%20the%20Rakhine%20State.pdf.

ASEAN Parliamentarians for Human Rights, 2015. "Parliamentarians Call on ASEAN Leaders to Address the Rohingya Crisis and the Escalating Risk of Atrocity Crimes in Myanmar," April 22, http://aseanmp.org/2015/04/22/parliamentarians-call-on-asean-leaders-to-address-the-rohingya-crisis-and-the-escalating-risk-of-atrocity-crimes-in-myanmar/.

ASEAN Secretariat, 2009. *A Bridge to Recovery: ASEAN's Response to Cyclone Nargis* (Jakarta: ASEAN Secretariat, July).

BBC News, 2007. "Nuns in Burma Anti-Junta Rallies," September 23, http://news.bbc.co.uk/2/hi/asia-pacific/7009005.stm.

BBC News, 2008. "France Angered by Burmese Delays," May 17, http://news.bbc.co.uk/2/hi/asia-pacific/7405998.stm.

BBC News, 2017. "Myanmar Says 'No Evidence' of Rohingya Genocide," January 4, www.bbc.com/news/world-asia-38505228.

Channel News Asia, 2015. "ASEAN's Non-Interference Policy Must Be Reviewed: Former Malaysian Minister," April 24, www.channelnewsasia.com/news/business/asean-s-non-interference/1804054.html.

Glauert, Rik, 2017. "Govt 'Deeply Concerned' by UN Report of Arakan State Human Rights Abuses," *The Irrawady*, February 9, www.irrawaddy.com/news/burma/govt-deeply-concerned-un-report-arakan-state-human-rights-abuses.html.

Hoge, Warren, 2007. "UN Report Finds 31 Killed in Myanmar Crackdown," *New York Times*, December 7.

Humaniti, 2015. "Former ASEAN Leaders Issue Letter on Myanmar Intolerance," *Burma Partnership*, April 22, www.burmapartnership.org/2015/04/former-asean-leaders-issue-letter-on-myanmar-intolerance/.

International Federation of Red Cross and Red Crescent Societies, 2011. "Myanmar: Cyclone Nargis 2008 Facts and Figures," May 3, www.ifrc.org/en/news-and-media/news-stories/asia-pacific/myanmar/myanmar-cyclone-nargis-2008-facts-and-figures/.

Latiff, Rozanna, 2017. "Malaysian PM Sends Off Aid Ship Bound for Muslim Rohingyas in Myanmar," *Reuters*, February 3.

Lewa, Chris, 2010. "Unregistered Rohingya Refugees in Bangladesh: Crackdown, Forced Displacement, and Hunger," The Arakan Project, February 11, 3–4.

MacKinnon, Ian, and James Sturcke, 2009. "After 20 Days Adrift, Burmese Boat People Land with Tales of Abuse and Starvation," *The Guardian*, February 4.

McPherson, Poppy, 2007. "6,700 Rohingya Muslims Killed in One Month in Myanmar, MSF Says," *The Guardian*, December 15.

Mon, Ye, and Shoon Naing, 2016. "ASEAN FMs Pledge Support on Rakhine," *Myanmar Times*, December 20.

Morada, Noel M., 2016. "Southeast Asian Regionalism, Norm Promotion and Capacity Building for Human Protection: An Overview," *Global Responsibility to Protect* 8, nos. 2–3: 111–32.

Muntarbhorn, Vitit, 2017. "'ASEAN Human Rights Law' Taking Shape," *Bangkok Post*, May 11, https://www.bangkokpost.com/opinion/opinion/1247414/asean-human-rights-law-taking-shape.

Mydans, Seth, 2008. "Myanmar Faces Pressure to Allow Major Aid Effort," *New York Times*, May 8.

Parameswaran, Prashanth, 2016. "Southern Thailand Peace Talks to Resume (Again) in Malaysia," *The Diplomat*, September 1, http://thediplomat.com/2016/09/southern-thailand-peace-talks-to-resume-again-in-malaysia-amid-violence/.

Radio Free Asia, 2012. "Rohingya Raised at ASEAN Meeting," July 13, www.rfa.org/english/news/myanmar/rohingya-07132012163418.html.

Roughneen, Simon, 2017. "Plight of the Rohingya Strains ASEAN Unity," *Nikkei Asian Review*, February 9, https://asia.nikkei.com/Politics/Plight-of-the-Rohingya-strains-ASEAN-unity.

Sheany, 2017. "Indonesia Ready to Help Myanmar Achieve Political Stability: Jokowi," *JakartaGlobe*, April 29, http://jakartaglobe.id/news/indonesia-ready-help-myanmar-achieve-political-stability-jokowi/.

Sipalan, Joseph, and Ebrahim Harris, 2017. "OIC Envoy Calls for UN Intervention to Avoid Genocide of Rohingya Muslims," *Reuters*, January 18.

Sokhean, Ben, 2017. "CPP Spokesman Warns That Army Will Not Stay Neutral," *Cambodia Daily*, May 18, https://www.cambodiadaily.com/editors-choice/cpp-spokesman-warns-that-army-will-not-stay-neutral-129894/.

Thayer, Carl, 2014. "ASEAN and UN Peacekeeping," *The Diplomat*, April 25, http://thediplomat.com/2014/04/asean-and-un-peacekeeping/.

5
AFRICAN EXPERIENCES OF R2P IMPLEMENTATION

Frank O. Okyere

Introduction

Africa is often credited with playing a pioneering role in generating momentum for the development and advancement of the Responsibility to Protect (R2P) agenda. Beginning with Francis Deng's "sovereignty as responsibility" thesis (Cohen and Deng 1998), through Kofi Annan's (2000) well-known "two concepts of sovereignty" speech at the Millennium Assembly, to the African Union's (AU's) transition from non-interference to non-indifference,[1] Africa or Africans have visible prints in the movement to protect populations from heinous crimes and serious abuses. Thus, the idea of reframing state sovereignty from a rights-based application to one of responsibility is not strange to the African continent. Notwithstanding, the R2P project in Africa faces daunting challenges which can be partly argued to be derived from conceptual incongruity that has further engendered implementation deficits at the regional and state levels.

Conceptually, the inherent weakness of the "modern" African state[2] grossly undermines the idea of locating the state at the core of protection responsibility. This is reflected in the fact that the state has often been a perpetrator rather than protector. For instance, in the last decade, more than a dozen African countries have experienced atrocity crimes with the active involvement, instigation, or connivance of the state.[3] This raises critical questions about why most African states are notorious for atrocity crimes, and what (state) structures will be most appropriate for effective prevention.

Indeed, the superimposition of a post-colonial state structure on pre-existing traditional systems of governance continues to engender structural problems – not only in atrocity prevention, but in human protection and human security in general. State agents are, in many cases, not perceived as legitimate actors for the provision of basic protection to local populations, especially in deprived, marginalized, and under-governed areas. Consequently, most African populations have required protection from abuses committed by state agents, instead of being protected by the state. It is thus not surprising that the African continent is host to the highest recorded cases of atrocity crimes since R2P was adopted in 2005. In spite of this, little has been done to articulate the concept of the state in relation to atrocity prevention; neither has significant effort been made to address the structural barriers impeding R2P's implementation in Africa.

Further aggravating these challenges, the implementation of R2P on the African continent in recent times has evoked negative sentiments that threaten to jeopardize the established political consensus on atrocity prevention. While progress has been made in creating and strengthening mechanisms for protecting populations from serious abuses in some jurisdictions, implementation of R2P in Libya and Côte d'Ivoire have bred regional apathy to R2P and consequent gravitation toward less contentious concepts like human security and protection of civilians at the regional level. Since Libya, the AU has strategically avoided any association with R2P by emphasizing distinctions between R2P and Article 4(h) of the Constitutive Act of the African Union (hereafter, Constitutive Act). It can be argued that the AU's apathy reflects the general sentiments of its member states following the fallout from the interventions in Libya and Côte d'Ivoire. This does not only risk relegating the principles of R2P to the periphery of the human protection discourse, but also threatens to reverse progress made in mobilizing political will of member states for atrocity prevention.

Addressing these challenges would require a changed approach to implementing R2P on the African continent. This chapter discusses the implementation of R2P at three interconnected levels in Africa: regional, national (state), and local. It highlights unique factors which affect efforts at protecting populations at each level, and how a change in approach may be necessary for effective implementation of R2P. The chapter proceeds on the axiom that while R2P is a universal norm, its application must be underpinned by domestic exigencies. In this regard, it contends that the state in its present posture does not offer the most effective avenue for implementing R2P in Africa due to structural deficiencies debilitating against it. At the very least, a reconfiguration of the state will be critical for the purposes of atrocity prevention in Africa, which may necessitate (re)conceptualizing the state to recognize the traditional hybrid governance systems which operate in practically every African community, and command the legitimacy necessary for exercising real sovereign authority over populations. Ultimately, such an inclusive approach will strengthen the resilience of societies to inhibit atrocity risk in a timely manner.

The argument for effective implementation of R2P

The original concept of R2P theorized by the International Commission on Intervention and State Sovereignty in 2001 was quite expansive (ICISS 2001). Indeed, it was so broad that some United Nations (UN) member states fiercely opposed the inclusion of R2P in the World Summit Outcome document in 2005 (United

Nations General Assembly 2005; Strauss 2009). Other dissenters expressed concern about the possibility for R2P to be used to pursue the foreign interests of strong states or to intervene in the domestic affairs of small and weak states (Kikoler 2009). The UN's attempt to limit its scope to allow for broad consensus and acceptance to legitimize its implementation likewise drew criticisms from academics and policy-makers, with one scholar describing it as "R2P-Lite" (Weiss 2012, 750).

In hindsight, it can be argued that broad consensus was achieved at the expense of conceptual clarity, making it practically difficult to translate the concept of "state responsibility" into a meaningful preventive strategy. More than a decade after acceptance, implementation of R2P has been a challenge for the UN, regional organizations, and member states. Of particular concern to this chapter is its implementation at the regional and state levels. The increasing ferocity of violence and attendant humanitarian crises in Africa demonstrates that the political rhetoric and broad acceptance is not matched by effective implementation. One reason is arguably the failure to address fundamental flaws inhibiting the state from fulfilling its primary responsibility. More precisely, it is taken for granted that each state possesses the character for effective atrocity prevention, glossing over pertinent factors that affect the state's predisposition to deliver on this responsibility. By claiming each state has the responsibility to protect populations, without scrutinizing what constitutes the state or the minimum characteristics it must exhibit, the principle of R2P risks severe implementation challenges. As will be argued later in this chapter, the crucial factors necessary for effective implementation of R2P have eluded most African states. Yet local sources of resilience, which are effective for prevention, are neither appreciated nor fully utilized. As acknowledged by former UN Secretary-General Ban Ki-moon in his 2016 report on mobilizing collective action, effective preventive strategies require partnerships at the local, national, regional, and international levels (Ban 2016). Nonetheless, further expositions on R2P have largely focused on the international, regional, and national level, ignoring the all-important role of the local level. The result has been a palpable failure, especially in Africa, where modern states – which are recognized by the international community – lack the rudiments for effective prevention.

The relevance and potential of regional organizations to assist states to deliver on their responsibility was also considered during the elaboration of the R2P concept. The World Summit Outcome explicitly named regional organizations as possible cooperation partners for a timely and decisive response to the manifest failure of states to protect their populations from mass atrocities. Accordingly, UN member states agreed to take collective action "in accordance with the Charter, including Chapter VII, on a case-by-case basis and in cooperation with relevant regional organizations" (United Nations General Assembly 2005, 30) in such situations. Organizations that are active in certain regions can establish mechanisms to assist in implementing R2P through peaceful interventions (Kabau 2012). When describing the roles of regional and sub-regional arrangements, Ban articulated that they are capable of developing "norms, standards, and institutions that promote tolerance, transparency, accountability, and the constructive management of diversity" (Ban

2011, 7). Regional and sub-regional organizations such as the AU, the Economic Community of Central African States (ECCAS), the Economic Community of West African States (ECOWAS), the International Conference on the Great Lakes Region (ICGLR), the Intergovernmental Authority on Development (IGAD) in East Africa, and the Southern African Development Community (SADC), have supported their member states in the implementation process, and offer a number of mechanisms and legal frameworks on the matter.

Notwithstanding the previously mentioned factors, the continued discord between the UN and regional organizations like the AU on how R2P ought to be applied has created a gap in the R2P implementation chain. The AU itself has not been able to establish the institutional framework to translate the normative principle into practical implementation. One reason for this is the political contention surrounding the principle, which makes the AU inclined to prioritize the promotion of a broader human security agenda over the responsibility to protect. The AU has deliberately avoided any reference to R2P or Article 4(h) in any of its documents, even in cases where it has deployed peace support operations in response to violence and potential atrocity crimes.

It is instructive to note that regional organizations, the AU in this case, can only go as far as providing assistance to states in the implementation of R2P – and given the existing impediments, the regional level may not offer the best prospects for implementing R2P effectively, even in the provision of the stated assistance.

Implementing R2P at the regional level

The AU is cited for its pioneering role in adopting measures which are essentially aligned with the principles of R2P. Through Article 4(h) of the Constitutive Act, the AU transitioned from a non-interventionist posture to one of non-indifference. This has encouraged member states to implement preventive mechanisms in their national frameworks and to establish individual early-warning capabilities. Further, the 2005 Ezulwini Consensus reached within the AU represents a common African position that found it vital "to reiterate the obligation of states to protect their citizens" (African Union Executive Council 2005, 6). The document clearly reflects upon the common agreement to support the first aspect of R2P. Occupying a leading role on the continent, the AU has prompted the different Regional Economic Communities (RECs) to create structures in the area of early warning and early response at the national level (Koko 2013). In West Africa, ECOWAS has, for example, encouraged member states to protect their citizens and strengthen the human security network through becoming part of its overarching Conflict Prevention Framework. In addition, ECOWAS's Protocol Relating to the Mechanism for Conflict Prevention, Management, Resolution, Peace-Keeping and Security (hereafter, ECOWAS Protocol), which stipulates international cooperation in the areas of conflict management, early warning, and peacekeeping operations, has led to national action.[4] The Protocol initiated the establishment of the ECOWAS Warning and Response Network for conflict prevention through monitoring zones in the sub-region. IGAD, SADC, and ECCAS have in a similar manner introduced their individual early-warning mechanisms (African Task Force on the Prevention of Mass Atrocities 2016). With respect to the specific crimes listed under the R2P norm – namely, genocide, war crimes, ethnic cleansing, and crimes against humanity – individual legal frameworks have been created. Member states of the 2006 ICGLR, for instance, adopted the Protocol for the Prevention and the Punishment of the Crime of Genocide, War Crimes and Crimes against Humanity and All Forms of Discrimination (hereafter, ICGLR Protocol). Thus, one can highlight that the RECs appear to commonly agree upon the necessity for enhancing the states' early-warning capabilities and for the creation of legal and policy frameworks to prevent atrocity crimes and address peace and security within the regions.

In providing assistance for states under stress or imminent atrocity crimes, several cases have highlighted the role that regional organizations can play in mitigating tension to prevent the escalation of violence – and hence, the suffering of the civilian population. During the violent 2007 presidential elections in Kenya, for example, the AU, through its Panel of Eminent African Personalities, took active part in the mediation of the crisis through engagement with the different parties. Supported by the AU, SADC subsequently took over the mediation efforts and agreement was signed at the final stage (Veber 2014). The regional bodies hence play a vital role in supporting states in their responsibility to protect the civilian population. Additionally, there exists a strong conviction that RECs "can provide support to various preventative and responsive measures when faced with severe humanitarian crises" (Barqueiro, Seaman, and Towey 2016, 46).

Regional organizations also play a role in the protection of civilians through non-peaceful or forceful interventions. Organizations have adopted legal frameworks which stipulate an intervention in cases where member states are unwilling or incapable to protect their own citizens. ECOWAS, for example, acknowledges its responsibility to "intervene to alleviate the suffering of the populations and restore life to normalcy in the event of crises, conflict and disaster."[5] This provision is in line with Article 4(h) of the Constitutive Act. The article permits the AU to intervene in member states in light of the occurrence of war crimes, genocide, and crimes against humanity. The Ezulwini Consensus highlights the common viewpoint of African states on the matter:

> Since the General Assembly and the Security Council are often far from the scenes of conflicts and may not be in a position to undertake effectively a proper appreciation of the nature and development of conflict situations, it is imperative that Regional Organisations, in areas of proximity to conflicts, are empowered to take actions in this regard. The African Union agrees with the Panel that the intervention of Regional Organisations should be with the approval of the Security Council; although in certain situations, such approval could be granted "after the fact" in circumstances requiring urgent action.
>
> *(African Union Executive Council 2005, 6)*

Regional experiences and challenges

Implementation of R2P at the regional level faces challenges. Experience with the implementation of R2P by regional organizations shows that there exist challenges when it comes to transforming norms into actions on the ground. The doctrine is widely accepted in a normative way. But regional organizations have struggled to translate the norm into actionable strategy. The AU, in particular, has deliberately avoided making specific reference to R2P during crisis intervention efforts, despite its historical leanings toward the principle (Aning and Okyere 2018). This is attributed to the fallouts from interventions in Libya and Côte d'Ivoire, fueling the AU's desire to promote the less contentious human security concept over R2P. The reluctance of the AU to activate its "right" of intervention creates two major challenges for implementation. First, it narrows the opportunities to access crisis situations through what Alex Bellamy describes as an atrocity-prevention lens (Bellamy 2011). Thus, very important early signals necessary for atrocity prevention are missed. Second, and as a consequence, it limits the tools available to the AU for intervention. As is commonly agreed, not all conflict prevention strategies are suitable for atrocity prevention.

The AU's response to the crisis in Burundi is the only exception, where an explicit reference to Article 4(h) was made. Even so, the proposed intervention force failed to deploy as it faced a recalcitrant regime determined to cling to power at any cost. Indeed, as the AU learned in Burundi, the state has often been the biggest impediment to external interventions for atrocity prevention. In its bid to stay in power, the government of Burundi declared any external intervention without its explicit consent as an "invasion and occupation force" and thus, a serious provocation (Mohammed 2015). This was in spite of Article 4(h), which enables the AU to intervene – without state consent – in grave circumstances.

Further, interventions by international or regional bodies for atrocity prevention have often been reactive, occurring only after the fact. In Libya, the AU failed to propose forceful intervention even in the face of a credible threat of atrocity crimes. AU deployment of an intervention force to crisis situations, such as in Mali and the Central African Republic (CAR), have occurred after the onset of violence and atrocity crimes. Admittedly, prompt and decisive responses have usually been hampered by bureaucratic processes and geopolitical dynamics pertaining at those levels. Thus, the significance of R2P tends to get lost in transition when approached from a regional or international perspective.

Peaceful means to ensure adherence to R2P, such as mediation efforts and the suspension of membership from regional organizations, have also proven to yield varying results. The ECOWAS Protocol, for example, includes the Council of the Wise and special mediators to respond to erupting conflicts. During the 2010–2011 electoral crisis in Côte d'Ivoire, the Protocol's mechanism was utilized in such a way that ECOWAS set up a high-level delegation for a mediation initiative. Furthermore, the REC deliberately took a stance on the election results by supporting Alassane Ouattara as the winner. The organization has nevertheless been criticized for a lack of unity in its approach, since certain states encouraged Laurent Gbagbo to stay in power (IRIN 2011). The AU likewise backed Ouattara as the victor, and both bodies finally suspended Côte d'Ivoire's membership (Kode 2016). Yet, the violence did not end with the suspension of membership and mediation efforts did not bring about the end of the conflict. Referring to the violent events following the coup in Guinea in 2008, Kwesi Aning and Samuel Atuobi (2012) write that the suspension of members might be an appropriate initial step to show public discontent, yet it does not evoke compliance or ensure a better situation on the ground.

There also appear to be challenges in the actual application of forceful measures by the AU. As mentioned previously, the Constitutive Act includes a provision on forceful intervention where member states manifestly fail to uphold their responsibility to protect. While the case of Libya in 2011 has cast doubt on the extent of Pillar Three and the R2P doctrine in general, other situations have even questioned the use of regional legal frameworks allowing for military intervention (Okyere, Aning, and Nelson 2014). The Darfur crisis is one of the cases that evidently showed the reluctance of the AU to invoke Article 4(h). Despite the Sudanese government's involvement in atrocities against the civilian population, the AU failed to take a lead and insisted on consent by the member state. It is therefore said that "despite the AU's adoption of a more interventionist charter than its predecessor the Organisation of African Unity, the norm of non-interference continues to trump human rights concerns" (Williams and Bellamy 2005, 42–43). This apparent custom of support among the African rulers, even in the event of mass atrocities taking place, hampers the implementation of R2P in its final stage.

Yet, one has to consider the attempts that ECOWAS has made to restore life to normalcy in the event of crises. In January 2017, when Adama Barrow defeated incumbent president Yahya Jammeh in The Gambia, ECOWAS issued an ultimatum to Jammeh after mediation efforts for the ultimate installment of Barrow failed. Even though the UN Security Council did not authorize the use of force under Chapter VII of the UN Charter, which would have made a military intervention by ECOWAS legal under international law, the regional body still entered the country with its troops, forcing Jammeh out (Helal 2017). This example shows that the threat of the use of force can prevent or halt a crisis, if it is backed by a credible capacity to use force, which is (usually) mostly lacking. Nevertheless, the AU and RECs must balance forceful interventions with their obligations under international law. The threat of the use of force alone can, in itself, constitute non-compliance with the UN Charter when not authorized by the Security Council or constituting self-defense, even though as stated in the Ezulwini Consensus, *prior consent* remains a subject of debate.

All the mentioned regional organizations directly or indirectly address the common responsibility to protect the civilian population. This is reflected in ECOWAS's Conflict Prevention Framework, in the ICGLR Protocol, and in the ECCAS Protocol, which establishes the Peace and Security Council for Central Africa. Nonetheless, "the operationalization of this burgeoning norm does not appear to convey any greater regional responsibility to protect civilians than well-established regional norms" (Barqueiro, Seaman, and Towey 2016, 46). In addition to a lack of consensus and political will in regard to the enforcement action under R2P, regional organizations have to deal with a lack of resources and capabilities.

National (state-level) experiences in implementing R2P

The adoption of the principle of "state responsibility to protect populations" by the General Assembly was a ground-breaking moment, as the United Nations embraced an approach that vitally flips the discourse on state sovereignty. The doctrine of R2P is unique, since it emphasizes sovereignty by giving the primary responsibility to protect to the individual states. Ultimately, nation-states are the primary actors in atrocity prevention. For the state to be effective in atrocity prevention, however, it must possess three fundamental features: capacity, legitimacy, and political will.

Capacity

The state must possess the ability to mitigate risks leading to mass atrocities, which can be undertaken through structural reforms, an inclusive political system, economic stability, and the rule of law (Claes 2013). Most states lack the capacity to implement the context-specific measures required for building national preventive capacity (Bellamy 2011). Hence, states commonly address the immediate manifestations of atrocities, rather than the drivers and triggers. The lack of – or inadequate capacity for – prevention remains the biggest impediment to R2P implementation in Africa.

Legitimacy

Legitimacy is perceived in both popular support and ability of the state to provide critical social services and protection. Illegitimate means of attaining or maintaining political power, and the lack of capacity to provide social services, creates a vacuum for exploitation by non-state actors. This can mean the occupation of territory by armed groups, such as witnessed in CAR, or transnational criminal groups, as experienced in Mali. With the changing dynamics in conflict and security, control of territory and "legitimate" use of force are no longer the exclusive domain of the nation-state – and as more actors emerge to challenge the authority of the state, the protection space will continue to shrink, exposing more populations to the risk of atrocity crimes. Without legitimacy, no state can effectively exercise sovereign authority over populations.

Political will

States may have the capacity and legitimacy, but lack the will, to implement the principles of R2P. Political will to implement measures for atrocity prevention has also been found to be lacking on many levels in Africa. This is in spite of the broad acceptance of R2P and rhetoric used by government officials at international gatherings such as the UN Human Rights Council, the Global R2P Focal Points meetings, and General Assembly meetings. Reality on the ground points to efforts by state authorities to frustrate, sometimes purposely, attempts to operationalize the principles of R2P. For instance, Kenya and Burundi, where cases of atrocity crimes were reported, have threatened to withdraw from the Rome Statute of the International Criminal Court. In his 2016 report on the responsibility to protect, Ban (2016, 8) admitted:

> although Member States have repeatedly emphasized their support for the prevention of atrocity crimes, this has not been sufficiently translated into concrete support for preventive strategies – even when there have been credible assessments of imminent threats to populations.

Nature of the state and its implications for atrocity prevention

A combination of these three conditions engenders serious state weakness that limits its ability to assume those responsibilities ascribed by the World Summit Outcome. Experience has shown that the post-colonial African state usually lacks these elements in various permutations, constraining its ability to protect populations and making it a source of threat to the population. The very nature of the post-colonial African state means that it "is not always positioned at the centre of protection, governance, and control" (Aning and Okyere 2016, 356). When it comes to the implementation of R2P at the national level, the operationalization cannot only be hampered by a lack of political will, but furthermore by the lack of capacity. "Most African states are vulnerable to mass atrocities because of their unique and peculiar institutional weaknesses" (Aning and Okyere 2015, 3); "they are weak, beset with corruption, and unable to control their territories and prevent abuse by state or private agents" (Aning and Okyere 2015, 5). In countries like CAR, Libya, and Mali, where the rule of law, in the form of law enforcement and justice systems, is barely functioning in vast parts of the country, the protection responsibilities are mostly not fulfilled. The average citizen has practically no interaction with the state except through sporadic local extortions by security forces (Lloyd 2010). In CAR, for instance, a near collapse of the state resulting from the 2013 civil war has exposed millions to atrocity crimes. Impunity reigns as the justice and law enforcement apparatus has ceased functioning and perpetrators of atrocity crimes are rewarded with amnesty and appointment to important government positions. And despite a glaring lack of capacity or legitimacy, responsibility for the protection of CAR's population is yet ascribed to the state.

Another dimension of state weakness manifests in the extreme measures to which political leaders resort in order to attain or maintain political power. Legitimacy is limited to the loyalties purchased from political allies and security forces. Existing state institutions are simply exploited to sustain the political regime. Events in Burundi, Cameroon, Democratic Republic of Congo, Egypt, Guinea, Libya, and Togo are a few of the instances where state enforcement apparatus has been unleashed on civilians in the pursuit of the parochial interests of political elites. In Kenya, the very institutions tasked with protecting the population were used to commit atrocities against innocent civilians in the aftermath of the 2007 elections (Halakhe 2013). The experience of Guinea in September 2009 – when security forces, notably the elite presidential guard, were used to murder, rape, and torture peaceful protesters – further demonstrates how the state, through the security agencies, can occasion the commission of crimes against humanity – even in "peacetime" (Human Rights Watch 2009).

These weaknesses of the state have engendered the growth of non-state armed groups and organized criminal networks that sometimes substitute for the state, especially in remote and ungoverned or under-governed spaces. Accompanying the spread of non-state armed groups are the deliberate targeting of civilians and brazen violation of international humanitarian law. This has often caused the state to prioritize regime security over human security, and in the process perpetuate serious abuses against civilians. Mali is a fitting example of how weak state structures led to the marginalization of segments of the population, giving rise to secessionist movements and organized criminal networks that also perform some state functions in the north of the country. As the state attempted to wrestle control from these forces, the ensuing militarization of the three northern regions of Gao, Kidal, and Timbuktu led to abuses by state agents that eventually escalated an already precarious situation, leading to the commission of atrocity crimes by both state agents and armed militia groups (Karlsrud 2016).

These examples provide ample evidence that the post-colonial African state, by its peculiar nature, is not best suited for effective implementation of R2P. The identified flaws make many African states vulnerable to the commission of mass atrocities. Faced with an institutional weakness that makes the state prone to violence, the countries are furthermore limited in the national implementation of the R2P principles. Effective implementation of R2P in Africa will necessitate further interrogating non-traditional actors that have long played the role of the state – sometimes concurrently with the state – in under-governed or marginalized spaces where populations are in dire need of protection.

Local "non-state" actors in atrocity prevention

The original formulation of R2P did not formally ascribe any deliberate or specific role to non-state actors. This has been found to limit the opportunities for effective prevention in Africa. As mentioned previously, in cases where the state is not able or willing to govern its territory effectively, there appears a void in which atrocity prevention is more difficult. In remote areas where the state is barely present, tasks that would fall under Pillar One of R2P are taken up by local non-state actors. In general, non-state actors – be they armed groups, religious leaders, traditional authorities, or civil society institutions – can fulfill roles previously ascribed to state authorities. They are capable of establishing an organized system through service provision, often legitimizing themselves through a sense of identity, provision of critical social services, or through violent acts. Anne Marie Baylouny (2010, 137) finds that "those able to regulate and organize relations, minimize conflict, and create peaceful order among the inhabitants have influence." Thus, several local non-state actors can contribute to atrocity prevention with a varying degree of influence. It has become widely evident that traditional leaders, religious authorities, and civil society are important to mitigate tension and create resilient structures at the local level. They have a vast knowledge of context-specific issues, are on site, and are known within the communities. "Through existing nontraditional security and justice mechanisms, they can be effective in early warning and response by resolving potential situations of mass atrocity and sharing information about local conditions with state authorities" (Aning and Okyere 2015, 6).

Traditional leaders can take over government functions, and thus contribute to a more stable environment which is less prone to violence. Local institutional structures can be created through the utilization of traditional leaders. An example is the traditional leaders of South Africa. After an initial removal of functions occupied by traditional leaders over land, the powers were given back so that land was managed on behalf of the government (Parliamentary Monitoring Group 2014). An allocation of responsibilities increases trust and inclusiveness of different groups, and can decrease tensions within the country. Furthermore, this can ensure clear regulation of land distribution and thus avoid the all-too-common resurrection of violence due to land disputes. The Parliamentary Monitoring Group (2014) of South Africa noticed that "democratisation of governance, decision-making, law-making processes and decision implementation was impossible without effective traditional leadership participation, particularly in the development of rural communities."

Religious leaders are essential non-state actors in atrocity prevention. In several regions, religious institutions are considered to possess moral authority that enables them to pronounce on critical issues and influence individuals (Bercovitch and Jackson 2009). When the power indirectly given to religious leaders is utilized in a manner that reinforces peace and stability, they can build resilience at the grassroots level. An example that illustrates activities by religious institutions in the area of conflict prevention was a meeting of forty religious and community leaders in Addis Ababa in 2016. Practical actions to increase resilience to hate speech were discussed, and an Action Plan for Africa was drafted. Among the concrete steps to be undertaken to counter incitement were the training of religious actors to spot root causes and drivers, cooperation with the media, and the engagement of people at risk of radicalization (World Council of Churches 2016). In general, they are highly respected individuals within their communities. Thus, they have the capability to influence attitudes and opinions toward atrocity-prevention mechanisms. In addition, they can contribute to compliance with national standards and legal norms and enhance trust among community members. They therefore take on roles that lead to the mitigation of tension, based on the fact that the civilian population listens to their counsel.

Civil society institutions can substitute for state responsibilities and therefore contribute to a more stable environment where the government has lost influence (legitimacy) or lacks capacity. A World Bank report highlights the crucial role of civil society organizations in cases where the government is absent or weakened. The report states that they "play a critical role in providing services to citizens, and at times substitute for public institutions and become primary providers of basic social services" (Africa Regional External Affairs Unit 2007, 1). Sierra Leone is utilized as a case study, and offers insight into the successful provision of basic services, ultimately improving the environment and preventing further escalation over basic needs. Civil society organizations have supported Sierra Leone throughout the war and in the recovery phase after 2002. They have contributed to the consolidation of peace, the improvement of economic stability, and the enhancement of government capabilities. These efforts are contributing to a more stable and peaceful environment through the creation of sustainable mechanisms that foster resilience.

Beyond individual non-state actors, experiences on the African continent demonstrate that state and non-state partnerships have proven an effective recipe for atrocity prevention and conflict prevention in general. The National Peace Council in Ghana offers a fitting example of how a decentralized, bottom-up, and culturally driven approach to conflict/atrocity prevention can be most effective. Ghana's Infrastructure for Peace consists of a "National Peace Committee, regional and district peace councils and as an innovative element, government-affiliated peace promotion officers at the regional and district level" (Giessmann 2016, 27). Through a legal framework, the National Peace Council Act of 2011, and the creation of institutional structures to increase the interaction of stakeholders in the areas of dialogue, conflict mitigation, and reconciliation, the National Peace Council has successfully negotiated several sensitive conflict issues that otherwise could have precipitated serious abuses and, consequently, atrocity crimes. Overall, the mechanism created in Ghana has been successful as a conflict prevention and mitigation body and thus has served a useful lesson for many countries.

In Liberia, where the presence of the state is limited to major cities, the *Palava Hut* system of conflict resolution, justice, and reconciliation offers the best avenue for preventing potential situations of atrocity crimes. While this system has mainly operated at the local level, Liberia's post-war reconciliation experiences reveal that the *Palava Hut* system can be scaled up and broadened when supported by the state. Other African countries have similar structures in place that could be further leveraged for atrocity prevention.

In general, it can be said that the creation of a society resilient to atrocity crimes needs to include local non-state actors with their context-specific expertise, knowledge, and – ultimately – legitimacy. They are the ones making it possible to address causes and symptoms of mass atrocities where the state is unwilling or unable to do so. Ultimately, in implementing R2P, especially on the African continent, its effectiveness will largely depend on how the conception of the state can be redefined or rearticulated to recognize the so-called non-state actors that have assumed some of the traditional roles played by the state.

Conclusion

The centrality of the state in protecting populations from mass atrocity crimes cannot be called to question. The state has control over the use of force, resources, and territory – the very essence of sovereignty. Nonetheless, experience during the recent past has shown that the state also presents the most serious threat to populations in Africa, due to structural weaknesses working against it. The three identified areas of fundamental state deficiency – capacity, legitimacy, and political will – cannot simply be wished away. They require deliberate policy shifts. Despite these factors, the approach to atrocity prevention in Africa has been lopsided, mostly state-centric, without recourse to the contextual dictates. This over-concentration on state responsibility limits the capacity for atrocity prevention, and exposes populations to serious abuses where the state is weak, absent, or the instigator or perpetrator of atrocity crimes.

Granted, the United Nations and regional bodies are consigned to dealing with state authorities. However, a smart shift in approach is required for effective atrocity prevention in Africa. This chapter has exposed the limitations of atrocity-prevention efforts at the regional and national levels. It has also argued that effective implementation of R2P in Africa requires a reconfiguration of the state to accommodate local sources of resilience that offer the best opportunity to extend protection to remote and isolated spaces on the continent. In other words, atrocity prevention will best succeed where a hybrid governance structure is promoted to compensate for the identified weaknesses of the state.

Notes

1 Constitutive Act of the African Union, 2000, Article 4(h).
2 The "modern African state" refers to post-colonial state structures that have been established to govern African countries.
3 These include Burundi, the Central African Republic, Côte d'Ivoire, the Democratic Republic of Congo, Egypt, Eritrea, Guinea, Kenya, Libya, Mali, Nigeria, Somalia, South Sudan, and Sudan. See Global Centre for the Responsibility to Protect (n.d.).
4 See ECOWAS Protocol Relating to the Mechanism for Conflict Prevention, Management, Resolution, Peace-Keeping and Security, 1999.
5 See ibid., Article 40.

References

Africa Regional External Affairs Unit, 2007. "The Civil Society Landscape in Sierra Leone: Understanding Context, Motives and Challenge," Report No. 06062007AFRSL (Washington, DC: World Bank, June 5), http://siteresources.worldbank.org/INTSIERRALEONE/Data and Reference/22088623/SL(CSO)Study.pdf.

African Task Force on the Prevention of Mass Atrocities, 2016. *African Regional Communities and the Prevention of Mass Atrocities* (Budapest: Budapest Centre for Mass Atrocities Prevention).

African Union Executive Council, 2005. "The Common African Position on the Proposed Reform of the United Nations: 'The Ezulwini Consensus'," Ext/EX.CL/2 (VII), March, www.un.org/en/africa/osaa/pdf/au/cap_screform_2005.pdf.

Aning, Kwesi, and Samuel Atuobi, 2012. "The Economic Community of West African States and the Responsibility to Protect," in W. Andy Knight and Frazer Egerton, eds, *The Routledge Handbook of the Responsibility to Protect* (New York: Routledge), 216–31.

Aning, Kwesi, and Frank Okyere, 2015. "Responsibility to Prevent in Africa: Leveraging Institutional Capacity to Mitigate Atrocity Risk," Policy Analysis Brief (Muscatine, IA: Stanley Foundation, January).

Aning, Kwesi, and Frank Okyere, 2016. "The African Union," in Alex J. Bellamy and Tim Dunne, eds, *The Oxford Handbook of the Responsibility to Protect* (Oxford: Oxford University Press), 355–72.

Aning, Kwesi, and Frank Okyere, 2018. "The African Union and the Responsibility to Protect," in Emma Birikorang, Frank Okyere, and Kwesi Aning, eds, *Annual Review of Peace Support Operations in Africa 2017* (Accra: Kofi Annan International Peacekeeping Training Centre), 125–36.

Annan, Kofi A., 2000. "We the Peoples: The Role of the United Nations in the 21st Century," Millennium Report (New York: United Nations).

Ban Ki-moon, 2011. "The Role of Regional and Subregional Arrangements in Implementing the Responsibility to Protect: Report of the Secretary General," A/65/877–S/2011/393, June 28.

Ban Ki-moon, 2016. "Mobilizing Collective Action: The Next Decade of the Responsibility to Protect: Report of the Secretary-General," A/70/999 – S/2016/620, July 23.

Barqueiro, Carla, Kate Seaman, and Katherine Teresa Towey, 2016. "Regional Organizations and Responsibility to Protect: Normative Reframing or Normative Change?" *Politics and Governance* 4, no. 3: 37–49.

Baylouny, Anne Marie, 2010. "Authority Outside the State: Non-State Actors and New Institutions in the Middle East," in Anne L. Clunan and Harold A. Trinkunas, eds, *Ungoverned Spaces: Alternatives to State Authority in an Era of Softened Sovereignty* (Stanford, CA: Stanford University), 136–52.

Bellamy, Alex J., 2011. "Mass Atrocities and Armed Conflict: Links, Distinctions, and Implications for the Responsibility to Prevent," Policy Analysis Brief (Muscatine, IA: Stanley Foundation, February).

Bercovitch, Jacob, and Richard Jackson, 2009. *Conflict Resolution in the Twenty-First Century: Principles, Methods, and Approaches* (Ann Arbor, MI: University of Michigan Press).

Claes, Jonas, 2013. "Atrocity Prevention at the State Level: Security Sector Reform and Horizontal Equality," Peace Brief No. 144 (Washington, DC: United States Institute of Peace, April 23).

Cohen, Roberta, and Francis M. Deng, 1998. *Masses in Flight: The Global Crisis of Internal Displacement* (Washington, DC: Brookings Institution Press).

Giessmann, Hans J., 2016. *Embedded Peace: Infrastructures for Peace: Approaches and Lessons Learned* (New York: UN Development Programme, Berlin: Berghof Foundation, Bern: Swiss Agency for Development and Cooperation).

Global Centre for the Responsibility to Protect, n.d. "Populations at Risk," www.globalr2p.org/regions/.

Halakhe, Abdullahi Boru, 2013. "'R2P in Practice': Ethnic Violence, Elections and Atrocity Prevention in Kenya," Occasional Paper Series No. 4 (New York: Global Centre for the Responsibility to Protect).

Helal, Mohamed, 2017. "Crisis in The Gambia: How Africa is Rewriting Jus ad Bellum," *Opinio Juris*, January 24, http://opiniojuris.org/2017/01/24/crisis-in-the-gambia-how-africa-is-rewriting-jus-ad-bellum/.

Human Rights Watch, 2009. "Bloody Monday: The September 28 Massacre and Rapes by Security Forces in Guinea," December 17, www.hrw.org/report/2009/12/17/bloody-monday/september-28-massacre-and-rapes-security-forces-guinea.

ICISS (International Commission on Intervention and State Sovereignty), 2001. *The Responsibility to Protect: Report of the International Commission on Intervention and State Sovereignty* (Ottawa: International Development Research Centre).
IRIN, 2011. "Briefing on AU and ECOWAS," February 15, www.irinnews.org/2011/02/15/briefing-au-and-ecowas.
Kabau, Tom, 2012. "The Responsibility to Protect and the Role of Regional Organizations: An Appraisal of the African Union's Interventions," *Goettingen Journal of International Law* 4, no. 1: 49–92.
Karlsrud, John, 2016. "Mali," in Alex J. Bellamy and Tim Dunne, eds, *The Oxford Handbook of the Responsibility to Protect* (Oxford: Oxford University Press), 786–800.
Kikoler, Naomi, 2009. "Responsibility to Protect," Keynote Address to the Conference on Protecting People in Conflict and Crisis: Responding to the Challenges of a Changing World (Oxford: Refugee Studies Centre, University of Oxford, September), 1–17.
Kode, David, 2016. *The Complexities of Democracy-Building in Conflict-Affected States: The Role of ECOWAS and the African Union in Côte d'Ivoire* (Stockholm: International Institute for Democracy and Electoral Assistance), www.idea.int/sites/default/files/publications/democracy-building-in-conflict-affected-states-the-role-of-ecowas-and-au-in-cote divoire.pdf.
Koko, Sadiki, 2013. "Warning Whom, For Which Response?" *African Security Review* 22, no. 2: 54–67.
Lloyd, Robert B., 2010. "Conflict in Africa," *Journal of the Middle East and Africa* 1, no. 2: 171–86.
Mohammed, Omar, 2015. "Burundi Says an Intervention by the African Union Will Be an Act of 'Invasion'," December 21, https://qz.com/578780/burundi-says-an-intervention-by-the-african-union-in-the-country-will-be-an-act-of-invasion/.
Okyere, Frank, Kwesi Aning, and Susan Nelson, 2014. "Article 4(h): Translating Political Commitment into Collective Action," in Dan Kuwali and Frans Viljoen, eds, *Africa and the Responsibility to Protect: Article 4(h) of the African Union Constitutive Act* (Abingdon: Routledge), 278–86.
Parliamentary Monitoring Group, 2014. "Roles and Functions of Traditional Leaders: Department of Traditional Affairs Briefing," November 4, https://pmg.org.za/committee-meeting/17800/.
Strauss, Ekkehard, 2009. *The Emperor's New Clothes? The United Nations and the Implementation of the Responsibility to Protect* (Baden-Baden: Nomos).
United Nations General Assembly, 2005. "2005 World Summit Outcome," A/RES/60/1, October 24.
Veber, Maruša, 2014. "Regional Organisations and the Responsibility to Protect: Challenging the African Union's Implementation of the Responsibility to Protect," UNU–CRIS Working Paper W-2014/14 (Bruges: United Nations University–Institute on Comparative Regional Integration Studies).
Weiss, Thomas G., 2012. "R2P After 9/11 and the World Summit," *Wisconsin International Law Journal* 24, no. 3: 741–60.
Williams, Paul D., and Alex J. Bellamy, 2005. "The Responsibility to Protect and the Crisis in Darfur," *Security Dialogue* 36, no. 1: 27–47.
World Council of Churches, 2016. "'An Action Plan for Africa' on the Role of Religious Leaders in Preventing Incitement to Violence," May 10, www.oikoumene.org/en/press-centre/news/201can-action-plan-for-africa201d-on-the-role-of-religious-leaders-in-preventing-incitement-to-violence.

6

EUROPE'S ENGAGEMENT WITH R2P IN A TRANSITIONAL INTERNATIONAL ORDER

Edward Newman and Cristina G. Stefan

Introduction

In 2013, the European Parliament launched a major initiative to solidify and operationalize European Union (EU) support for the Responsibility to Protect (R2P) doctrine and to formulate a "European consensus" on the issue (this chapter draws upon Newman and Stefan 2019). In 2016, the EU appointed a Focal Point to coordinate its activities in this area, the first regional organization to do so. The European External Action Service launched its "Atrocity Prevention Toolkit" in January 2019, designed to coordinate European responses to atrocities in a proactive and coherent manner. These initiatives are taking place in parallel with broader efforts on the part of European foreign policy elites to project a more active global role for the EU in conflict resolution, security, and normative leadership, as reflected in the EU's 2016 "Global Strategy" (European Commission 2016).

However, these moves follow signs of collective ambivalence within the EU toward the R2P principle since it was established in 2005. The slow pace with which the EU has adopted R2P, in spite of the support of key individual members, is indicative of political tensions, uncertainties, and bureaucratic path dependency in the organization at a time when there are also doubts about the international role of the EU. This chapter explores the EU's engagement with the R2P principle and considers whether this can form an important aspect of its external engagement, including its international normative role. Our analysis focuses on two layers of concurrent normative contestation which problematize the EU's role in this area: first, at the global level, and second, internally within the EU. In the first section, we introduce the theoretical context of global normative contestation around issues such as R2P, often associated with liberal, Western values. We set this against the background of the "normative power Europe" debate in international perspective in order to assess the EU's role in promoting R2P globally, at a time when many argue that the EU's normative authority is in decline and rising powers are increasingly resisting aspects of the liberal international order. The second section focuses on internal normative contestation processes taking place within the EU. Despite support for R2P among key European states, the collective internalization of R2P in Europe has been slow. The third section explores the EU's potential to take a meaningful leadership role on R2P, despite the challenges identified within each of the two layers of contestation. We explore whether there is potential for the EU to speak with one voice on R2P-related issues, further to the 2013 European Parliament's call for consensus. As a test, the response of the EU to the contemporary refugee "crisis" does not augur well both for European collective action around R2P, or in terms of normative credibility in global perspective. Can the latest attempt of the EU to marshal a collective European response to the R2P initiative – after a decade of ambivalence – be successful, and what are the implications of this for the EU's normative leadership globally?

R2P and the EU

At the World Summit in 2005, United Nations (UN) member states agreed upon a responsibility to protect their populations from genocide, war crimes, ethnic cleansing, and crimes against humanity, and to prevent such crimes, including their incitement. The World Summit Outcome document stipulated that the international community should encourage and help states to exercise this responsibility and support the UN in establishing an early-warning capability. The agreement stated that the international community, through the UN, also has the responsibility to help to protect populations from these atrocities where national authorities are manifestly failing to do so (United Nations General Assembly 2005, paragraphs 138, 139).

European states have been fundamentally important in driving the R2P movement internationally, both in terms of its contested normative emergence and its controversial operationalization. There is a close normative and political fit between the EU and R2P in line with the Union's constitutive values, its international activities, and the commitment of its members – in theory, at least – to the highest standards of human rights and justice (Knudsen 2013). The substance of R2P resonates strongly with the themes of justice, liberalism, and cosmopolitanism which lie at the heart of the European political tradition. R2P's Pillar One calls for states to meet their existing commitments to international human rights with respect to human protection – rights that European states have been at the forefront of codifying and promoting since the end of the Second World War. These are at the core of the EU's founding treaties, underpinned by the EU Charter of Fundamental Rights of 2000, and form the core of European society. There is wide European commitment to the idea that "in the twenty-first century, more than ever, sovereignty entails responsibility," and that the responsibility to protect populations from egregious human rights abuses is a shared and a transboundary one (European Commission 2008, 12).

European countries played a leading role in facilitating the emergence of the R2P principle and in achieving broad commitment to it from states at the UN

World Summit (Badescu 2011, 106–27). In subsequent years, R2P has had some limited visibility in key EU external action realms, including humanitarian aid, European security strategy, and development assistance. It has also been a minor reference point in EU debates about its security and foreign policy. The Common Foreign and Security Policy, and the Common Security and Defense Policy, have made explicit reference to R2P as part of a broader commitment to international law. The European Council has also explicitly endorsed the R2P principle, in particular in relation to preventive action (Council of the European Union 2009). Specific EU milestones such as the EU Programme for the Prevention of Violent Conflicts (the Gothenburg Programme, 2001), the European Consensus on Development (2005), and the European Consensus on Humanitarian Aid (2008) form the broader background for European support of the R2P principle, as well as the Lisbon Treaty agenda which gave rise to external action and "European foreign policy" as a key aspect of the EU's identity.

R2P has not, however, been a key policy platform for the EU and most of the institutional endorsements of R2P between 2005 and 2013 have been quite cursory or insubstantial. As others have observed, R2P has not been internalized into the foreign policy apparatus of the EU, or indeed, that of the EU member states (see ahead) (Brockmeier, Kurtz, and Junk 2014; De Franco, Meyer, and Smith 2015). There has been, therefore, good reason for skepticism as to whether the R2P principle would, or could, be a focus in the EU's pursuit of a global role in the promotion of justice and normative change. This is underpinned by the changing global context: the rise in prominence of non-liberal states, a retreat in liberal internationalism in the West, and doubts about the global reach of the EU following the United Kingdom's decision to exit the Union.

However, in 2013, the European Parliament (2013) produced the most substantive European statement on R2P to date, and in 2016, an EU Focal Point on R2P was established. In 2019, the "Atrocity Prevention Toolkit" – which makes specific reference to R2P, and represents a clear step toward operationalization – was launched. These measures have firmly put R2P back on the radar of the EU, at a time when the EU has faced major challenges in terms of responding to humanitarian crises overseas – including in Iraq, Libya, and Syria – and an unprecedented humanitarian refugee crisis. The European Parliament's statement called for stronger European coordination on R2P and for a number of actions which would integrate R2P into the different areas of activity of the EU, including conflict prevention, international trade, and development assistance. It also situated R2P in the context of the EU's collective identity and its aspirations as a global actor. The key question that this development poses is therefore whether this renewed vision of Europe's support of R2P is politically feasible, and whether it can overcome the divisions which have hampered Europe's internalization of R2P since 2005. In turn, in a transitional international order characterized by normative contestation and the relative decline of the reach of Western authority, what are the prospects for European normative leadership with reference to R2P?

R2P and European normative leadership

An examination of the EU's approach toward R2P provides an interesting focus for broader questions about Europe's increasingly active – but often controversial – foreign policy and its role within the evolving international order. The European Parliament observed that "the EU has always been an active promoter of R2P on the international stage" and simultaneously that "it needs to strengthen its role as a global political actor, upholding human rights and humanitarian law and also reflecting that political support in its own policies" (European Parliament 2013, paragraph T). In its consideration of R2P, the European Parliament (2013, preamble and paragraph I) also made note of "expectations as to its future engagement for a more peaceful world order based on the rules of international law" and the fundamental importance of the "further development and the legitimacy of the principle of R2P." In this context, the EU's responses to humanitarian challenges in cases such as Libya, Iraq, Mali, and Syria, and the associated refugee crisis, will play a critical part in defining the EU's place in the world. This comes at a time when the EU is attempting to project an assertive political presence in international affairs, following the Lisbon Treaty and the establishment of the European External Action Service.

The European Parliament's request for a "Consensus on R2P" reflected a number of important features which provide an insight into the EU's fledgling attempts to form an international political role, as well as the region's collective political culture (European Parliament 2013). First, in terms of the normative context, R2P is approached from the perspective of European constitutive values, objectives, and policies, as enshrined in the Treaty on European Union, as well as with reference to core international agreements such as the UN Charter, the Universal Declaration of Human Rights, the Genocide Convention, and the Rome Statute of the International Criminal Court. Thus, R2P is seen as an emerging international norm within the liberal tradition and as part of the evolving international legal apparatus designed to protect human rights, including the interlinkages between R2P and the International Criminal Court (Fisher and Stefan 2016), another international initiative of which European countries have been at the forefront (European Parliament 2013, paragraph R). The EU goes further than many other actors in seeing the R2P principle as a legal doctrine, and not only as a political concept. Moreover, the European conceptualization of R2P also places it firmly in the context of broader processes and norms relating to international justice, even though the specific focus of R2P relates to a narrow range of crimes. Thus, the emerging European conception of R2P is not confined to the obligation to respond to war crimes, crimes against humanity, and genocide, but is embedded in broader, interlinked, political, social and legal norms. The fundamental significance of this relates to the belief – inherent in European society – that individual security, liberty, and human rights are the bedrock of a stable order.

Second, the European approach to R2P reflected in the European Parliament document is embedded in an evolving and increasingly conditional sovereignty norm in which the needs and rights of people are gradually transcending the conventional Westphalian model of international society. Again, this reflects the liberal political and social heritage of Western Europe. It is therefore very notable that the European Parliament aligned itself to the earlier, more radical, expression of R2P found in the International Commission on Intervention and State Sovereignty (ICISS) report, and not only the 2005 UN World Summit Outcome, which outlined a more conservative vision. The ICISS report argued that a "modern" understanding of state sovereignty is evolving in the context of changing norms: the world is moving from a territorial-based sovereignty – where those in power control sovereignty – to popular sovereignty, in the context of principles of democratic entitlement and solidarism. Accordingly,

> sovereignty implies a dual responsibility: externally – to respect the sovereignty of other states, and internally, to respect the dignity and basic rights of all the people within the state. . . . Sovereignty as responsibility has become the minimum content of good international citizenship.
>
> *(ICISS 2001, 8)*

Notably, the ICISS version of R2P did not rule out international action outside the UN – if the Security Council "fails to discharge its responsibility to protect in conscience-shocking situations crying out for action" (ICISS 2001, 55) – whereas this was explicitly ruled out in the 2005 World Summit agreement. The European Parliament (2013, paragraphs C, G) – unlike many other global actors – sees a clear thread of continuity between the ICISS agenda which was a response to atrocities in the 1990s, and the twenty-first century R2P agenda. In contrast, most – or all – non-Western support for R2P has stressed the pluralist, Westphalian framework of the 2005 agreement (Stefan 2017). The EU's apparent position on R2P – at least in the European Parliament – will therefore likely fuel international normative contestation around humanitarianism and human protection, if it is projected in an assertive manner.

The EU approach to R2P also emphasizes the prevention of atrocities, in line with the broader EU apparatus that is designed to prevent conflict (European Parliament 2013, paragraphs H, N, O). In this context, war crimes, crimes against humanity, and genocide are seen as crimes that tend to occur in situations of armed conflict, and a strong conflict – prevention capacity is something tangible that the EU can contribute to R2P, based upon its comprehensive approach to external conflict. The Gothenburg Programme and many subsequent developments within the EU's external affairs machinery have provided the EU with a leadership role globally in preventing intrastate armed conflict, and this experience and capacity provides an important basis for the EU engagement in support of R2P. This also means that the EU's approach to upholding R2P can be applied to a broad range of issues which are known to be relevant to the onset of violent conflict, relating to governance, economic development, poverty and inequality, gender equality, and democratic rights.

Indeed, the European Parliament (2013, paragraph M) advocated in favor of approaching R2P in the context of a broad range of directly or indirectly relevant policy areas, including development cooperation, aid, and crisis management. This represents a shift in R2P debates more broadly, because it focuses upon the underlying sources and driving forces of instability and armed conflict, all of which the EU has considerable international experience in addressing. At the same time, it does raise a challenge of policy coherence, since there is a real potential for conflicts of interests and tensions between different norms across these broad policy areas.

Despite contributing to international normative contestation, the EU did not get involved, collectively, in any significant attempt to promote and operationalize R2P post-2013. This was regardless of calls by the UN Secretary-General for an increased role to be played by regional actors. According to the normative aspirations that the EU has adopted, the effectiveness and legitimacy of the European response to atrocities will play a major role in defining the region's collective stature and credibility as a "responsible" global actor, and in affirming Europe's commitment to justice. Yet fundamental questions remain about the extent to which the EU can meaningfully embrace R2P as an external action platform, and whether the principle can contribute to the EU's troubled normative identity. While we tackle the lack of internal consensus in a later section, we focus now on the "normative power Europe" debates.

Normative power Europe?

The concept of "normative power" has been a focus of earlier discussions about Europe's capacity to shape norms related to human rights and justice, and it provides a useful context for an analysis of the EU's potential to play a leadership role in support of R2P. According to this, the EU's constitutive principles – reflected in a history of European agreements and a commitment to international human rights instruments – mean that certain values are internalized within collective European society and policy (Manners 2002; Weiler and Wind 2003; Sjursen 2006). In particular, peace, freedom, democracy, the rule of law, and respect for human rights are considered to be foundational and indivisible to the collective European identity, and in turn provide a normative worldview which has an impact externally through European external policy and through various forms of diffusion (Manners 2002, 2006). As Ian Manners (2002, 252) argues, "the most important factor shaping the international role of the EU is not what it does or what it says, but what it is."

These values not only constitute the European identity, but in theory, they contribute to a worldview that guides Europe's interaction with external partners – for example, in promoting and supporting democracy, human rights, and good governance – and that represents a standard of practice to which those who wish to do business with Europe aspire. For those societies in the European neighborhood who wish to join the EU community, these standards constitute a necessary benchmark. From this perspective, Europe's role as a global actor takes into account – in theory – not only the interests of Europe and European states, but a cosmopolitan commitment to certain standards of human welfare globally.

According to this, Europe is therefore inherently normative as a function of its constitutive principles, and there is ample evidence of the diffusion effect of liberal values in a range of policy areas, in particular in the near abroad and the European neighborhood, but also further afield. Moreover, these values have been shown to play a role in areas such as conflict resolution (Tocci 2007), promoting the abolition of the death penalty, democracy promotion, and other movements. This debate is relevant to the EU's engagement with R2P since the success of the principle rests, in part, upon its normative traction in international politics, and its promotion by normative leaders. However, an effective role in support of R2P would clearly rest not only upon what the EU is, but also what it does. If the EU is to make this a key policy platform for its global role, it will need to be underpinned by the normative reach and credibility of Europe.

The concept of "normative power Europe" is relevant to R2P in a number of ways, and especially in terms of the emphasis placed by the EU upon atrocity prevention. Norm diffusion is at the heart of the concept, and insofar as the success of R2P will rest in large part upon its emergence as a norm, the EU has the potential to contribute to this process if its "normative power" has meaning and can be used as a vehicle for R2P. R2P seeks, above all, to normalize the idea that states have a responsibility to prevent egregious human rights abuses within their territory, and to accept an *international* responsibility to protect in certain circumstances. If the EU has the "ability to shape conceptions of the 'normal' in international relations" (Manners 2002, 239), then its embrace of R2P could signal a leadership role in promoting these twin concepts. If R2P is to gain normative traction globally, the support of a unified Europe will be important – or even decisive – given that the most powerful and the emerging states are ambivalent about the concept.

However, the idea of the normative power of Europe has been challenged on many fronts, and these challenges remain valid in terms of Europe's promotion of R2P. The concept of normative power – how to define and measure it – has been questioned (Forsberg 2011; Kavalski 2013; Laïdi 2008). The internal diversity of the European Union, in particular after waves of enlargement, presents a wide range of values and interests which defy the idea of a fixed, coherent, value system. From a realist perspective, questions have similarly been raised about the tension between the interests of the most powerful European states and their commitment to a common European position in external action (Hyde-Price 2006), something clearly in evidence when the EU has attempted to respond to humanitarian crises.

Many scholars have also raised concerns about the legitimacy of the "normative power" concept, whether promoted by example or through policies. It is all too easy to see in Europe's "normative power" an assumption of superiority over "other" systems of justice and politics which it seeks to "civilize" (Diez 2005; Pace 2007; Laïdi 2008). The history of Europe and its engagement with regions across the globe – including colonization – raises sensitivities in terms of its own capacity to proselytize in relation to political and social organization, and this legacy must be taken into account by European stakeholders in any attempt to promote the EU's role in global debates about justice and R2P.

Challenges pertaining to internal contestation

In addition to the global normative contestation which divides states, there is also evidence of normative contestation *within* Europe in terms of how to respond to egregious human rights abuse. The experience of the EU's engagement in sensitive foreign policy challenges in Libya, Iraq, Syria, and Ukraine, among others, and especially in the refugee "crisis" of 2015–2016, provides ample evidence of this. As a result, the EU has arguably not been a global normative leader in promoting the responsibility to protect framework, despite the leadership of some European powers in promoting human rights internationally. These internal challenges relate both to the institutional machinery and political dynamics of the EU, and to differences among members in relation to international humanitarian action. Such challenges speak directly to the difficulties of norm localization *within* a liberal community, which is not commonly discussed in the relevant norm contestation literature. It is therefore far from certain whether the EU can overcome the internal differences and embrace R2P as a coherent policy platform. We identify six challenges as defining the EU's engagement with R2P. These internal challenges explain many of the difficulties that the organization has experienced in terms of engaging with the R2P principle.

First, there remain divisions across and within EU members regarding the scope and operationalization of R2P, and in particular, the role of military force in preventing or stopping egregious human rights violations; European states have arguably never reached a consensus on this (Brockmeier, Kurtz, and Junk 2014). Some leading EU countries – notably the United Kingdom and France – actively support the concept of military humanitarian intervention, whether within the framework of R2P or not, while others, such as Germany and other north European countries, have major reservations about military intervention. Some states believe that, while R2P is something to be supported in principle, they prefer to retain autonomy to act according to their own view of humanitarian necessity. This has led to situations in which the United Kingdom and France have been essentially outside the European framework in undertaking or supporting military action, and other European countries have adopted very different stances. Germany's abstention from the 2011 UN Security Council resolution which authorized armed force in Libya is one such illustration. The R2P agreement and its operationalization has therefore exposed internal European divisions relating to global justice more broadly, and doubts remain as to whether the principle is something that Europe can engage with to strengthen its normative reach and global presence.

Second, the EU has been slow to internalize R2P into external action machinery, as others have suggested (Task Force on the EU Prevention of Mass Atrocities 2013; De Franco, Meyer, and Smith 2015). According to this argument, low levels of bureaucratic receptivity within the EU explain why the Union has not been more active in promoting the R2P principle. Existing foreign policy directives and policies, developed over some years and through long political negotiations, have resulted in a focus upon conflict prevention, development assistance, human rights, and democracy promotion. A reformulation of external action framed around the principle of R2P is not readily achieved, or not necessarily welcome among the European Commission's foreign policy technocrats. Even within the EU, the added value of R2P is therefore not universally accepted. European External Action Service staff believe they are working fully in support of R2P on a daily basis, even if they do not label it as such, and they are quite surprised that anyone would doubt this.[1] The "Global Strategy" included just one indirect reference to R2P, with no attempt to indicate how the principle might be operationalized through the various policy programs of the EU. This occurred just a few years after the European Parliament outlined a substantive strategy for the EU's engagement with R2P. The European Genocide Network is further illustration of this mentality. Following a 2002 European Council decision, this network of national contact points was established to investigate genocide, crimes against humanity, and war crimes. The network meets regularly, issues reports, and is the driving force behind initiatives such as the EU Action Plan on Impunity, but notably does not reference R2P in its work, and apparently does not have R2P on its radar.[2]

Third, the EU's credibility in terms of its leadership role in promoting humanitarian values – including R2P – can be questioned in relation to "internal" standards and practices, and this has resulted in some reluctance on the part of European leaders and officials to project R2P as a strategy.[3] The EU's fledgling R2P position is directed outward to external humanitarian tragedies, without much introspection or consideration of the policies and standards within European countries. Minority rights, attitudes toward hate crimes and incitement, and policies – including asylum and resettlement – toward people feeling egregious deprivation have all raised questions about Europe's commitment to humanitarianism, if not its double standards. Do European policies toward those seeking asylum from R2P crimes live up to the political commitment to R2P, for example? In this sense, Europe's role as a normative actor globally in relation to R2P is potentially in tension with the policies or standards of justice within European countries, and this affects the credibility and legitimacy of its role. The "EU's enduring power of attraction" and the "soft power" that the High Representative of the Union for Foreign Affairs and Security Policy speaks of is not fully convincing (Mogherini 2016), and in reality there is – unofficially, of course – hesitation among European foreign policy technocrats about projecting normative leadership globally.[4] In a transitional order characterized by normative contestation and the relative decline of the reach of liberalism – underscored by the United Kingdom's Brexit vote and the election of US President Donald J. Trump – questions are raised about the prospects for European normative leadership with reference to R2P. The European Council President suggested that "the challenges currently facing the European Union are more dangerous than ever before in the time since the signature of the Treaty of Rome" (Tusk 2017); European confidence in terms of global normative leadership is in retreat.

Fourth, it is far from certain if European citizens are engaged with Europe's role as a normative actor with respect to R2P, or whether this represents an area of democratic deficit. A further challenge in terms of Europe's normative power and its standing as a global actor therefore relates to "internal" legitimacy, in particular related to the views of citizens in European countries. Public opinion forms the basis of democratic policymaking, but there are real doubts about the level of public support for the EU's humanitarian role, particularly if it involves the use of armed force. During consultations for the new "Global Strategy," R2P was simply not on the radar of most member state representatives, suggesting a low level of visibility for R2P at the national level.

Fifth, there is ample evidence that "external" EU geopolitical interests and national interests within EU members displace normative values – including those relating to R2P – when these come into conflict. This, again, raises questions about policy coherence and credibility. European trade and energy ties to the Middle East and Russia, for example, are arguably often in tension with – and transcend – the EU's human rights commitments.

Sixth and finally, the EU's engagement with R2P, in the context of its broader external policies, raises significant problems related to policy coherence. Recent experience has demonstrated how these political and institutional challenges have made it difficult to formulate a coherent and consistent European response to pressing humanitarian crises. Integrating R2P into EU development assistance, conflict prevention, and humanitarian activities, and the EU's work in strengthening and promoting international human rights compliance, generates multiple tensions. European missions such as the EU Rule of Law Mission in Kosovo and the EU Military Operation in Bosnia and Herzegovina have also demonstrated the difficulties of aligning the EU's normative values – in terms of justice promotion – with strategic goals. It is not certain that EU members individually and the Union collectively are upholding – and contributing to – standards of global justice in their response to severe human rights abuse.

Europe's prospects for taking up a meaningful leadership role on R2P

In this section, we discuss the prospects for Europe's leadership role making an impact on the promotion of norms relating to human protection, despite the two sets of challenges identified previously. We argue that there is potential for the EU to speak with one voice on R2P-related issues, if it picks up from where the European Parliament left it in 2013. This was the most significant moment when the European Parliament placed R2P on the EU's radar, calling for "consensus" on the topic.

The refugee crisis of 2015–2016 arguably presented a test for the EU to demonstrate a leadership role in humanitarian assistance relevant to R2P through prioritizing Pillar Two, the responsibility to assist those escaping mass atrocity situations by seeking asylum in Europe. It provided the revival of the normative power

Europe concept, triggered by a global crisis that Europe was forced to address given that it occurred in its backyard. "Normative power Europe" *in practice* develops from Manners' (2002) conceptualization as the ability to persuade others through processes of norm diffusion, except that it is *inward*-looking; it implies persuading its own Schengen Area member states to reach a common European foreign policy on the issue of refugees. Europe's claim of authority is directly related to the competence level it has shown, collectively, in addressing the biggest crisis that Europe faces at the moment, which is the essence of social processes of normative power in practice. Competence in this sense emphasizes locally generated resources to find long-term resettlement places for those displaced by past and ongoing crises.

The refugee crisis has provided the EU with the one "window of opportunity" to show leadership on issues to which it has long been committed, in line with the liberal values it embraces. The EU can take up a meaningful role in implementing R2P through prioritizing Pillar Two. If the EU fails to seize it, though, its "normative power" will likely diminish considerably. Indeed, providing a collective response to the refugee crisis *is* one key way to exercise the responsibility to protect. The UN Secretary-General argued that full implementation of international refugee law was required in order to fulfill R2P: "protection of refugees and the internally displaced," "by supporting requests for asylum or protecting refugees in safe facilities ... by regional or international actors" represents one way to fulfill the responsibility to assist, under R2P's Pillar Two (Ban 2014, paragraph 65). In 2008, others suggested that "there may be no easier way for the international community to meet its responsibility to protect than by providing asylum and other international protection on adequate terms" (Barbour and Gorlick 2008, 532).

While the EU is not very likely to experience any of the four core crimes covered by the R2P framework, it can certainly respond to refugee and asylum seekers escaping such crimes in their countries. The leadership needed in this case is one "based on values" of the type Austria and Germany showed when they opened their borders to allow in thousands of refugees from Hungary. Focusing on the discourse of assisting refugees as part of the R2P prescriptions could translate into socializing more EU officials into embracing R2P, through policy first and then practice. However, the refugee crisis triggered very sparse references to R2P among government officials, practitioners, and diplomats. Some academics, however, have argued that safe passage and granting asylum are both key to fulfilling R2P (for example, Bellamy 2015; Newman 2018).

While the EU has indeed seen the refugee crisis as quite distinct – conceptually – from R2P and therefore has refrained from referring to the principle in this context, several references to R2P in recent EU policy documents are more encouraging. For instance, the R2P principle was referenced in the EU's "New European Consensus on Development" (European Commission 2017, paragraph 66). Nevertheless, the response to the refugee crisis has generated controversy and has implications for the EU's credibility as a humanitarian actor in normative terms. A key aspect of the interdiction efforts were agreements with third countries to take in or prevent the onward journey of large numbers of refugees as a way of diverting them from Europe. An agreement with Turkey in March 2016 to accommodate approximately 2 million Syrians who were in Turkey at that time – and thus blocked onward transit – in return for financial and political incentives was particularly controversial. Irrespective of the necessity of such measures, the response has raised questions regarding the "normative power" of Europe.

Conclusions

The EU is facing broad challenges which raise doubts about its capacity and desire to promote norms, and this has implications for R2P. A more active external action profile does not necessarily mean more actively promoting normative principles. While the EU cannot be expected to be the savior of the norm, there is still significant potential for it to provide R2P with global traction, but only if the regional body assumes leadership by speaking with one voice on promoting norms related to human protection, starting with responsibilities to assist refugees, in accordance with Pillar Two.

The principal problem relevant to the EU's engagement with R2P is that norms are more likely to play a role for EU *external* action when they align with traditional policy goals and when the EU is dealing with relatively weak regions and countries. This pragmatism surely problematizes the attraction of Europe's soft power and exposes the inherent contradictions between external policies which seek to balance norms and political self-interests at the same time, and the conflict between collective principles and national political agendas. Thus, the issue is not just normative versus material interests, but also conflicts between norms.

As this debate has evolved, it has generated more reflective, sometimes self-critical viewpoints on Europe's normative contribution to international order, which has acknowledged the limitations and constraints of the EU's foreign policy more broadly. It is widely believed that there is no single, monolithic, European identity or value system, and the development of Europe's normative role should not be thought of as cumulative and linear.

Similarly, it is not universally assumed that Europe's influence and contributions to global norms of justice are progressively strengthening or that the EU necessarily "does good" in terms of its contributions to global justice. On the contrary, there is evidence that the normative influence of Europe – on issues related to justice, as well as a wide range of policy areas – is at a crossroads. The question of what the European Union should represent in international politics – in terms of peace, justice, and international order – needs to be revisited in light of a multifaceted transformation within Europe and the world.

The President of the European Commission's 2016 State of the Union address suggested that "our European Union is, at least in part, in an existential crisis" (Juncker 2016). The "Global Strategy" similarly stated that "we live in times of existential crisis, within and beyond the European Union. Our Union is under threat. Our European project, which has brought unprecedented peace, prosperity and democracy, is being questioned" (European Commission 2016, 7). The reasons for this alarm are clear for all to see.

The attitude in the EU among members and policy staff is one of "pulling ourselves together," and preventing the unraveling of the European project in an inhospitable environment. This involves focusing upon core European interests, not global norms, and toughening up on security. Even if the EU was not facing severe internal crises, the changing international order is less and less conducive to Europe playing a global leadership role. If "normative power Europe" ever had traction, it is certainly in retreat, in the context of global norm contestation and a changing power constellation. The "Global Strategy" emphasized the need for a "rules-based global order . . . guided by clear principles" and an "idealistic aspiration," but the subtext seems to increasingly reflect a power-political worldview (European Commission 2016, 8).

The prioritization of, and preoccupation with, hard economic interests, the desire to avoid political conflict with partners *and* adversaries – including the United States, Russia, India, and China – has brought the realization that principles such as R2P are something of a luxury. Moreover, from the external perspective, the persuasion of the EU as a normative actor is in doubt within this transitional international order in which liberal internationalism is in retreat.

On the face of it, the EU has already moved toward the operationalization of R2P – with the appointment of an R2P Focal Point, a very active group of national Focal Points, and the publication of its own "Atrocity Prevention Toolkit." However, in the context of broader pressures and changes, there are formidable constraints upon the EU's normative traction in this policy area and these constraints are largely beyond the EU's control.

Notes

1   Interviews, New York, June 2016, and Brussels, November 2016.
2   Interview, The Hague, November 2016.
3   Interviews, New York, June 2016, and Brussels, July 2016.
4   Interviews, Brussels, July 2016.

References

Badescu, Cristina Gabriela, 2011. *Humanitarian Intervention and the Responsibility to Protect: Security and Human Rights* (Abingdon: Routledge).
Ban Ki-moon, 2014. "Fulfilling our Collective Responsibility: International Assistance and the Responsibility to Protect: Report of the Secretary-General," A/68/947–S/2014/449, July 11.
Barbour, Brian, and Brian Gorlick, 2008. "Embracing the 'Responsibility to Protect': A Repertoire of Measures Including Asylum for Potential Victims," *International Journal of Refugee Law* 20, no. 4: 533–66.
Bellamy, Alex J., 2015. "Safe Passage and Asylum Key to Fulfilling the Responsibility to Protect," *IPI Global Observatory*, September 8, http://theglobalobservatory.org/2015/09/syria-refugees-unhcr-aylan-kurdi/.

Brockmeier, Sarah, Gerrit Kurtz, and Julian Junk, 2014. "Emerging Norm and Rhetorical Tool: Europe and a Responsibility to Protect," *Conflict, Security and Development* 14, no. 4: 429–60.

Council of the European Union, 2009. "EU Priorities for the 64th UN General Assembly," 10809/09 (Brussels: Council of the European Union, June 9).

De Franco, Chiara, Christoph O. Meyer, and Karen E. Smith, 2015. "'Living by Example?' The European Union and the Implementation of the Responsibility to Protect (R2P)," *Journal of Common Market Studies* 53, no. 5: 994–1009.

Diez, Thomas, 2005. "Constructing the Self and Changing Others: Reconsidering 'Normative Power Europe'," *Millennium: Journal of International Studies* 33, no. 3: 613–36.

European Commission, 2008. "Report on the Implementation of the European Security Strategy: Providing Security in a Changing World," S407/08 (Brussels: European Commission, December 11).

European Commission, 2016. "Shared Vision, Common Action: A Stronger Europe. A Global Strategy for the European Union's Foreign and Security Policy" (Brussels: European External Action Service).

European Commission, 2017. "The New European Consensus on Development: 'Our World, Our Dignity, Our Future'" (Brussels: European Commission, June 8).

European Parliament, 2013. "European Parliament Recommendation to the Council of 18 April 2013 on the UN Principle of the 'Responsibility to Protect' ('R2P')," 2012/2143(INI) (Brussels: European Parliament).

Fisher, Kirsten J., and Cristina G. Stefan, 2016. "The Ethics of International Criminal 'Lawfare'," *International Criminal Law Review* 16, no. 2: 237–57.

Forsberg, Tuomas, 2011. "Normative Power Europe, Once Again: A Conceptual Analysis of an Ideal Type," *Journal of Common Market Studies* 49, no. 6: 1183–204.

Hyde-Price, Adrian, 2006. "'Normative' Power Europe: A Realist Critique," *Journal of European Public Policy* 13, no. 2: 217–34.

ICISS (International Commission on Intervention and State Sovereignty), 2001. *The Responsibility to Protect: Report of the International Commission on Intervention and State Sovereignty* (Ottawa: International Development Research Centre).

Juncker, Jean-Claude, 2016. "State of the Union Address 2016: Towards a Better Europe – A Europe that Protects, Empowers and Defends," Strasbourg, September 14, http://europa.eu/rapid/press-release_SPEECH-16-3043_en.htm.

Kavalski, Emilian, 2013. "The Struggle for Recognition of Normative Powers: Normative Power Europe and Normative Power China in Context," *Cooperation and Conflict* 48, no. 2: 247–67.

Knudsen, Tonny Brems, 2013. "The Responsibility to Protect: European Contributions in a Changing World Order," in Knud Erik Jørgensen and Katie Verlin Laatikainen, eds, *Routledge Handbook on the European Union and International Institutions: Performance, Policy, Power* (Abingdon: Routledge), 157–70.

Laïdi, Zaki, ed., 2008. *EU Foreign Policy in a Globalized World: Normative Power and Social Preferences* (Abingdon: Routledge).

Manners, Ian, 2002. "Normative Power Europe: A Contradiction in Terms?" *Journal of Common Market Studies* 40, no. 2: 235–58.

Manners, Ian, 2006. "Normative Power Europe Reconsidered: Beyond the Crossroads," *Journal of European Public Policy* 13, no. 2: 182–99.

Mogherini, Federica, 2016. "Statement by HR/VP Federica Mogherini on the Occasion of the International Day of Democracy," Brussels, September 26, https://eeas.europa.eu/headquarters/headquarters-homepage/32212/statement-hrvp-federica-mogherini-occasion-international-day-democracy_en.

Newman, Edward, 2018. "The Limits of Liberal Humanitarianism in Europe: The 'Responsibility to Protect' and Forced Migration," *European Review of International Studies* 4, nos. 2–3: 59–77.

Newman, Edward, and Cristina G. Stefan, 2019. "Normative Power Europe? The EU's Embrace of the 'Responsibility to Protect' in a Transitional International Order," *Journal of Common Market Studies* 25 July, https://doi.org/10.1111/jcms.12953.

Pace, Michelle, 2007. "The Construction of EU Normative Power," *Journal of Common Market Studies* 45, no. 5: 1041–64.

Sjursen, Helene, 2006. "The EU as a 'Normative' Power: How Can This Be?" *Journal of European Public Policy* 13, no. 2: 235–51.

Stefan, Cristina G., 2017. "On Non-Western Norm Shapers: Brazil and the Responsibility While Protecting," *European Journal of International Security* 2, no. 1: 88–110.

Task Force on the EU Prevention of Mass Atrocities, 2013. *The EU and the Prevention of Mass Atrocities: An Assessment of Strengths and Weaknesses* (Budapest: Budapest Centre for the International Prevention of Genocide and Mass Atrocities).

Tocci, Nathalie, 2007. *The EU and Conflict Resolution: Promoting Peace in the Backyard* (Abingdon: Routledge).

Tusk, Donald, 2017. "'United We Stand, Divided We Fall': Letter by President Donald Tusk to the 27 EU Heads of State or Government on the Future of the EU Before the Malta Summit," January 31, www.consilium.europa.eu/en/press/press-releases/2017/01/31-tusk-letter-future-europe/?utm_source=dsms-auto&utm_medium=email&utm_campaign=%22United+we+stand%2c+divided+we+fall%22%3a+letter+by+President+Donald+Tusk+to+the+27+EU+heads+of+state+or+government+on+the+future+of+the+EU+before+the+Malta+summit.

United Nations General Assembly, 2005. "2005 World Summit Outcome," A/RES/60/1, October 24.

Weiler, J. H. H., and Marlene Wind, eds, 2003. *European Constitutionalism Beyond the State* (Cambridge: Cambridge University Press).

PART III
Atrocity prevention

7
ATROCITY PREVENTION, NATIONAL RESILIENCE, AND IMPLEMENTATION

Stephen McLoughlin

In this chapter, I discuss how strengthening national resilience contributes to the implementation of the Responsibility to Protect (R2P). The idea of strengthening national resilience was identified by former United Nations (UN) Secretary-General Ban Ki-moon as a key component in operationalizing Pillar One of R2P. While there is evidence that the international community is becoming more effective at providing timely and decisive action in cases of imminent or manifest failure of state responsibility, a focus on the role of domestic actors in addressing risk holds the potential to reduce the number of circumstances where atrocities are perpetrated, offsetting the possibility of dangerous risk escalation.

Pillar One entails the responsibility that the state has for the protection of its population from genocide, crimes against humanity, ethnic cleansing, and war crimes (Ban 2009, 10). Implementation in terms of Pillar One requires a consideration of what domestic actors do to carry out their responsibility to protect. Ban (2015, 6) identified a number of recommendations in relation to shifting the principle "from the conceptual to the practical." For Pillar One, this means three areas: encouraging greater adoption of a range of legal mechanisms related to mass atrocities, strengthening national resilience to prevent mass atrocities, and expanding and supporting national Focal Points (Ban 2015, 7–9). These priorities put the focus on the role that domestic actors can play in strengthening protection through the prevention of mass atrocities.

The purpose of this chapter is to explore the relationship between atrocity prevention, national resilience, and R2P implementation. I argue that recent scholarly interest in the question of how and why mass atrocities are avoided raise strong possibilities for implementation, particularly in relation to strengthening national resilience. I explain this in three parts. First, I chart the conceptual development of Pillar One. While R2P emerged out of the debate in the 1990s about how the international community should respond to humanitarian emergencies such as those in Rwanda, Kosovo, and Srebrenica, the concept has been broadened to consider the question of how national actors can prevent such emergencies from occurring in the first place. I explore the development of the concept of prevention – particularly long term, or structural – and highlight how policy-based articulations tended to overlook the role that domestic actors play in such processes. Second, I provide an overview of the growing scholarly interest in why genocide and other mass atrocities do not occur in particular situations, despite the presence of risk factors. By asking this question, we gain a better understanding of what local and national actors do to prevent these crimes. This is of central importance to the principle of R2P, but yet, it is only recently that a clear picture of such dynamics has emerged. Third and finally, I consider how national resilience contributes to implementation. I argue that knowledge of existing practices of risk mitigation is slowly being utilized to develop an atrocity-prevention lens, which then facilitates the dissemination of knowledge and insights related to national resilience. While such processes are nascent, I explore ways in which these practices are beginning to influence domestic practice.

Prevention and Pillar One

Interest in prevention – both in relation specifically to mass atrocities, and conflict more broadly – has been growing since the end of the Cold War. This is evidenced in the establishment of a number of key offices and initiatives. In 2004, the UN Secretary-General established the Office of the Special Adviser on the Prevention of Genocide (United Nations Security Council 2004). In 2012, former US President Barack Obama set up an Atrocities Prevention Board, stating that mass atrocities were a national security concern (White House 2012). Increased support over the last couple of decades for the UN Department of Political Affairs in the form of better capacity to carry out its preventive functions, such as early warning and mediation, is further evidence of a growing commitment to and diversification of efforts to prevent conflict and mass atrocities. Yet while prevention lies at the heart of the UN's commitments (United Nations 1945; Hampson, Wermester, and Malone 2002, 1), it was not until the 1980s that attempts were made to establish institutional capacity for conflict prevention.

Prevention was identified in Boutros Boutros-Ghali's (1992) report "An Agenda for Peace," which mapped ways that the UN could address unfolding challenges of security (see also Luck 2006, 5). This report, and its follow-up "Supplement to An Agenda for Peace" (Boutros-Ghali 1995), emphasized the necessity to better coordinate actors and resources for preventive diplomacy, as well as post-conflict rebuilding that prioritized addressing each conflict's underlying causes (Boutros-Ghali 1995; Menkhaus 2004, 421). Yet the 1990s were characterized by failures of prevention, with some pointing to the absence of early warning and a lack of flexibility in mandates, meaning that opportunities were lost to prevent, or at least mitigate, atrocities in places such as Rwanda and Srebrenica (United Nations 1999).

Despite this, prevention as a concept was more clearly defined and delineated as the decade unfolded. In 1997, the Carnegie Commission on Preventing Deadly Conflict released a report, *Preventing Deadly Conflict*, which repackaged preventive action into two key areas: operational and structural prevention. Operational prevention (also known as direct prevention) referred to strategies such as preventive peacekeeping and preventive diplomacy, with the aim of averting highly tense situations from escalating into violent conflict. Structural prevention entails strategies that deal with the underlying or root causes of violent conflict (Hamburg and Vance 1997, xix). This dual approach to prevention was endorsed by the UN in its series of reports on conflict prevention that appeared between 2001 and 2006, mapping out and making recommendations in relation to institutional approaches to such action (see Annan 2001, 2003, 2006). In the first of these reports, Kofi Annan (2001, 18, 24) advocated the creation of a "culture of prevention" in the UN system, recommending that agencies, departments, and programs adopt a "prevention lens" in all projects that involved activities that overlapped with operational or structural prevention. This approach to prevention was also endorsed in the International Commission on Intervention and State Sovereignty's report, *The Responsibility to Protect*, which first proposed the principle of R2P. In addition to early warning, it promoted the need to develop strategies for both "direct prevention" and "root cause prevention" (ICISS 2001, 22–27). R2P, in other words, was premised on effective prevention.

Structural prevention lies at the heart of Pillar One in R2P. As the "2005 World Summit Outcome" document points out, the foundation of the principle is the declaration that "[e]ach individual State has the responsibility to protect its populations from genocide, war crimes, ethnic cleansing and crimes against humanity" (United Nations General Assembly 2005, paragraph 138). Embedded in this is the assumption that it is better for such crimes not to occur in the first place. When risk escalates to dangerous levels, the need for international involvement in preventive efforts also tends to rise. It is then, by observing how domestic actors respond to the root causes of conflict, that we develop a better understanding of what Pillar One responsibility looks like.

Yet there are two key problems with the concept of structural prevention that have implications for R2P and Pillar One. The first problem is that it assumes that the existence of root causes – or structural risk factors – indicates an inevitable progression toward a violent outcome. This then prompts the assumption that the removal of such structural risk factors then results in effective mass atrocity prevention (see McLoughlin 2014a, 415). This is often reflected in the literature through the positioning of "root causes" as the first of a number of phases that lead to the perpetration of violence. Such stages often develop from "potential violence" or "pre-violence" – which indicate the presence of root causes or risk, before progressing to "escalation" or "gestation" (see Draman 2003, 234; Rothchild 2003, 44–46; Stanton 1996). However, suggesting that the amelioration of root causes is necessary for effective prevention does not correspond with what is known about the structural risk factors associated with mass atrocities. As pointed out in the next section, the scholarship about the causes of genocide and other mass atrocities – although varied in its findings – finds general consensus in the claim that the existence of "root causes" does not mean that a violent outcome is inevitable. Indeed, more often than not, countries that contain risk do not go on to commit mass atrocities, which suggests the possibility that local and national actors are committing to action which has, as one effect, the mitigation of risk. Precisely why risk does not escalate in these cases, and what can be learned from asking such a question, has the potential to yield insights for prevention, particularly in relation to Pillar One.

The second problem is that until recently, research and policymaking has focused mostly on the role that international actors play, consequently overlooking what domestic actors do to mitigate risk. In the broader literature on structural prevention, key preventive actors are for the most part external to the places that are subject to risk. The UN, Western liberal-democratic states, international non-governmental organizations, and regional organizations are typically identified as the key players, and domestic actors such as local organizations, communities, and national governments are overlooked (McLoughlin 2014a, 419). This is not to say that such publications do not mention domestic actors. On the contrary, some of the UN's key documents on prevention place great emphasis on these actors. For example, the first report on prevention released by Annan (2001, 2) stressed that "the primary responsibility for conflict prevention rests with national government, with civil society playing a role." In subsequent reports, the same point is made repeatedly. However, beyond this general acknowledgment, there is almost no indication as to how domestic actors can or have carried out effective strategies of prevention.

These limitations are problematic for R2P, particularly in relation to Pillar One. R2P starts with the acknowledgment that the primary responsibility lies with states themselves to protect their population from atrocity crimes, yet at the time of the World Summit, there was little understanding of what responsible sovereignty looked like, especially in the face of risk – much was known about the absence of such responsibility, but less about its presence (McLoughlin 2014a, 420). Very little research had been conducted on what steps states take to uphold such a responsibility despite the well-acknowledged fact that the presence of risk (or "root causes") only rarely escalated to dangerous levels. Addressing that lacuna would go some way to adding clarity to how responsible sovereignty is carried out.

This poses a problem for R2P, particularly in terms of Pillar One implementation. The role of domestic actors lies at the center of the pledge that states made at the 2005 World Summit. Therefore, the key question to ask in terms of prevention is: how are domestic actors implementing this responsibility? Given that mass atrocities occur rarely, even in the face of risk, there are indications that numerous insights could be gained by putting the focus on domestic actors. Yet by 2005, the question of what domestic actors do had received little more than lip-service in policy reports; and the question of why genocide and other mass atrocities do not occur despite the presence of risk was largely overlooked.

This lacuna was acknowledged by Ban (2009) in his first report on R2P, "Implementing the Responsibility to Protect." It provided a conceptual unpacking of the World Summit pledge, in order to map out practical possibilities for prevention and reaction. While pointing out that the role that the international community can play in long-term prevention is at best "supplemental," it provided little guidance as to the role of domestic actors, stating that "[m]ore research and analysis are needed on why one society plunges into mass violence while its neighbours remain relatively stable" (Ban 2009, 10–11). The challenge, then, was to develop a more comprehensive understanding of why it is that some states avoided mass violence, in order to more effectively identify domestically driven processes of prevention, which give better shape to the idea of responsible sovereignty.

The Secretary-General's 2013 report

The first document released by the UN to explore the role of domestic actors in R2P was Secretary-General Ban's 2013 report, "The Responsibility to Protect: State Responsibility and Prevention" (Ban 2013). Distinguishing itself by proposing a risk resilience framework which aims not to provide a prescriptive list of strategies that vulnerable states should adopt, the report considers how it is that states experiencing risk have avoided escalation of that risk. The framework is based on insights already gained from countries that have achieved some level of success in managing situations that are associated with the risk of mass atrocities. The report identifies key risk factors associated with mass atrocities. These include discrimination against identity-based groups, the will to target a minority group, the presence of armed groups with the capacity to commit atrocity crimes, circumstances that facilitate the perpetration of mass atrocities (such as policies of persecution), lack of government capacity to prevent atrocity crimes, and the perpetration of violence that could be construed as precursors to more systematic violence (Ban 2013). While this is not an exhaustive list of causal factors associated with atrocity crimes, it broadly represents an overview of long-term and proximate causes that accompany such violence. Prevention itself is a contextually specific process which occurs at moments right across the risk spectrum, from low to moderate cases of identity-based discrimination, to dangerous mobilization following major upheaval. Successful strategies of prevention need to be based on an understanding of the causes of mass atrocities.

However, whereas earlier approaches to prevention identified strategies that advocated external actors as primary agents, the 2013 report's starting point was very different. Instead of proposing new strategies, it drew on insights of various domestic contexts that have effectively managed risk in the past. In doing so, the report asked the question why atrocity crimes do not occur in the face of risk, and looked at the role of domestic actors as a key source of insight. To answer this question, the report compiled a series of lessons learned from a variety of domestic contexts, to contribute to their list of "national sources of resilience." These include constitutional protections, democracy, state obligations to criminalize violence associated with atrocity crimes, transitional justice mechanisms (where needed), security sector reform, and measures that address real or perceived inequalities (Ban 2013). The report explored examples from a diverse range of countries, which illustrated how such strategies and processes can provide a protective effect on mass atrocity risk. The examples show how particular such processes are to specific national and local contexts, providing a glimpse of the importance of local and national actors in developing their own strategies in efforts to build national resilience.

This risk/resilience framework marked the first time that a UN report on prevention explored in detail the ways that local and national agents have an impact on prevention. While the primacy of domestic actors has always been emphasized in documents on prevention (largely in relation to conflict more generally), the precise role that domestic actors play had been largely unknown. In presenting these national sources of resilience, the report built a repertoire of domestic action based on strategies and policies that have had some impact on the risk of mass atrocities.

By presenting a framework for prevention which considers the impact of domestically driven prohibitive factors in relation to mass atrocity risk, the 2013 report corresponds well with some of the scholarly key findings about genocide and mass violence. The report points out that "[s]ocieties can exhibit multiple sources of risk but not experience atrocity crimes" (Ban 2013, 4). Likewise, there is broad agreement within the genocide scholarship that the existence of risk factors do not signal an inevitable path to outcomes of mass violence (see, for example, Harff 2003; Straus 2012; McLoughlin and Mayersen 2013). Indeed, when it comes to long-term – or structural – risk factors, the causal link becomes even more tenuous. While such risk factors may make societies more conducive to the future occurrence of genocide or other mass atrocities, they are not sufficient to lead to such violence. In general, the perpetration of mass atrocities is rare, even in the presence of risk, a point which can be gleaned from comparing the prevalence of risk to the number of violent outcomes. Genocide Watch, for example, compiled a list of countries that experienced varying levels of risk between 1945 and 2008 (Stanton 2016). For every country that reached the highest stage of risk (persecution), only one-third went on to perpetrate violent extermination. At lower levels of risk, the proportion of countries that experience a progression to genocide diminishes considerably (Stanton 2016). It is logical, therefore, that approaching prevention needs to be premised on this more nuanced understanding of risk.

Yet despite this clear consensus, the question of why risk (more often than not) *does not* lead to mass atrocities is largely overlooked in the field of comparative genocide studies. Research into the causes of genocide and other mass atrocities generally focus on why things go wrong. The general pattern has been to select past cases of mass violence in order to establish common preconditions and causal factors, which then form the basis of theoretical claims about such violence. The question of what other outcomes are possible when such preconditions exist in places where genocide and other atrocities do not materialize tends to be neglected. Consequently, we know a lot about why mass atrocities occur, but much less about how and why such violence is avoided in the face of risk. In relation to Genocide

Watch's database, we have a limited understanding of why it is that the majority of countries that have appeared on it have not reached the stage of extermination.

Interest in negative cases in comparative genocide studies

In recent years, researchers have devoted more attention to the question of why genocide and mass atrocities do not occur despite the presence of risk. This research provides insights into the variety of ways that various domestic actors manage risk and prevent atrocities. While prevention may not always be the immediate goal, prevention is often one of the positive consequences.

The work of Scott Straus has been pivotal in understanding why it is that states and territories that display extremely high risk manage to "pull back from the brink," while others perpetrate mass violence. He found that the most effective prohibitive factor against genocide was the forging of a "political vision that incorporates a role for multiple identities," which he regarded "as fundamental to the project of the state" (Straus 2015, 323). This goes beyond banning specific identities, as had been done in Rwanda post-1994. Rather it involves a national vision which recognizes and incorporates the diversity of identities that exist within a given territory (Straus 2015, 322). Exemplifying this were the inaugural leaders of Senegal and Mali, Leopold Senghor and Alpha Oumar Konaré. Senghor achieved three key outcomes in the first two decades of Senegal's independence. First, at a time when many other African states were retreating from democracy, he moved the country from a one-party system to a multi-party democracy, which was fully functioning by the mid-1970s. Second, he promoted a vision of inclusiveness as being a central part of Senegal's nascent identity as an independent state. Third, he built and fostered coalitions that helped his inclusive vision to materialize. This foundation of valuing and fostering plurality has had a protective effect on the Senegalese government's response to an internal rebellion in Casamance, in the south of the country.

Although not Mali's inaugural leader, Konaré forged similar values in the country, coming to power as he did at a time when Mali was transitioning away from authoritarian rule, and was enduring a rebellion in the north. His decade as president (1992–2002) was characterized by the use of dialogue and negotiation in order to bring an end to the conflict, which facilitated a negotiated settlement. He also made efforts to bring formerly marginalized groups into the policymaking process (Straus 2015, 189). This preference for dialogue, consensus, and inclusiveness helped to de-escalate the military crisis in the country's north in the mid-1990s, an outcome that Straus argues was not necessarily inevitable. Even when conflict flared up again in 2011, President Ahmed Sékou Touré continued to use dialogue and negotiation, which resulted in heavy constraints on the use of violence against both Tuareg and Arab members of the population, which ran contrary to the growing negative public sentiment against them (Straus 2015, 204).

Similarly, Deborah Mayersen (2014) argues that various strategies by vulnerable populations have been used. She explores two historical cases – the situation of the

Yemenite Jews in the first half of the twentieth century, and Iran's Bahá'í community since the 1979 revolution – where genocide was on the verge of happening, but was prevented. She found that both domestic and international actors assisted these populations to be empowered in the face of the high risk of genocide. During the 1930s in Germany and Austria, emigration was a strategy deployed effectively by the Jewish population in order to escape persecution and extermination. When the Second World War began in 1939, less than 40 percent of the original population remained in Germany. Similar levels of emigration occurred in Austria, where 110,000 of the country's 192,000 Jews had left by 1939, meaning that fleeing persecution was indeed an effective tool for genocide prevention for many people. A similar strategy was deployed by Yemenite Jews between 1900 and 1950. While persecution of this particular population was not as severe as in Central Europe, Jewish communities in the country – particularly in remote areas – experienced discrimination and persecution. In this case, the establishment of the state of Israel enabled nearly 50,000 Jews to be airlifted to the new state, with only a few thousand remaining. Following the 1979 Iranian revolution, many members of the Bahá'í religious community were the targets of a specific campaign by the new regime, involving arrests, abductions, and executions, which heightened the risk of genocide. In response, many Bahá'ís from around the world initiated a global campaign to highlight awareness of this treatment, which spurred the UN, numerous governments, and a range of other international organizations to release statements, pass resolutions, and apply pressure on the Iranian government to uphold human rights principles. While the discrimination against Bahá'ís in Iran has not abated, the campaign was regarded as being instrumental in placing limits on the regime's actions to the extent that "would seem to have restrained the large-scale massacres that earlier appeared imminent" (Kuper 1992, 139).

Historian Manus Midlarsky (2014, 454) has also explored a range of cases where genocide was expected to occur, but did not. Among these include the Greeks in the Ottoman Empire, particularly during the First World War; Irish Catholics in British-occupied Ireland following the First World War; and Jews in Poland during the Partitions in the late 1700s. These negative cases are linked by the "affinity variable" – the existence of "like-minded or ethnoreligiously similar populations" who would be influential enough to deter the genocidal motivations of potential perpetrators. For example, during the time of the Ottoman Empire, the Greek population was not targeted for extermination in the way that the Armenian population was, despite the fact that both groups had been active in becoming politically organized in the years preceding the war. Midlarsky argues that in some parts of the Empire – especially given their settlement in many coastal areas around the Black, Mediterranean, and Aegean seas – the Greeks were arguably a greater threat than the Armenian population. However, the Greek community, unlike the Armenians, had a large affine population nearby. As the Ottoman Empire suffered territorial losses in the nineteenth century, the newly independent state of Greece emerged. It grew in power as further Ottoman lands around its growing borders broke away. The consequences, therefore, of targeting the Ottoman Greeks invited the possibility of provoking another opponent into action. This, argues Midlarsky, pressured the Ottomans into restraint. The Greeks did not completely escape violence – indeed, there were massacres by the Turks along the Black Sea coast and in Smyrna (Izmir), but they were considerably less widespread.

While most of these investigations involved cases at the high-end of the risk spectrum, my work has investigated cases involving moderate risk, in order to understand how structural preconditions such as discrimination, human rights violations, and horizontal inequality can be managed over the long term. The importance of this approach is that few, if any, cases of mass atrocities have occurred in the absence of such long-term structural risk factors. While most scholars overlook cases of prevention that do not involve heightened states of risk, it is important to better understand how it is that countries with such structural challenges manage risk over the long term, and are able to avoid the kind of upheaval that spurs dangerous risk escalation. Most of my research has concentrated on post-colonial African states, where statebuilding unfolded within pre-determined borders that contained diverse groups, languages, and cultures. Much of the insights I identify – especially in relation to Botswana, Tanzania, and Zambia – are context-specific, and thus cannot be taken as models to be applied uniformly across other polities. Nevertheless, some key commonalities exist. First, the manner in which independence was forged appears to be important. In the three aforementioned states, liberation movements were largely non-violent, and were led by individuals who and organizations that promoted inclusive national identities. Second, in all three countries, this relatively peaceful and amicable path to independence was then followed through with policies that embodied this inclusiveness, particularly by prioritizing all-encompassing policies and services (McLoughlin 2014b, 159). While the ambition of the equitable service provision often surpassed the resources available to governments (particularly in Zambia and Tanzania), the commitment to this ideal ensured that no one single group profited disproportionately from the spoils of governance.

The architects of this inclusivity were the three countries' inaugural leaders – Seretse Khama of Botswana, Kenneth Kaunda of Zambia, and Julius Nyerere of Tanzania. They were responsible for forging and fostering inclusive national identities, which were largely successful in transcending ethnic and religious differences. In Zambia, Kaunda promoted the idea of "humanism" (Burdette 1988, 77; Hall 1969, 48–50), while in Tanzania Nyerere (1968, 12) promoted *Ujamaa* (see also Svendsen 1970, 79). Khama of Botswana put the principle of harmony and non-racialism at the heart of his vision of the country. In practical terms, these visions determined behavior and motivated strategies in varying ways. In Tanzania, for example, the country's roughly equal numbers of Christians and Muslims underpinned the leadership structure of the governing party Tanganyika African National Union (TANU),[1] the composition of the party matched this demographic breakdown, and since independence in 1962, the leaders of the governing party have alternated between Muslim and Christian (see Rasmussen 1993, 23–24). In Zambia in the 1960s, Kaunda was alarmed about the growing factional divisions within the governing United National Independence Party, and correspondingly reshuffled ministerial portfolios on a regular basis to mitigate against the possibility of any single identity group gaining dominance at an institutional level (see Burdette 1988, 71–72; Molteno 1974, 69; Posner 2005). Although these examples occurred far upstream from the possibility of mass violence, they are instructive for the long-term stability of states, especially relatively new states that face high identity-based challenges.

This research offers a glimpse of a diverse range of processes – largely initiated by domestic actors – which have had some success in mitigating risk, from moderate to extreme risk scenarios. Even when atrocities are unfolding, there are ways to place limits on the number of people who are targeted, both by facilitating emigration, and through the presence of affine populations. In cases where such atrocities appeared imminent, countries like Mali and Senegal provide insights into the way that political leaders have worked to place limits on violent conflict to ensure civilians were not deliberately targeted. These strategies were in part motivated by inclusive ideologies that censured the vilifying of minority groups, and that fostered broad and equitable visions of statehood. Leaders advocating inclusive ideologies had a positive impact on scenarios of moderate risk, which enabled countries like Zambia, Tanzania, and Botswana to avoid entrenched and institutionalized forms of inequality and discrimination. While such observations have hitherto arisen from a small number of cases, it is clear that this growing interest in negative cases offers a broad set of insights into processes of risk mitigation, initiated mostly by domestic actors, in a variety of situations across the risk spectrum.

How does this provide more clarity in policy terms? It shifts the emphasis on preventive strategies away from the need for international actors to come up with solutions to a perceived problem, and challenges them to better understand local and national sources of resilience that already build resilience in the face of risk. Such sources of resilience are policies, processes, and strategies that have already been implemented, and which have had some positive effect in managing risk associated with mass atrocities. The question of implementation and R2P must put this at the center of its concerns. Implementation is not reserved just for cases of weakened or failed responsibility, but must be at the heart of how responsible sovereignty can slowly diminish the need for international action.

Pillar One and implementation

In the last decade, the growing interest in the role that domestic actors play in mitigating risk associated with mass atrocities has yielded some developments in policy documents. As discussed earlier, key among these is Ban's 2013 report. Beyond the UN, other policy-oriented reports are also linking insights about national resilience to policy options for prevention. Chief among these are those published by The Stanley Foundation, which initially flagged the need to better understand resilience in a 2011 report on atrocity prevention (Bellamy 2011). This was followed by two reports that developed the idea of building state capacity and resilience for the prevention of mass atrocity crimes (Simon 2012; Bellamy 2016b), not only emphasizing the importance of local and national actors, but also pointing out that long-term prevention is primarily and overwhelmingly carried out by local and national actors.

How do these developments contribute to the implementation of R2P? As pointed out in the introduction, the Secretary-General sees the building of national resilience for prevention as a key component of Pillar One implementation. The question is: how does this translate into a shift "from the conceptual to the practical" (Ban 2015, 6)? In one sense, it is an easy question to answer – insights about strengthening national resilience are based on actions, strategies, and policies that are *already* in existence, and that have had some demonstrable positive impact in relation to the mitigation of mass atrocity risk. These existing insights have the potential to drive further action, and this is where the idea of resilience can contribute to the implementation of R2P. There are four ways this can happen.

The first is to continue to develop awareness of existing practice; that is, to examine cases where risk associated with mass atrocities has been or is being mitigated due to national sources of resilience. The policy interest in resilience has arisen from a desire to understand what domestic actors are already doing to prevent mass atrocities over the long term. Given that our understanding of why atrocities do not occur – and how domestic actors mitigate risk – is relatively nascent, there is a need to build on our understanding of domestically driven processes of risk mitigation. This forms the bedrock of the principle of R2P, which is premised on the notion that responsibility for protection against atrocity crimes rests first and foremost with the state. However, while much is known about when and why this responsibility manifestly fails, much less is known about what responsible sovereignty looks like in practice, particularly in countries that contain risk associated with mass atrocities. Thus, one way of moving "from the conceptual to the practical" is to understand and identify effective practice in relation to risk mitigation.

The second is to utilize these insights by developing an atrocity-prevention lens. According to Alex Bellamy, an atrocity-prevention lens is "an approach that focuses on injecting atrocity-prevention considerations into existing policies, programs, and capabilities, and, when necessary, 'convening' or 'coordinating' these assets for prevention purposes" (Bellamy 2016a, 69), While Bellamy considers something comparable to the kind of authority given to the UN's Genocide Prevention and R2P offices, there is no reason why the idea of an atrocity-prevention lens could not be utilized more widely by a broader range of actors. In relation to Pillar One, the "analytical capability" of an atrocity-prevention lens operates in two main ways (Bellamy 2016a, 69). First, it can be utilized as a means of understanding how various policies, strategies, and processes may have the potential to exacerbate mass atrocity risk. Second, it provides a means of highlighting how certain domestic processes strengthen resilience in the face of such risk. To these ends, governments, community leaders, and civil society organizations could all benefit from adopting such a lens. For example, part of the Ghanaian National Peace Council's mandate includes working closely with government in order to support peacebuilding initiatives. The Council has a "peace-building support unit" which operates within the Ministry of the Interior, overseeing a range of internal security matters and providing feedback both to the Council as well as the Ministry itself (Awinador-Kanyirige 2014, 2–3), and thus implementing an atrocity-prevention lens.

The third is to use both domestic and international fora to disseminate such knowledge about how various sources of resilience have effectively mitigated risk in a variety of contexts. There are numerous examples of domestically driven processes of risk mitigation, and knowledge of such processes has the potential to provide insights for other states and communities facing comparable challenges. While risk in every country is context-specific, and requires its own particular responses, knowledge about what has worked in other places could provide local and national opportunities to adopt and tailor similar practices. This is beginning to happen at a regional and international level. The R2P Focal Points initiative is an example of how such dissemination could work. There are currently fifty-nine national Focal Points, whose objective involves working nationally and internationally to "prevent and halt mass atrocities" (Global Centre for the Responsibility to Protect 2016). According to Ban (2015, 9), one of the network's strengths is to "enable a richer sharing of lessons learned between regions." The more frequently that lessons about risk and resilience are shared among other interested actors and stakeholders, the more likely such insights will be translated into further preventive strategies.

The fourth involves influencing and changing domestic practice, based on a more thorough understanding of "what works" in terms of comparable challenges in other contexts. However, this is difficult to identify in general terms. Because resilience refers to a diverse range of processes initiated by a variety of different actors, often depending on unique circumstances, the question of how resilience influences domestic practice is far from straightforward. The extent to which this has started to occur is unclear, as it is only recently that scholars have begun to draw links between certain domestic processes and resilience against mass atrocities. Such processes are, for the most part, implemented for other purposes, with resilience against mass atrocities arising as a positive effect. Moreover, processes that strengthened resilience in one time period may not be adequate for unfolding challenges in another.

Conclusion

As the principle of R2P moves "from the conceptual to the practical," the key challenge at the Pillar One level is how domestic actors can become more robust agents of prevention. Ban's 2013 report on Pillar One emphasized the fact that no country is entirely immune to risk, which means that the challenge of effective risk mitigation and long-term prevention is universal. While effective prevention ultimately leads to a diminishing number of cases where the perpetration of mass atrocities is imminent or underway, one of the problems with implementing effective policies of prevention has been the tendency to measure success through the absence of violence. In policy terms, this is only helpful in those cases when mass atrocities are on the verge of being committed, and where the causal connection with a violent outcome is very strong. However, this holds less sway in situations where such violence is not about to break out. This means that there is a need to measure effective strategies of prevention not simply by the absence of violence, but through the existence of processes that effectively mitigate risk over the long term. The idea of strengthening state resilience offers a means to do this – putting the focus not only on the role of domestic actors, but also challenging the idea that successful prevention is simply the unfolding of a non-event. This is important for the question of R2P and implementation because it provides a better understanding of what types of action contribute to lower levels of risk.

Nevertheless, recent convergence of policy and scholarly interest in understanding how atrocities are avoided provide some clear possibilities for R2P and implementation in three key ways.

First, research into negative cases provides greater clarity to our understanding of which roles local and national actors can play when faced with challenges associated with mass atrocity risk. This research has highlighted that when atrocities do not unfold in an environment containing risk, then a range of meaningful strategies, policies, and actions are being adopted by a variety of actors, depending on context and resources at hand.

Second, this improved understanding of how local and national actors effectively mitigate risk has challenged earlier articulations of structural prevention, which had put the focus on the role of international actors while overlooking the key role that domestic actors play. While reports on both conflict and atrocity prevention typically acknowledge the central responsibility that domestic actors carry, there had been little exploration of how this responsibility actually occurred in practice. Now, with greater insights into these domestically driven processes of risk mitigation, more detailed articulations of these processes are arising in reports on prevention. The UN's 2013 report on Pillar One, with its risk/resilience framework, exemplifies this.

Third and finally, with policy articulations of resilience and the dissemination of this knowledge comes greater possibilities for other domestic actors to learn from and tailor such insights to their own circumstances. Initiatives such as the R2P national Focal Points provide platforms for different states to share their own experiences, and to learn from the insights of others. In this way, the idea of resilience can contribute to the implementation of R2P. Yet our understanding of risk mitigation and negative cases in the scholarship is patchy at best – we have only just started to understand the myriad ways that domestic actors have contributed to the avoidance of mass atrocities across different contexts and levels of risk. More research is needed to further develop not only our knowledge of negative cases, but also the extent to which this knowledge is influencing ongoing strategies of structural prevention.

Note

1 TANU changed its name to Chama Cha Mapinduzi in 1977.

References

Annan, Kofi, 2001. "Prevention of Armed Conflict: Report of the Secretary-General," A/55/985, June 7.
Annan, Kofi, 2003. "Interim Report of the Secretary-General on the Prevention of Armed Conflict," A/58/365–S/2003/888, September 12.

Annan, Kofi, 2006. "Progress Report on the Prevention of Armed Conflict: Report of the Secretary-General," A/60/891, July 18.

Awinador-Kanyirige, William A., 2014. "Ghana's National Peace Council," Policy Brief (New York: Global Centre for the Responsibility to Protect).

Ban Ki-moon, 2009. "Implementing the Responsibility to Protect: Report of the Secretary-General," A/63/677, January 12.

Ban Ki-moon, 2013. "The Responsibility to Protect: State Responsibility and Prevention: Report of the Secretary-General," A/67/929–S/2013/399, July 9.

Ban Ki-moon, 2015. "A Vital and Enduring Commitment: Implementing the Responsibility to Protect: Report of the Secretary-General," A/69/981–S/2015/500, July 13.

Bellamy, Alex J., 2011. "Mass Atrocities and Armed Conflict: Links, Distinctions and Implications for the Responsibility to Prevent," Policy Analysis Brief (Muscatine, IA: The Stanley Foundation).

Bellamy, Alex J., 2016a. "Operationalizing the 'Atrocity Prevention Lens': Making Prevention a Living Reality," in Sheri P. Rosenberg, Tibi Galis, and Alex Zucker, eds, *Reconstructing Atrocity Prevention* (Cambridge: Cambridge University Press), 61–80.

Bellamy, Alex J., 2016b. "Reducing Risk, Strengthening Resilience: Toward the Structural Prevention of Atrocity Crimes," Policy Analysis Brief (Muscatine, IA: The Stanley Foundation).

Boutros-Ghali, Boutros, 1992. "An Agenda for Peace: Preventive Diplomacy, Peacemaking and Peace-Keeping: Report of the Secretary-General," A/47/277, June 17.

Boutros-Ghali, Boutros, 1995. "Supplement to An Agenda for Peace: Position Paper of the Secretary-General on the Occasion of the Fiftieth Anniversary of the United Nations," A/50/60–S/1995/1, January 25.

Burdette, Marcia M., 1988. *Zambia: Between Two Worlds* (Boulder, CO: Westview Press).

Draman, Rasheed, 2003. "Conflict Prevention in Africa: Establishing Conditions and Institutions Conducive to Durable Peace," in David Carment and Albrecht Schnabel, eds, *Conflict Prevention: Path to Peace or Grand Illusion?* (Tokyo: United Nations University Press), 233–53.

Global Centre for the Responsibility to Protect, 2016. "Global Network of R2P Focal Points," www.globalr2p.org/our_work/global_network_of_r2p_focal_points.

Hall, Richard, 1969. *The High Price of Principles: Kaunda and the White South* (Harmondsworth: Penguin).

Hamburg, David, and Cyrus R. Vance, 1997. *Preventing Deadly Conflict: Final Report* (Washington, DC: Carnegie Commission on Preventing Deadly Conflict).

Hampson, Fen Osler, Karin Wermester, and David M. Malone, 2002. "Introduction: Making Conflict Prevention a Priority," in Fen Osler Hampson and David M. Malone, eds, *From Reaction to Conflict Prevention: Opportunities for the UN System* (Boulder, CO: Lynne Rienner), 1–11.

Harff, Barbara, 2003. "No Lessons Learned from the Holocaust? Assessing Risks of Genocide and Political Mass Murder Since 1955," *American Political Science Review* 97, no. 1: 57–73.

ICISS (International Commission on Intervention and State Sovereignty), 2001. *The Responsibility to Protect: Report of the International Commission on Intervention and State Sovereignty* (Ottawa: International Development Research Centre).

Kuper, Leo, 1992. "Reflections on the Prevention of Genocide," in Helen Fein, ed., *Genocide Watch* (New Haven, CT: Yale University Press), 135–61.

Luck, Edward C., 2006. *UN Security Council: Practice and Promise* (New York: Routledge).

Mayersen, Deborah, 2014. "Rethinking Approaches to Prevention Under the Responsibility to Protect: Agency and Empowerment within Vulnerable Populations," *Global Responsibility to Protect* 6, no. 4: 483–507.

McLoughlin, Stephen, 2014a. "Rethinking the Structural Prevention of Mass Atrocities," *Global Responsibility to Protect* 6, no. 4: 407–29.

McLoughlin, Stephen, 2014b. *The Structural Prevention of Mass Atrocities: Understanding Risk and Resilience* (London: Routledge).

McLoughlin, Stephen, and Deborah Mayersen, 2013. "Reconsidering Root Causes: A New Framework for the Structural Prevention of Genocide and Mass Atrocities," in Bert Ingelaere, Stephan Parmentier, Jacques Haers, and Barbara Segaert, eds, *Genocide, Risk and Resilience: An Interdisciplinary Approach* (Basingstoke: Palgrave Macmillan), 49–67.

Menkhaus, Ken, 2004. "Conflict Prevention and Human Security: Issues and Challenges," *Conflict, Security and Development* 4, no. 3: 419–63.

Midlarsky, Manus I., 2014. "International Affinity and the Prevention of Genocide: Implications for R2P," *Global Responsibility to Protect* 6, no. 4: 453–82.

Molteno, Robert, 1974. "Cleavage and Conflict in Zambian Politics: A Study of Sectionalism," in William Tordoff, ed., *Politics in Zambia* (Manchester: Manchester University Press), 62–106.

Nyerere, Julius K., 1968. *Ujamaa: Essays on Socialism* (Dar es Salaam: Oxford University Press).

Posner, Daniel N., 2005. *Institutions and Ethnic Politics in Africa* (Cambridge: Cambridge University Press), 56–69.

Rasmussen, Lissi, 1993. *Christian–Muslim Relations in Africa: The Cases of Northern Nigeria and Tanzania Compared* (London: British Academy Press).

Rothchild, Donald, 2003. "Third-Party Incentives and the Phases of Conflict Prevention," in Chandra Lekha Sriram and Karin Wermester, eds, *From Promise to Practice: Strengthening UN Capacities for the Prevention of Violent Conflict* (Boulder, CO: Lynne Rienner), 35–66.

Simon, David J., 2012. "Building State Capacity to Prevent Atrocity Crimes: Implementing Pillars One and Two of the R2P Framework," Policy Analysis Brief (Muscatine, IA: The Stanley Foundation).

Stanton, Gregory H., 1996. "The 8 Stages of Genocide," www.genocidewatch.org/genocide/8stagesofgenocide.html.

Stanton, Gregory H., 2016. "Genocides, Politicides, and Other Mass Murder Since 1945, with Stages in 2008," *Genocide Prevention Advisory Network*, www.gpanet.org/content/genocides-politicides-and-other-mass-murder-1945-stages-2008.

Straus, Scott, 2012. "Retreating from the Brink: Theorizing Mass Violence and the Dynamics of Restraint," *Perspectives on Politics* 10, no. 2: 343–62.

Straus, Scott, 2015. *Making and Unmaking Nations: War, Leadership, and Genocide in Modern Africa* (Ithaca, NY: Cornell University Press).

Svendsen, Knud Erik, 1970. "The Present Stage of Economic Planning in Tanzania," in Anthony H. Rweyemamu, ed., *Nation-Building in Tanzania: Problems and Issues* (Nairobi: East African Publishing House), 79–89.

United Nations, 1945. "Charter of the United Nations," www.un.org/en/charter-united-nations/.

United Nations, 1999. "Report of the Independent Inquiry into the Actions of the United Nations During the 1994 Genocide in Rwanda," S/1999/1257, December 19.

United Nations General Assembly, 2005. "2005 World Summit Outcome," A/RES/60/1, October 24.

United Nations Security Council, 2004. "Letter Dated 12 July 2004 from the Secretary-General Addressed to the President of the Security Council," S/2004/567, July 13.

White House, 2012. "Fact Sheet: A Comprehensive Strategy and New Tools to Prevent and Respond to Atrocities," April 23, https://obamawhitehouse.archives.gov/the-press-office/2012/04/23/fact-sheet-comprehensive-strategy-and-new-tools-prevent-and-respond-atro.

8
ATROCITY PREVENTION IN PRACTICE
Studying the role of Southeast Asian women in atrocity prevention

Sara E. Davies

Introduction

The prevention of atrocities is the primary goal of the Responsibility to Protect (R2P) principle. It is also widely recognized that R2P is best implemented in ways that build upon existing sources of national resilience and empower populations at risk. R2P has particular significance in highlighting situations where there are populations at risk owing to practices of discrimination. Acts of sexual and gender-based violence in conflict and non-conflict situations that are widespread and systematic are war crimes, crimes against humanity, and acts of genocide, according to the 1998 Rome Statue; and threats to international peace and security, as first articulated in United Nations (UN) Security Council Resolution 1325 (2000) and reaffirmed in Resolution 1820 (2008). The targeting of individuals for gender-based violence is attributable to the context-specific forms of gender discrimination and gender inequality in politically unstable and conflict situations (Davies and True 2015).

To promote a gendered approach to R2P that addresses these sources of risk, prevention work must focus on the elimination of discrimination, interrupting the continuum of violence against women, and the strengthening of women's participation in the sectors necessary to deliver sustainable peace and conflict prevention. To date, atrocity prevention has focused on the UN organization and state-level institutions responsible for prevention work. However, regional organizations also play a necessary and important role in R2P prevention work. This chapter examines the contribution made by feminist scholars and activists within the Southeast Asian region who have been concerned with gender inequality and gender discrimination with a view to enhancing the participation of women in protection roles, and also in preventing gender-based violence in conflict.

The chapter proceeds in three parts. First, it explores the relationship between R2P and the Women, Peace and Security (WPS) agenda. Here, I identify how the prevention of atrocities has become a shared focus between the two agendas leading to some consensus on areas for mutually supportive engagement. Second, I demonstrate how this engagement has taken place in the Southeast Asian region, specifically looking at how women's human rights advocates within the Association of Southeast Asian Nations (ASEAN) region have promoted alignment between the R2P principle and the WPS agenda. Third, the chapter provides some suggestions for future areas of engagement and activism.

Policy and research alignment between R2P and WPS

R2P contains three pillars:

1 All states have a responsibility to protect their populations from genocide, war crimes, crimes against humanity, and ethnic cleansing, including prevention of these crimes and their incitement.
2 The international community, including neighboring states and regional organizations, has a responsibility to encourage and assist the state with meeting its protection obligations.
3 The international community has a responsibility to use diplomatic, humanitarian, and other peaceful measures to protect populations and to take timely and decisive action in accordance with the UN Charter if a state is manifestly failing to protect its population from these four crimes.

Since the adoption of the 2005 World Summit, there has been a significant proliferation of research and debate about how R2P should be implemented. Timely and decisive response – Pillar Three of R2P – is still primarily associated with the principle (Ralph 2018, 195). However, "pragmatic approaches" have also evolved to discuss the responsibility to prevent mass atrocities in the first place (Ralph 2018, 196). This has led to UN Secretary-General reports on the realization of Pillar One and Pillar Two: the responsibility of regional organizations, state-level institutions, and UN agencies (Ban 2011, 2013, 2014), to prioritize the prevention of atrocity crimes. These reports all note that Pillar Three responses come inevitably too late, and in such environments, the protection of populations can be immensely difficult. The 2017 report goes so far as to suggest the need to turn away from the UN Security Council as the principal agency capable of advocating the R2P principle and develop a broader approach that entails the whole gamut of thematic agendas and human rights instruments available to support prevention (Guterres 2017). Prevention creates the best conditions for stability and prosperity, which enable populations to be protected effectively and inclusively. Since the first UN Secretary-General's report on R2P in 2009 (Ban 2009), there has been a deliberate shift toward acknowledgment that patterns of human rights violations and gender discrimination constitute upstream atrocity risks. Both UN Secretaries-General Ban Ki-moon (2007–2016) and António Guterres (Jan 2017 to present) have called for institutional reform, including at the state level, to protect vulnerable populations from human rights violations that could give rise to future atrocity crimes.

On the specific topic of gender inequality and its relationship to the commission of R2P crimes, successive reports of the UN Secretary-General have noted that the prevention of mass atrocity crimes requires engagement with the conditions that perpetuate gender inequality and gender discrimination, and that the violation of women's human rights creates disproportionate vulnerability to atrocity crimes – specifically those that constitute sexual and gender-based violence. These insights prompted advocacy and research on how to engage with and promote the prevention, protection, and participation framework outlined by the United Nations WPS agenda and the R2P principle (Bond and Sherret 2006; Davies and Teitt 2012). The WPS agenda was first introduced in 2000 under UN Security Council Resolution 1325. Since then, the UN Security Council has endorsed seven additional WPS resolutions: 1820 (2008), 1888 (2009), 1889 (2009), 1960 (2010), 2106 (2013), 2122 (2013), and 2422 (2015). Included among the provisions endorsed in these resolutions are the importance of women's leadership and political participation in peace and security institutions; the introduction of gender-specific measures to protect women during conflict and instability, including against sexual and gender-based violence; the need to address impunity for such sexual and gender-based violations; recognition of the vital role that women and civil society organizations play in conflict prevention and peacebuilding; and the need for more systematic plans of action at the national, regional, and international levels to advance gender equality and women's rights protection (*Security Council Report: Monthly Forecast* 2017).

Promoting greater awareness and inclusion of the WPS agenda in all R2P prevention and response activities has increasingly become a core focus for several R2P partners and institutions. In the region, aligning existing women's political inclusion and empowerment activities with atrocity prevention has been a core focus of the University of Queensland's Asia Pacific Centre for the Responsibility to Protect (APCR2P), which created one of the earliest teaching and research programs on the alignment of WPS and R2P. Today, it is common practice for the WPS agenda and R2P principle to be discussed as both aligned and mutually constitutive in country-level workshops conducted by the Centre across the Asia-Pacific. Moreover, the Centre began some of the earliest "Track 2" diplomatic and research discussions on the R2P prevention pillar, which saw the region turn quite early to aligning R2P with a prevention (rather than intervention) focus and aligning prevention activities with gender empowerment. The Centre convened a High-Level Advisory Panel on the Responsibility to Protect in Southeast Asia, whose report identified, as early as 2013, the need to advance a human protection mandate to assist states with realizing their responsibility to protect (High-Level Advisory Panel on the Responsibility to Protect in Southeast Asia 2014). This led to recommendations by the High-Level Panel for further engagement with those regional institutions responsible for human protection: the ASEAN Inter-Governmental Commission on Human Rights (AICHR), the ASEAN Commission on the Promotion and Protection of the Rights of Women and Children (ACWC), and the ASEAN Institute for Peace and Reconciliation (AIPR) (Asia Pacific Centre for the Responsibility to Protect 2017b, 2).

These early attempts to create linkages between two mutually distinct but complimentary agendas – R2P and WPS – were not without controversy, and there has always been a need to be respectful of fundamental differences in approach and emphasis between civil societies, as well as governments. However, this work has laid the foundation for the research being produced and encouraged within the R2P stream today, such as the European Centre for the Responsibility to Protect's creation of the Women Network on the Responsibility to Protect, Peace and Security (ECR2P n.d.), Global Action to Prevent War, the Women's International League for Peace and Freedom's Concept Note on Integrating Gender Perspectives into the Third Pillar of the Responsibility to Protect (GAPW, n.d.) and the growth of publications on the topic (Harris Rimmer 2014; Hewitt 2016; Murphy and Burke 2015; Trillò 2015; Gilgan 2017; Spitka 2017). It may even be said that through the volume of research produced, there has emerged a shared normative understanding of "prevention" between R2P and WPS (Bellamy and Davies 2019) that conceptualizes the prioritization of a preventive relationship to be directed at addressing the following:

1   *Sexual and gender-based violence can constitute acts of genocide, war crimes, ethnic cleansing, and crimes against humanity.* At their most basic, R2P and WPS share important goals in common, not least, the elimination of these crimes. As Secretary-General Guterres (2017, 9) noted:

> Accountability for the prevention of atrocity crimes can be strengthened by open reflection and inclusive dialogue on national experiences and the practical steps needed to strengthen atrocity prevention. The perspectives of women and youth should be included in risk assessments and the design of measures to close atrocity-prevention gaps.

2   *There is a strong explanatory relationship between endemic gender inequality and high rates of political violence and one-sided violence against civilians.* As Secretary-General Ban (2013, 5) observed:

> Gender discrimination and inequality increase underlying risks associated with sexual and gender-based violence, which can constitute genocide, war crimes and crimes against humanity.... Specific gender discrimination practices include the denial or inadequate protection of basic rights relating to physical security and the status of women, compulsory birth control and unequal access to services and property.

3   *Sexual and gendered violence may be among the first types of mass atrocity crimes committed against populations to achieve political ends.* These crimes can occur before, during, and after conflict, as Syria, Mali, Myanmar, Sri Lanka, and the recent Yazidi tragedy in Iraq demonstrate. There is a history – and cases exist today – of gendered crimes being used as tools of political violence to achieve exclusion and displacement (Davies and True 2015).

4   *R2P and WPS share a common focus on prevention and in the development of tools at the international, regional, national, and societal levels to empower women and prevent mass atrocities.* This means that there is opportunity to align the R2P principle and the WPS agenda on the targets and tools needed to prevent mass atrocity crimes, which demands action to address structural gender inequality and gender discrimination.

From these areas of strategic engagement, we may identify five elements where policy and research collaboration have been taking place between R2P and WPS. First, operational synergies have been created such as the UN Security Council's Informal Expert Group on Women, Peace and Security, which hears briefings and reports on country situations where there is the risk of atrocities or a history of atrocities. Such a mechanism lifts both WPS and R2P out of their silos to be understood holistically with reference to countries that require the attention of the Security Council (*Security Council Report: Monthly Forecast* 2017; Guterres 2017, 22).

Second, there has been recognition that widespread sexual and gender-based violence constitutes an atrocity crime and should therefore be core business for R2P. Successive Secretary-General reports on R2P since 2009 have referred to ending impunity for sexual and gender-based violence and the responsibility of states, international organizations, and regional organizations in supporting the documentation and prevention of these crimes. Identifying regional organizations as being important interlocutors between domestic constituencies and international organizations in the translation and promotion of a shared WPS and R2P agenda was a particularly significant expansion of the locations to have discussions about gender inclusion in the prevention of violence and atrocities.

Third, there has been more visibility of R2P advocates championing gender responsiveness and engagement. The UN Secretary-General's second special advisor on R2P (2014–2016), Jennifer Welsh, incorporated gender discrimination and gender rights abuses indicators into the work of the UN Office on Genocide Prevention and R2P, particularly in relation to country-specific recommendations and statements on high-risk situations (see United Nations 2014).

Fourth, there has been greater discussion about the need for states to ratify international human rights instruments into domestic legislation; in particular, for states to become parties to the Rome Statute of the International Criminal Court, to fully implement the Convention on the Elimination of All Forms of Discrimination Against Women (CEDAW) and its Optional Protocol into domestic legislation, and to commit to refugee protection norms under the 1951 Convention Relating to the Status of Refugees (Guterres 2017, 15).

Fifth, greater attention has been paid to identifying women bureaucrats, women civil society organizations, and women parliamentarians as agents of protection and change. The European Centre for the Responsibility to Protect's Women Network on the Responsibility to Protect is a recent example that illustrates that the R2P agenda is no longer gender blind (Bond and Sherret 2006). However, having a shared focus – prevention and attention to gender empowerment – still requires the negotiation of a shared agenda among a diverse membership. The steps taken within the ASEAN context to build a network and agree to a shared agenda is next examined in the chapter.

ASEAN as a champion of R2P and WPS engagement

As mentioned earlier, practical prevention measures at the state level have been identified to support the mutual prevention goals of R2P and WPS. They include ratifying the international human rights treaties and protocols into domestic legislation (specifically, but not exclusively, on matters of violence against women, gender, and race discrimination, sexual and reproductive rights, rights of children, and rights of refugees), treating the Human Rights Council Universal Periodic Review on human rights mechanisms as an opportunity to improve prevention and protection strategies, and prioritizing security and justice reform to promote both gender equality and end impunity for gender-based crimes (United Nations 2014).

At the regional level, there are additional opportunities to draw attention to high-level commitments made by states to end human rights violations, promote gender inclusion in peace and conflict processes, and end violence against women. Since the adoption of the ASEAN Charter in 2009, ASEAN's institutional capacity to support protection (if not always the political will to follow through) has expanded considerably. This is most obviously seen in the establishment of the ACWC (2010), a formal reporting mechanism which meets twice annually to promote, advocate, build capacity, and assist states with the development and implementation of policies that protect the rights of women and children. Since the creation of this body, member states have made the following commitments through ASEAN joint statements and declarations:

1   The Declaration on the Elimination of Violence Against Women in the ASEAN Region (2012), and the ASEAN Regional Plan of Action on the Elimination of Violence Against Women (2015); progressed by the ACWC and the AICHR.
2   Affirmation of the WPS agenda by ASEAN representatives at the annual UN WPS thematic session.
3   All ASEAN members signed the 2014 United Nations Declaration of Commitment to End Sexual Violence in Conflict; and the foreign ministers of Indonesia, the Philippines, and East Timor issued a joint ministerial statement declaring their role as Preventing Sexual Violence Initiative champions (Teitt 2014).
4   The issue of a Joint Statement on Promoting Women, Peace and Security in ASEAN (hereafter, Joint Statement) at the 31st ASEAN Summit in November 2017 (ASEAN 2017b).

These regional commitments have given momentum to regional activists who are seeking reform from within ASEAN members. However, discussion often turns to *how* to translate the statements and regional-level engagements to support local-level implementation of prevention. At the regional level, an ongoing concern is that despite the increasingly frequent use of empowerment language in discussing women's inclusion in peace and security processes, the risk remains that action and policies to support WPS implementation remains cut off from peace and security fora; and in turn, from explicit discussions about the prevention of mass atrocities. Within ASEAN, for example, all meetings and matters pertaining to women are discussed in the Socio-Cultural Community of the ASEAN tri-sector community arrangement. The Political-Security Community and the Economic Community will make reference to women's rights or women's economic empowerment, but the Blueprint (for action) and Plan of Action have (to date)[1] remained located within the Socio-Cultural Community (Davies, Nackers, and Teitt 2014).

Yet it would be wrong to presume that declarations and statements alone sum up the work of ASEAN WPS and R2P champions. In August 2014, I was convener (with APCR2P's deputy director, Sarah Teitt) of a workshop with nearly forty attendees – WPS and R2P "champions" – from ASEAN member states (Asia Pacific Centre for the Responsibility to Protect 2014a). Those in attendance represented a cross-section of civil society, researchers, bureaucrats, and human rights advocates. The workshop focused on the co-promotion of the principle of R2P and the WPS agenda. Individuals in attendance had identified themselves in their work capacity as R2P and/or WPS advocates. At the end of the workshop, participants took part in a survey and a shared report which suggested themes and approaches for future engagement. The discussion focused on three thematic areas: regional architecture, focused on advancing WPS through national and regional level institutions and mechanisms; capacity-building – the role of national human rights institutions and civil society networks; and the prioritization of WPS through local, state, and regional advocacy networks.

Why is it important to study one particular workshop that was held in 2014? Since this workshop, the APCR2P has continued to proactively engage in promoting and sharing capacity-building work between R2P and WPS advocates within the ASEAN region (Asia Pacific Centre for the Responsibility to Protect 2015, 2017a), first at the regional level and increasingly at the state level (Cambodia, Indonesia, the Philippines, and recently Myanmar). Giving attention to listening and sharing different understandings of WPS and R2P led to the development of a stakeholders' agenda that facilitated more formal collaboration between the APCR2P and the ACWC. This collaboration explored at a meeting in Brisbane in 2017 the linkages between atrocity prevention, gender empowerment, and the elimination of discrimination (ASEAN 2017a). After this meeting, there was agreement that this relationship should be an annual occurrence with attention devoted to particular themes that fall under the mandate of the ACWC. This path of cooperation is an important illustration of how WPS and R2P champions may pursue shared prevention emphases to promote and elevate agendas such as gender human rights protection, end impunity for atrocity crimes, and include women in peace and conflict processes within the region. The following sections draw on the experiences and discussions aired at that first meeting and explored in subsequent encounters, and provide a good sense of the diverse range of actions associated with work on advancing the nexus between the WPS and R2P agendas (Asia Pacific Centre for the Responsibility to Protect 2014b).

Theme 1: preventing violence against women through national and regional architecture

Advancing WPS at the state level: WPS National Action Plans

WPS National Action Plans (NAPs) provide governments with an opportunity to articulate priorities, coordinate policy, and evaluate the implementation of Resolution 1325 at the national level. WPS NAPs are not the only policy tool required to implement gender mainstreaming, but they are intended to elucidate the range of government agencies and other stakeholders that are responsible for promoting women's participation and gender equality, particularly in peace and security institutions (True 2016). Under-Secretary Maria Cleofe Gettie Sandoval, of the Philippines' Office of the Presidential Adviser on the Peace Process, shared lessons from the Philippines' experience in crafting and implementing their Resolution 1325 NAP.

As a first step, advocates for the Philippines NAP drew on international commitments made by the Philippines government (including CEDAW, the Beijing Platform for Action, and Resolutions 1325 and 1820) to call for national measures to implement policies aimed at gender equality and women's political inclusion. Three elements of domestic legislation and policy development formed the cornerstone of the Philippines WPS NAP:

1. Republic Act 9710 (known as the "Magna Carta of Women"), which is a comprehensive women's human rights law that includes provisions for increasing women's participation in the management of armed conflict.
2. The *Philippine Development Plan 2011–2016*, in which Chapter 9 affirms the Philippines' government's commitment to Resolutions 1325, 1820, 1888, and 1889, and expressly commits to the implementation of Resolution 1325, "which entails close collaboration with the CSOs [civil society organizations] to fully comply with the government's commitment to increase participation of women in peace processes and address sexual violence against women in armed conflict situations" (National Economic and Development Authority 2011, 297).
3. Executive Order No. 865, which created a National Steering Committee on Women, Peace and Security to implement Resolutions 1325 and 1820 and which is comprised of nine agencies: the Office of the Presidential Adviser on the Peace Process, the Philippine Commission on Women, National Defense, Social Welfare and Development, Justice, Interior and Local Government, Foreign Affairs, the National Commission on Indigenous Peoples, and the National Commission on Muslim Filipinos.

These three measures provided the mandate for designing the Philippines WPS NAP, which was adopted in March 2010 and included two main pillars: protection and prevention, and empowerment and participation. The enabling policy environment and the WPS NAP translated into WPS projects and activities in gender and development plans, budgets, and reporting mechanisms. These are geared at enhancing the capacity of government agencies and other actors to mainstream prevention and protection through gender-responsive and conflict-sensitive policies, programs, and support services for women and children in conflict situations. The overall aim is for women in conflict and post-conflict situations to be protected and empowered, and to play a decisive role in peace and security processes and mechanisms.

At the time, given the importance of the Bangsamoro peace process in the Mindanao civil conflict in the Philippine archipelago, Under-Secretary Sandoval indicated that the task ahead was to establish *institutional* posts for continuing implementation of the Philippines NAP with a priority placed on gender budgeting, to develop gender-sensitive development projects (through the Philippines government's program to extend development projects and increase livelihood and job opportunities in isolated and conflict-affected communities), to collect disaggregated data in conflict-affected areas (sex, age, and ethnicity) to establish baselines and set benchmarks, and to work with civil society to address violence in the context of armed conflict and to increase women's participation in peacebuilding in the Philippines.

In 2016, President Rodrigo Duterte came to office having made a number of sexist and misogynist comments about women. In his first year as president, the Philippines government found itself in a serious battle against Islamic rebels in Marawi City. When he announced his decree on martial law, the president said he would protect soldiers who raped women during this period. His comment in February 2018 was the suggestion that Philippines soldiers should shoot female rebels in the vagina (Ellis-Peterson 2018). These comments, which could be interpreted as an order by a president, amount to crimes of sexual and gender-based violence and crimes against humanity under the 1998 Rome Statue. At the same time, President Duterte has been leading a "war against drugs" campaign since taking office in 2016, which has led to widespread extra-judicial killings that are now under investigation by the International Criminal Court prosecutor Fatou Bensouda (BBC 2018).

Addressing gender inequity and reforming the state structures that permit formal and informal gender inequality practices is vital to the development of national and societal-level tools that empower women and address gender equity. The political context in which these four areas are to be progressed is a real obstacle since the election of Duterte. However, at the same time, the introduction of these measures and indicators such as sex-disaggregated data collection, and the support of civil society in its outreach programs, have been potentially vital prevention pillar responses under the WPS agenda and the R2P prevention agenda that have assisted with understanding the harm and enhancing the early-warning indicators of human rights violations since Duterte's election.

Advancing WPS within the region: ASEAN architecture

While Under-Secretary Sandoval offered insights into the progress required to further implement WPS at the national level, Yuyun Wahyuningrum (Senior Advisor on ASEAN and Human Rights at the Indonesian non-governmental organization Coalition for International Human Rights Advocacy) provided an analysis of opportunities to advance WPS within ASEAN institutions and mechanisms. "Yuyun reflected that with the achievement of peace amongst ASEAN member states, the Political-Security Community is well placed to be receptive to concerted advocacy to move WPS commitments forward" (Asia Pacific Centre for the Responsibility to Protect 2014b, 9). This ambition was realized with the adoption of the 2017 Joint Statement. It is still too early to judge the implications of this statement, but it is worth examining what Yuyun suggested could be achieved by attaching WPS to the Political-Security Community.[2] At the time, Yuyun pointed out that although the majority of ASEAN's engagement in women's matters was "siloed"/located within the Socio-Cultural Community, the institutions were not designed to maintain this silo. There is an existing link to the Political-Security Community in that both the AIPR and the AICHR are attached to the work of the Political-Security Community.

Yuyun argued that the most effective advocacy strategies leverage the mandate of various ASEAN institutions and mechanisms, in particular, through locating WPS champions among the membership of these bodies. Noting the experience of the Indonesia-based Human Rights Working Group in advocating for greater human rights protection in ASEAN, she offered three suggestions to help further advance WPS in ASEAN. First, the WPS agenda must be made more visible in all the ASEAN institutions by a continual mention of WPS in advocacy documents and submissions, and through establishing WPS dialogue partners within particular institutions mentioned earlier. Second, advocates should seek to lobby ambassadors with credentials to ASEAN to become champions, and encourage these representatives to highlight the importance of WPS at bilateral or multilateral meetings. The Indonesian Ministry of Foreign Affairs is known to be particularly well-disposed to raising WPS as a matter of political security in the ASEAN processes. Third, the drafting of ASEAN's new blueprint for 2025 provides an opportunity to ensure that WPS is visible in this important document (Asia Pacific Centre for the Responsibility to Protect 2014b).

The inclusion of WPS did not occur at the time of the blueprint's publication in 2015 (ASEAN 2015). Reference to women within the document was focused in the Socio-Cultural Community pillar; women's inclusion and participation was primarily discussed in the same way that other minority groups were referenced. Ending the silence around women's experience of conflict, their exclusion or marginalization from peace processes, and their risk of atrocities because of their gender, was not raised in this document. The continuation of stereotypical depictions of women in the peace and security sector as women in need of protection, and women discussed in the same context as children, the disabled, the elderly, and the displaced, were in the document. References such as these removes their agency and their right to participate, and promotes the idea that failure to participate is on account of gender, age, or disability rather than violence and access to financial resources and political power. The adoption of the 2017 Joint Statement has the potential to close this gap and promote an understanding of WPS that is broader than the protection mechanism. Furthermore, it has the potential for the region to seriously engage, through the ASEAN Political-Security Community, in the prevention of discriminatory harms that give rise to violence and conflict.

Theme 2: preventing violence against women through capacity-building

Discussions about preventing violence against women through capacity-building focused on noting the existing contribution of women's rights and gender equality institutions, and the role of civil society networks which are often on the front line in reporting violence against women when state structures do not yet accommodate such reporting.

National institutions like Komnas Perempuan (Indonesia's National Commission on Violence Against Women) have a vital role to play here. Komnas Perempuan was established in response to women's civil society organizations' demand for accountability for sexual violence experienced by Chinese women in mass riots in May 1998. Similar to the development of the Philippines WPS NAP, advocates for a national mechanism for women's human rights in Indonesia drew on international commitments and legal frameworks – namely, Indonesia's obligations under CEDAW and the Convention against Torture. Established by presidential decree, the key purpose of Komnas Perempuan has been to prevent and address violence against women, and to protect and enforce women's human rights. In addition to international agreements, the work of Komnas Perempuan is enabled by (and in turn strengthens) state policies for ensuring women's human rights, including the Law on the Elimination of Domestic Violence, policies at the national and provincial levels regarding holistic services for women victims of violence, the Law on Elimination of Human Trafficking Crimes, the policy for 30 percent quota for women in parliament, and the Law on Witness and Victim Protection. The commission serves as a resource center for women's rights and violence against women; as a negotiator and mediator between government, victims' communities, and women's rights organizations; as an initiator of gender-sensitive policy reform; and as a monitoring body and rapporteur on gender-based violence.

Desti Murdijana, vice chairperson of Komnas Perempuan, has stressed that women's human rights institutions attempt to fulfill both a preventive and capacity-building role in the following ways:

1   *Raising public awareness.* Working with the media promotes public participation in strategic campaigns, and connects local, national, and international advocacy to promote women's solidarity (i.e., movements for defenders of women's human rights).

2   *Supporting survivors.* This is achieved by strengthening national mechanisms for integrated services to victims, strengthening the Witness and Victims Protection Agency, supporting local mechanisms for recovery and survivor support, and providing letters of support for legal cases of violence against women.
3   *Advocating for legal reform.* It is helpful to provide recommendations for addressing violence against women to the Executive, support the women desk in parliament, and create curriculum and training modules for the judicial branch.
4   *Enhancing monitoring and reporting.* This can be achieved by strengthening fact-finding on violence against women, issuing annual reports on violence against women, presenting independent reports to international human rights mechanisms, and supporting community-based monitoring.
5   *Research and data.* The collection of data encourages strategic religious institutions to analyze how religious teachings can address the issues of violence against women and break the silence, benchmarks the prevalence of violence against women (Indonesia does not have statistics on violence against women), and provides an evidence base on "what works" to address violence against women.

However, Desti emphasized that the security sector remains resistant to gender-sensitive and gender-responsive reform within post-authoritarian Indonesia. She also noted that this was not particular only to Indonesia, but reflected a regional resistance to strengthen gender-reform mechanisms within security institutions. Regional mechanisms are an important area in which to promote normative discussions on these issues and could be tasked with "feeding" back experiences into national-level mechanisms in order to buttress nascent local normative developments and to provide additional layers of accountability (Asia Pacific Centre for the Responsibility to Protect 2014b).

In the context of countries with ongoing conflict and a government undergoing tremendous political and bureaucratic reform, attention to and prevention of violence against women often relies almost entirely on the reporting practices of women civil society networks. The Gender Equality Network (GEN) in Myanmar is an excellent case in point, which – among other things – has worked to define and address violence against women in Myanmar (also see Faxon, Furlong, and Phyu 2015). GEN was established following Cyclone Nargis in 2008, and remains an interagency network of over 100 civil society organizations, non-governmental organizations, international non-governmental organizations, and technical specialists. The network is unique in that its membership includes women's ethnic groups which are part of the Myanmar government peace process (Nationwide Ceasefire Agreement), as well as ethnic groups that are not yet signatories.

GEN's promotion of building capacity to address violence against women has led to a focus in particular on three important outcomes. First, the National Strategic Plan for the Advancement of Women (2013–2022), which is based in twelve areas of the Beijing Platform for Action and three key areas of CEDAW, has been developed. The plan was launched in October 2013 as a whole-of-government approach, with the Ministry of Social Welfare as the government stakeholder for the plan. The challenge has been to maintain engagement in development and execution of that plan across the provinces. Second, the draft Prevention of Violence Against Women Bill (which was before Myanmar Parliament as of early 2018) has been advanced. GEN's work involved publishing briefing papers on legal reform related to addressing violence against women; building capacity on good practices for violence against women legislation; holding consultations with parliamentarians, government stakeholders, and key civil society organizations; and developing a "roadmap" with key government agencies for drafting the law. There is a plan to communicate details of the law, once passed by parliament, which includes a public notice of the law and reaching out to health and police departments within provinces about the existence of the new law. In an environment whereby the government continues to manage its relationship with the military (which has constitutional control of Home Affairs, the military, and Border Ministry, as well as a 30 percent quota in the upper and lower parliament) GEN sought to release all drafts of the law to its network to ensure there was transparency in the law-making process given the role of women civil society organizations networks in campaigning for this law. This remains a delicate balance between engagement and staying within the boundaries imposed by the 2008 Myanmar Constitution. Third and finally, intersectional awareness has been raised. Given the long history of ethnic conflict and divisions, even prior to Myanmar's independence in 1948, GEN recognizes that there is an ongoing need for civil society organizations (in the absence of the state fulfilling this role) to conduct and disseminate research on cultural norms, social practices, and gender equality with the purpose of building awareness, understanding, and tolerance.

Although civil society networks can achieve noteworthy positive outcomes, they also confront significant challenges, especially in politically tense environments. As a result, there is a need to create opportunities to elevate their work at the regional and international levels, to assure their personal security, and to enable their continued networking with local human rights defenders.

Domestically, the region has a number of locations where unequal gender stereotypes and unequal gender relations are being fueled by political campaigns. In Myanmar, ethnicity is strongly associated with gender stereotypes. Among ethnic groups, struggling for political and economic representation, women supply the next generation of fighters and political activists (Davies and True 2017). The WPS agenda is discussed more frequently in the context of the peace process and in the federal parliament, where there was a 10 percent increase of women elected in the 2016 elections (Shwe et al. 2017, 2). But women's representation is minimal in the security and justice sectors. In addition, not every woman in Myanmar is equal before the law. Since the introduction of the "race and religious laws" in 2015, Myanmar women face a range of prohibitions on who they may marry and how many children they may have, depending on their husband's ethnicity and religion. It affects whether the marriage is registered, which in turn affects whether the children may receive citizenship (Marler and Aguilar 2018). These laws were directed in particular to promote the Bamaar ethnic and Buddhist majority in Myanmar, and to deliberately isolate and stigmatize the Rohingya and Muslim populations. These laws contributed to existing patterns of mistreatment and violations, particularly against the Rohingya population, illustrated in the forced displacement of thousands into Bangladesh in 2017 and 2018 to seek safety from serious human rights violations, according to the UN Special Rapporteur on the Situation of Human Rights in Myanmar (Lee 2018).

In 2018, the Indonesian Parliament was to adopt legislation that not only moves toward criminalizing sex between homosexuals, but also outlaws sex between unmarried couples (Knight 2018). For a number of years, prominent clerics and politicians have openly supported a sequence of attacks against homosexuals, and police have led raids against businesses known to support the homosexual community (nightclubs, publishing houses, and civil society organizations). The proposed legislation would put in place harmful discriminatory practices that would legally permit threats and intimidation against LGBT (lesbian, gay, bisexual, and transgender) individuals and activists. In addition, the proposed outlawing of sex outside marriage will perpetuate regressive gender stereotypes and enforced social norms on gender relations. The virginity test for female police officers in some Indonesian districts is one example of the stigma and discrimination that women face if they wish to be part of the security sector in Indonesia (Human Rights Watch 2017). The proposed legislation, coupled with the intimidation and violence against individuals on the basis of their gender, should be interpreted as direct threats to the safety of women and sexual minorities from gender-based violence (Davies and True 2015). These situations are precisely where mutual advocates from R2P and WPS may identify populations at risk and solutions to prevent their exclusion and/or harm.

Theme 3: prioritizing regional networks on the WPS agenda

How to prioritize a regional WPS agenda is a question often discussed by academics and activists keen to promote the hard-won gains they have individually and collectively made in advancing an ASEAN experience of WPS promotion, but who are also conscious that not all states are ready to embark on their WPS NAPs. As such, a regional model would lay the foundations for what individual states need to consider.[3]

Lourdes Veneracion-Rallonza (2019) has noted the overall lack of progress in discussing WPS and gender empowerment in the security sector within ASEAN, illustrating her argument with the nascent attempt to progress the integration of WPS in the Philippines security sector. Veneracion-Rallonza noted that training in the security sector had primarily focused on "protection and prevention." Note that the terms were used collectively rather than individually,[4] indicating a potentially problematic interpretation of how protection was being conflated with prevention rather than each being identified as having separate but mutually supportive goals to be fulfilled by the security sector. Training on "protection and prevention" had focused on women's physical security, including harassment, sexual violence, and reproductive health; psychological trauma; and economic burdens – vulnerability to labor exploitation and trafficking of internally displaced women/girls. However, there remains very limited space within ASEAN militaries to advocate a progressive understanding or training programs on gender mainstreaming and women's participation within the military without subscribing to gender stereotypes (women as the peacemakers and medics, and female peacekeepers' [sole] function as facilitating community engagement with local women). Moreover, it remains unknown at present what opportunities exist for a collective ASEAN engagement with WPS and R2P within the defense forces, what harm has been done by Duterte – for example, publicly condoning and encouraging militaries to engage in acts of sexual violence – and whether joint activities can be seriously promoted when the Myanmar military continues to face no inquiry, let alone charges, for the serious allegations of crimes committed by their forces against civilian populations.

There is great utility in referring to the CEDAW, the CEDAW Optional Protocol, and Resolution 1325, as legal instruments in order to open spaces for dialogue on gender and protection. In national dialogues across the region, emphasis has often been placed on how UN member states, such as Indonesia, are obliged to uphold both CEDAW and Resolution 1325, and to develop relevant programs and policies to implement their commitments. However, patience and dedicated advocacy is required. The Indonesian NAP process began in 2004 with consultations and the formation of a drafting team. The NAP was drafted between 2011 and 2014 through a series of consultations, and was facilitated by the enactment of a presidential decree that allowed for budget allocation to integrate the NAP into the National Medium Term Development Plan. In the Indonesian case in particular, the real task is to raise public awareness to facilitate implementation at both the national level *and* in local governments. Particularly in sites of conflict and post-conflict, such as West Papua and Aceh provinces, the prevalence of violence and discrimination against women remain sites of high risk – and limited opportunities for engagement to prevent or protect.

Future areas of alignment and engagement for R2P and WPS: ASEAN contributions

In March 2017, the APCR2P invited all the ACWC members to attend a five-day session in Australia to discuss, engage, and exchange on the WPS agenda. Consultations occurred between the ACWC members and the Australian government's Department of Foreign Affairs and Trade, Federal Police, and the Department of Defence (Asia Pacific Centre for the Responsibility to Protect 2017a). ACWC members exchanged information and views on their country situations, their government and legislative context, and their individual work in the areas of government, civil society, and/or academia. Responsibility of the region to advance the WPS agenda at the state and regional level were the themes of discussion. Crucially, the outcome of this meeting was that the ACWC formally noted that the WPS agenda would become a strong component of their work, which had up until that time been primarily focused on the introduction of domestic legislation concerning violence against women. The opportunity to exchange had also led to a realization of the need to "contribute to better promotion and protection of the rights of women and children and the responsibility of each ASEAN Member State to protect women and children's peace and security, and the whole population" (ASEAN 2017a).

After this event, the ACWC's recommendation that a Joint Statement on Promoting Women, Peace and Security in ASEAN be proposed was adopted at the 31st ASEAN Summit in November 2017 in the Philippines (ASEAN 2017b). The statement was crucial for two reasons. First, it significantly advanced how women were described and characterized in the ASEAN setting. The language in the statement did not refer to women as primarily victims in need of protection. This has been a particularly important development for promoting a vision of the WPS agenda in the ASEAN region which does not conceptualize women's inclusion in peace and security as the victims or, equally essentialist, the peacemakers. Second, it provided a clear mandate for the engagement and participation of ASEAN institutions, such as the ACWC, in the promotion of a WPS agenda.

Women participate in political, economic, security, and justice sectors in a variety of roles and power hierarchies. The journey for WPS at the global level, in particular, has been to ensure that the four pillars – prevention, participation, protection, and relief and recovery – are achieved with equal attention. As Coomaraswamy (2015) noted, the agenda has had a problematic history with states and the Security Council focusing their attention primarily on the protection pillar. This means that:

> the capacity to provide gender-sensitive conflict early warning, support women's engagement in conflict resolution, deliver adequate immediate and long-term recovery services to women and girls affected by conflict or crisis, or provide the Security Council with adequate intelligence about gender-specific threats, challenges and opportunities for women's engagement in different processes will continue to fall short of expectations and needs.
>
> *(Coomaraswamy 2015, 282)*

The prioritization of protection above the other pillars is an understandable but problematic focus for preventing conflict. It is similar to the problem faced by the R2P principle with emphasis on protection over prevention. As such, there is an opportunity and need for the two agendas to create normative consensus on the prioritization of preventing conflict, atrocities, and gender discrimination as essential to achieving protection. The practical difficulty in promoting a shared agenda is not a clash of egos or offices, but how to achieve a shared vision that does not suffer political rejection and a loss of engagement in *both* agendas.

These concerns are real and legitimate. As the preceding discussion has shown, while there is progress within the ASEAN membership, there is also a serious pushback against unhindered female participation in the political and security spaces. There are gender stereotypes that fuel discriminatory laws and practices in the region, which justify harm and exclusion of women from participating in the political and security space, let alone ensuring that women are protected in these spaces. Gender stereotypes place particular groups of women and men at risk in the region, particularly homosexual and transgender communities. There are significant obstacles concerning how women's participation in peace and security is viewed; both WPS and R2P advocates must walk a fine line.

This makes the adoption of the 2017 Joint Statement all the more significant. It is an opportunity to remind states of their commitments to this statement – to the need to ensure the participation of women and the prioritization of their engagement in peace and conflict prevention processes in particular, to the need for men and boys to be active participants in the WPS agenda, and to the need for the promotion of gender equality to end social exclusion, discrimination, and isolation.

We may see how this difficult road of promoting the WPS agenda as a national responsibility to protect obligation is working in the case of the Philippines. Despite President Duterte's harmful talk of gender stereotypes and promotion of gender violence to *increase* his popularity, the hard work of promoting WPS in this political environment continues. Since the removal of the Islamic rebels in Marawi City in the second half of 2017, the government and civil society have worked to connect women's civil society networks with the security sector to address the specific relief and recovery needs of women, and to ensure women's voices and experience are being incorporated into the reconstruction and recovery effort (Permanent Mission of the Republic of the Philippines to the United Nations 2017). It was *in the Philippines* that the first Joint Statement was signed. Duterte's election and popularity certainly illustrates a disconnection between WPS language, WPS commitments, and local-level practice. However, it is equally important to remember that the Philippines remains the site of civil society and a Philippines bureaucracy, which continues to fight for resources and political commitments to WPS. The Joint Statement was vital for WPS champions within this country.

At the regional level, there is renewed potential from adopting broader WPS language in the Joint Statement. The ASEAN Political-Security Community was listed in the statement as a future partner for realizing WPS in the region, as were fora such as the ACWC and the AIPR. The inclusion of these institutions potentially legitimate discussion on member state practices that exclude, marginalize, or harm women – and in turn, harm regional peace and security.

Conclusion

The principle concern among the R2P and WPS champions is how to ensure complementarity without creating political or reputational "risk" to either agenda. Despite the apparent benefits of linking legislation and policy on violence against women with WPS National Action Plans, activists tend to emphasize differences rather than complimentary agendas to ensure their own political space, budgets, and resources. Likewise, in the case of security sector reform engagement in WPS, prior emphasis on protection, at the exclusion of the other equally important pillar of prevention, was a source of frustration. Network building has contributed to breaking down these barriers to promote a WPS agenda that has been adopted by the ASEAN political leadership and, significantly, it was achieved without sacrificing language such as participation, equality, or prevention, and included a range of (new and old) institutions identified as responsible actors for WPS implementation in the region.

The priority going forward will be twofold – first, to maintain the advocacy strength and participation in the ACWC network; and second, to pay serious attention to integrate the discussions of the ACWC at the country level, and to relate their work and developments to the research and engagement of the AIPR. Given that the Joint Statement now creates this formal link, it is time to consider how the region may develop meaningful indicators of progress on women's inclusion in the political, economic, justice, and security sectors.

There is no doubt that the ASEAN region provides an important example of how to promote an R2P–WPS dialogue that is mutually beneficial and that does *not* compromise the advancement of either agenda. An R2P agenda, which seriously engages with gender inclusion in the prevention pillar and seeks out the participation of WPS champions in the region, should be cognizant of the national politics and persuasive arguments that need to be put forward to support continued engagement and exchange to protect populations.

Notes

1 It is possible that the 2017 Joint Statement will help to change practice and that the Political-Security Community may begin to introduce a regular item on WPS in annual meetings.
2 In addition to the ACWC, the AICHR, the ASEAN Ministerial Meeting on Women, and the AIPR.
3 Many of them have only recently completed NAPs on violence against women, and as such, many attendees from the government sector expressed uncertainty about how to both differentiate and identify the need for another NAP to their Executive.
4 Resolution 1325 (2000) put forward four pillars to realize the WPS agenda: prevention, participation, protection, and relief and recovery.

References

ASEAN, 2015. *ASEAN 2025: Forging Ahead Together* (Jakarta: ASEAN Secretariat).
ASEAN, 2017a. "The ASEAN Commission on the Promotion and Protection of the Rights of Women and Children (ACWC) to Advance Gender, Peace and Security Agenda in the Region," Brisbane, March 31.
ASEAN, 2017b. "Joint Statement on Promoting Women, Peace and Security in ASEAN," Manila, November 16.
Asia Pacific Centre for the Responsibility to Protect, 2014a. "ASEAN and the Prevention of Violence Against Women," *Spotlight on R2P* 12, August.
Asia Pacific Centre for the Responsibility to Protect, 2014b. "ASEAN and the Prevention of Violence Against Women in Conflict and Humanitarian Situations: Report and

Recommendations of the 20 August 2014, Jakarta, Indonesia Workshop" (Brisbane: Asia Pacific Centre for the Responsibility to Protect).

Asia Pacific Centre for the Responsibility to Protect, 2015. "Toward a Culture of Prevention: Advancing Women, Peace and Security in ASEAN," *Spotlight on R2P* 21, August.

Asia Pacific Centre for the Responsibility to Protect, 2017a. "Convenors of APPAP Working Group on Gender and Atrocities Prevention Facilitate Fellowship Program for ASEAN Commission on the Promotion and Protection of the Rights of Women and Children," *Spotlight on R2P* 38, March.

Asia Pacific Centre for the Responsibility to Protect, 2017b. "High Level Advisory Panel on the Responsibility to Protect Public Seminars in Southeast Asian Capitals," *Spotlight on R2P* 41, August: 1–5.

Ban Ki-moon, 2009. "Implementing the Responsibility to Protect: Report of the Secretary-General," A/63/677, January 12.

Ban Ki-moon, 2011. "The Role of Regional and Subregional Arrangements in Implementing the Responsibility to Protect: Report of the Secretary-General," A/65/877–S/2011/393, June 28.

Ban Ki-moon, 2013. "Responsibility to Protect: State Responsibility and Prevention: Report of the Secretary-General," A/67/929–S/2013/399, July 9.

Ban Ki-moon, 2014. "Fulfilling Our Collective Responsibility: International Assistance and the Responsibility to Protect: Report of the Secretary-General," A/68/947–S/2014/449, July 11.

BBC, 2018. "Philippines Drugs War: ICC Announces Initial Inquiry into Killings," February 8.

Bellamy, Alex J., and Sara E. Davies, 2019. "A Cross-Cutting Agenda: Responsibility to Protect and Women, Peace and Security," in Sara E. Davies and Jacqui True, eds, *The Oxford Handbook of Women, Peace and Security* (New York: Oxford University Press), 585–97.

Bond, Jennifer, and Laurel Sherret, 2006. *A Sight for Sore Eyes: Bringing Gender Vision to the Responsibility to Protect Framework* (Santo Domingo: United Nations International Research and Training Institute for the Advancement of Women, March).

Coomaraswamy, Radhika, 2015. *Preventing Conflict, Transforming Justice, Securing Peace: A Global Study on the Implementation of United Nations Security Council Resolution 1325* (New York: United Nations).

Davies, Sara E., and Sarah Teitt, 2012. "Engendering the Responsibility to Protect: Women and the Prevention of Mass Atrocities," *Global Responsibility to Protect* 4, no. 2: 198–222.

Davies, Sara E., and Jacqui True, 2015. "Reframing Conflict-Related Sexual and Gender-Based Violence: Bringing Gender Analysis Back In," *Security Dialogue* 46, no. 6: 495–512.

Davies, Sara E., and Jacqui True, 2017. "The Politics of Counting and Reporting Conflict-Related Sexual and Gender-Based Violence: The Case of Myanmar," *International Feminist Journal of Politics* 19, no. 1: 4–21.

Davies, Sara E., Kimberly Nackers, and Sarah Teitt, 2014. "Women, Peace and Security as an ASEAN Priority," *Australian Journal of International Affairs* 68, no. 3: 333–55.

ECR2P (European Centre for the Responsibility to Protect), n.d. "Women Network on the Responsibility to Protect, Peace and Security," https://ecr2p.leeds.ac.uk/women-network/women-network-on-the-responsibility-to-protect-peace-and-security/.

Ellis-Peterson, Hannah, 2018. "Philippines: Rodrigo Duterte Orders Soldiers to Shoot Female Rebels 'In the Vagina'," *The Guardian*, February 13.

Faxon, Hilary, Roisin Furlong, and May Sabe Phyu, 2015. "Reinvigorating Resilience: Violence against Women, Land Rights, and the Women's Peace Movement in Myanmar," *Gender & Development* 23, no. 3: 463–79.

GAPW (Global Action to Prevent War), n.d. "Women as Solutions to and Victims of the Threat of Mass Atrocities: Integrating Gender Perspectives into the Third Pillar of the Responsibility to Protect," Background Concept Note, www.globalactionpw.org/wp/wp-content/uploads/background-concept-note.pdf.

Gilgan, Chloë M., 2017. "Exploring the Link Between R2P and Refugee Protection: Arriving at Resettlement," *Global Responsibility to Protect* 9, no. 4: 366–94.

Guterres, António, 2017. "Implementing the Responsibility to Protect: Accountability for Prevention: Report of the Secretary-General," A/71/1016–S/2017/556, August 10.

Harris Rimmer, Susan, 2014. "Feminist Ripostes to the Responsibility to Protect," Public lecture given at the Gender Institute's Feminist Theory Now Series, The Australian National University, Canberra, July 22, http://genderinstitute.anu.edu.au/feminist-ripostes-responsibility-protect-doctrine.

Hewitt, Sarah, 2016. "Overcoming the Gender Gap: The Possibilities of Alignment Between the Responsibility to Protect and the Women, Peace and Security Agenda," *Global Responsibility to Protect* 8, no. 1: 3–28.

High-Level Advisory Panel on the Responsibility to Protect in Southeast Asia, 2014. "Mainstreaming the Responsibility to Protect in Southeast Asia: Pathway Towards a Caring ASEAN Community," Report presented at the United Nations, New York, September 9.

Human Rights Watch, 2017. "Indonesia: No End to Abusive 'Virginity Tests'," November 22.

Knight, Kyle, 2018. "Criminalizing Indonesia's LGBT People Won't Protect Them," *Human Rights Watch*, February 14.

Lee, Yanghee, 2018. "End of Mission Statement by Special Rapporteur on the Situation of Human Rights in Myanmar," Seoul, February 1, www.ohchr.org/EN/NewsEvents/Pages/DisplayNews.aspx?NewsID=22619&LangID=E.

Marler, Isabel, and Macarena Aguilar, 2018. "What's Attracting Women to Myanmar's Buddhist Nationalist Movement?" *Open Democracy*, January 30.

Murphy, Ray, and Róisín Burke, 2015. "Sexual and Gender-Based Violence and the Responsibility to Protect: Where Does Gender Come In?" *Irish Studies in International Affairs* 26: 227–55.

National Economic and Development Authority, 2011. *Philippine Development Plan 2011–2016* (Pasig City: National Economic and Development Authority).

Permanent Mission of the Republic of the Philippines to the United Nations, 2017. "PH Highlights Key Role of Women in Gov't Response to Marawi at Security Council Meeting," October 27.

Ralph, Jason, 2018. "What Should Be Done? Pragmatic Constructivist Ethics and the Responsibility to Protect," *International Organization* 72, no. 1: 173–203.

Security Council Report: Monthly Forecast, 2017. "Hindsight: Women, Peace and Security – Closing the Security Council's Implementation Gap," April: 2–3.

Shwe Sein Latt, Kim N. B. Ninh, Mi Ki Kyaw Myint, and Susan Lee, 2017. *Women's Political Participation in Myanmar: Experiences of Women Parliamentarians, 2011–2016* (Myanmar: The Asia Foundation, April).

Spitka, Timea, 2017. "Drawing the Red Lines: Gender and Responsibility to Protect in BiH and Israel/Palestine," in *The Responsibility to Protect at 10: The Challenge of Protecting the World's Most Vulnerable Populations* (Waltham, MA: Brandeis University), https://brandeis.edu/ethics/pdfs/internationaljustice/r2p/march%202015%20p apers/r2p-spitka.pdf.

Teitt, Sarah, 2014. "ASEAN and the Prevention of Sexual Violence in Conflict and Humanitarian Situations: From Commitment to Practical Action in Southeast Asia," *AP R2P Brief* 4, no. 6: 1–8.

Trillò, Tommaso, 2015. "Gender Identity, Gender Based Violence, and the Responsibility to Protect," Working Towards Prevention Working Paper No. 1 (Budapest: Budapest Centre for the International Prevention of Genocide and Mass Atrocities), www.genocide prevention.eu/wp-content/uploads/2015/07/Tommaso-Trillo-GBV-07-April-153.pdf.

True, Jacqui, 2016. "Explaining the Global Diffusion of the Women, Peace and Security Agenda," *International Political Science Review* 37, no. 3: 307–23.

United Nations, 2014. *Framework of Analysis for Atrocity Crimes: A Tool for Prevention* (New York: United Nations).

Veneracion-Rallonza, Lourdes, 2019. "WPS and the Association of South East Asian Nations," in Sara E. Davies and Jacqui True, eds, *The Oxford Handbook of Women, Peace and Security* (New York: Oxford University Press), 388–401.

PART IV
International legal accountability

9

LINKING HUMAN RIGHTS ACCOUNTABILITY AND COMPLIANCE WITH R2P IMPLEMENTATION

Ekkehard Strauss

Introduction

In this chapter, I propose a closer link between human rights accountability and compliance, and the implementation of the Responsibility to Protect (R2P). Following a review of recent discussions on the application of R2P to the situations in Libya, Côte d'Ivoire, and Syria in 2011, I share some observations on the relationship between human rights law and R2P in general before reviewing the possibilities for using a closer link between human rights accountability and the implementation of R2P.

Application of R2P to Libya, Côte d'Ivoire, and Syria

In March 2011, the United Nations Security Council (UNSC) authorized member states "to take all necessary measures ... to protect civilians and civilian populated areas under threat of attack in the Libyan Arab Jamahiriya" (Resolution 1973 [2011], S/RES/1973 [2011], March 17, 2011). Based on this mandate, NATO took command of all military operations in Libya and, during the following seven months, aircraft attacked command centers and convoys of the Libyan Army until, on October 20, Muammar Gaddafi died after being captured by rebel forces following NATO attacks on his convoy.

In Libya, the so-called Arab Spring experienced in some countries in North Africa encouraged people to organize public demonstrations, starting in Benghazi on February 15, 2011, and to demand more individual and collective freedom and an end of Gaddafi's rule. The protest spread to Misrata and Tripoli in the following days, and the Libyan Air Force and Navy started to attack civilian areas in Benghazi. Based on the tribal structure of society, armed resistance began, and local movements formed and started to engage the Libyan Army in all main cities, involving heavy weapons captured during previous attacks. By taking large urban centers like Benghazi, the rebels carried warfare into areas that were densely populated by civilians. The African Union and the League of Arab States unanimously condemned the action of the regime, and the defected permanent representative of Libya to the United Nations (UN) in New York called on the UNSC to authorize military action to protect the population of Benghazi (Global Arab Network 2011).

On February 26, the UNSC "[r]ecall[ed] the Libyan authorities' responsibility to protect its population" (Resolution 1970 [2011], S/RES/1970 [2011], February 26, 2011). On the day before the adoption of the resolution, the Human Rights Council (HRC) held a special session on the situation in Libya and condemned not only the "indiscriminate armed attacks," but also extra-judicial killings, arbitrary arrests, detention and torture of peaceful demonstrators. In order to improve the human rights situation, the HRC requested some concrete, measurable steps from Libya, including the release of detainees, cessation of intimidation, persecution, and arbitrary arrests of individuals, unblocking of the internet and telecommunication networks, and access of human rights monitors.

Resolution 1970 (2011), while referring to the HRC resolution of the previous day, only included the access of international human rights monitors and the lifting of restrictions on all forms of media in its concrete demands of Libya, before referring the situation to the International Criminal Court and imposing a general arms embargo, travel ban, and asset freeze with no particular reference to their relationship with ongoing mass atrocities. The UNSC also committed to review Libya's action related to implementing the resolution, but did not include any progress indicators such as those established by the HRC. On the ground, the rebels formed a National Council to act as a representative of the Libyan people. Meanwhile, their offensive was repelled by a loyalist counter-offensive, which led to the encirclement of the main cities held by the rebels, including Benghazi. Gaddafi threatened, when retaking Benghazi and Misrata, to go house by house and attack the "cockroaches" (*Economist* 2011).

On March 22, the UNSC deplored the failure of Libya to comply with its earlier demands of Resolution 1970 (2011) and, without reference to sources, condemned the gross and systematic violations of human rights, including arbitrary detentions, enforced disappearance, torture, and summary executions. Resolution 1973 (2011) outlined its objectives – to protect civilians and unimpeded passage of humanitarian assistance – which did not directly respond to the human rights violations indicated earlier, since they could continue in areas under the control of the Gaddafi regime that were not experiencing active fighting. Notwithstanding these limited objectives, the UNSC authorized action under Chapter VII of the UN Charter not only to establish a ceasefire and end all attacks on civilians, but stressed as second operational priority "to find a solution to the crisis which responds to the legitimate demands of the Libyan people" (Resolution 1973 [2011]).

While lauded initially as a precedent for the application of R2P, critical voices rose shortly after the NATO operation "Unified Protector" had begun, and appear to prevail in academic analysis. Others interpreted the application of R2P by the UNSC to the situations in Libya and Côte d'Ivoire during the same months as a "high water mark" before an inevitable demise (Rieff 2011).

In Côte d'Ivoire, President Laurent Gbagbo refused to accept the result of the November 28, 2010 presidential elections and exploited ethnic tensions to stay in power. Members of his regime manipulated young Ivorians to violence and instrumentalized unresolved rural land issues, causing large-scale violations of human rights (Human Rights Council 2011a). Credible reports of extra-judicial and summary executions; rape, acts of torture, and other cruel, inhumane, and degrading treatment; enforced disappearances, arbitrary arrests and detentions; attacks against religious buildings; and acts of intimidation, harassment, and extortion reached the international media. By March 2011, elected President Alassane Ouattara established his preliminary offices in the Golf Hotel, which was under siege by Gbagbo's supporters, while Côte d'Ivoire's military, supported by the United Nations Operation in Côte d'Ivoire (UNOCI), fought Gbagbo's supporters in the streets of Abidjan who were trying to reach the Presidential Palace, where the former president and his closest allies remained under the protection of the Presidential Guard.

On March 30, 2011, the UNSC had recalled to Côte d'Ivoire "its authorization ... given to the UNOCI ... to use all necessary means to carry out its mandate to protect civilians under imminent threat of physical violence" and adopted a travel ban and asset freeze "against those individuals who obstruct peace and reconciliation in Côte d'Ivoire, obstruct the work of UNOCI and other international actors in Côte d'Ivoire and commit serious violations of human rights and international humanitarian law" (Resolution 1975 [2011], S/RES/1975 [2011], March 30, 2011).[1]

The African Union and the Economic Community of West African States condemned the post-election crisis in Côte d'Ivoire (African Union 2011; Economic Community of West African States 2011). The UNSC increased the authorized number of troops for UNOCI by 2,000 to 11,000 (Resolution 1968 [2011], S/RES/1968 [2011], February 16, 2011), and reaffirmed "the primary responsibility of each State to protect civilians" and "the responsibility of Côte d'Ivoire to promote and protect all human rights and fundamental freedoms" (Resolution 1975 [2011]). The UNSC welcomed the HRC resolution on the situation in Côte d'Ivoire (adopted March 25), but only referred to its content with regard to the dispatch of an independent international commission of inquiry. However, the HRC did not request Côte d'Ivoire to take any measurable action against particular human rights violations other than to cease them altogether (Human Rights Council 2011b).

While the application of R2P in the situation of Côte d'Ivoire appears to have been accepted generally, notwithstanding the unclear wording of the respective resolutions by UN organs, the criticism regarding Libya is explicit and considered by many to be the main reason for the lack of effective UNSC action on the situation in Syria since March 2011. The main criticism of the application of R2P to the situation in Libya was already apparent from the explanations of votes after the adoption of Resolution 1973 (2011) (United Nations Security Council 2011). It was related, first, to the lack of credible information on the situation on the ground (which was not comparable to Rwanda, Darfur, Congo, Bosnia, or other situations of deliberate massacre) (Kuperman 2015), and to the consequences of urban warfare between the Libyan Army and armed rebels, which were inflated to mass atrocities perpetrated by the Gaddafi regime against the civilian population. Second, the BRICS (Brazil, Russia, India, China, and South Africa) members of the UNSC, in particular Russia and China, claimed that NATO had exceeded its authority to protect civilians and moved toward regime change only days into the operation. Third, the military intervention did not resolve the conflict in Libya, but led to a protracted civil war with no clear solution in sight.

Meanwhile, in Syria, violent repression of protests in the main urban centers throughout the country developed, in different phases, into a protracted civil war with the intervention of regional and international actors and mass atrocities being committed by all sides on a regular basis (see, for example, Adams 2015). While the human rights situation was well documented, at least since the first special session of the HRC on April 29, 2011 (see United Nations General Assembly 2011a for details) and the presentation of the first report of an independent international commission of inquiry (United Nations General Assembly 2017, 2011b), on August 22, the UNSC was not able to agree even on the three recurrent measures taken in comparable situations – a referral to the International Criminal Court, an arms embargo, and targeted sanctions against the main perpetrators. China and Russia vetoed draft resolutions in this regard, including the imposition of sanctions for the alleged use of chemical weapons by the Bashar al-Assad regime (see Security Council Report 2017). The lack of unity in the UNSC to take action against mass atrocities being committed in Syria provoked a controversial discussion about the agreement on R2P and its practical consequences (see, for example, Murray and McKay 2014).

R2P sought to clarify when, where, and how the international community has a responsibility to protect populations within the territory of a state when the state itself has failed to meet these responsibilities. More than ten years after the adoption of R2P by the General Assembly (UNGA), there remain, on the one hand, concerns at the selective application of R2P and, as a consequence, the potential for its subjective use by strong powers against weaker, mainly developing states, to impose their political agenda. On the other hand, there are legitimate concerns that necessary measures to prevent and respond to mass atrocities are not taken due to political considerations, which are allowed to prevail over international law for lack of conceptual clarity on the application of R2P. It still remains unclear which methodology is involved when distinguishing between the situations requiring the application of R2P and other situations of conflict and violence. In the course of comprehensive research led by the late Sheri Rosenberg, it was observed that not one interlocutor identified a current standard to decide on the application of R2P in a particular situation (Rosenberg and Strauss 2012).

Nevertheless, in the meantime, advocates of R2P claim that the UNSC referred to R2P in sixty-seven resolutions and twenty-one presidential statements (Global Centre for the Responsibility to Protect 2018). The majority emphasize the responsibility of the state concerned for the protection of civilians or, less frequently, a responsibility to protect populations. Sometimes there is a general reference to paragraphs 138 and 139 of the "2005 World Summit Outcome" document (United Nations General Assembly 2005). However, the factual and legal reference for employing one expression or the other remains unclear. The same lack of clarity prevails in the thirty resolutions of the HRC (Global Centre for the Responsibility to Protect 2017). In its statements on R2P, the HRC, in general, follows the statements of other UN entities rather than leading the discussion on its application. Apparently, the lack of unity among member states prevails as to where the discussion on the implementation of R2P is best placed. The HRC does not appear to be among the first choice of member states.

Other UN human rights mechanisms and the High Commissioner for Human Rights use R2P as a reference point to express an elevated level of gravity in situations already in high public attention, to advocate for member states' intervention to halt already ongoing mass atrocities, and to bring alleged perpetrators to justice. R2P is used as a different expression of the obligations of states to prevent and punish mass atrocities, rather than as a new principle (for a more detailed analysis, see Strauss 2016).

The UN Secretary-General (UNSG) has identified further clarification related to the bases for undertaking collective action in response to situations where states are manifestly failing to protect populations as an outstanding conceptual issue for member states (Ban 2016, paragraph 19). He has also stressed the need to strengthen accountability to prevent mass atrocities in order to ensure their prevention in practice (Guterres 2017). He has elaborated on the legal obligation, the national moral and political responsibility to prevent mass atrocities through the application of R2P, and the role of national, regional, and international processes and institutions. However, in the absence of recommendations for a practical methodology to establish accountability of particular actors in specific situations, there remains space for a range of political, economic, and legal factors to be taken into consideration for the application of R2P. R2P remains open to different interpretations.

The application of human rights accountability and compliance, at the very least, would require states to explain their reasoning for the application of R2P to particular situations from a common normative reference point. Human rights standards could be used to identify situations requiring the application of R2P, facilitate the identification, sequencing, and measuring of national and international mitigating measures, and provide demonstrable evidence to determine whether a state is "manifestly failing" to meet its obligations to protect populations.

The general relationship between R2P and states' human rights obligations

Status of discussion on the implementation of R2P and states' human rights obligations

In 2009, the UNSG outlined a three-pillar strategy for advancing the agenda mandated by heads of state and government at the 2005 World Summit (Ban 2009).[2]

Member states and the UNSG have underscored from the outset that the provisions of the 2005 World Summit are firmly anchored in well-established principles of international law. The outline of the three-pillar strategy was not intended to detract in any way from the much broader range of obligations existing under international humanitarian, human rights, refugee, and criminal law.

The UNSG clarified subsequently that the pillars were not designed to operate in a sequence, but that the use of particular preventive and responsive tools should follow a sequential logic. The implementation of R2P requires a continuum of steps moving from prevention to response tailored to the specific circumstances of each case. While there is broad consensus that the scope of R2P should be limited to the three crimes (genocide, war crimes, and crimes against humanity) and ethnic cleansing, the response should employ all humanitarian, development, security, and human rights interventions available to member states, the UN system, regional and sub-regional organizations, and their civil society partners.

In his reports on the implementation of R2P, the UNSG explicitly referred to examples of human rights policies and practices that are contributing, or could contribute, to implementing Pillars One and Two. In addition, all high commissioners sought to integrate the interpretation of R2P into the understanding of obligations and limits deriving from international human rights law. Louise Arbour, for example, elaborated on the characteristics of human rights monitoring needed to support the prevention of genocide. She argued that, properly designed, a monitoring mechanism could provide authoritative early warning of situations at risk of degenerating into genocide, as such situations were almost invariably preceded and characterized by a discernable escalation of systematic or gross violations of human rights (Arbour 2008).

While common sense suggests that many of the elements of good governance tend to serve the same objectives as the obligation to prevent mass atrocities, mitigating measures as part of the implementation of R2P should be measurable by linking them through indicators to specific risk factors for mass atrocities, which derive primarily from specific human rights obligations. Thus, the mainstreaming of a methodological "mass-atrocity lens" into all development, humanitarian, and security policies as recommended repeatedly, should be a narrower and clearly defined set of general human rights mainstreaming (for a similar proposal for the national level, see Ralph 2014).

Legal basis

R2P stands as a practical and normative response to past failures to prevent genocide and other forms of mass atrocities. From a normative point of view, the challenge for establishing human rights accountability to the implementation of R2P is to effectively implement obligations of states under international human rights, humanitarian, and refugee law to an exceptional situation at risk of the three crimes being committed.

The general basis for applying human rights accountability to the implementation of R2P is the character of international human rights conventions to establish *erga omnes* obligations. International law draws an essential distinction between such obligations of a state toward the international community as a whole and those arising vis-à-vis another state from a bilateral treaty. By their very nature, international human rights obligations are the concern of all states, and in view of the importance of the rights involved, all states could claim a legal interest in their protection (see Posner 2009).

The specific basis is *ius cogens* international legal obligation of states to prevent genocide, war crimes, and crimes against humanity (for details, see Strauss 2009). The application of human rights accountability to R2P in practice would progressively develop a list of relevant violations. In order to escape the discussion on possible causal links between observed violations and their deterioration into mass atrocities, which would inevitably open the door for the political discussions standing in the way of applying R2P today, prevention of mass atrocities can be built on existing preventive legal obligations as established in the case law of UN human rights mechanisms and international courts and tribunals.

The interpretation of international human rights law has led, over time, to the identification of obligations for their effective implementation and the prevention of their violation. The term "prevention" appears, *inter alia*, in the title, the preamble, and the substantive articles of various human rights conventions.[3] Most treaty bodies have interpreted the obligation to prevent as a general obligation to avoid the repetition of similar violations in the future,[4] and some conventions contain the obligation to implement specific legal, administrative, or other means to prevent violations or their causes. This includes the obligation to monitor abstract risk situations (for example, the monitoring of compulsory labor to prevent it from turning into slavery) and the obligation to investigate any suspicion. Legal measures include the reform of inadequate national provisions. In this context, some conventions include the obligation to systematically collect information on violations. Other measures include the provision of educational, health, economic, or social services to potential victims or perpetrators. Another approach includes educational measures for potential perpetrators, victims, or the population at large. These measures are obligatory for the state party, even before any violation has occurred.

In addition, the general obligations to respect and ensure the rights of a treaty have been interpreted to contain a positive duty to take steps toward effective implementation as much as a duty to refrain from acts of violation.[5] On this basis, the obligations of state actors encompassed within any human rights have been broken down into obligations to "respect" rights by not committing direct violations against individuals, to "protect" individuals from violations of their rights by non-state actors, and to "fulfill" rights when the state must step in and provide the content of the right.

The question of whether the positive duties include a duty to prevent violations has been interpreted differently by different treaty bodies. All treaty bodies concluded, though, that states may be held liable for their failure to take adequate measures to prevent violations or for their lack of appropriate responses when violations have occurred by non-state actors (see, for example, United Nations 2004). At the time of the existence of a real and immediate risk to the life of an identified individual or individuals, a state is obliged to take measures within the scope of its powers which can be expected to avoid the risk. Thus, the rationale for the legal obligation of protecting human rights and the normative basis of R2P are identical.

Toward a concept of human rights accountability and compliance for the application of R2P

It is clear from the objectives of R2P that, notwithstanding the reference to genocide, war crimes, crimes against humanity, and ethnic cleansing, it cannot apply only at the stage at which responsibility under international criminal law could be established. Instead, R2P requires the prospective assessment of future developments based on present facts and circumstances.

Similar challenges are faced in the national and international implementation of human rights obligations, including, for example, the obligation of *non-refoulement*, and are successfully addressed by human rights treaty bodies. In drawing the appropriate parallels, a situation should be considered in the context of R2P, if its examination establishes a "real risk" that exceptionally grave human rights violations – as described in genocide, war crimes, crimes against humanity, and ethnic cleansing – are occurring or could occur in the future. According to the methodology applied by human rights treaty bodies, the risk is considered "real" if potential victims can be identified and related to possible scenarios involving any of the three crimes. Any situation could be assessed for risks of mass atrocities based on this standard (for details of this approach, see Rosenberg 2013).

Within this approach, human rights "accountability," defined as the factor of being responsible, would be used to identify "risks," defined as the possibility of mass atrocity crimes being committed due to particular human rights violations and their underlying "factors," defined as circumstances contributing to the possibility, with the aim of identifying "threats," defined as risks of mass atrocities reaching the "real" threshold of R2P; that is, concrete victims, their potential violations, and the perpetrators can be identified within concrete scenarios. Once the situation was identified and the main risk factors are known, one could arrive at a list of mitigating measures and corresponding human rights obligations that could be recommended and implemented at different stages of a developing crisis. In addition to the specific standards applicable to genocide, war crimes, ethnic cleansing, and crimes against humanity, human rights obligations contained in treaties and customary law are directly relevant for this list, in particular as far as they have been made applicable for the respective state through recommendations of human rights mechanisms; in particular, the Universal Periodic Review. The impact of measures taken by the government can be monitored against the timelines and indicators established on the basis of the respective human rights obligations.

In this regard, the Experts Group on Darfur set an important precedent. The group identified four priority areas – human rights protection, humanitarian access, accountability and justice, and monitoring of implementation of recommendations – and for each, selected a number of recommendations, identified steps that could be considered indicators for their implementation, and assessed the length of time (between three and twelve months) needed for their implementation. The respective matrix was shared with the government of Sudan, which agreed with a substantial number of recommendations, although it remained unclear sometimes what specific steps it agreed to undertake for their implementation. The status of implementation annexed to the final report of the group offers a wealth of generic measures to address mass atrocities, which could be used to define a continuum of steps in other situations (United Nations General Assembly 2007a, 2007c).

The question of whether a state is "manifestly failing" should be determined based on the information of relevant human rights violations, the state of implementation of measurable steps to mitigate risk factors, and their impact on the real risk that exceptionally grave violations of human rights could occur in the future. Based on the continuum of steps, the compliance of national governments and the international community can be established. Manifest failure occurs when foreseeable consequences have not been addressed and the risk level prevails or increases. Failure to meet the timelines for action or to take action effectively would mean that the respective state is failing to meet its international obligations to protect its people from mass atrocities and would guide decision-makers within the UN toward replacing action by the state where and as far as it is failing.

US targeted airstrikes against Islamic State of Iraq and Syria (ISIS) in Iraq to prevent possible mass atrocities against the Yazidi population trapped on Mount Sinjar, while largely ignored by the advocates of R2P, may be among the most important precedents so far for the application of R2P as promoted here. Planes from Iraq, the United Kingdom, and the United States had dropped humanitarian aid on the mountain before the US began airstrikes against ISIS positions on August 9, 2014 in order to break the siege and allow the trapped people on Mount Sinjar to escape into safety. On August 12–13, a dozen US Marines and special forces joining the British Special Air Service already in the area informed White House security advisers that only 4,000–5,000 people remained, had sufficient food and water available, and would be rescued by Kurdish Peshmerga soon. Based on this information, President Barack Obama decided to discontinue the airstrikes, as they had achieved their objective (NBC News 2014; Deutsche Welle 2014).

Implementation mechanisms

Regarding the application of human rights accountability to the implementation of R2P, there remains a disconnection between the legal interpretation of the international obligations to prevent genocide, war crimes, crimes against humanity, and related human rights violations, and the mandate of the international mechanisms and institutions tasked with responding to mass atrocity risks. In the absence of a central instance charged with the binding interpretation of international human rights law in a particular situation, only the UNSC could enforce its interpretation with measures according to Chapter VII.

Consequently, the proposed concept can assist relevant actors to determine whether a situation falls within the application of R2P. It could be used by governments; political bodies of regional and international organizations, including UN human rights mechanisms; and civil society, which are all called upon to make assessments as to the applicability of R2P, and assist common and coordinated approaches to implement R2P. Most member states would agree that an assessment of credible information by independent and impartial actors or bodies provides the best basis upon which to take a decision regarding collective action to protect populations from atrocity crimes. Over the years, a variety of mechanisms have provided that information, including commissions of inquiry and fact-finding missions, the United Nations High Commissioner for Human Rights, the special procedures mandate holders of the HRC, the human rights treaty bodies, and the special advisers, envoys, and representatives of the UNSG. However, the impact of these reports on deliberations in the UNSC is limited, *inter alia*, by a lack of common standards to determine the risks and the relevant elements of threats.

The HRC demonstrated its ability to address situations of ongoing massive human rights violations when member states agreed to put the situation on its agenda. In May 2008, the HRC reviewed the human rights situation in Sri Lanka (for details, see United Nations General Assembly 2008). At that time, the government had abrogated the ceasefire with the Liberation Tigers of Tamil Eelam and had started a military campaign, which, between September 2008 and May 2009, caused serious and widespread violations of international humanitarian and human rights law (see Panel of Experts on Accountability in Sri Lanka 2011). However, four months prior, only three out of fifty-six member states participating in the discussion referred to the conflict situation and called for restraint in counter-terrorism measures. One member state urged the protection of civilians, and another the prevention of sexual violence against women in the conflict zone. Some member states submitted general recommendations, including to "take measures" to protect civilians, to "prevent" cases of disappearances and killings, and to "punish" violations of international humanitarian and human rights law.

The outcome of the first two cycles of the Universal Periodic Review showed the requirement of a mass atrocity-prevention element within the list of issues and questions raised with the respective government. The same is true for the consideration of periodic state party reports under relevant human rights treaties such as the International Covenant on Civil and Political Rights; the International Covenant on Economic, Social and Cultural Rights; the International Convention on the Elimination of All Forms of Racial Discrimination; the Convention against Torture; the Convention on the Elimination of All Forms of Discrimination against Women; and the Convention on the Rights of the Child. Member states should be requested to include an analysis of a list of agreed risk factors related to large-scale violence in their reports and, based on the discussion, concrete recommendations for mitigating particular risks should be submitted. In addition, member states should report on their contribution to prevent mass atrocities around the world. Presently, the recommendations remain too abstract and lack a measurable preventive effect on mass atrocities. In addition, the UNSC needs to develop processes to address situations to prevent future mass atrocities outside the periodic Universal Periodic Review.

The HRC lacks the power to implement its decisions and recommendations if a member state refuses to cooperate. Therefore, the developing practice of the HRC to transmit reports of fact-finding and assessment mechanisms to the UNGA and the UNSG could increase its impact, if those organs would use their respective capacities in a complementary way. The HRC should also transmit its reports to the UNSC regarding those situations already on its agenda of country situation or thematic agenda items, in particular protection of civilians in armed conflict and threats to international peace and security. In April 2014, the UNSC commemorated the twentieth anniversary of the genocide in Rwanda under the latter agenda item and requested the UNSG "to ensure greater collaboration between existing early-warning mechanisms for genocide prevention and other serious international crimes, in order to help to detect, assess and respond to sources of tension and points of risks or identify vulnerable populations" (Resolution 2150 [2014], S/RES/2150 [2014], April 16, 2014, 4). The development of a generic repertoire of measures, similar to the aide memoire on protection of civilians (United Nations Office for the Coordination of Humanitarian Affairs 2014), would assist the HRC and the UNSC to respond to the causes of mass atrocities and gross human rights violations that are more detailed and fine-tuned than is the present menu of investigations and responses, which can mainly be applied after the fact. This could be built from the list of the 2007 high-level mission on human rights in Darfur (United Nations General Assembly 2007b).

Some treaty bodies developed early-warning and early-action procedures to prevent and respond to violations of treaty obligations. In 1993, the Committee on the Elimination of All Forms of Racial Discrimination formulated a procedure to address serious, massive, or persistent patterns of racial discrimination, in some cases with genocidal dimensions (United Nations General Assembly 1993, Annex III). The procedure leads to a formal decision expressing the views of the committee, which often include detailed recommendations to halt further human rights violations. Based on almost identical provisions, country visits can be carried out confidentially by the Committee against Torture and its Subcommittee, by the Committee on the Elimination of Discrimination against Women (Articles 8, 9), and by the Committee on Economic, Social and Cultural Rights (Article 11). The Human Rights Committee can request reports from states parties at any time that it deems appropriate, which forms the basis of its emergency procedure developed in 1991. These findings could be shared with the UNSC, the HRC, and the UNGA, when the respective country situation reaches their attention.

As proposed to the UNSG by the United States Holocaust Memorial Museum, the capacity of the United Nations Office on Genocide Prevention and the

Responsibility to Protect to monitor and assess mass atrocity crimes should be strengthened by directing the office to explore new joint assessment efforts with the Department of Political and Peacebuilding Affairs, the Office of the United Nations High Commissioner for Human Rights (OHCHR), and other relevant entities, which should include human rights mechanisms, based on a joint standard of human rights accountability.

It has also been proposed to reconstitute the Advisory Committee on the Prevention of Genocide as a new Advisory Committee on Preventing Mass Atrocities, with a new panel of senior members, and to provide them with a mandate to act as an accountability mechanism for the UNSG by reviewing his or her work annually (Gowan, Woocher, and Solomon 2016). The members of the original Advisory Committee were appointed by Kofi Annan in early 2006 and met twice in order to support the Special Adviser on the Prevention of Genocide in developing response options to particular country situations and to provide advice on how genocide prevention could be made more effective within the UN.[6] In October 2006, the committee proposed some modest steps to the UNSG and his successor, which have been partially implemented. On the basis of this experience and taking into account the changes to the early-warning and prevention work within the UN, the committee could be useful in assisting in particular the Department of Political and Peacebuilding Affairs, the OHCHR, and the United Nations Development Programme in developing response strategies to country situations at risk of mass atrocities deriving from the broader human rights screening within the Human Rights up Front (HRuF) policy (for the latter, see Kurtz 2015). The Inter-Agency Task Force on a country situation could seek strategic guidance from the committee on the way forward in applying R2P in addressing a particular at-risk situation through a continuum of steps.

However, the UNSC remains the most important organ to lead the implementation of R2P on a particular county situation. Instead of the present practice of referring to R2P in general terms, the Council should express concern at the lack of sufficient protection manifest in particular violations established through the proposed approach, request concrete measures to be taken and establish a review mechanism, and rely on the findings related to human rights accountability and compliance rather than its own assessment. The UN Charter (Article 34) and Resolution 1366 (2001) provide a framework for such discussions (Resolution 1366 [2001], S/RES/1366 [2001], August 30, 2001).

Reviewing UNSC action on the implementation of R2P on the basis of human rights accountability

Based on the more abstract considerations presented earlier, it could be worth returning to the challenges for UNSC action in the situations of Libya, Côte d'Ivoire, and Syria, and imagining the application of human rights accountability to the implementation of R2P. The UNSC would be required to clearly express the application of R2P by using the wording related to Libya and some other past situations and "recalling the [Libyan authorities'] responsibility to protect its population" rather than the unclear wording in the resolutions regarding Côte d'Ivoire, which make it doubtful whether the application of R2P was agreed. Similar to the standard wording "[a]cting under" used in the final preambular paragraph of every resolution to clarify the legal basis, this would highlight the normative basis of the action taken by the Council and clarify that its members established a real risk of mass atrocities being committed in the respective member state.

The use of R2P as a normative basis for UNSC action in a particular situation should then trigger a particular approach of defining a continuum of steps to prevent and halt an expected cause of events. The decision of the UNSC should be based on the assessment of the situation on the ground based on the real risk standard. The required information and analysis would be available from UN sources on the ground, the periodic reviews of country situations in the context of the HRuF policy, and reports from monitoring mechanisms such as commissions of inquiry, special rapporteurs, or treaty bodies.

Resolution 1970 (2011) established measures expected to motivate the Gaddafi regime to change its approach. However, the International Criminal Court referral, the arms embargo, the travel ban, and the assets freeze were not linked to concrete action to halt and prevent particular violations relevant for R2P with clear indications of accountability and timelines for their implementation, but were mainly used to punish past behavior. For Benghazi, this could have included the call for an immediate ceasefire, the creation of a humanitarian corridor, and the opening of a political dialogue as proposed by the African Union (for more details, see Bachman 2016).

The authorization of military intervention in Resolution 1973 (2011) is similarly loosely formulated and not different from authorizations of the past. The application of R2P will pose the challenge of limited and targeted military action and the Libyan case is an example of the difficulties in implementing this approach within existing doctrine. According to analysts, including from within NATO, the protection of civilians was largely ensured ten days into the campaign (see, for example, House of Commons Foreign Affairs Committee 2016, paragraphs 44, 45–49). However, for lack of operational guidance, attacks continued and followed the pattern of Kosovo for lack of better precedent by starting to target infrastructure, installations, and convoys – including retreating military units – which may be considered legitimate targets according to international humanitarian law, but did not contribute to the objectives outlined in the resolution. The Independent International Commission on Kosovo had recommended closing the gap between legality and legitimacy and, with the NATO intervention in mind, had called for a principled framework to guide future interventions (Independent International Commission on Kosovo 2000). With a view to the overwhelming account by the military personnel involved in the campaign, it is not evident that there were secret orders from the beginning to "take out" Gaddafi and change the regime in Libya (this is argued, for example, by Zenko 2016). While the general reluctance of the UNSC to include detail on military action in its authorization could be justified by the unpredictability of the development of military engagement and the lack of expertise in the UNSC to remotely control such action, a clear link between the action requested from the government and the military action could have prevented the expansion observed in Libya.

Inevitably, due to the lack of accountability mechanisms for human rights violations, there will remain a gap between the options for targeted sanctions and military intervention and the need for particular sanctions, including judicial means. However, some of these gaps could be covered by calling on regional organizations and bilateral partners to support the implementation of the continuum of steps through concrete measures based on their obligations under Chapters VII and VIII of the UN Charter.

Another important weakness of the Libyan intervention, which is used repeatedly by member states to oppose the application of R2P in general and an intervention in Syria in particular, is the aftermath of the NATO campaign; that is, the lack of creating a stable and democratic state. However, while the responsibility to rebuild is an integral part of R2P, an intervention based on the assessment of the real risk of mass atrocities being committed cannot be limited by considerations of the possibility to create a stable and democratic state in the future (for a similar line of argument, see Hamid 2016). The proportionality of the intervention derives from a comparison of the potential situation after the intervention with the potential situation without the intervention. Only the action required by the concrete scenario can be considered legitimate within R2P, and while outside intervention to prevent or halt events from unfolding may create new dynamics between a government and its population, the political consequences and decisions on the future of the political system must remain a sovereign decision of the member state.

Notwithstanding the differences among Council members on R2P, since the adoption of Resolution 1973 (2011), the UNSC has adopted various resolutions to prevent mass atrocities in South Sudan, Yemen, Libya, Mali, Sudan, and the Central African Republic (see Global Centre for the Responsibility to Protect 2018), including Resolution 2150 (2014) reaffirming the commitment of the UN to R2P. It may be worth mentioning that an intervention in Syria would not even require an agreement on the application of R2P. With a view to the spill-over effects of the intrastate conflict into neighboring states, the region, and even the world regarding the refugees, an intervention would be justified by the past practice of the UNSC as applied in Iraq in 1990, in Congo, and in Bosnia and Herzegovina.

Conclusions

R2P still lacks a precedent for its application, which demonstrates the difference between the old ways of humanitarian intervention and a new norm able to convert words into deeds. Libya appears as yet another example where military intervention was authorized by the UNSC only when all its members agreed and received the accord of the respective regional organizations and powers. Resolution 1970 (2011) was not the strong step in affirming the responsibility of states to protect their people, as well as the legitimate role of the Council to step in when they failed to meet that responsibility, as hoped by France (United Nations 2011). So far, R2P seems to be able to do precisely the reverse of its ambition (see Orford 2011, 2).

The systematic application of human rights accountability in the implementation of R2P as outlined here would, first, increase the likelihood that all relevant stakeholders would be encouraged to focus discussions of an at-risk situation to appropriate action and facilitate the debate on whether a situation falls within R2P. The application would, second, add legitimacy, transparency, and accountability to the application of the three pillars of R2P to a given situation and the conclusion when a state is "manifestly failing" to protect its populations. This could, third, result in greater consistency and predictability of action taken by the international community in the implementation of R2P. Relevant actors would be encouraged to provide justifications for action or inaction measured against human rights standards and accountability.

At the same time, it must be stated that there is a general trend among member states in the UNSC, the UNGA, and the HRC of gradual withdrawal from international standards on human rights, democracy, and the rule of law with the justification of exceptional security or economic challenges. It has become increasingly difficult to agree on joint action in support of human rights protection and mass atrocity prevention, even in extreme cases like Syria, South Sudan, and Myanmar. It is not evident that human rights accountability can overcome the problem of lack of political will among member states to implement R2P. On the other hand, in a situation of deep divide within the UN, R2P could support the creation of a basic consensus on the common minimum denominator within the human rights pillar of the Charter in the interest of retaining the credibility of an organization indispensable for contributing to today's challenges of international security, climate change, counter-terrorism, and development.

Acknowledgments

This chapter is based on a presentation delivered to the conference on Implementing the Responsibility to Protect: Domestic Process and Foreign Assistance, The Australia National University, Canberra, October 27, 2016. The views expressed herein are those of the author and do not necessarily reflect the views of the United Nations.

Notes

1. The targeted sanctions were imposed according to the criteria set out in Resolution 1572 (2004), S/RES/1572 (2004), November 15, 2004.
2. Pillar One outlines the primary responsibility of the state to protect its population from genocide, war crimes, crimes against humanity, and ethnic cleansing. Pillar Two is the international community's responsibility to help and encourage states to fulfill their R2P. Pillar Three is the international community's responsibility to take action to protect populations from these described crimes.

3   See, for example, the International Convention on the Elimination of All Forms of Racial Discrimination, preambular paragraph 10 and Article 3; the Convention on the Suppression and Punishment of the Crime of Apartheid, preambular paragraph 5; the International Convention against Apartheid in Sports, preambular paragraph 3; the Convention against Discrimination in Education, Article 3; the Slavery Convention, Article 2; the Supplementary Convention on the Abolition of Slavery, the Slave Trade, and Institutions and Practices Similar to Slavery, Article 3; and the Convention against Torture, Article 2.
4   See, for example, *Bradley McCallum v. South Africa*, A/66/40, Vol. II (2011), Part I, Annex VI, section WW, 559–67.
5   See most recently United Nations Economic and Social Council (2017), which deducted an obligation to prevent effectively infringements of economic, social, and cultural rights from the general obligation to protect (paragraph 16).
6   The Advisory Committee was composed of Sadako Ogata, Romeo Dallaire, Gareth Evans, Zackari Ibrahim, Monica Andersson, and Desmond Tutu.

References

Adams, Simon, 2015. "Failure to Protect: Syria and the UN Security Council," Occasional Paper No. 5 (New York: Global Centre for the Responsibility to Protect, March).

African Union, 2011. "Communique of the 265th Meeting of the Peace and Security Council," PSC/PR/COMM.2(CCLXV), March 10.

Arbour, Louise, 2008. "The Responsibility to Protect as a Duty of Care in International Law and Practice," *Review of International Studies* 34, no. 3: 445–58.

Bachman, Jeff, 2016. "Revisiting the 'Humanitarian' Intervention in Libya," *Huffpost*, www.huffingtonpost.com/jeff-bachman/revisiting-the-humanitari_b_9445270.html.

Ban Ki-moon, 2009. "Implementing the Responsibility to Protect: Report of the Secretary-General," A/63/677, January 12.

Ban Ki-moon, 2016. "Mobilizing Collective Action: The Next Decade of the Responsibility to Protect: Report of the Secretary-General," A/70/999-S/2016/620, July 22.

Deutsche Welle, 2014. "US Rescue Operation for Yazidis on Iraq's Mount Sinjar 'Less Likely'," August 14.

Economic Community of West African States, 2011. "Final Communiqué of the Thirty-Ninth Session of the Authority of Heads of State and Government," March 24.

Economist, 2011. "The Lessons of Libya," May 19.

Global Arab Network, 2011. "Libyan Ambassador to UN Urges International Community to Stop Genocide," February 21.

Global Centre for the Responsibility to Protect, 2017. "R2P References in United Nations Human Rights Council Resolutions," November 16, www.globalr2p.org/media/files/hrc-resolutions-r2p-16-november-2017.pdf.

Global Centre for the Responsibility to Protect, 2018. "R2P References in United Nations Security Council Resolutions and Presidential Statements," January 18, www.globalr2p.org/media/files/unsc-resolutions-and-statements-with-r2p-table-as-of-18-january-2018.pdf.

Gowan, Richard, Lawrence Woocher, and Daniel Solomon, 2016. *Preventing Mass Atrocities: An Essential Agenda for the Next UN Secretary-General* (Washington, DC: United States Holocaust Memorial Museum).

Guterres, António, 2017. "Implementing the Responsibility to Protect: Accountability for Prevention: Report of the Secretary-General," A/71/1016-S/2010/556, August 10.

Hamid, Shadi, 2016. "Everyone Says the Libya Intervention Was a Failure: They're Wrong," Brookings, April 12.

House of Commons Foreign Affairs Committee, 2016. "Libya: Examination of Intervention and Collapse and the UK's Future Policy Options," Third Report of Session 2016–2017 (London: House of Commons, September 14).

Human Rights Council, 2011a. "Report of the International Commission of Inquiry on Côte d'Ivoire," A/HRC/17/48, July 1.

Human Rights Council, 2011b. "Situation of Human Rights in Côte d'Ivoire," A/HRC/RES/16/25, April 13.

Independent International Commission on Kosovo, 2000. *The Kosovo Report: Conflict, International Response, Lessons Learned* (Oxford: Oxford University Press).

Kuperman, Alan J., 2015. "Obama's Libya Debacle: How a Well-Meaning Intervention Ended in Failure," *Foreign Affairs* 94, no. 2: 66–77.

Kurtz, Gerrit, 2015. *With Courage and Coherence. The Human Rights Up Front Initiative of the United Nations* (Berlin: Global Public Policy Institute).

Murray, Robert W., and Alasdair McKay, eds, 2014. *Into the Eleventh Hour: R2P, Syria and Humanitarianism in Crisis* (Bristol: E-International Relations).

NBC News, 2014. "Obama Authorizes 'Targeted' Airstrikes Against ISIS in Iraq," August 8.

Orford, Anne, 2011. *International Authority and the Responsibility to Protect* (Cambridge: Cambridge University Press).

Panel of Experts on Accountability in Sri Lanka, 2011. "Report of the Secretary-General's Panel of Experts on Accountability in Sri Lanka," March 31.

Posner, Eric A., 2009. "Erga Omnes Norms, Institutionalization, and Constitutionalism in International Law," *Journal of Institutional and Theoretical Economics* 165, no. 1: 5–23.

Ralph, Jason, 2014. "Mainstreaming the Responsibility to Protect in UK Strategy: Improving the Government's Response to the Threat of Mass Atrocity," UNA – UK Policy Briefing 2 (London: United Nations Association).

Rieff, David, 2011. "R2P RIP," *New York Times*, November 7.

Rosenberg, Sheri P., 2013. *A Common Standard for Applying the Responsibility to Protect* (New York: Benjamin N. Cardozo School of Law).

Rosenberg, Sheri, and Ekkehard Strauss, 2012. "A Common Approach to the Application of the Responsibility to Protect," in Daniel Fiott, Rober Zuber, and Joachim Koops, eds, *Operationalizing the Responsibility to Protect: A Contribution to the Third Pillar Approach* (Brussels: Madariaga-College of Europe Foundation, Global Action to Prevent War, the Global Governance Institute, and the International Coalition for the Responsibility to Protect), 55–72.

Security Council Report, 2017. "Chronology of Events: Syria," August, www.securitycouncilreport.org/chronology/syria.php.

Strauss, Ekkehard, 2009. "A Bird in the Hand Is Worth Two in the Bush – On the Assumed Legal Nature of the Responsibility to Protect," *Global Responsibility to Protect* 1, no. 3: 291–323.

Strauss, Ekkehard, 2016. "UN Human Rights Council and High Commissioner for Human Rights," in Alex J. Bellamy and Tim Dunne, eds, *The Oxford Handbook of the Responsibility to Protect* (Oxford: Oxford University Press), 315–34.

United Nations, 2004. "General Comment No. 31 [80], The Nature of the General Legal Obligation Imposed on States Parties to the Covenant," CCPR/C/21/Rev.1/Add.13, May 26.

United Nations, 2011. "In Swift, Decisive Action, Security Council Imposes Tough Measures on Libyan Regime, Adopting Resolution 1970 in Wake of Crackdown on Protesters," Meetings Coverage, Security Council, SC/10187/REV.1, February 26.

United Nations Economic and Social Council, 2017. "General Comment No. 24 on State Obligations under the International Covenant on Economic, Social and Cultural Rights in the Context of Business Activities," E/C.12/GC/24, August 10.

United Nations General Assembly, 1993. "Report of the Committee on the Elimination of Racial Discrimination," A/48/18, September 15.

United Nations General Assembly, 2005. "2005 World Summit Outcome," A/RES/60/1, October 24.

United Nations General Assembly, 2007a. "Human Rights Situations that Require the Council's Attention: Final Report on the Situation of Human Rights in Darfur . . .," A/HRC/6/19, November 28.

United Nations General Assembly, 2007b. "Implementation of General Assembly Resolution 60/251 of 15 March 2006 Entitled 'Human Rights Council': Report of the High-Level Mission on the Situation of Human Rights in Darfur Pursuant to Human Rights Council Decision S-4/101," A/HRC/4/80, March 9.

United Nations General Assembly, 2007c. "Implementation of General Assembly Resolution 60/251 of 15 March 2006 Entitled 'Human Rights Council': Report on the Situation of Human Rights in Darfur . . .," A/HRC/5/6, June 8.

United Nations General Assembly, 2008. "Universal Periodic Review: Report of the Working Group on the Universal Periodic Review: Sri Lanka," A/HRC/8/46, June 5.

United Nations General Assembly, 2011a. "Report of the Human Rights Council on Its Seventeenth Special Session," A/HRC/S–17/2, October 18.

United Nations General Assembly, 2011b. "Report of the Independent International Commission of Inquiry on the Syrian Arab Republic," A/HRC/S–17/2/Add.1, November 23.

United Nations General Assembly, 2017. "Report of the Independent International Commission of Inquiry on the Syrian Arab Republic," A/HRC/36/55, August 8.

United Nations Office for the Coordination of Humanitarian Affairs, 2014. *Aide Memoire for the Consideration of Issues Pertaining to the Protection of Civilians in Armed Conflict* (New York: United Nations).

United Nations Security Council, 2011. "Security Council Approves 'No-Fly Zone' Over Libya, Authorizing 'All Necessary Measures' to Protect Civilians, by Vote of 10 in Favour with 5 Abstentions," 6498 Meeting (Night), March 17, www.un.org/press/en/2011/sc10200.doc.htm.

Zenko, Micah, 2016. "The Big Lie About the Libyan War," *Foreign Policy*, March 22.

10
LINKING THE PAST AND THE PRESENT

The contribution of transitional justice to security after complex conflicts

Susanne Karstedt and Michael Koch

Introduction: moving into the territory of contemporary conflicts

Transitional justice has been one of the most visible and successful normative, legal, and policy innovations at the international level. With its proliferation across the globe to more variegated settings and conflicts, transitional justice has expanded and adapted its scope, mechanisms, and tools to diverse situations of conflict and violence, and to a range of different actors and situations. As transitional justice mechanisms responded to the challenges that arose from the changing contours of mass atrocities at the turn of the twenty-first century and to the context in which they presently take place, transitional justice moved into the increasingly difficult territory of complex conflicts, multiple forms of violence, and a diversity of actors.

In the spread, prevalence, and actor involvement in contemporary mass atrocities, processes are operating that defy hierarchical models and clear-cut typologies of perpetrators, bystanders, collaborators, and victims (for an overview, see Karstedt 2013, 385–386). Transitional justice in post-conflict situations has to deal with legacies of deeply ingrained, long-term, and repeated cycles of violence. Christian Gerlach describes such a situation as an "extremely violent society," where an "overall acclimation to violence" has occurred that facilitates and precipitates events of mass atrocity crimes. Atrocities emerge from the "grassroots nature" (Gerlach 2010; Gerlach and Werth 2009, 172) of other types of violence, committed by an array of perpetrator groups, among them militias and paramilitary groups, rebel groups, or warlord armies. In contrast to the authoritarian setting with a strong state as perpetrator, and its abuse of the monopoly of force, contemporary atrocities take place in a setting of fragile or weak states, where the monopoly of violence has been lost, institutions are dysfunctional, and security forces act according to their own or in the interest of (competing) elite groups (for the paradox of state strength and weakness, see Karstedt 2014b, 2014c).

What can transitional justice achieve in the aftermath of such complex conflicts as just one of the subclusters of activity that are core tasks in such a post-conflict situation (World Bank 2011), and how does it work in the context of peace negotiations, disarmament, and other peacekeeping and peacemaking activities? Further, what can transitional justice contribute to the United Nations (UN) framework of Responsibility to Protect (R2P) as adopted by the United Nations General Assembly (2005), and to the protection of citizens and civilians from atrocity crimes and massive human rights violations, in particular their recurrence in the aftermath of conflicts? This chapter aims to link transitional justice, a backward-looking mechanism, to the R2P agenda, which is decisively focused on the present and future. Do transitional justice processes help to prevent future violence? Or do they instigate violence by fueling conflicts and resentment among victim and perpetrator groups, or within the wider community?

In answering these questions, we focus on one particular outcome of transitional justice processes – the reduction of different types of violence (see Karstedt with Koch 2016).[1] Even if institutional stability, the rule of law, or democratic inclusion have been defined as objectives of transitional justice processes (United Nations Security Council 2004), and have also been included in the three pillars of the R2P framework – state responsibility, international assistance and capacity-building, and timely and decisive response (Ban 2009) – the securitization of citizens first and foremost implies the reduction of violence, and the freedom from fear of violence in their daily lives. The analysis is based on a sample of complex conflicts, i.e., conflicts with multiple parties involved, between 1976 and 2012, thus representing the typical forms of conflict as previously outlined. The selection of transitional justice mechanisms is based on the definition given by the UN Secretary-General in his 2004 report to the Security Council and comprises international and domestic trials, truth commissions, amnesties, and disarmament (disarmament, demobilization, and reintegration – DDR) (United Nations Security Council 2004, 4).[2] We first provide a brief overview of the relationship between transitional justice mechanisms and the R2P framework, and then proceed to the study itself.

Justice, protection, and peace: uneasy relationships

Like all other justice mechanisms, transitional justice is essentially a backward-looking social process and institution. International and domestic trials and courts, tribunals, amnesties, truth commissions, and redress schemes, to name the core of transitional justice mechanisms as described by the UN Secretary-General in 2004 (United Nations Security Council 2004), are designed to address the wrongs of the past. Often taking place a long time after the event (Karstedt 2014a), with extremely long trials or procedures, and being highly selective with regard to cases brought forward and perpetrators standing trial, they have been deemed ineffectual in preventing such events from occurring in the first place. The very nature of transitional justice processes does not seem to make it suitable for galvanizing and implementing effective responses and international action to intervene in, and to prevent, mass atrocities.

The R2P framework explicitly includes transitional justice mechanisms and tools of justice with decisive roles in its agenda, as defined in the UN Secretary-General's report to the General Assembly in 2009 (Ban 2009). In Pillar One, the responsibility of states to end impunity for such crimes and to assist in international justice proceedings is detailed (paragraphs 17–19); in Pillar Three, which outlines tools of timely and decisive responses, the deterrent effect of referral to international criminal justice institutions is invoked (paragraph 53), in particular with regard to the prevention of incitement to atrocity crimes (paragraph 54). Building on the assertion by the Secretary-General that justice and peace "are not mutually exclusive objectives, but rather mutually reinforcing imperatives" (United Nations Security Council 2004, 1), the framework of R2P assigns to transitional justice a preventive role which is based on two functions of criminal law. First is its "rational function" of deterring future crimes among the general population and in particular within the group of potential perpetrators; and second is its expressive and normative function of confirming moral codes and legal norms by charging and sentencing perpetrators, which includes the social meaning and symbolism of justice.[3] The norms involved in the latter function are enshrined in the Rome Statute, and in particular the norms of non-violence against civilians and citizens (Sikkink 2011). Both functions rely on credible institutions and procedures of justice, the existence of institutions and mechanisms of justice, and the establishment of the rule of law (United Nations Security Council 2004).

There is surprisingly little evidence of a deterrent impact of international criminal law beyond anecdotal and case evidence.[4] In addition, such claims mostly ignore the little support for a deterrent effect of courts and sanctioning that has been found for "ordinary" criminal justice (for an overview, see Nagin 2013). We might assume that in the complex situations of violence and conflict with multiple actors, courts and sentences have an even less deterrent effect. Research on simulation models suggests that rather than deterrence by prosecution, separation of conflict parties reduces atrocity crimes and violence (Weidmann and Salehyan 2013; Epstein 2002). In a similar vein, there is a dearth of analysis and evidence about which ways the tools of R2P can achieve the desired outcome of averting mass atrocities, or reducing atrocity violence more generally (Welsh 2011, 261). Notwithstanding a growing body of evidence that interventions and peace operations significantly reduce the risk of recurrence of violence (Doyle and Sambanis 2006), and that the risk of recurring violence is much lower with the presence of a peacekeeping mission (Fortna 2008),[5] both scholars and practitioners are just beginning to understand how interventions into complex processes of violence can be used to protect civilians according to Pillar Three (Welsh 2011).

Consequently, transitional justice mechanisms and the tools of preventive humanitarian intervention are seen in an uneasy relationship in which "justice" poses a threat to "peace," and both seem to be irreconcilable (Ambos, Large, and Wierda 2009). As the International Criminal Court (ICC) signifies a shift toward justice (Langer 2015), it is the focus of such debates. The ICC is seen as an impediment to peace negotiations and agreements, in particular if its retributive function is emphasized (for an overview, see Clark 2011, 522). Indeed, the "interests of justice" have been given prerogative in a number of statements from the ICC prosecutor (Krzan 2016). Historically, this contrasts with preceding transitional justice processes in Latin America and South Africa in the 1990s, where the prosecution of perpetrators was rejected on the grounds that, due to its divisive and polarizing nature, justice could create new tensions and frictions at the time (Clark 2011, 539), only to be resumed decades later. Nonetheless, authors agree that the Rome Statute assigns a preventive and deterrent role to the ICC; however, whether the court can fulfill these functions remains doubtful (Holvoet and Mema 2015; Clark 2011). Official statements such as the Nuremberg Declaration on Peace and Justice assign a critical and decisive role to justice when securing sustainable peace (for the text of the Nuremberg Declaration on Peace and Justice, see United Nations General Assembly 2008).

To date, the relationship between justice and peace is under-researched, and mostly relies on evidence from case studies.[6] While case studies tend to corroborate incompatibility, a rare systematic study on the impact of the ICC on the duration of conflict qualifies such pessimistic conclusions. Alyssa Prorok (2017) found that ICC involvement in a conflict situation increased the duration of conflict, but only in the absence of domestic prosecution; credibility and threat of domestic prosecution reduced the exacerbating effects of ICC involvement; and the interactive effect between international and local justice facilitates if not peace, then at least the end of the conflict. Even if the overall record for peace operations seems to be positive, protective interventions or a peacekeeping presence have been found to have counterproductive effects on one-sided violence against civilians in complex conflicts. Thus, peace operations in ongoing conflicts can unintentionally increase the level of violence perpetrated by non-state actors (Hultman 2010). Given the lack of evidence on both preventive effects of transitional justice and the relationship between peace and justice, the role of transitional justice mechanisms within the R2P framework largely remains normative. In order to implement an integrated framework including justice mechanisms, we need to know how justice mechanisms contribute to security for citizens during and after complex conflicts.

The study

The aim of our research was to answer the following questions. First, do transitional justice mechanisms contribute to security by reducing violence after complex conflicts that include multipolar and horizontal violence by state and non-state actors? Or, second, do they have a counterproductive effect by increasing or stabilizing violence on a high level overall or among specific groups?

This analysis is based on a sample of complex conflicts and the countries in which they took place. The selected transitional justice processes are related to these conflicts with either a start during conflict or post-conflict. As such, the research provides a unique analysis that relates characteristics of the conflict, the post-conflict situation, and the operation and impact of transitional justice processes. It therefore allows for a detailed, conflict-related assessment of the potential of transitional justice processes in sixty-three countries between 1976 and 2012, of which forty-nine had a conflict-related transitional justice process and fourteen did not. Given the complex and highly destructive conflicts and the ensuing fragility of these countries post-conflict, it is astounding that nearly four out of five countries (78 percent) had a transitional justice process – a fact that speaks to the appeal, the hopes, and the perceived benefits of transitional justice processes.

According to Geoff Dancy (2010), we asked whether there was a "discernible difference" in terms of violence that could be attributed to the presence or absence of an overall transitional justice mechanism, including several mechanisms, or to the presence of a single mechanism. Four transitional justice mechanisms were included (following the United Nations Security Council's 2004 definition): trials, truth (and reconciliation) commissions (TRCs), DDR programs, and amnesties. As most countries in the sample used multiple mechanisms at different points of time, single mechanisms could not be assessed independent of the presence/absence of any other. Three different types of violence were used – direct conflict-related battle deaths, state violence, and terrorist attacks by non-state groups – as well as a combined index. The types of violence represent dyadic as well as one-sided violence, and state and non-state actors, and thus reflect the situation of complex conflicts.

Sample and data

The sample was selected with the purpose of including "horizontal violence" (violence by non-state actors) in order to represent the post-conflict environment in which contemporary transitional justice processes operate (de Greiff 2012). Our episodes of horizontal violence represent a selection of protracted, intense, and deadly conflicts, with numerous conflations of different types, which were representative for the decades at the end of the twentieth and beginning of the twenty-first centuries. Conflicts were selected above a threshold of intensity; if violence fell below the threshold, this was then defined as post-conflict, but did not imply the complete absence of violence (for these and the following details on sample and data, see Karstedt with Koch 2016). The selected types include episodes of ethnic and revolutionary war, as well as non-state conflicts between 1976 and 2012. States and governments were actors in most conflicts. The final sample included 124 conflicts, in sixty-three countries, covering the period 1976–2012. Twenty-seven countries were affected by such conflicts in Africa, twenty-three in Asia and Oceania, seven in the Americas, and six in Europe. In 2012, conflicts had ended in about three-quarters (forty-seven) of the sixty-three countries, while in sixteen countries, conflicts were still ongoing, i.e., at least one of the conflicts had not been resolved and continued above the threshold of intensity. For thirty-one countries, this involved a post-conflict situation after ethnic war, for thirty-seven a post-conflict situation after revolutionary war, and for twenty-two a post-conflict situation after a non-state conflict; most of the countries emerged from a series and conflagrations of different types of conflicts.

Transitional justice mechanisms were identified that were related to these conflicts, irrespective of a start within or post-conflict. As international criminal justice procedures were conducted only for a minority of countries and conflicts, domestic and national transitional justice processes were selected; this provided a sample of homogeneously contextualized procedures. The mechanisms including trials, TRCs, and amnesties that had taken place in these countries were collected from the Transitional Justice Database Project.[7] We included DDR programs, as these are increasingly counted as transitional justice-related mechanisms (Dancy 2011), and used the data set compiled by Lilli Banholzer (2014). In order to have at least a five-year follow-up period for assessing the impact of transitional justice processes up to 2012, we included transitional justice procedures up to the end of 2007, resulting in 158 mechanisms, which were used by forty-nine countries. Of these, sixty-four took place in Africa, thirty-nine in Asia, thirty-eight in the Americas, and seventeen in Europe. This included 37 percent (fifty-eight) trials, 15 percent (twenty-four) TRCs, 15 percent (twenty-four) DDRs, and 33 percent (fifty-two) amnesties. Even if trials and amnesties are the dominant mechanisms, other mechanisms are widely and frequently used. Nine post-conflict countries had no transitional justice process at all, and five had ongoing conflicts without any transitional justice process. A number of countries had no transitional justice process after one conflict, but used such a process after another conflict; others used transitional justice mechanisms after all conflicts. Transitional justice processes were used broadly and mostly independently of the type of conflict. The post-conflict setting accommodates transitional justice processes generally, as well as its different components. "Drivers" as well as "spoilers" of transitional justice processes are not concentrated in particular post-conflict settings, but are present in all of them (Skaar and Wiebelhaus-Brahm 2013; Sriram 2013).

All additional data were collected with the aim of covering the sample throughout the time periods as far as possible.[8] We used a combined measure – the Violent Societies Index (VSI) – with three components: conflict-related violence, state violence, and terrorist attacks.[9] State violence was measured by the Political Terror Scale (PTS) – a combined index of state-sanctioned killings, torture, disappearances, and political imprisonment; terrorist attacks comprising a count of such attacks in each country; and battle deaths in state-based internal armed conflicts which measures violence by armed groups. Besides the VSI, these components were also used as stand-alone measures of violence.[10]

Results

In a first step, we compared whether the presence of a transitional justice process made a difference at all; this presents a kind of baseline. In order to isolate an impact of transitional justice processes, we then analyzed three sets of conditions: the timing and sequencing of the transitional justice process; the involvement of the different parties and actors in the transitional justice process; and the external factors shaping the post-conflict/conflict environment in which the transitional justice processes took place. We thus combined both external factors with characteristics of the transitional justice process itself in this analysis.

Presence of transitional justice after conflict

We compared post-conflict situations only, with a transitional justice process and without, and included transitional justice processes with and without amnesties (trials, TRCs, and/or DDRs only). Violence was measured at the end of the conflict, and five years later.[11] As Table 10.1 shows, with a transitional justice process including amnesties present, overall violence – and in particular state violence and terrorist attacks – are significantly reduced during the five-year period after the end of the conflict.

In contrast, if a transitional justice process is completely absent during the first five post-conflict years, violence levels are not significantly reduced, although they mostly subside. The significant reduction of violence can presumably be attributed to the presence of amnesties within the transitional "mix"; we do not find any significant impact on violence levels if amnesties are excluded, and only trials, TRCs, and/or DDRs are included. Further analyses show that the presence of each specific mechanism during this period, whether amnesty, trial, TRC, or DDR, does not have any significant impact on combined and specific levels of violence.

We further analyzed trajectories of overall and state violence for fifteen years after the start of a transitional justice process in thirty countries for which data were available for such a long period (not shown here); consequently, most of the trajectories of the countries included already start during the conflict.[12] The results of the trend analysis corroborate our findings from a shorter period as shown. Two-thirds of the countries had downward trajectories both for the combined index of violence and for state violence. About 70 percent of these downward trends were significant; i.e., these countries experienced a sizable and decisive reduction of all violence and in particular state repression. The minority, one-third, had an upward trajectory, with a significant increase of overall violence for more than half of these countries, and of state violence for one-third. In this group, countries with non-state conflicts are concentrated.

As the presence of a non-state conflict signals higher levels of violence, trajectories out of violence might actually depend on the level of violence at the start of the transitional justice process. However, downward trajectories of overall violence, as well as state violence, are more – and not less – frequent in the group of countries with high levels of violence at the start of the transitional justice process. In contrast, about half of the countries with lower levels of overall violence and state violence at this point have an upward trend with significantly increasing violence for the majority of this group. Generally, transitional justice processes do not obstruct downward trends of violence, and high levels of violence are not an adverse condition for downward trends of violence after the start of transitional justice processes, but to the contrary.

TABLE 10.1 Transitional justice processes and post-conflict violence five years after the end of conflict

Types of violence	Transitional justice process						No transitional justice process		
	Amnesties included (28 countries) violence			Amnesties excluded (22 countries) violence			(13 countries) violence		
	End of conflict	Five years post-conflict	Significance	End of conflict	Five years post-conflict	Significance	End of conflict	Five years post-conflict	Significance
Violent Societies Index	6.7	4.8	**	6.7	5.9	ns	6.1	5.5	ns
State violence (Political Terror Scale)	5.0	4.1	**	5.0	4.6	ns	5.0	4.6	ns
Battle deaths per 100,000	1.0	0.2	ns	1.0	0.9	ns	0.8	0.1	ns
Terrorist attacks (count per year)	15.4	7.0	*	17.4	20.0	ns	7.8	10.4	ns

Level of significance: * p < .05. ** p < .01. *** p < .001; ns = not significant.
The Violent Societies Index is a combined index of state violence (Political Terror Scale), battle deaths, and terrorist attacks; it is based on standardized values of each of its three components between 0 and 9; the combined index has a range between 0 and 27, with higher values indicating higher levels of overall violence. For details, see Karstedt with Koch (2016, Appendix 3).

Sources for violence indicators – State violence: Gibney, Cornett, and Wood (2015); combined scale from two sources, standardized values between 0 and 9, higher values indicate higher levels of state violence (computations by authors); Battle deaths: Uppsala Conflict Data Program (n.d.); Terrorist attacks: START (2015).

Other sources: Uppsala Conflict Data Program (2015); Olsen, Payne, and Reiter (2010); Banholzer (2014); own computations.

Timing of the start of transitional justice

Transitional justice processes are already starting during the conflict. Consequently, the actual timing of the implementation of a transitional justice process might shape the potential impact of the process. We compared all transitional justice processes independent of whether or not they included amnesties that started before the end of the conflict and afterwards. Violence was assessed both for the first five years after the start of the transitional justice process, and up to ten years later; mean values across both periods were used as impact indicators. As Table 10.2 shows, transitional justice processes that start post-conflict have a significantly better record on all violence indicators than those that start during the conflict. This difference is sustained into the period of 6–10 years after the start of the transitional justice process. It therefore can be ruled out that this is an impact of the presence/proximity of the conflict itself, as this would mostly apply for the first five years. Independent of the inclusion of amnesties, timing has long-term consequences for the levels of violence up to a decade, and a later start generally seems to be more beneficial. An early start of transitional justice processes – in particular also for trials and TRCs as stand-alone or combined mechanisms (not shown here) – does not have comparative advantages.

TABLE 10.2 Start of transitional justice during and post-conflict: violence 1–5 and 6–10 years after the end of conflict

Types of violence	Post-conflict violence 1–5 years			Post-conflict violence 6–10 years		
	Start transitional justice process			Start transitional justice process		
	During conflict (40 countries)	Post-conflict (17 countries)	Significance	During conflict (27 countries)	Post-conflict (18 countries)	Significance
Violent Societies Index	10.8	6.3	***	11.2	5.2	***
State violence (Political Terror Scale)	7.0	4.8	***	7.2	4.1	***
Battle deaths per 100,000	10.9	0.9	**	9.3	2.0	*
Terrorist attacks (count per year)	62.4	15.0	*	90.7	13.1	†

Level of significance: † $p < .1$. * $p < .05$. ** $p < .01$. *** $p < .001$.
Sources: See Table 10.1.

External factors and conditions: spoilers and drivers

We controlled for external factors that might make the post-conflict environment more adverse for transitional justice processes and/or were related to the measurement of impact. These included the legacy of conflict in terms of type, duration and extensity of the previous conflict, stability and quality of the institutional environment, and ethnic discrimination as a structural and political obstacle for an ongoing transitional justice process, as one might assume in particular after an ethnic war. We find that transitional justice processes can achieve a similar impact (if at all) both in advantageous as well as in highly disadvantageous post-conflict situations; i.e., situations with little stability, high ethnic discrimination, and a legacy of particularly extensive, deadly, and long conflicts.

State and non-state actors: trials and amnesties

At the core of the debate about justice and peace is the presupposition that prosecution and trials, as well as amnesties, give rise to different motivation and justification for violence among both state and non-state actors, and thus also fuel particular types of violence. The former might instigate revenge by the groups whose representatives are on trial, and the latter might encourage continuous violence because of impunity for perpetrators from either side. Our data show that trials and amnesties for state and non-state agents fairly evenly involve both groups, and are spread across the conflict and post-conflict periods. We therefore compared the presence/absence of trials and amnesties for state and non-state actors independent of whether they started during conflict or post-conflict, and assessed the level of violence for the first five post-conflict years. Neither trials of state agents nor of non-state agents had a significant impact on levels of violence. Independent of the group charged, trials do not counteract or interfere with violence reduction in the post-conflict setting.

In contrast, amnesties for state agents, as well as non-state agents, had an impact on violence levels. As Table 10.3 shows, amnesties for both groups increase the level of violence during the first five post-conflict years. Importantly, these are the only instances of significantly higher levels of violence, rather than no change at all or reduction in our sample. Violence by state agents and agencies is at significantly higher levels when amnesties are granted to both groups, but amnesties for state agents also coincide with significantly higher levels of overall violence as measured by the VSI, and fatalities in combat situations (battle deaths). Quite substantive, however, non-significant increases of terrorist attacks are observed for amnesties for both groups. Amnesties for both groups seem to interact in this process of a build-up of violence. When amnesties are granted to state actors, this might be seen as encouragement by this group further to engage in both repressive and conflict violence; when amnesties are granted to non-state actors, this might serve as justification for state agents for further repressive action, state violence, and military action. The higher levels of fatalities in combat might also indicate increasing involvement of non-state actors if they see amnesties granted to state actors.

TABLE 10.3 Amnesties for state and non-state agents: post-conflict violence (1–5 years)

Types of violence	Post-conflict violence: 1–5 years					
	State agents			Non-state agents		
	No amnesty (31 countries)	Amnesty (16 countries)	Significance	No amnesty (26 countries)	Amnesty (21 countries)	Significance
Violent Societies Index	6.0	7.5	*	6.1	7.0	ns
State violence (Political Terror Scale)	5.0	5.8	*	4.9	5.7	*
Battle deaths per 100,000	0.3	0.9	†	0.3	0.8	ns
Terrorist attacks (count per year)	12.3	24.6	ns	12.9	21.0	ns

Level of significance: † $p < .1$. * $p < .05$; ns = not significant.
Sources: See Table 10.1.

Conclusion: a place for justice

Three results stand out that generally support – but also qualify – the role of justice within the R2P framework and in the context of multipolar and horizontal violence. It should be noted that these results refer to national and within-country transitional justice processes, which might account for their timing – often during conflict – and the conditions of their start – mostly when violence has already subsided.

First, transitional justice processes have the potential to start, contribute, and provide momentum to the overall reduction of all types of violence up to ten years after the end of a conflict. They do this independently of adverse conditions; transitional justice processes achieve a reduction of violence both in advantageous and in highly disadvantageous post-conflict situations; i.e., situations with little stability, high ethnic discrimination, and a legacy of particularly extensive, deadly, and long conflicts. Both duration of conflict and the inclusion of a non-state conflict significantly increase the levels of violence, and thus create a potentially difficult environment for transitional justice processes. Nonetheless, transitional justice processes and different mechanisms were used broadly and mostly independently of the type and intensity of the conflict, and "drivers" as well as "spoilers" of transitional justice processes were not found to be concentrated in particular post-conflict settings.

During the five post-conflict years, transitional justice processes which include amnesties make a significant difference, while stand-alone trials, TRCs, and DDRs or any combination of these do not. It is the combination of mechanisms, which includes amnesties, that makes a difference, as amnesties by themselves are not unambiguously beneficial. There is no evidence in our data that transitional justice processes interfere with, disturb, or counteract the reduction of violence. This applies to all single mechanisms, amnesties, trials, TRCs, and DDRs. Importantly, we provide evidence that even in the aftermath of the most complex conflicts, transitional justice processes including trials or trials specifically neither increase violence generally nor rekindle the conflict; if combined with amnesties, they rather have the potential to reinforce a downward trend of all types of violence. These results mirror the findings by Dancy and his colleagues, who also found that the combination of trials and partial amnesties have the greatest benefits "as the cumulative effect of trials and partial amnesties can take hold" (Dancy et al. 2013, 1). This is, one would posit, a major achievement in a complex post-conflict situation. The results thus give credibility to the "accountability and justice model" and lend support to its role even in the aftermath of the most complex situations. Justice and peace (as non-violence or less violence) are not incompatible, and like peace agreements, justice mechanisms (trials and amnesties)[13] have the potential to reduce violence and keep it at low(er) levels in the majority of conflict situations.

Second, our data show that timing of transitional justice processes matters. The R2P framework, in particular Pillar Three, emphasizes "timely" reactions toward imminent, emerging, or ongoing atrocity crimes, which involves intervention and preventive measures during conflicts. We find that the majority of trials start during conflict, while TRCs evenly start before and after the end of the conflict. In the post-conflict situation, transitional justice processes with and without amnesties start when violence has significantly subsided; a less violent and more secure environment seems to be a requirement for transitional justice processes to take off. Importantly, transitional justice processes with a post-conflict start have a significantly better record on all violence indicators than those that start during the conflict, independent of the inclusion of amnesties. Timing has long-term consequences for the levels of violence, up to a decade. A later start generally seems to be more beneficial than an early start of transitional justice processes – in particular also for trials and TRCs as stand-alone or combined mechanisms. Our results on the national level corroborate those found for the ICC; early intervention by the ICC is prohibitive for ending conflict violence (Prorok 2017). The potential contribution of transitional justice processes toward the R2P framework seems to be contingent on timing, and the relationship between justice and peace predicated on which type of justice mechanism is used when.[14] In particular, these results add a cautionary note on using transitional justice mechanisms as part of Pillar Three; if started during the conflict as a mainly deterrent device, they might have counterproductive consequences in the long run.

Third, our results for amnesties as a justice mechanism are mixed. On the one hand, they seem to be a necessary precondition for a significant reduction of violence within a whole package of transitional justice mechanisms. While trials of state and non-state agents do not counteract or interfere with violence reduction in the post-conflict situation (although they do not significantly reduce violence), amnesties for both groups increase the level of violence during the first five post-conflict years. This is the more important, as it is the only instance in our analyses where we find a significant increase of violence. Taken together, these results cast doubt on an overall and generally beneficial impact of amnesties, which historically have been chosen as a way out of the dilemma of justice and peace due to their supposed impact on long-term peace and stability (Clark 2011, 539). As state and non-state actors are fairly evenly involved in trials during conflict and post-conflict, without advantages for either of the groups, even-handed trials and prosecution should be seen as an option to achieve a reduction of violence on par with amnesties. The data do not lend support to a forced choice between justice and peace, but confirm a violence-reducing effect of fair and even-handed justice as emphasized within the R2P framework.

Notwithstanding its limited focus on violence and its reduction as an indicator of security for citizens, the study has generated preliminary evidence for the place of justice within the R2P framework, and a baseline that justice mechanisms do not interfere with a reduction of one-sided and horizontal violence in complex conflicts. We do not provide evidence as to the (causal) processes reducing violence, whether they relate to a deterrent or an expressive and symbolic function of justice. Even if a role for justice is clearly emerging within the R2P framework, expectations and assumptions need to become more realistic and based on evidence in order to support its edifice.

Acknowledgment

This chapter is based on Karstedt with Koch (2016). The research was partially funded by the International Center for Transitional Justice.

Notes

1 Which, in addition, includes legal institutional/rule of law quality and political capacity/stability as measured outcomes of transitional justice processes.
2 "Transitional justice consists of both judicial and non-judicial processes and mechanisms, including prosecution initiatives, facilitating initiatives in respect of the right to truth, delivering reparations, institutional reform and national consultations." United Nations Secretary-General (2010, 2).
3 For an overview of deterrence in international criminal law, see Karstedt (2014a). Sikkink (2011) claims for Latin America that prosecution had a deterrent effect on state agents committing gross violations of human rights. On expressivism in international criminal law, see Meijers and Glasius (2013); both functions are different from a mere acceptance of laws.
4 Kenya is often cited as a case, as is the impact of the Thomas Lubanga Dylio trial on the recruitment of child soldiers in the Democratic Republic of the Congo. See Holvoet and Mema (2015); Pauletto and Patel (2010).
5 Peace agreements are successful in terminating violence in two-thirds of the cases, while violence recurs and is resumed within a five-year period in a minority of 32 percent of the cases; however, if violence is resumed it is at a reduced level of overall violence. Human Security Report Project (2012, 175–76).

6 For example, on Uganda, see Clark (2011). For a number of case studies, see Ambos, Large, and Wierda (2009).
7 Reparations or lustrations were not included, due to insufficient documentation. The Transitional Justice Database further provided information on trials and amnesties which included state and non-state agents. State agents are those serving the government, while groups opposing the government are counted as non-state actors, both at the time of the crime. For details, see Karstedt with Koch (2016).
8 Additional indicators were used to control for structural conditions of the post-conflict situation and the environment in which transitional justice processes operate, such as discrimination of ethnic groups, as this might be an aggravating factor for transitional justice processes and their impact. For details, see Karstedt with Koch (2016).
9 For further general information on construction and sources, see Karstedt (2012); this article uses a different standardization of the components and the overall VSI.
10 The VSI as used in the report and in this chapter is based on standardized values of each of its three components between 0 and 9; the combined index has a range between 0 and 27, with higher values indicating higher levels of overall violence. The PTS is combined from two sources, the US State Department and Amnesty International country reports; we calculated a scale from both sources ranging from 0 to 9, and higher values indicate higher levels of state violence. Terrorist attacks were retrieved from the START (Study of Terrorism and Responses to Terrorism) Global Terrorism Database, and counted per country and year. Battle deaths in state-based internal armed conflicts is a measure of violence by armed groups, which includes the state as well as paramilitary groups and guerrillas. Data were retrieved from the Peace Research Institute Oslo (PRIO) Battle Death data set and from the University of Uppsala Department of Conflict and Peace Research Conflict Data Program, and calculated as rates per 100,000. For details, see Karstedt with Koch (2016).
11 The period between six and ten years post-conflict was not included, as numbers were too small for meaningful comparisons.
12 This left only a small number of post-conflict countries with ten-year trajectories after the start of the transitional justice process; the results for this group mirrored the results of the group of thirty countries with fifteen-year trajectories.
13 Transitional justice processes that start both during conflict and post-conflict are dominated by "justice mechanisms," trials, and amnesties, which are at the core of the majority of transitional justice processes.
14 But on the timing of transitional justice processes in Latin America and their impact on the stabilization of democracy, see Dancy and Wiebelhaus-Brahm (2015).

References

Ambos, Kai, Judith Large, and Marieke Wierda, 2009. *Building a Future on Peace and Justice: Studies on Transitional Justice, Peace and Development: The Nuremberg Declaration on Peace and Justice* (Berlin: Springer).

Ban Ki-moon, 2009. "Implementing the Responsibility to Protect: Report of the Secretary-General," A/63/677, January 12.

Banholzer, Lilli, 2014. "When Do Disarmament, Demobilisation and Reintegration Programmes Succeed?" Discussion Paper (Bonn: German Development Institute).

Clark, Janine Natalya, 2011. "Peace, Justice and the International Criminal Court: Limitations and Possibilities," *Journal of International Criminal Justice* 9, no. 3: 521–45.

Dancy, Geoff, 2010. "Impact Assessment, Not Evaluation: Defining a Limited Role for Positivism in the Study of Transitional Justice," *International Journal of Transitional Justice* 4, no. 3: 355–76.

Dancy, Geoff, 2011. "Choice and Consequence in Strategies of Transitional Justice," in Christopher J. Coyne and Rachel L. Mathers, eds, *The Handbook on the Political Economy of War* (Cheltenham: Edward Elgar), 397–431.

Dancy, Geoff, Bridget Marchesi, Tricia Olsen, Leigh Payne, Andrew Reiter, and Kathryn Sikkink, 2013. "Stopping State Agents of Violence or Promoting Political Compromise? The Powerful Role of Transitional Justice Mechanisms," Paper presented at the 2013 American Political Science Association annual meeting, Chicago, IL, August.

Dancy, Geoff, and Eric Wiebelhaus-Brahm, 2015. "Timing, Sequencing, and Transitional Justice Impact: A Qualitative Comparative Analysis of Latin America," *Human Rights Review* 16, no. 4: 321–42.

De Greiff, Pablo, 2012. "Justice in Context: Transitional Justice and Paradigms of State and Conflict," Unpublished Concept Paper for International Center for Transitional Justice, New York, March.

Doyle, Michael W., and Nicholas Sambanis, 2006. *Making War and Building Peace: United Nations Peace Operations* (Princeton, NJ: Princeton University Press).

Epstein, Joshua M., 2002. "Modeling Civil Violence: An Agent-Based Computational Approach," *Proceedings of the National Academy of Sciences of the United States of America* 99, no. 3: 7243–50.

Fortna, Virginia Page, 2008. *Does Peacekeeping Work? Shaping Belligerents' Choices After Civil War* (Princeton, NJ: Princeton University Press).

Gerlach, Christian, 2010. *Extremely Violent Societies: Mass Violence in the Twentieth-Century World* (Cambridge: Cambridge University Press).

Gerlach, Christian, and Nicolas Werth, 2009. "State Violence –Violent Societies," in Michael Geyer and Sheila Fitzpatrick, eds, *Beyond Totalitarianism: Stalinism and Nazism Compared* (Cambridge: Cambridge University Press), 133–79.

Gibney, Mark, Linda Cornett, and Reed Wood, 2015. "The Political Terror Scale," www.politicalterrorscale.org/.

Holvoet, Mathias, and Medlir Mema, 2015. "The International Criminal Court and the Responsibility to Protect," in Daniel Fiott and Joachim Koops, eds, *The Responsibility to Protect and the Third Pillar: Legitimacy and Operationalization* (Basingstoke: Palgrave Macmillan), 21–38.

Hultman, Lisa, 2010. "Keeping Peace or Spurring Violence? Unintended Effects of Peace Operations on Violence against Civilians," *Civil Wars* 12, nos. 1–2: 29–46.

Human Security Report Project, 2012. *Human Security Report 2012: Sexual Violence, Education, and War: Beyond the Mainstream Narrative* (Vancouver: Human Security Press).

Karstedt, Susanne, 2012. "Contextualizing Mass Atrocity Crimes: The Dynamics of 'Extremely Violent Societies'," *European Journal of Criminology* 9, no. 5: 499–513.

Karstedt, Susanne, 2013. "Contextualizing Mass Atrocity Crimes: Moving Toward a Relational Approach," *Annual Review of Law and Social Science* 9: 383–404.

Karstedt, Susanne, 2014a. "The End of Impunity? Global Law-Making and Atrocity Crimes," *Zeitschrift für Rechtssoziologie* 34, nos. 1–2: 125–48.

Karstedt, Susanne, 2014b. "Organizing Crime: The State as Actor," in Letizia Paoli, ed., *The Oxford Handbook of Organized Crime* (Oxford: Oxford University Press), 303–20.

Karstedt, Susanne, 2014c. "State Crime: The European Experience," in Sophie Body-Gendrot, Mike Hough, Klára Kerezsi, René Lévy, and Sonja Snacken, eds, *The Routledge Handbook of European Criminology* (Abingdon: Routledge), 125–53.

Karstedt, Susanne, with Michael Koch, 2016. "Transitional Justice and Complex Conflicts: Legacies of Multipolar and Horizontal Violence," Report for the International Center for Transitional Justice, New York, unpublished.

Krzan, Bartłomiej, 2016. "International Criminal Court Facing the Peace vs. Justice Dilemma," *International Comparative Jurisprudence* 2, no. 2: 81–8.

Langer, Johannes, 2015. "Peace vs. Justice: The Perceived and Real Contradictions of Conflict Resolution and Human Rights," *Criterios* 8, no. 1: 165–89.

Meijers, Tim, and Marlies Glasius, 2013. "Expression of Justice or Political Trial? Discursive Battles in the Karadžić Case," *Human Rights Quarterly* 35, no. 3: 720–52.

Nagin, Daniel S., 2013. "Deterrence in the Twenty-First Century," *Crime and Justice* 42, no. 1: 199–263.

Olsen, Tricia D., Leigh A. Payne, and Andrew G. Reiter, 2010. *Transitional Justice in Balance: Comparing Processes, Weighing Efficacy* (Washington, DC: United States Institute of Peace).

Pauletto, Elettra, and Preeti Patel, 2010. "Challenging Child Soldier DDR Processes and Policies in the Eastern Democratic Republic of Congo," *Journal of Peace, Conflict and Development* 16: 35–57.

Prorok, Alyssa K., 2017. "The (In)compatibility of Peace and Justice? The International Criminal Court and Civil Conflict Termination," *International Organization* 71, no. 2: 213–43.

Sikkink, Kathryn, 2011. *The Justice Cascade: How Human Rights Prosecutions Are Changing World Politics* (New York: W.W. Norton).

Skaar, Elin, and Eric Wiebelhaus-Brahm, 2013. "The Drivers of Transitional Justice: An Analytical Framework for Assessing the Role of Actors," *Nordic Journal of Human Rights* 31, no. 2: 127–48.

Sriram, Chandra Lekha, 2013. "Spoilers of Justice," *Nordic Journal of Human Rights* 31, no. 2: 248–61.

START (Study of Terrorism and Responses to Terrorism), 2015. "Global Terrorism Database," www.start.umd.edu/gtd/.

United Nations General Assembly, 2005. "2005 World Summit Outcome," A/RES/60/1, October 24.

United Nations General Assembly, 2008. "Letter Dated 13 June 2008 from the Permanent Representatives of Finland, Germany and Jordan to the United Nations Addressed to the Secretary-General," A/62/885, June 19.

United Nations Secretary-General, 2010. "Guidance Note of the Secretary General: United Nations Approach to Transitional Justice," March.

United Nations Security Council, 2004. "The Rule of Law and Transitional Justice in Conflict and Post-Conflict Societies: Report of the Secretary-General," S/2004/616, August 23.

Uppsala Conflict Data Program, n.d. "Battle-Related Deaths Dataset (v.5–2015)," ucdp.uu.se/.

Uppsala Conflict Data Program, 2015. "Non-State Conflict Dataset (v2.5–2014)," ucdp.uu.se/.

Weidmann, Nils B., and Idean Salehyan, 2013. "Violence and Ethnic Segregation: A Computational Model Applied to Baghdad," *International Studies Quarterly* 57, no. 1: 52–64.

Welsh, Jennifer, 2011. "Civilian Protection in Libya: Putting Coercion and Controversy Back into RtoP," *Ethics and International Affairs* 25, no. 3: 255–62.

World Bank, 2011. *World Development Report 2011: Conflict, Security, and Development* (Washington, DC: World Bank).

PART V
Peacekeeping, civil–military assistance, and stabilization

PART V

11
IMPLEMENTING R2P THROUGH UNITED NATIONS PEACEKEEPING OPERATIONS

Opportunities and challenges

Charles T. Hunt and Lisa Sharland

Introduction

In the mid-1990s, the inability of United Nations (UN) peacekeepers to prevent or halt genocide in Rwanda or avert the Srebrenica massacres in Bosnia was instrumental in the genesis of the Responsibility to Protect (R2P) doctrine (Bellamy 2009; Evans 2008). Indeed, these events ensure that R2P is inextricably linked and entangled with the history of UN peacekeeping.

Since then, UN peacekeeping operations[1] have often been sent, in part, to respond to the commission of mass atrocity crimes. For example, in July 2007, following allegations of genocide and other crimes against humanity, a faltering African Union (AU) mission was eventually replaced by a joint African Union–United Nations Mission in Darfur (UNAMID). In April 2014, following mass atrocities including ethnic cleansing in the Central African Republic (CAR), regional troops were "re-hatted" to create a United Nations Multidimensional Integrated Stabilization Mission in the Central African Republic (MINUSCA). On other occasions, missions have been *in situ* as acts of genocide, war crimes, crimes against humanity, and ethnic cleansing have unfolded around them. Following Côte d'Ivoire's disputed presidential elections in December 2010, the United Nations Operation in Côte d'Ivoire (UNOCI) was besieged as atrocities were committed. Elsewhere, the UN's statebuilding mission in South Sudan was forced into a sudden course correction when widespread and systematic attacks on civilians accompanied the outbreak of civil war in December 2013. On each occasion, the Security Council initially authorized or adjusted these missions under Chapter VII of the UN Charter to use all necessary means to protect civilians from physical violence.

In addition to protection of civilians (POC) mandates, resolutions authorizing UN peacekeeping operations in places like CAR, Mali, and the Democratic Republic of the Congo (DRC) have also referenced the host state's primary responsibility to protect its population from harm and requested that missions in Sudan/South Sudan support efforts to target perpetrators of, and pursue accountability for, mass atrocity crimes. It is understandable, therefore, that UN peacekeeping operations are seen as a crucial mechanism for implementing R2P in practice. UN Secretaries-General have repeatedly identified UN peacekeeping missions as an appropriate instrument for operationalizing R2P (Ban 2009, 2014; Guterres 2017). Scholars, too, have argued that many core objectives of UN peacekeeping operations are consonant with R2P and that therefore these could be mutually reinforcing frameworks for action to protect civilians from the most egregious of human rights abuses (Hunt and Bellamy 2011; Berdal 2015; Williams 2016b; Nasu 2011).

The broad notion of POC in the context of this chapter pertains to the protection of civilians from harm resulting directly or indirectly from armed conflict. It is often referred to as a legal concept due to its firm roots and long tradition in international humanitarian, human rights, and refugee law. However, it can also be understood as a normative framework for alleviating the effects of armed conflict on civilian populations. POC in armed conflict emerged as a thematic agenda of the Security Council after Resolution 1265 (1999), paragraph 10 stated a willingness to "respond to situations of armed conflict where civilians are being targeted or humanitarian assistance to civilians is being deliberately obstructed," further pledging to consider "appropriate measures" for doing so. That agenda item has included efforts to improve the capabilities of peacekeeping operations with protection mandates.

The emergence and content of R2P has been covered elsewhere in this volume (see Cecilia Jacob and Martin Mennecke's Introduction). However, it is useful to briefly discuss the relationship between R2P and POC. Conceptually, R2P and the better established POC agenda are closely linked but distinct concepts. The POC agenda is wider than R2P because it applies to protection of civilians from all violations of international humanitarian and human rights law in situations of armed conflict. However, some aspects of R2P's prevention components extend beyond POC. For instance, not all mass atrocities occur in times of armed conflict. Despite significant overlap between protecting civilians from mass atrocities and civilian protection in conditions of armed conflict,[2] the two objectives are distinct, have different prerequisites and, in many cases, different strategies are likely to be needed (for elaboration on different strategies, see Hunt and Bellamy 2011, 5–7).

Consequently, there are synergies – but also important differences and distinctions – between R2P and POC, whether as legal concepts or thematic Security Council agendas (van Steenberghe 2014; Lie and de Carvalho 2012; Francis, Popovski, and Sampford 2012; for more detail, see Williams 2016b). However, the focus of this chapter is not on POC in armed conflict, but on POC as an operational concept for UN peacekeeping operations (Tardy 2012). The emergence of this POC operational concept as a center of gravity for modern UN peacekeeping has led many to identify synergies between this and the R2P framework, and add further weight to the case of R2P implementation by peacekeepers.

Seeking to pursue R2P objectives through UN peacekeeping operations, in particular under the POC operational concept, presents a number of political, principled, and practical challenges. UN peacekeeping is predicated on a holy trinity of principles that enable its passage in Security Council resolutions, contributions by major troop and financial providers, and acceptance by host governments and conflicting parties. Codified in the 2008 "capstone doctrine," these are that peacekeeping operations: (1) are deployed with the consent of the main parties to the conflict; (2) act impartially; and (3) use the minimum amount of force necessary to defend the mission and the mandate (United Nations 2008). It is argued that a combination of this principled consensus and the fact that these missions are authorized under resolutions of the Security Council also affords UN peacekeeping missions their unique legitimacy and has enabled their effectiveness (see Hurd 1999). The imperative in R2P to act without host-state consent when it is manifestly failing to fulfill its primary responsibility (as a last resort) is at odds with the established principles of UN peacekeeping (United Nations Department of Peacekeeping Operations/Department of Field Support 2015, 19).[3] In this sense, R2P may bring an intolerable level of political toxicity to UN peacekeeping operations, with significant ramifications for their future viability. Similarly, UN peacekeeping operations are perennially beset by shortfalls in resources and the political will that are essential to implementing their ambitious mandates (Bellamy and Hunt 2015). Relying on these over-stretched and under-resourced missions to realize the great expectations of R2P may be unrealistic and ethically untenable.

This chapter explores the political, principled, and practical challenges associated with the implementation of R2P through UN peacekeeping. It proceeds in three main parts. The first section traces the evolution of the POC agenda in UN peacekeeping missions in order to identify issues of contention among member states, particularly as they relate to the principles of peacekeeping and the concept of host-state consent in the context of implementing R2P. The second section draws on examples from the UN peacekeeping missions in South Sudan and the DRC, to identify a range of opportunities as well as challenges emerging from comprehensive POC strategies and practices in the field. The third section lays out a number of areas that, if strengthened, could enhance the implementation of R2P through the UN's peace operations going forward.

The chapter argues that UN peacekeeping already offers many opportunities for pursuing and realizing R2P goals. However, it also cautions that any overreach or attempts to characterize peacekeeping as a vehicle for implementing R2P in full, unconditionally, may jeopardize the unique legitimacy and effectiveness of UN peacekeeping.

The protection of civilians in UN peacekeeping: politics, principles, and policies

Although POC is now central to the work of UN peacekeeping, it was not institutionalized as part of traditional peacekeeping in the first fifty years of operation. The "observe, monitor and report" missions that largely characterized the period from 1948 until the end of the Cold War had no explicit reference to "protection of civilians" in their mission mandates (Holt and Taylor, with Kelly 2009, 42). Most missions during this period were focused on managing interstate conflicts, and observing ceasefires and the implementation of peace agreements. Yet that slowly started to shift during the 1990s following the failure of UN peacekeeping missions to protect civilians from appalling violence, including in contexts where mass atrocity crimes took place, such as Rwanda and Srebrenica (United Nations 1999a, 1999b).

These tragic events served as catalysts for further discussion and debate in New York about the role of UN peacekeeping in protecting civilians. By 1999, the Security Council was beginning to focus on the protection of civilians in armed conflict as a thematic issue, as exemplified by Resolution 1265 (1999).[4] At the same time, the Council was facing pressure to deploy peacekeeping missions into conflicts of an internal and intrastate nature, in contexts such as Sierra Leone and the DRC. Haunted by the failures of peacekeeping in the 1990s, and informed by thematic developments on POC, the Council authorized the first UN peacekeeping operation with an explicit mandate to protect civilians in Sierra Leone in October 1999. Referring to Chapter VII of the UN Charter, that mandate stated that:

> UNAMSIL [United Nations Mission in Sierra Leone] may take the necessary action to ensure the security and freedom of movement of its personnel and, within its capabilities and areas of deployment, to afford protection to civilians under imminent threat of physical violence, taking into account the responsibilities of the Government of Sierra Leone and ECOMOG [Economic Community of West African States Monitoring Group].
>
> *(Resolution 1270 [1999], paragraph 14)*

Similar language was used by the Security Council in various configurations, usually under Chapter VII of the Charter, to mandate UN peacekeeping missions in the DRC, Liberia, Côte d'Ivoire, Burundi, Sudan, Darfur, Lebanon, Chad, and CAR, to protect civilians in the decade that followed (Holt and Taylor, with Kelly 2009, 45). In other words, POC language started to become institutionalized into new and revised multidimensional peacekeeping missions from 1999 onwards.

Despite the considerable progress that including POC in peacekeeping mandates represented at the strategic level, there was limited progress during this decade at the operational and tactical levels, where the Security Council was reliant on member states and the UN Secretariat to take the concept forward. This was largely attributable to the limited discussion between the Security Council, the UN Secretariat, and member states about what implications this newly mandated language would have on the ground in terms of operational planning, force generation, guidance, and training. This meant no overarching policies on POC were put in place for missions, or for military, police, and civilian components.

Furthermore, while the Security Council had reached agreement on the need for peacekeeping missions to protect civilians, there had been very little discussion with the major troop and police contributing countries (T/PCCs) about what

POC entailed on the ground. That meant there were no standard pre-deployment training, no performance measures, and no accountability frameworks. The limited POC successes during this decade were therefore generally a consequence of good mission leadership or exceptional individuals, rather than consistent policies or directions provided by headquarters (Holt and Taylor, with Kelly 2009).

By 2008, it was clear that there had been limited progress on the ground to improve efforts by peacekeeping missions to protect civilians, or enhance understanding of the concept (Holt and Taylor, with Kelly 2009). This lack of understanding extended to the relationship between POC and R2P, meaning that efforts to improve the implementation of POC mandates were often confused or held hostage to concerns about the concept of R2P.[5] For example, oversimplified interpretations of Pillar Three as a license for non-consensual intervention when a government was failing to uphold its responsibility to protect was seemingly at odds with established principles of UN peacekeeping – namely, consent of the host government to the deployment of a mission. These concerns and misunderstandings resulted in worry among UN peacekeeping officials that hard-won consensus on POC may be jeopardized and its consolidation in the field challenged,[6] and significant disagreement among member states when the debates that had been taking place in the Council reached the General Assembly through the Special Committee on Peacekeeping Operations (C34) in 2008.

Debating politics and principles

There was no reference to "protection of civilians" as a mandated task in any C34 report prior to 2009. The issue had not garnered significant attention in the early part of the decade as part of the committee's consideration of "the whole question of peace-keeping in all their aspects."[7] As the premier General Assembly body engaged in providing proposals, recommendations, and conclusions on a range of peacekeeping issues, the absence of wider discussion on POC reflected a lack of awareness about the need for further concrete guidance to operationalize the mandate. It also reflected wider confusion in the peacekeeping community about the distinct differences between POC and R2P.

Efforts to discuss the roles and responsibilities of T/PCCs when it came to POC in the C34 met with hostility. Many of the countries in the Non-Aligned Movement (which included most major T/PCCs), as well as Russia and China, initially opposed the inclusion of explicit language on the need for POC guidance in the C34 report. There were a range of reasons put forward during negotiations in the years that followed.[8] Some T/PCCs felt it was an affront to them and a criticism of their efforts on the ground, where they argued they were already protecting civilians (despite evidence to the contrary emerging from the field). Others argued that peacekeepers were already being asked to do too much and did not have the resources or capabilities to carry out such mandates. Many major T/PCCs argued that the demands placed on them were unreasonable, particularly when those demands were coming from countries that were not willing to deploy significant numbers of personnel into the field (primarily Western and European countries). Many countries also relied on the argument that a more "holistic" rather than military approach was needed to find peace, as this would ultimately result in civilians being protected.

Perhaps of greatest concern, however, was the mistaken argument that POC went beyond the three peacekeeping principles. In line with similar concerns about consent for intervention under R2P, there was a partly mistaken belief that inclusion of POC would diminish the importance of host-state consent and diminish the impartiality of peacekeepers. Despite both POC and R2P fulfilling similar objectives at the operational and tactical levels, this meant that debate and discussions on R2P were often not clearly differentiated from discussions on POC within a peacekeeping context.

Despite these challenges, however, the debates started to move forward, with 2009 representing a watershed year for POC. The C34 agreed to introduce into its report a sub-heading – "Other mandated tasks, including the protection of civilians" – followed by four paragraphs (United Nations 2009, paragraphs 125–128). The Security Council also adopted Resolution 1894 (2009) on protection of civilians, recognizing in paragraph 22 the need for "comprehensive operational guidance" and requesting that the Secretary-General develop "an operational concept for the protection of civilians." The UN membership was beginning to slowly accept the importance of POC in peacekeeping, although there were still significant reservations and caveats in place on how that debate moved forward.

Developing policy and addressing ground realities

The inclusion of language on POC in the 2009 C34 report (United Nations 2009), along with the requests of the Security Council, provided the UN Secretariat with sufficient scope to advance work to develop guidance and eventually, policy, on POC. This was an important step forward in clarifying and articulating how POC differed from R2P. In setting out what tasks constituted POC, it became much clearer how POC could actually enable the implementation of the less controversial aspects of R2P, particularly as it related to R2P Pillar Two activities; that is, the international community assisting member states with their responsibility to protect.

The release of the draft operational concept on POC in 2010 provided the first clear articulation of how peacekeeping missions and peacekeepers were expected to support the host government in upholding their responsibility to protect the civilian population. It identified three tiers: (1) protection through political process; (2) providing protection from physical violence; and (3) establishing a protective environment (United Nations Department of Peacekeeping Operations/Department of Field Support 2010).

There is significant resonance between Tier 3 and efforts to implement R2P under Pillar Two, particularly in terms of ensuring that a mission was preparing a country to sustain efforts to protect the civilian population. Tasks such as supporting the political process, disarmament, demobilization and reintegration, rule of law, and supporting security sector reform were articulated as part of Tier 3 POC tasks. In conducive mission environments such as Liberia and Haiti, for example, there has been considerable scope for peacekeeping missions to fulfill R2P Pillar Two objectives. Yet this is not necessarily the case in contexts where the conditions are less conducive, or the host government is obstructing the work of the peacekeeping mission. As the case study of South Sudan demonstrates in the next section, the crisis of December 2013 resulted in the mission significantly reducing the scope of its mandate from one focused on statebuilding to one almost exclusively focused on efforts to physically protect civilians. On the one hand, this shows how the POC operational concept also offers opportunities to envisage how peacekeeping could produce the timely and decisive responses envisaged under Pillar Three of R2P. On the other hand, such challenges have led some commentators to question whether a definition of POC that includes capacity-building tasks (as defined under Tier 3) may be too wide for the purposes of fulfilling POC objectives in peacekeeping (Di Razza 2017; Chappuis and Gorur 2015).

While recent challenges in contexts such as South Sudan have focused attention on the scope of POC, most of the initial politics and controversy was focused around the use of force through efforts to implement Tier 2. While the POC operational concept was not explicit on what actions a peacekeeping mission should take if it was required to confront host-government forces in the field, further guidance was much clearer on the matter, meaning POC has continued to remain contentious in discussions in New York. For example, the Framework for Drafting Comprehensive Protection of Civilians (POC): Strategies in UN Peacekeeping Operations acknowledged that "missions are authorized to use force against any party, including elements of government forces, where such elements are themselves engaged in physical violence against civilians" (United Nations Department of Peacekeeping Operations/Department of Field Support 2011, 3). Other documents are similarly very clear on the topic (United Nations Department of Peacekeeping Operations 2015; United Nations Department of Peacekeeping Operations/Department of Field Support 2015).[9]

Nonetheless, these developments, which are essential in clarifying expectations for peacekeepers on the ground when it comes to POC, continue to highlight an ongoing challenge for UN peacekeeping missions when they are operating in environments where the host government or forces associated with the host government may be a perpetrator of attacks against civilians. In effect, by acting in these situations, peacekeeping missions are filling the gap where host governments are failing to uphold their responsibility to protect. While this may demonstrate that UN peacekeeping missions can fulfill and support R2P objectives, such actions may diminish the unique value and legitimacy of peacekeeping. With the erosion of host-government consent taking place in contexts such as South Sudan and the DRC, this prompts wider questions about what roles peacekeeping can have in operationalizing R2P.

Protection in practice: examples from South Sudan and the Congo

South Sudan: statebuilding and POC

The United Nations Mission in Sudan (UNMIS) was deployed in 2005 to oversee the implementation of the peace agreement that concluded decades of armed struggle in the protracted north–south civil war in Sudan. The mission chaperoned South Sudan through its referendum and passage to independence in July 2011. In Resolution 1996 (2011), the United Nations Mission in South Sudan (UNMISS) was established to support the capacity of the newly established government to assume functions of state responsibilities by the newly independent country. However, the outbreak of a new civil war in December 2013 forced the UN into a course correction with Resolution 2155 (2014). The case of UNMISS raises at least three key challenges to seeing peacekeeping missions as a vehicle for implementing R2P.

First, the 2013 descent into civil war and the perpetration of systematic attacks against civilians by government forces, as well as opposition fighters, highlights the inherent tension for POC in peacekeeping. The original mandate pursuing peacebuilding primarily through state capacity-building is consistent with Tier 3 of the UN's POC operational concept – that is, creating a protective environment – and was articulated at the time and in subsequent Secretary-General reports as a shining example of R2P Pillar Two international assistance to a state in upholding its responsibility to protect (Ban 2014; Giffen 2016).[10] However, this backfired when the security institutions that the mission was supporting became the chief abusers rather than protectors of civilians. The idea that UNMISS could simultaneously build the capacity of the South Sudanese security forces and protect civilians from them was untenable and led to the Security Council restructuring the mission to suspend direct assistance to the state institutions and instead focus on four key goals: support the delivery of humanitarian assistance, monitor and report on human rights abuses, protect civilians from physical violence, and support the implementation of the January 23, 2014, Agreement on Cessation of Hostilities (Malan and Hunt 2014, 16). This example reveals a tension between statebuilding objectives and peacekeepers' responsibility for the physical protection of vulnerable civilian populations (Tier 2) and the relative weighting and prioritization of these tasks. This presents major problems for UN peacekeeping missions when host states are implicated in abuses against civilians. It also limits the utility of peacekeeping as a vehicle to implement R2P.

Second, the mission's decision to "open the gates" to hundreds of thousands of civilians fleeing violence undoubtedly saved lives. However, this created de facto internally displaced persons camps within UN bases, and it is now impossible for UNMISS to evict the hundreds of thousands of civilians whose safety depends on the relative sanctuary this provides. These "POC sites" absorb huge quantities of mission attention and resources to sustain. Even then, as with other "safe haven" concepts before them, the POC sites arguably create unrealistic expectations that peacekeepers simply cannot meet in both the scale and quality of assistance with current resources (United Nations Security Council 2016). Responding to threats and attacks on civilians in the vicinity of – and occasionally within – the sites in practice is fraught with difficulty for UN troops and police. Similarly, providing for internal security of the sites has produced legal and jurisdictional challenges for UN police who do not have the executive mandate to arrest and detain. Moreover, millions more beyond the gates are left exposed, even further out of reach, and denied even the limited coverage that UNMISS could otherwise achieve. All of this means that despite the short-term benefits of the POC sites, this approach may reduce the effectiveness of the mission to provide physical protection more broadly.

Third, despite authorization to use all necessary means to protect civilians, irrespective of the source of the threats (Resolution 2155 [2014], paragraph 4[a][i]),[11] UNMISS has proven unable (or unwilling) to act on it effectively. Two major incidents in 2016 illustrated this "inaction" starkly. In February 2016, the POC site in Malakal was attacked by external armed elements (including government Sudan People's Liberation Army forces), during which at least thirty inhabitants were killed, 123 others were wounded, and a large portion of the site was destroyed (Center for Civilians in Conflict 2016a, 2016b; United Nations Secretary-General 2016a). Despite a UN investigation that handed down recommendations for preventing similar future failures, when violence broke out again in Juba in July 2016, the main UN compound installation and adjacent POC sites were attacked, resulting in the deaths of tens of civilians and the injury of many more, including acts of sexual violence in the vicinity of the POC sites (United Nations Secretary-General 2016b; Center for Civilians in Conflict 2016b). Accounts at the time reported peacekeeper "inaction" including desertion of posts and reluctance or refusal to follow orders (Patinkin 2016; Human Rights Watch 2016b). A subsequent independent special investigation identified a range of shortcomings that contributed to the failings, including confusion over command and control and rules of engagement, as well as coordination issues between uniformed and non-uniformed components of the mission. However, perhaps the most significant finding emphasized the risk averse and "inward-looking" posture of peacekeepers when it came to fulfilling POC responsibilities (United Nations Security Council 2016). The POC sites also become a microcosm for tensions between the mission and the host government. The reluctance on the part of some T/PCCs to respond to violations by host-government forces has left the mission in a difficult position whereby the mandate is not backed up by troops on the ground. In this context, relying on peacekeepers to provide the "timely and decisive" responses to vulnerable populations required under R2P's Pillar Three is likely to be inadequate.

UNMISS has been mandated as a force for protection regardless of from where the threats to civilians emanate. However, the reliance on host-state consent for freedom of movement and even continued existence of the mission constrains what peacekeepers can do to prevent, halt, and respond effectively to mass atrocities in and around their areas of deployment, let alone across the wider territory of South

Sudan. Indeed, it highlights a more general point that when peacekeeping missions are deployed in the context of ongoing fighting that imperils civilians, it is extremely difficult for peacekeepers to achieve their circumscribed protection aims, let alone the great expectations of the responsibility to protect (Giffen 2016).

Democratic Republic of the Congo: robust POC

The DRC – in particular, its eastern provinces on the shores of Lake Kivu – has been the site of repeated episodes of mass atrocity crimes (Stearns 2011; Prunier 2008). In addition to the Opération des Nations Unies au Congo (ONUC) mission (1960–1964), there have been multiple incarnations of UN peacekeeping missions in the DRC since Resolution 1279 (1999) mandated the establishment of the United Nations Organization Mission in the Democratic Republic of the Congo (MONUC) in 1999 to oversee the Lusaka peace agreement that brought to an end the Congolese civil war. MONUC was one of the earliest missions to include the now commonplace POC mandate, and POC was made the mission's priority task in Resolution 1856 (2008).[12] Reflecting a new phase of the post-war transition, MONUC was transformed into the United Nations Organization Stabilization Mission in the Democratic Republic of the Congo (MONUSCO) in Resolution 1925 (2010). MONUSCO was mandated to support the government of the DRC in its stabilization and peace consolidation efforts, and was authorized to use all necessary means to protect civilians. Following the overrun of Goma by *Mouvement du 23 Mars* (M23) fighters in November 2012,[13] the Security Council broke with tradition and authorized a Force Intervention Brigade (FIB), with the mandate to "carry out targeted offensive operations ... unilaterally or jointly with the FARDC [Forces Armées de la République Démocratique du Congo]" with the aim of neutralizing armed groups. Although not exclusively justified for POC purposes, it was part of the Security Council's rationale that envisaged FIB as "contribut[ing] to the objective of reducing the threat posed by armed groups on state authority and civilian security in eastern DRC and to make space for stabilization activities" (Resolution 2098 [2013], paragraph 12[b]).

Three points are worth noting here. First, despite early successes in defeating the M23 rebel group, the robust approach to providing protection to civilian populations (that is, by removing major threats to their safety) also yielded negative side effects (Tull 2018; Hunt 2017). For instance, it was hoped that FIB would bring a more proactive and robust approach to POC across the whole mission under the notion of "one mission, one force, one mandate." Yet in some instances, the arrival of FIB prompted other contingents or so-called "framework brigades" to adopt a more passive and reactive "garrison mentality" – becoming less, not more, likely to respond to civilian insecurity – disowning the POC agenda viewed as the domain of FIB (Day 2017). It has also been argued that the passivity of the framework brigades had a negative feedback effect on the proactivity and robustness of FIB (Tull 2018). These same shortcomings extend across the mission and have been exposed by ongoing attacks against civilians in the Beni territory of eastern DRC since October 2014 – despite the large presence of MONUSCO peacekeepers stationed nearby (Human Rights Watch 2016a).

Second, the DRC has been a laboratory for POC experimentation. For instance, MONUSCO has been the breeding ground for the development of Joint Protection Teams, the Community Liaison Assistant concept, the Community Alert Network, and the experimentation with more mobile rapidly deployable units such as Company and Temporary Operating Bases (Weir and Hunt 2011). These initiatives have enhanced existing POC efforts and hold promise for making missions better at responding rapidly and effectively. Perhaps most importantly, many of these mechanisms and tools offer potential to improve prevention through early warning and empowering local communities to develop self-protection strategies (Gorur and Carstensen 2016). However, efforts to export POC mechanisms from DRC to other missions such as Mali and CAR have met with limited success, highlighting how POC efforts need to be context specific.

Third, MONUSCO's strategy to counter armed groups revealed a tension between support to the Congolese government and POC mandate. The mission is not only supporting government institutions, but at times – FIB in particular – conducting joint military operations to restore and extend state authority. Given that government forces are responsible for as many as 60 percent of the human rights violations against civilians in the DRC (United Nations 2017), the case of MONUSCO (as with UNMISS) throws up thorny questions regarding the desirable degree of partnership with host governments. If missions cannot curtail the worst abuses of the host government and are at times complicit – notwithstanding the mitigation efforts of the UN's human rights due diligence policy – in their misconduct, this poses a question about the utility of UN peacekeeping as a vehicle for implementing R2P. For both peacekeeping and R2P, this raises a fundamental question: how can you build a protective environment (POC Tier 3, and broader R2P Pillars Two and Three) without emboldening an abusive and intransigent host government?

The occurrence of atrocity crimes in the DRC makes MONUSCO an obvious bulwark for advancing R2P objectives. Furthermore, the mission has provided a petri dish for trialing new approaches and developing innovative tools for POC that have brought some improvements in the planning for, management of, and response to POC needs. However, in addition to financial and human resource constraints, lessons from FIB have emphasized that there are no military solutions to political problems. Despite the obstruction by a recalcitrant host government, these events demonstrate how current thinking and practice in peacekeeping missions such as MONUSCO offer only limited promise for implementing R2P.

An agenda for protection

As the case studies of South Sudan and the DRC have demonstrated, UN peacekeeping missions are already fulfilling some aspects of R2P, yet there are inherent risks and challenges if peacekeeping is relied on too heavily to fulfill these objectives. If R2P is to be implemented through UN peacekeeping, then this requires the overall endeavor of UN peacekeeping to become more effective, and peacekeeping missions need to better prioritize POC. As this section details, reforms are already underway to implement these improvements through aspects of the reform agenda emerging from the High-Level Independent Panel on United Nations Peace Operations (2015). Such improvements are likely to have the most success in environments where the peacekeeping mission is able to deliver its mandate without interference from the host government or parties to the conflict. The more challenging aspect to address, however, relates to how peacekeeping missions deliver on their POC mandate in environments where their role is contested or challenged, in particular by the host government, as demonstrated by the case studies of South Sudan and the DRC. Failure to manage these risks carefully may actually diminish the ability of UN peacekeeping as an institution to protect civilians.

Strengthening peacekeeping and enhancing implementation of POC

If a UN peacekeeping mission is effective and successful in fulfilling its mandate to protect civilians, then it will also support the implementation of R2P. This is likely to have most success in environments where the host government and parties to the conflict provide their unreserved support for the peacekeeping mission, as this will allow for a mandate that delivers not only on the physical protection of civilians in instances where the government is unable to do so (Pillar Three), but also that supports efforts to develop the government's capacity to protect civilians (Pillar Two). This has largely been the case in the contexts of recent missions that have closed down or entered a transition phase, such as in Liberia, Côte d'Ivoire, and Haiti. In other words, a peacekeeping mission can support the country in fulfilling its responsibility to protect through all pillars of R2P, which also aligns with the three tiers of protection identified in the UN POC policy.

In contexts where there is host-government support for the mission, the main impediment to delivering on the implementation of R2P often rests with some of the challenges currently facing UN peacekeeping. As the High-Level Independent Panel on United Nations Peace Operations' report pointed out, there are still significant reforms that need to take place if UN peacekeeping is to live up to its objectives and deliver on the ground. Closing that gap between expectation and delivery requires improvements in "assessments and planning capabilities, timely information and communication, leadership and training as well as more focused mandates" (High-Level Independent Panel on United Nations Peace Operations 2015, ix). Reforms that focus on improving the UN's force-generation processes, developing crisis responses, and strengthening mission leadership are likely to have an impact on the ability of missions to deliver and react to situations on the ground where civilians are under threat. It also requires consistent and concerted effort to implement key reforms as they relate to various cross-cutting issues, whether it be women, peace and security (e.g., deployment of women protection advisers and gender advisers to the field), or preventing sexual exploitation and abuse.

Greater effort is also needed to articulate the POC roles and responsibilities of different actors on the ground. There has been considerable investment by the UN in the last decade to develop guidance and training materials to prepare different mission components when it comes to POC. This has included the development of scenario-based training materials, as well as specific guidance for military and police components. In response to the events in Malakal and Juba in South Sudan in 2016, the UN undertook a review of the directions given to senior mission leaders on mandate implementation, piloting a crisis management tabletop exercise for civilian heads of mission, with a similar exercise for Force Commanders in the process of being implemented (United Nations Security Council 2017, 6). Ultimately, improving the guidance and preparation for peacekeepers prior to and during deployment will contribute to physical protection as well as creating a protective environment, which will have positive impacts on the pursuit of R2P goals.

Such initiatives, however, also need to be accompanied by the political commitment of member states to support UN peacekeeping. Recent high-level summits and ministerial meetings hosted in New York, London, and Vancouver, which have focused on capability gaps in peacekeeping by encouraging member states to commit more personnel and equipment, are steps in the right direction. Yet one of the major challenges remains garnering the will to act on what is already a sufficiently expansive POC mandate and robust rules of engagement (Cammaert and Klappe 2015). The Kigali Principles on the Protection of Civilians – a non-binding set of eighteen pledges for effective implementation of POC – is one initiative that has already gained both high-level and widespread support that could be pushed further and used in tandem with other mechanisms to promote and potentially follow through on accountability measures for non-compliance. Such initiatives were to be complemented by work undertaken with the UN Secretariat to develop an accountability framework on POC as part of planned revisions to the Department of Peacekeeping Operations and Department of Field Support (DPKO/DFS) policy on the protection of civilians in 2018.

Managing the challenge of host-state consent

Even if the overall effectiveness of peacekeeping improves through the reforms outlined in this chapter, the political context into which a mission deploys is likely to affect the ability of a mission to implement its POC mandate and ultimately whether it is able to support certain aspects of R2P. In conditions that are less conducive to the delivery of a peacekeeping mandate – either because of a lack of resources or capabilities, or because the host government and parties to the conflict challenge the mission mandate (as in the cases of South Sudan and the DRC) – then it is likely that the mission will struggle to fulfill its POC mandate.

The issue of host-government consent to the deployment of a peacekeeping mission remains one of the most challenging contexts for POC and for realizing the value-add for R2P. While a government may agree to the initial deployment of a mission, that support or acquiescence is likely to shift throughout the duration of the peacekeeping mission. In some cases, host authorities may seek to put restrictions on elements of the mandate, as was the case with the initial decision to deploy a Regional Protection Force into South Sudan (Williams 2016a). This resulted in a lack of unanimity in the Security Council when it came to the reauthorization of the peacekeeping mandate for UNMISS, demonstrating fractures in the Council over the strategic direction of the mission. Host governments may also seek other means to obstruct the protection efforts of a mission; for example, by denying access of peacekeepers to particular parts of the country. Such efforts not only prevent a peacekeeping mission from fulfilling its mandate but may enable atrocities to take place with little detection.

If the nature of host-government consent shifts throughout a mission, or the government becomes obstructionist, then it is highly unlikely that the mission will be able to deliver on any capacity-building mandate. This is also the case in contexts where there may be a mandate to support security sector reform or conduct joint operations (such as with the FARDC in the DRC), and the host-government forces are found to be committing human rights abuses. Cooperating and working with the host government in these contexts may result in UN peacekeeping becoming complicit in human rights abuses against civilians. As a consequence in these contexts, the Security Council has prioritized efforts by the mission to physically protect the civilian population. Or put in an R2P context, Pillar Three takes primacy over Pillar Two. Considered in the context of R2P, this may mean that there is an emphasis on Pillar Three activities early in the mission, when there is a need to physically protect civilians from mass atrocities, with a focus on capacity-building and supporting the state (Pillar Two) when the security situation on the ground has stabilized and there is an opportunity to rebuild.

These contexts are far from ideal for UN peacekeeping. Providing physical protection, as is the case in the POC sites in South Sudan, may be a stop-gap measure until the political process moves forward and space is opened up to build a more protective environment. Alternatively, it may open up political space that allows the political process to move forward. But in both instances, it means the Security Council in particular needs to be engaged and focused on maintaining some degree of consent by the host government, or else the unique legitimacy that has framed UN peacekeeping is likely to diminish.

Developing a political consensus on the future of peacekeeping

Some member states have expressed concerns about the waning consent in some peacekeeping missions, identifying a challenge for UN peacekeeping, particularly when it comes to POC, and ultimately, R2P. It is evident that there needs to be a broader discussion among the UN membership about the applicability of UN peacekeeping principles. While the High-Level Independent Panel on United Nations Peace Operations' report acknowledges their importance, it also notes "these principles must be interpreted progressively and with flexibility in the face of new challenges, and they should never be an excuse for failure to protect civilians or to defend the mission proactively" (High-Level Independent Panel on United Nations Peace Operations 2015, x). As outlined in the previous section, developments on the ground in South Sudan, the DRC, and other mission contexts have raised questions about the outer limits of peacekeeping (High-Level Independent Panel on United Nations Peace Operations 2015, 12); in other words, whether there are types of environments that may not be suitable for UN peacekeeping missions, but that may be fulfilled by other types of missions. Greater clarity is needed on what is expected of peacekeeping missions in these challenging contexts, particularly if expectations about protection of civilians are to be met.

One such example is the debate around missions that have some of the characteristics of peace enforcement operations. The experimentation, expansion, and emergence of new operational concepts, such as FIB in the DRC, presents the opportunity for more robust enforcement and intervention modalities that could have protection at their core. While many have cautioned against UN peace operations "creeping" into the territory of enforcement operations (Hunt 2017), the development of a new doctrine or modality for stabilization missions (or indeed, coercive human protection operations) authorized by the Security Council may offer a number of benefits. First, this would distinguish between, and provide distinct frameworks for, operations that abide by the established principles of peacekeeping and those that do not. Second, this may also offer succor to those that fear that Security Council resolutions authorizing the use of force for human protection may be abused by the Permanent Five members. A new doctrine with more stringent reporting requirements (such as those usually placed upon parallel forces authorized under the same resolutions as peacekeeping missions) could allay fears – evident in the Brazilian "Responsibility While Protecting" concept – about transparency and accountability when implementing enforcement mandates. But that goes beyond the scope of peacekeeping missions.

In the absence of developing a new type of UN deployable mission, partnerships between the UN, regional organizations, and member state-led parallel forces provide a valuable vehicle for managing and responding to conflict-related violence and atrocities. In particular, African (sub-)regional organizations such as the AU and the Economic Community of West African States have launched early interventions to stabilize situations where mass atrocities were occurring or highly likely such as in Mali and CAR. Similarly, other regional organizations continue to mount extra-regional missions in support of regional and UN missions – for instance, the European Union in Mali and CAR. It is important that the lessons from the deployment, re-hatting, and inter-operation of these missions are identified and learned. The development of effective systems and processes for managing, resourcing, and communicating between these efforts are critical to realizing the goals of peacekeeping and the R2P alike. Similarly, further analysis and dialogue on these approaches will enable the spirit of the recommendations emerging from the High-Level Independent Panel on United Nations Peace Operations on the "spectrum of peace operations" and partnerships to be realized with protection of civilians as the priority.

Conclusion

This chapter has examined some of the challenges and opportunities for implementing R2P through UN peacekeeping – particularly relating to POC mandates. When R2P implementation is understood simply as doing whatever one can to prevent and avert mass atrocities, UN peacekeeping missions already do much to contribute to R2P objectives.[14] Indeed, the three-tiered POC operational concept offers a convenient framework for conceptualizing actions that are consonant with the obligations under the three-pillar framework of the R2P. Tier 1 of the POC operational concept includes elements of preventive action that resonate with R2P's Pillar One (prevention and host-state responsibility); POC's Tier 3 focus on capacity-building toward the creation of a protective environment provides an avenue for the international assistance envisaged under R2P's Pillar Two (international assistance); and POC's Tier 2 focus on provision of physical protection from threats provides the enabling platform for timely and decisive responses required under R2P's Pillar Three. UN peacekeeping can provide a valuable mechanism to provide political leverage, respond to mass atrocities, and support host governments to fulfill their responsibility to protect. Through strengthening existing capacities and the measured development of new strategies there is a great deal of potential to enhance their ability to prevent atrocities.

UN peacekeeping missions can therefore be vital for the implementation of R2P under particular circumstances. However, they should not be made subordinate to the objectives of and obligations under R2P. As has been shown, these objectives are only aligned when host governments are willing to support and consent to a peace operation. Unfortunately, some of the most challenging missions facing the UN at present – in places such as South Sudan and the DRC – are beholden to the political demands of host governments that often do not want the peacekeeping mission there. Grappling with the thorny issues around consent and the question of what peacekeeping missions should do when host governments are complicit in atrocities will be critical to the future credibility of UN peacekeeping missions as well as their utility in realizing R2P.

Bringing an atrocities-prevention lens and agenda to UN peacekeeping is not without political challenges and risks. It may further unrealistically raise expectations, alter the political calculus of parties to conflicts, and potentially challenge the consensus on peacekeeping principles and the partnership among T/PCCs, the Security Council, peacekeeping financiers, and host states that enables the unique endeavor of peacekeeping to protect civilians on the ground. Peacekeeping operations have much to offer in implementing R2P, but will not if their future viability is called into question. It is therefore vital that efforts to pursue R2P goals through UN peacekeeping do so in ways that do not jeopardize their principled consensus. For the millions of civilians who currently rely on peacekeepers for their everyday safety and for those who will do so in future, this is something that should be avoided at all costs.

Acknowledgments

The authors are extremely grateful to the editors and Aditi Gorur for their helpful comments on earlier drafts of this chapter. Some of the research that contributed to this chapter was funded through an Australian Research Council Discovery Early Career Researcher Award (DE170100138) and an Australian Research Council Discovery Project (DP160102429).

Notes

1. By "peacekeeping operations," the authors refer to a wide range of mission types deployed under a UN flag, drawing on the concept of the "spectrum of peace operations" set out in the High-Level Independent Panel on Peace Operations (2015). However, most examples drawn on in this chapter are UN peacekeeping missions with explicit mandates on the protection of civilians.
2. Particularly when the former are commissioned in the context of the latter.
3. Although note that the capstone doctrine distinguishes between consent at the strategic level from the main parties to the conflict, which peacekeepers must obtain, and consent at the tactical level for actions undertaken in pursuance of the mandate, which peacekeepers need not necessarily obtain United Nations (2008, 32). In practice, several peacekeeping missions have operated without meaningful consent of the host-state government and have undertaken actions to which the host-state government objected. See further Sebastián and Gorur (2018).
4. The UN Security Council held its first thematic debate and adopted a Presidential Statement on the protection of civilians in armed conflict in February 1999. United Nations Security Council (1999). It then adopted the first Resolution (1265) on the protection of civilians in armed conflict in September 1999.
5. See, for example, statement by Morocco during debate in United Nations Security Council (2009a, 17–19); and statement by Sudan during debate in United Nations Security Council (2009b, 34–5).
6. See recognition of this in Ban (2012, paragraph 21).
7. See United Nations General Assembly Resolution 2006(XIX), February 18, 1965, which established the Special Committee on Peacekeeping Operations.
8. This section draws on discussions that took place during one author's participation in negotiations in the Special Committee on Peacekeeping Operations between 2010 and 2013. See also the statement by Aljowaily (2010).
9. "*[U]ntil state security forces are able and willing to protect civilians*, the mission must be prepared to intervene unilaterally to prevent, pre-empt or put an end to threats of physical violence. Weighing circumstances on the ground, missions must bear in mind that they are mandated to protect civilians irrespective of the source of threat, including when elements of the host government are themselves responsible for threatening civilians with physical violence" (United Nations Department of Peacekeeping Operations/Department of Field Support 2015, 13, emphasis in original).
10. Indeed, the original mandate framed this in R2P language, tasking UNMISS to: "Support the Government of the Republic of South Sudan in exercising its responsibilities for conflict prevention, mitigation, and resolution and protect civilians through: . . . Advising and assisting the Government of the Republic of South Sudan, including military and police at national and local levels as appropriate, in fulfilling its responsibility to protect civilians, in compliance with international humanitarian, human rights, and refugee law." See Resolution 1996 (2011), paragraphs 3(b), 3(b)(iv).
11. A similar linguistic shift had occurred in resolutions on Cote d'Ivoire in 2011 when government forces were perpetrating abuses. See Hunt (2016).
12. Paragraph 6 "*[e]mphasizes* that the protection of civilians . . . must be given priority in decisions about the use of available capacity and resources, over any of the other tasks" (emphasis in original).

13 The M23 was an armed group operating primarily in North Kivu, comprised of elements of the *Congrès national pour la défense du peuple* disgruntled at the outcomes of a March 23, 2009, peace deal.
14 This notion of R2P as a "duty of conduct" is the preferred formulation of former R2P Special Advisor to the Secretary-General, Jennifer Welsh. See Welsh (2014).

References

Aljowaily, Amr, 2010. "Challenges in Applying Protection Mandates," in International Forum for the Challenges of Peace Operations, *Challenges Forum Report 2010: Challenges of Protecting Civilians in Multidimensional Peace Operations* (Stockholm: Edita Vastra Aros AB), 137–44.

Ban Ki-moon, 2009. "Implementing the Responsibility to Protect: Report of the Secretary-General," A/63/677, January 12.

Ban Ki-moon, 2012. "Report of the Secretary-General on the Protection of Civilians in Armed Conflict," S/2012/376, May.

Ban Ki-moon, 2014. "Fulfilling Our Collective Responsibility: International Assistance and the Responsibility to Protect: Report of the Secretary-General," A/68/947–S/2014/449, July 11.

Bellamy, Alex J., 2009. *Responsibility to Protect: The Global Effort to End Mass Atrocities* (Cambridge: Polity Press).

Bellamy, Alex J., and Charles T. Hunt, 2015. "Twenty-First Century UN Peace Operations: Protection, Force and the Changing Security Environment," *International Affairs* 91, no. 6: 1277–98.

Berdal, Mats, 2015. "United Nations Peacekeeping and the Responsibility to Protect," in Ramesh Thakur and William Maley, eds, *Theorising the Responsibility to Protect* (Cambridge: Cambridge University Press), 223–48.

Cammaert, Patrick C., and Ben Klappe, 2015. "Application of Force and Rules of Engagement in Peace Operations," in Terry D. Gill and Dieter Fleck, eds, *The Handbook of the International Law of Military Operations* (Oxford: Oxford University Press), 151–58.

Center for Civilians in Conflict, 2016a. *A Refuge in Flames: The February 17–18 Violence in Malakal POC* (Washington, DC: Center for Civilians in Conflict), https://civiliansinconflict.org/wp-content/uploads/2017/09/ViolenceMalakalPOC_LowResSingle.pdf.

Center for Civilians in Conflict, 2016b. *Under Fire: The July 2016 Violence in Juba and UN Response* (Washington, DC: Center for Civilians in Conflict), https://civiliansinconflict.org/wp-content/uploads/2017/09/civic-juba-violence-report-october-2016.pdf.

Chappuis, Fairlie, and Aditi Gorur, 2015. "Reconciling Security Sector Reform and the Protection of Civilians in Peacekeeping Contexts," Civilians in Conflict Issue Brief No. 3 (Washington, DC: Stimson Center and the Geneva Center for the Democratic Control of Armed Forces).

Day, Adam, 2017. "The Best Defense Is No Offense: Why Cuts to UN Troops in Congo Could Be a Good Thing," *Small Wars Journal*, http://smallwarsjournal.com/jrnl/art/the-best-defense-is-no-offense-why-cuts-to-un-troops-in-congo-could-be-a-good-thing.

Di Razza, Namie, 2017. "Reframing the Protection of Civilians Paradigm for UN Peace Operations," Issue Brief (New York: International Peace Institute).

Evans, Gareth, 2008. *The Responsibility to Protect: Ending Mass Atrocity Crimes Once and for All* (Washington, DC: Brookings Institution Press).

Francis, Angus, Vesselin Popovski, and Charles Sampford, eds, 2012. *Norms of Protection: Responsibility to Protect, Protection of Civilians and Their Interaction* (Tokyo: United Nations University Press).

Giffen, Alison, 2016. "South Sudan," in Alex J. Bellamy and Tim Dunne, eds, *The Oxford Handbook of the Responsibility to Protect* (Oxford: Oxford University Press), 857–75.

Gorur, Aditi, and Nils Carstensen, 2016. "Community Self-Protection," in Haidi Willmot, Ralph Mamiya, Scott Sheeran, and M. Weller, eds, *Protection of Civilians* (Oxford: Oxford University Press), 409–27.

Guterres, António, 2017. "Implementing the Responsibility to Protect: Accountability for Prevention: Report of the Secretary-General," A/71/1016-S/2017/556, August 10.

High-Level Independent Panel on Peace Operations, 2015. "Uniting our Strengths for Peace: Politics, Partnerships and People," Report (New York: United Nations).

Holt, Victoria, and Glynn Taylor, with Max Kelly, 2009. *Protecting Civilians in the Context of UN Peacekeeping Operations: Successes, Setbacks and Remaining Challenges* (New York: United Nations).

Human Rights Watch, 2016a. "DR Congo: Protect Civilians in Beni from Attack: Nearly 700 Dead since Massacres Began 2 Years Ago," October 7, www.hrw.org/news/2016/10/07/dr-congo-protect-civilians-beni-attack.

Human Rights Watch, 2016b. "South Sudan: Killings, Rapes, Looting in Juba: Arms Embargo, Additional UN Sanctions Needed," August 15, www.hrw.org/news/2016/08/15/south-sudan-killings-rapes-looting-juba.

Hunt, Charles T., 2016. "Côte d'Ivoire," in Alex J. Bellamy and Tim Dunne, eds, *The Oxford Handbook of the Responsibility to Protect* (Oxford: Oxford University Press), 693–716.

Hunt, Charles T., 2017. "All Necessary Means to What Ends? The Unintended Consequences of the 'Robust Turn' in UN Peace Operations," *International Peacekeeping* 24, no. 1: 108–31.

Hunt, Charles T., and Alex J. Bellamy, 2011. "Mainstreaming the Responsibility to Protect in Peace Operations," *Civil Wars* 13, no. 1: 1–20.

Hurd, Ian, 1999. "Legitimacy and Authority in International Politics," *International Organization* 53, no. 2: 379–408.

Lie, John Harald Sande, and Benjamin de Carvalho, 2012. "Conceptual Unclarity and Competition: The Protection of Civilians and the Responsibility to Protect," in Benjamin de Carvalho and Ole Jacob Sending, eds, *The Protection of Civilians in UN Peacekeeping: Concept, Implementation and Practice* (Baden-Baden: Nomos), 47–61.

Malan, Mark, and Charles T. Hunt, 2014. "Between a Rock and a Hard Place: The UN and the Protection of Civilians in South Sudan," ISS Paper 275 (Pretoria: Institute for Security Studies).

Nasu, Hitoshi, 2011. "Operationalizing the Responsibility to Protect in the Context of Civilian Protection by UN Peacekeepers," *International Peacekeeping* 18, no. 4: 364–78.

Patinkin, Jason, 2016. "Rampaging South Sudan Troops Raped Foreigners, Killed Local," Associated Press, August 16, http://bigstory.ap.org/article/237fa4c447d74698804be210512c3ed1/rampaging-south-sudan-troops-raped-foreignerskilled-local.

Prunier, Gérard, 2008. *Africa's World War: Congo, the Rwandan Genocide, and the Making of a Continental Catastrophe* (Oxford: Oxford University Press).

Sebastián, Sofía, and Aditi Gorur, 2018. *UN Peacekeeping and Host-State Consent: How Missions Navigate Relationships with Governments* (Washington, DC: Stimson Center).

Stearns, Jason K., 2011. *Dancing in the Glory of Monsters: The Collapse of the Congo and the Great War of Africa* (New York: Public Affairs).

Tardy, Thierry, 2012. "The Dangerous Liaisons of the Responsibility to Protect and the Protection of Civilians in Peacekeeping Operations," *Global Responsibility to Protect* 4, no. 4: 424–48.

Tull, Denis M., 2018 "The Limits and Unintended Consequences of UN Peace Enforcement: The Force Intervention Brigade in the DR Congo," *International Peacekeeping* 25, no. 2: 167–90.

United Nations, 1999a. "Report of the Independent Inquiry into the Actions of the United Nations During the 1994 Genocide in Rwanda," S/1999/1257, December 15.

United Nations, 1999b. "Report of the Secretary-General Pursuant to General Assembly Resolution 53/35: The Fall of Srebrenica," A/54/549, November 15.

United Nations, 2008. *United Nations Peacekeeping Operations: Principles and Guidelines* (New York: Peacekeeping Best Practices Section, United Nations).

United Nations, 2009. "Report of the Special Committee on Peacekeeping Operations and Its Working Group," 2009 Substantive Session (23 February–20 March 2009), A/63/19, March 24.

United Nations, 2017. "Report of the Secretary-General on the United Nations Organization Stabilization Mission in the Democratic Republic of the Congo," S/2017/206, March 10.

United Nations Department of Peacekeeping Operations, 2015. *Protection of Civilians: Implementing Guidelines for Military Components of United Nations Peacekeeping Missions* (New York: United Nations).

United Nations Department of Peacekeeping Operations/Department of Field Support, 2010. "Draft DPKO/DFS Operational Concept on the Protection of Civilians in United Nations Peacekeeping Operations," www.peacekeeping.org.uk/wp-content/uploads/2013/02/100129-DPKO-DFS-POC-Operational-Concept.pdf.

United Nations Department of Peacekeeping Operations/Department of Field Support, 2011. *Framework for Drafting Comprehensive Protection of Civilians (POC): Strategies in UN Peacekeeping Operations* (New York: United Nations).

United Nations Department of Peacekeeping Operations/Department of Field Support, 2015. *DPKO/DFS Policy: The Protection of Civilians in United Nations Peacekeeping* (New York: United Nations).

United Nations Secretary-General, 2016a. "Note to Correspondents on the Special Investigation and UNHQ Board of Inquiry into the Violence in the UNMISS Protection of Civilians Site in February 2016," June 21, www.un.org/sg/en/content/sg/note-correspondents/2016-06-21/note-correspondents-special-investigation-and-unhq-board.

United Nations Secretary-General, 2016b. "Note to Correspondents: Board of Inquiry Report on Malakal," August 5, www.un.org/sg/en/content/sg/note-correspondents/2016-08-05/note-correspondents-board-inquiry-report-malakal.

United Nations Security Council, 1999. "Statement by the President of the Security Council," S/PRST/1999/6, February 12.

United Nations Security Council, 2009a. "Protection of Civilians in Armed Conflict, 6151st Meeting," S/PV.6151 (Resumption 1), June 26.

United Nations Security Council, 2009b. "Protection of Civilians in Armed Conflict, 6066th Meeting," S/PV.6066 (Resumption 1), January 14.

United Nations Security Council, 2016. "Executive Summary of the Independent Special Investigation into the Violence in Juba in 2016 and the Response by the United Nations Mission in South Sudan," S/2016/924, November 1.

United Nations Security Council, 2017. "Letter Dated 17 April 2017 from the Secretary-General Addressed to the President of the Security Council," S/2017/328, April 17.

van Steenberghe, Raphaël, 2014. "The Notions of the Responsibility to Protect and the Protection of Civilians in Armed Conflict: Detecting Their Association and Its Impact upon International Law," *Goettingen Journal of International Law* 6, no. 1: 81–114.

Weir, Erin A., and Charles T. Hunt, 2011. "DR Congo: Support Community-Based Tools for MONUSCO," Field Report (Washington, DC: Refugees International).

Welsh, Jennifer M., 2014. "Implementing the 'Responsibility to Protect': Catalyzing Debate and Building Capacity," in Alexander Betts and Phil Orchard, eds, *Implementation and World Politics: How International Norms Change Practice* (Oxford: Oxford University Press), 124–43.

Williams, Paul D., 2016a. "Key Questions for South Sudan's New Protection Force," *IPI Global Observatory*, September 12, https://theglobalobservatory.org/2016/09/south-sudan-regional-protection-force-kiir-unmiss/.

Williams, Paul D., 2016b. "The R2P, Protection of Civilians, and UN Peacekeeping Operations," in Alex J. Bellamy and Tim Dunne, eds, *The Oxford Handbook of the Responsibility to Protect* (Oxford: Oxford University Press), 524–44.

12

CIVIL–MILITARY RELATIONS AND R2P

The Afghan experience

William Maley

Afghanistan does not often feature in discussion of venues notorious for mass atrocity crime in the period since the Second World War. The Cambodian genocide under the Khmer Rouge, ethnic cleansing in Bosnia, the Rwandan genocide of 1994, and the persecution of the Rohingyas of Myanmar in 2017 are much more likely to attract attention as paradigm cases to which a global responsibility to protect might apply (see Kiernan 2008; Cigar 1995; Barnett 2002; Ibrahim 2018). Yet the omission of Afghanistan is curious. Afghanistan has experienced more than four decades of disruption since the communist coup of April 1978 that undermined its fragile political order. Mass killings began right after the coup (see Barry 1980), and a careful 1991 study estimated that unnatural deaths in Afghanistan between 1978 and 1987 totaled 876,825 (Khalidi 1991), or more than 240 deaths every day for ten years straight. This was enough to prompt discussion of whether genocide had taken place (Fein 1993). And while mayhem on such a scale no longer occurs, Afghanistan is hardly in a "post-conflict" phase. On December 28, 2017, a large number of civil society activists gathered at the Tebyan cultural center in Babah Sharbat street in the Afghan capital, Kabul, for a seminar to mark the thirty-eighth anniversary of the Soviet invasion of Afghanistan in December 1979. Attending a seminar is not usually considered a high-risk activity, but this was not a normal day. Bombers associated with the Islamic State of Iraq and Syria (ISIS) terrorist group had identified the cultural center as a target, and moved with lethal precision to strike it. At least forty-one attendees were killed, and many more injured (Abed, Faizi, and Mashal 2017). Sadly, this was anything but an isolated incident: rather, it was but one of a string of recent attacks on Shiite Muslims, predominantly from the vulnerable Hazara community that has had a long experience of persecution and marginalization (see Ibrahimi 2017). These come alongside mass-casualty attacks mounted by the Taliban, notably one on January 27, 2018, in the Shahrara neighborhood in Kabul that used an ambulance perfidiously packed with explosives to kill at least ninety-five residents of Kabul going about their daily business (Mashal and Sukhanyar 2018).

Yet Afghanistan since 1978 has hardly been a neglected part of the world, although there have been particular periods – notably, that between the collapse of the communist regime in April 1992 and the terrorist attacks in New York and Washington of September 11, 2001 – when Afghanistan has received perhaps less attention than it deserved. For most of the 1980s, it was a central theater in what some called the second Cold War, as the Soviet Union, which had invaded Afghanistan on December 27, 1979, saw its troops harried by Afghan resistance fighters (*Mujahideen*) who received support from the United States and other Western countries (see Maley 2002, 32–104). Furthermore, ever since the overthrow of the Taliban regime by the United States and its allies in Operation Enduring Freedom in November 2001, there has been a substantial international military presence in Afghanistan, now under the rubric of the non-combat "Operation Resolute Support," approved by NATO in June 2014, pursuant to which some 13,000 troops from thirty-nine NATO states and partners remain in the country. Indeed, the overthrow of the Taliban regime coincided almost exactly with the publication of the report of the International Commission on Intervention and State Sovereignty that introduced the idea of the Responsibility to Protect (R2P) – disaggregated into responsibilities to prevent, react, and rebuild – into both academic discourse and policy discussion (ICISS 2001).

This history, both remote and recent, highlights a number of difficult questions relating to the implementation of R2P, and my aim in this chapter is to draw some of these out. Over the last forty years, Afghanistan has experienced diverse forms of disruption: an internal struggle triggered by the 1978 coup, a war of resistance and a proxy war following the Soviet invasion, militarized rivalry between different groups after the collapse of the communist regime in April 1992, and a creeping invasion from Pakistan after 2001. In addition, Afghanistan has experienced an aggressive military occupation by Soviet troops; the US intervention following the September 11 attacks; and after the overthrow of the Taliban regime, a military operation to confront al-Qaeda, running in parallel with rebuilding of the Afghan armed forces and reconstruction efforts through mixed civil–military Provincial Reconstruction Teams (PRTs) leading up to the post-2014 transition of responsibility to Afghanistan and the Afghan state. The development of the PRTs highlighted an important aspect of Afghanistan's post-2001 transition: that the need for a substantial military – as well as civilian – presence showed that Afghanistan was not in a "post-conflict" phase, but rather was struggling with what Astri Suhrke and Arne Strand (2005, 142) have called "the logic of conflictual peacebuilding." An implication is that a "responsibility to rebuild" may arise in an environment where challenges to effective "rebuilding" remain considerable.

In this chapter, I argue that all these experiences suggest that the circumstances in which the invocation of a responsibility to protect might be contemplated can be quite confused or even murky, and that Afghanistan's experience since 2001 suggests that the exigencies of intervention can often militate *against* an intervention's serving to minimize the risk of mass atrocities, even if a "responsibility to rebuild" has been accepted by intervening powers. The chapter is divided into four sections. The first offers a picture of the experiences of the Afghan population in the period from 1978 to 2001, and demonstrates the massive social dislocation that flowed from events of that time. The second looks at the various dimensions of the post-2001 intervention, and shows that the objective of countering anti-Western terrorism, together with the emergence of Iraq as a new theater of military activity, compromised both the rebuilding of Afghanistan, and the neutralizing of threats facing ordinary Afghans. The third shows that civil–military engagement through PRTs was an ad hoc response to a need to move beyond Kabul, rather than a device for preventing mass atrocity crime, and that on occasion it facilitated the empowerment of unappetizing actors. The final section offers some brief conclusions.

The burden of the past: 1978–2001

Afghanistan, more than most states, has been the victim of stereotypical imageries that have tended to distract attention from the profound complexities marking its politics and society. For too long, the notion that it was a remote, isolated, and violent space, populated by wild tribesmen and shaped by rivalry between nineteenth century European powers in the so-called "Great Game," seemed to predominate. Those who painted such pictures often garnished their presentations with lines quoted from Rudyard Kipling, who never once set foot in Afghanistan, and echoes can occasionally be found even in writings of twenty-first-century British travelers, who from time to time seem to have been afflicted by a strong "Lawrence of Arabia" complex. Serious modern scholarship has either discredited such imagery, or made a strong case for heavily qualifying it. Afghanistan has been much less isolated from the wider world than many people think (see Crews 2015); the processes which led to state formation were much more complex than simple images of the Great Game would suggest (see Hanifi 2008; Hopkins 2008; Rahimi 2017), and the notion of Afghanistan as simply a "tribal society" crumbles in the face of an appreciation that substantial elements of its population, such as Tajiks in northern Afghanistan, are not organized along tribal lines at all. Nor are depictions of Afghanistan as wracked with tribal violence of much use in explaining its recent predicaments. Of course, there are notable examples of rivalry, feuding, and contestation in many parts of the country, in some cases pre-dating the wider conflicts triggered by the April 1978 coup (see, for example, the analysis offered in Martin 2014). But on the whole, for nearly half a century before the coup, Afghanistan was arguably the most peaceful country in Asia, with no disruptions even approaching the turmoil associated with the Second World War, the partition of India, or decolonization in Indochina.

This changed dramatically with the April 1978 coup and the December 1979 Soviet invasion. The coup in no sense reflected a demand within Afghan society for revolutionary change; on the contrary, it was a complex product of a range of different factors: the unhealthy dependence of the Afghan state on unstable sources of rentier income that had weakened its ability to meet people's needs, increasing division within the Afghan political elite following the overthrow of King Zahir Shah in a July 1973 palace coup, and the presence in strategic positions within the armed forces of Soviet-trained officers who had imbibed a crude variant of Marxism-Leninism during their training (see Rubin 2002b). They dubbed their coup the "Saur Revolution," as "Saur" (or Taurus) was the month in the Afghan zodiac calendar in which it took place. But the only revolution that occurred was a brutal "revolution from above" in which the new leaders embarked on ill-considered efforts to produce dramatic transformation of Afghan society, backed up with the threat or use of force.

Even before the Soviet invasion, the new regime put on display a taste for mass atrocity crimes. To give just two examples, in early 1979, a commando force, reportedly accompanied by Soviet advisers (see Girardet 1985, 107–10), murdered large numbers of residents of the village of Kerala in Kunar, and in the middle of the same year, Hazaras in the Kabul neighborhood of Chindawol were killed in large numbers as well (on the Kerala massacre, see Afghanistan Justice Project 2005, 19–20; on the massacre of Hazaras, see Barry 1980, 204). This rapid resort to coercion was a clear indicator of the failure of the regime to secure generalized normative support; that is, legitimacy. This, together with intense antagonism between different factions within the post-coup leadership, set the scene for the Soviet invasion. It is now reasonably clear that the Soviet leadership that took the decision to invade had hoped to be able to withdraw Soviet forces from Afghanistan within a relatively short period, but the effect of the invasion was to undermine the capacity of the USSR's chosen puppet, Babrak Karmal, to garner the kind of legitimacy required for the Soviets to be able to cut Afghanistan loose without putting at risk the regime they had installed. The result was a quagmire, and one in which coercive violence became a substitute for a coherent political strategy. Ultimately it proved self-defeating: as Marshal Sergei Akhromeev remarked at the November 1986 Politburo meeting at which the in-principle decision to withdraw from Afghanistan was taken, "we have lost the battle for the Afghan people" (Grossman 1993, 25). Yet social dislocation resulting from the invasion was enormous, and refugees fled Afghanistan in the millions (see Schmeidl and Maley 2008).

It was no secret that Soviet forces engaged in acts of the utmost brutality in Afghanistan. This was actually recognized in 1989, when the Supreme Soviet formally issued an amnesty for crimes committed by Soviet forces during the occupation (*Pravda* 1989). However, without Afghan collaborators, it would have been difficult for the USSR even to attempt to administer the parts of the country that it could dominate militarily. A secret police, described euphemistically as the "State Information Service" (*Khedamat-e Ettalaat-e Dawlati*) but known colloquially by its acronym KhAD, was directed from 1980 to 1985 by Dr Najibullah Ahmadzai, who subsequently replaced Karmal as president. Its reputation for brutality was both well documented and well deserved. Nonetheless, the limits of coercion as a tool of regime maintenance became very clear. Najibullah's regime survived the withdrawal of Soviet forces, but the cut-off of Soviet aid at the end of 1991 proved fatal, and the regime collapsed within four months.

The Afghan resistance forces that for the best part of a decade had been battling both the Soviet Army and the communist regime inherited the symbols of the state, but not functioning state instrumentalities and agencies capable of mobilizing resources, redistributing them, and regulating the behavior of the population. What resulted was a ferocious battle for control of the symbols, most importantly Kabul. Complicating this was the disposition of regional powers to support different groups from within the Afghan resistance – only Ahmad Shah Massoud "lacked a powerful foreign patron" (Rubin 2002b, 273); Pakistan supported the *Hezb-e Islami* of Gulbuddin Hekmatyar (which mainly played a spoiler role, relentlessly rocketing Kabul whenever it found the opportunity); Uzbekistan supported the militia of Abdul Rashid Dostam; and Iran supported the Shiite *Hezb-e Wahdat*. This may have appeared simply an outbreak of mindless violence, but it was actually driven by careful calculation. As the French analyst Gilles Dorronsoro put it, "[t]his new war's frequently shifting alliances give the impression of irrationality and chaos, but everything that has happened since 1992 has been the result of a rigorous political logic. The Afghan civil war is not 'primitive' or 'tribal,' but strongly political" (Dorronsoro 1995, 37; see also Christia 2012). Unfortunately, this offered no protection against mass atrocity crimes. Perhaps the worst was the so-called "Afshar massacre" of February 2003, which saw hundreds of ethnic Hazaras murdered, largely at the hands of members of the *Ittihad* militia loyal to Abdul Rab al-Rasoul Sayyaf (United Nations 1993, paragraph 58). Human Rights Watch (2005, 89) drew the grim conclusion that the "Ittihad troops apparently wanted to leave some evidence of their crimes—to terrorize the local population."

In the light of these cruelties, some observers were inclined to see the advent of the Taliban, a Pakistan-backed militia drawn from the ranks of religious students, as a harbinger of peace (see, for example, Fergusson 1997; Goldsmith 1997). This optimism proved misplaced, although for a while it survived the Taliban takeover of Kabul in September 1996. The Taliban brought "peace" to Kabul in the same sense in which Germany brought "peace" to Warsaw when it overran it in September 1939. What followed was the implementation of a deeply repressive system of rule which drew not so much on "village" values as on images of the village in the minds of orphans from refugee camps with little experience of the pragmatic dimensions of village life (see Maley 1998). Women in particular saw their opportunities for social life shrink dramatically, but those who suffered the most violence were Shiite Hazaras. In August 1998, the Taliban carried out a massacre in Mazar-e Sharif that the observer Ahmed Rashid (2000, 73) described as "genocidal in its ferocity." Some 2,000 Hazaras were murdered in just three days. A detailed picture of what happened was painted by UN official Rupert Colville:

> Some were shot on the streets. Many were executed in their own homes, after areas of the town known to be inhabited by their ethnic group had been systematically sealed off and searched. Some were boiled or asphyxiated

to death after being left crammed inside sealed metal containers under a hot August sun. In at least one hospital, as many as 30 patients were shot as they lay helplessly in their beds. The bodies of many of the victims were left on the streets or in their houses as a stark warning to the city's remaining inhabitants. Horrified witnesses saw dogs tearing at the corpses, but were instructed over loudspeakers and by radio announcements not to remove or bury them.
(Colville 1999)

It is unsurprising that nearly two decades later, some 80 percent of Afghans surveyed by the Asia Foundation (2017, 228) expressed "no sympathy at all" for the Taliban.

It is, of course, counterfactual, but nonetheless tempting, to reflect on whether the existence of a "responsibility to protect" doctrine before 2001 would have made any difference in Afghanistan's long period of suffering. The most plausible response is that it would not. In its post-2005 variant, R2P runs into difficulty when the prime offender is a permanent member of the United Nations (UN) Security Council, as was the case through the 1980s in Afghanistan following the Soviet invasion. Furthermore, there was an almost complete lack of interest after 1992 in the developing situation in Afghanistan, with Bosnia dominating the headlines and Afghanistan depicted as reverting to patterns of "tribal warfare" that had allegedly afflicted it since time immemorial. Ironically, some saw the Taliban as offering a *solution* to this "problem," and there was an almost willful reluctance to concede just how much misery the Taliban had caused. Until September 2001, there was no great disposition to confront the Taliban directly, although they had been sanctioned for accommodating Osama Bin Laden after the al-Qaeda attacks on the US embassies in Kenya and Tanzania in August 1998 (see Maley 2002, 207–9).

Developments after 2001

The overthrow of the Taliban regime occurred for political rather than humanitarian reasons. Nonetheless, the articulation of the R2P doctrine by the International Commission on Intervention and State Sovereignty in 2001 raised a number of questions pertinent to Afghanistan. One was whether post-2001 developments in Afghanistan would amount to the effective discharge of a "responsibility to prevent" mass atrocity crimes in the future. Another was whether the intervention of international forces would give effect to a "responsibility to rebuild." This latter question is addressed in the next section; this section focuses on the extent to which political and institutional changes since 2001 have provided a bulwark against future atrocities. At the outset, however, it is important to note that the idea of a responsibility to protect has not been central to Afghan political debates in the period since 2001. There has been quite a deal of discussion of human rights issues, and also of transitional justice, although that term itself is not one easily translated into Afghan languages. But to the extent that the idea of R2P has been of interest, it has been within a relatively narrow circle of analysts, and it has not been actively promoted to a wide audience.

The overthrow of the Taliban in 2001 was followed by a conference under UN auspices in Bonn at which non-Taliban political actors laid out a pathway for the reconstitution of the Afghan state. It provided for the establishment of an interim administration with up to twenty-nine departments, to be followed by a transitional administration, and the holding of a constitutional assembly (*Loya Jirga*) to draft a new constitution for the country. These objectives were broadly met. A consensus candidate, Hamid Karzai, was chosen to be chair of the interim administration, and a new constitution was adopted in January 2004, providing for a strongly centralized presidential system. An election was held later that year which saw Karzai elected as president with 55.4 percent of the vote. He held office until 2014, when he was succeeded by his former finance minister, Dr Ashraf Ghani. The 2004 constitution set in place an impressive range of human rights protections, and while the rule of law remained weak (see Mason 2011; Swenson 2017), the Afghan state did not function as an agent of persecution as it had during the communist period. President Karzai, however, did not prove a dynamic leader in terms of policy development and implementation, and too often members of his immediate family proved to be self-serving and kleptocratic (see Partlow 2016). The result was the emergence of a political system that was neopatrimonial in character, with formal bureaucratic structures entangled with the dispensing of patronage in complicated ways (see Maley 2018). Networks proved just as important as institutions in shaping political outcomes (see Sharan 2011, 2013, 2017; Sharan and Bose 2016), and those in the "right" networks enjoyed high levels of impunity.

A further factor complicating the mapping of political power in Afghanistan after 2001 has been the emergence or re-emergence of what have been called "warlords" or "strongman governors" (see Mukhopadhyay 2014; Englehart and Grant 2015; Malejacq 2016). Some of these have been well-known figures from the period of struggle against the Soviet Union, such as Ismail Khan in Herat. Others were related to such figures, such as Gul Agha Sherzai, whose father, Haji Abdul Latif, had been known in the 1980s as the "Lion of Kandahar." Some began their careers as leaders of what were essentially ethnic militias; Dostam provided a prominent example. While the word "warlord" was often used as a term of denigration, as it had been in China in the early twentieth century (see Pye 1971; Ch'i 1976), in the Afghan case some of these "warlords" enjoyed significant legitimacy in the eyes of elements of the Afghan population. This did not mean that they were necessarily appetizing figures; indeed, Dr Ghani, who invited Dostam to be a vice-presidential running mate at the 2014 election, had earlier referred to Dostam as a "known killer" (Nordland 2014). Yet perhaps more damaging to the standing of the Kabul government was a lower stratum of district strongmen and petty warlords with records of predation against the local population. Such figures often had limited legitimacy but relatively high spoiler capacity, and it was this that positioned them to increase their power when in early 2002, the United States and some of its allies blocked the expansion beyond Kabul of the International Security Assistance Force (ISAF) in order to conserve military assets for future use in Iraq. President Karzai was left with little option but to offer such petty warlords positions within the state as a way of pacifying them. The result, however, was to contaminate the standing of the state, fostering the impression that at best, it was indifferent to extractive corruption, and at worst, it was a party to this very phenomenon.

This was also one reason why transitional justice proved so difficult to deliver. This is an area where there is a genuine tension between different ethics: a consequentialist ethic which judges an action in terms of the results it can produce, and a deontological ethic which is concerned with conceptions of right and wrong. Ramesh Thakur, one of the principal authors of the R2P doctrine, has argued that "[p]eace is forward looking, problem solving and integrative, requiring reconciliation between past enemies within an all-inclusive community. Justice is backward looking, finger pointing and retributive, requiring trial and punishment of perpetrators of past crimes" (Thakur 2004, 287). He later argued that "[o]nly the previously traumatised and war-torn societies can make the delicate decisions and painful choices between justice for past misdeeds, political order and stability today, and reconciliation for a common future tomorrow" (Thakur 2017, 122). The difficulty here is that "societies" do not end up making the choices; rather, the choices end up being made by transitional political leaderships that often contain within their ranks some prime candidates for prosecution. Sayyaf has not been held accountable in any meaningful fashion for the 1993 Afshar massacre; he remains a prominent political figure to this day. And Hekmatyar, whose rocketing killed thousands of Kabul residents in the 1990s, was welcomed back to the city by the political leadership of the country in 2017, much to the disgust of many ordinary Afghans, and without any acknowledgment on his part of the suffering that he had caused them in the past (see Osman 2017; Mashal 2017; Docher 2017). Indeed, when in 2018 a mural was painted on a Kabul wall depicting the late Hamida Barmaki, a human rights activist killed in a 2011 supermarket bombing for which Hekmatyar's party had claimed responsibility, masked men – plainly Hekmatyar supporters – defaced the mural the following day. The price paid for accommodating such figures may prove to be high.

Does this mean that the threat of mass atrocity crime in Afghanistan has dissipated? The answer, alas, is no, and the explanation is fundamentally geopolitical. While the Taliban effectively collapsed as a movement at the end of 2001, it was revived in sanctuaries thoughtfully supplied by the Inter-Services Intelligence (ISI) directorate of the Pakistan Armed Forces. This was costly for Pakistan, in that it contributed to the emergence of the terrorist *Pakistani* Taliban, but key generals clearly thought it worthwhile as a means for minimizing Indian influence within Afghanistan. Just as the Taliban proved themselves capable of intense ferocity in the 1990s, so in more recent times have they shown no qualms about attacking civilian targets in blatant violation of the provisions of international humanitarian law. The bulk of civilian casualties have consistently been victims of the armed opposition, not the Afghan government or its international backers. As long as the Taliban remain active combatants, mass atrocity crimes will continue, most obviously through the detonation of bombs in public places. The solution to this problem lies not in offering political space to the Taliban, but in confronting their Pakistani backers. US policy under President Donald J. Trump has formally recognized that this is the case, but whether the Trump administration is capable of reinforcing this recognition with coherent policy settings is another matter. In addition, ISIS activists have also appeared in Afghanistan, posing a particular threat to Hazara Shia, who were killed in large numbers when ISIS bombed a peaceful demonstration in Kabul in July 2016 (Mashal and Nader 2016). Afghanistan is far from immune to the threat of mass atrocities.

Civil–military engagement and the responsibility to rebuild

Following the overthrow of the Taliban regime in 2001, two different sorts of security challenges presented themselves immediately in Afghanistan. The first was the need for some kind of internationally supplied security capability to protect the new interim administration, and to offer security commitments to ordinary people going about their day-to-day lives, until such time as an effective Afghan National Army and an effective Afghan National Police could be established. The second arose from the continued presence in Afghanistan of elements of the al-Qaeda organization that had plotted the September 2001 attacks on the United States. Thus, from the outset of international involvement in Afghanistan after 2001, two different missions operated in parallel. One was a counter-terrorism operation conducted by the United States – Operation Enduring Freedom – which was a continuation of the original mission to overthrow the Taliban. The second, put in place with authorization of the UN Security Council pursuant to Resolution 1386 of December 20, 2001, took the form of ISAF, the establishment of which had been anticipated by the Bonn Agreement of December 2001. Among those who had promoted the idea of the ISAF deployment, there was a widespread belief that to be effective, it would need to spread beyond its initial deployment point of Kabul into other parts of Afghanistan. Unfortunately, with US attention already drifting toward Iraq, this did not happen – and it was only in late 2003 that the wider deployment of ISAF was finally authorized, by which time a great deal of momentum had been lost. This was one factor that facilitated the reappearance of the Taliban, and it drove home very clearly the notion that providing security for ordinary people in Afghanistan was not the top priority for the international community. The existence of parallel missions on the ground was also a source of considerable confusion for ordinary people. Not understanding the fine detail of what was going on, it was easy for Afghans to find themselves utterly perplexed when uniformed personnel one day spoke of security, reconstruction, and human dignity, while (other) uniformed personnel the next day engaged in kinetic operations that involved bursting into private houses and striking fear into the occupants.

The uncertain security environment in Afghanistan created significant challenges for rebuilding. One was a challenge of coordination. The international actors who surged into Afghanistan from late 2001 had significant resources at their disposal, but on the whole much less immediate knowledge of the situation on the ground than had some of the non-governmental organization (NGO) personnel with years of experience in Afghanistan, often in extremely difficult circumstances. Very often, NGO personnel felt neither an obligation to pay obeisance to the resources which the new arrivals could command, nor any desire to repose under their collective umbrella, which ran the risk of associating NGOs in the minds of the population with some of the kinetic activities which international forces were pursuing. Furthermore, as the new Afghan state began to take shape, tension developed over whether the better approach was to channel reconstruction resources through the state, or bypass the state for the sake of the rapid realization of reconstruction objectives. Neither approach prevailed in its entirety, and the result was a proliferation of "aid paradoxes" where aid simultaneously built and undermined the new state (see Bizhan 2018; for more detail on reconstruction challenges, see Maley 2006, 78–100, 2018, 69–85). On the whole, the record of reconstruction projects has been somewhat mixed. There have been notable successes in the areas of education and public health, but at the same time, the reports of the office of the US Special Inspector-General for Afghanistan Reconstruction, established by the National Defense Authorization Act for Fiscal Year 2008, have highlighted significant examples of maladministration and waste of resources. The greater success of reconstruction has been indirect, through the opening of Afghanistan to the effects of globalization processes from which it was substantially insulated during the Taliban period (see Mohammadi 2014). The result is that Afghanistan's young population is connected to the world in ways that no previous Afghan generation had ever experienced, and while this has the effect of opening Afghanistan to radicalizing influences (see Akbar 2018), it has also created a generation with a much clearer vision of the wider world and where Afghanistan and Afghans sit within it.

In strict terms of civil–military relations – a complex phenomenon in the best of times (see Maley, Sampford, and Thakur 2003) – the main theaters of activity that emerged were the diverse PRTs that were established in various parts of Afghanistan (for more detailed discussion, see Maley and Schmeidl 2015). For more remote parts of Afghanistan, the PRTs had the potential to be the principal actors in the discharge of a responsibility to rebuild. Underlying their establishment was the conviction that civil and military actors, working *together*, could deliver better outcomes for ordinary Afghans than either would be able to do working separately. But beyond this, there was very little in the way of any best-practice PRT "model" to be rolled out. This was principally because the PRTs were essentially exercises in improvisation, although they owed something to the experience of the Civil Operations and Revolutionary Development Support Program in South Vietnam. Some twenty-seven PRTs were established in Afghanistan, thirteen led by the United States, with the balance being run by Washington's NATO and non-NATO allies. Quite rapidly, it became clear that there was little that united the different PRTs. There was no overarching mechanism to coordinate their activities, either through ISAF or through the line ministries of the Afghan government. How they performed depended very greatly upon the resource endowments provided by the states that were responsible for particular PRTs, as well as the operating environments in particular provinces and the cultures of the militaries that were deployed. When the environments were positive – as for example in Bamiyan, where the New Zealand Defence Force was located – significant developmental objectives could be achieved. Yet as one careful study has documented, where aid was injected as a force-multiplier in contested regions, the outcome was rather different: aid projects ran the risk of providing targets for the armed opposition to hit and of fueling competition rather than cooperation (see Sexton 2016). There were also significant questions relating to the durability of what was achieved by PRTs. Australia, for example, was involved for a number of years in PRT activity in Uruzgan (see Maley 2011, 2015; Khosa 2015), but it remains one of the most insecure provinces in the country, with the Taliban extremely active in many of its districts. Indeed, there is a danger that buildings established to house clinics and schools could end up one day serving as comfortable Taliban headquarters.

One other point about PRT activity deserves note. In Afghanistan, one is very likely to be judged by the company that one is seen to be keeping – and this created risk for PRTs, given the decidedly mixed character of local officials appointed in the environment of neopatrimonialism over which President Karzai had presided, not least of inadvertent alignment with potentially violent local actors. Some states proved much more attuned to this danger than did others. In Uruzgan, for example, Australia developed a relatively close relationship with a local strongman, Matiullah Khan; indeed, one Australian general went so far as to describe him as "our guy" (Oakes 2010). Matiullah, however, had ambitions of his own (see Filkins 2010; Schmeidl 2010), and his agenda did *not* necessarily coincide with Australia's. He was a member of the Popalzai tribe of Durrani Pushtuns, and his ascendancy risked being resented by many Durranis who were not Popalzai, by many Pushtuns who were not Durranis, and by many non-Pushtuns. As it turned out, Matiullah was not a good long-term investment, either: he was assassinated in Kabul in 2015 (Ahmed 2015). A responsibility to rebuild needs to be focused on methodical rebuilding of institutions, an endeavor which requires both adequate resources and firm long-term commitment from crucial states. Investing in "strongmen" is a dangerous quick fix.

Conclusion

The four decades of turmoil that Afghanistan has experienced commenced well before the crystallization of any idea of a global responsibility to protect, but the fact that political rather than humanitarian considerations have been the dominant driving forces behind even the post-2001 intervention suggests that giving effect to R2P faces significant challenges. One problem, which the earlier decades highlight, is that of mass atrocity killings in "slow motion," which may be very difficult to predict and hence to prevent (on problems in this sphere more broadly, see Rubin 2002a). It is doubtful whether too many *individual* events in Afghanistan's recent history have been on a scale comparable to the Rwandan genocide of 1994, but it is possible that over the *longue durée*, more Afghans suffered violent deaths than did Rwandans, not least as a result of the use of relatively high-technology weaponry against highly vulnerable targets. There is nothing particularly surprising about this; after all, the road toll globally claims more than a million lives annually, far more than the number of lives claimed by terrorist attacks, but receives much less attention, for cognitive reasons that are by now well understood (see Goodin 2006, 124–31). It does, however, raise the question of whether there are yet appropriate norms or sets of norms to deal with a situation of large-scale, but "slow-motion" killing, especially when carried out by the forces of a permanent member of the Security Council that can veto any action that might be appropriate under Chapter VI or VII of the Charter of the United Nations.

More recent developments in Afghanistan point to a different set of difficulties, related to the challenge of optimizing cooperation between civil and military actors as a device for discharging a responsibility to rebuild. Here, the lessons of the period after 2001 are fundamentally dispiriting. The intervention that overthrew the Taliban was not carried out with a predominant focus on rebuilding Afghanistan for the benefit of its people. Rather, the reconstruction of Afghanistan was seen as a means to an end; namely, the elimination of an environment conducive for the flourishing of anti-Western terrorist groups such as al-Qaeda. With the blocking of expansion beyond Kabul of ISAF, PRTs were established very much as "second-best" responses to the need to establish some kind of presence in rural Afghanistan. They were not set up in line with some overarching model; on the contrary, they displayed a great deal of variety in terms of ethos, resourcing, and commitment to long-term objectives. Some PRTs were reasonably successful in achieving local objectives, but a country as seriously damaged as Afghanistan cannot easily be rebuilt on a province-by-province basis. It is naïve to think that provincial-level cooperation can overcome the malign effects of a neopatrimonial political order, and an insurgency driven from sanctuaries on the territory of a meddlesome neighbor.

Those looking for a coherent model of civil–military engagement to give effect to a responsibility to rebuild as part of R2P will not find it in Afghanistan. They will need to look elsewhere. But the dispiriting Afghan experience should not be read as implying that effective and coordinated discharge of civil and military responsibilities in a disrupted state is irrelevant to a responsibility to rebuild. While the operational environment in Afghanistan was compromised by a range of factors, including the drift of US attention to Iraq and the resumption of Pakistani meddling, Afghanistan has suffered also because some PRTs proved markedly less effective than others. In this respect, ensuring appropriate civil–military engagement in aid of a responsibility to rebuild is but one part of the task of ensuring effective civil–military engagement more generally.

References

Abed, Fahim, Fatima Faizi, and Mujib Mashal, 2017. "Islamic State Claims Deadly Blast at Afghan Shiite Center," *New York Times*, December 28.

Afghanistan Justice Project, 2005. *Casting Shadows: War Crimes and Crimes Against Humanity: 1978–2001* (Kabul: Afghanistan Justice Project).

Ahmed, Azam, 2015. "Powerful Afghan Police Chief Is Killed in Targeted Suicide Attack," *New York Times*, March 20.
Akbar, Shaharzad, 2018. "Afghan Youth and 'Soft Radicalisation': Emerging Social Forces," in Srinjoy Bose, Nishank Motwani, and William Maley, eds, *Afghanistan – Challenges and Prospects* (Abingdon: Routledge), 143–56.
Asia Foundation, 2017. *Afghanistan in 2017: A Survey of the Afghan People* (Kabul: The Asia Foundation).
Barnett, Michael, 2002. *Eyewitness to a Genocide: The United Nations and Rwanda* (Ithaca, NY: Cornell University Press).
Barry, Michael, 1980. "Répressions et guerre soviétiques," *Les Temps Modernes* 408–9: 171–234.
Bizhan, Nematullah, 2018. *Aid Paradoxes in Afghanistan: Building and Undermining the State* (Abingdon: Routledge).
Ch'i, Hsi-Sheng, 1976. *Warlord Politics in China 1916–1928* (Stanford, CA: Stanford University Press).
Christia, Fotini, 2012. *Alliance Formation in Civil Wars* (Cambridge: Cambridge University Press).
Cigar, Norman, 1995. *Genocide in Bosnia: The Policy of "Ethnic Cleansing"* (College Station: Texas A&M University Press).
Colville, Rupert C., 1999. "One Massacre That Didn't Grab the World's Attention," *International Herald Tribune*, August 7.
Crews, Robert D., 2015. *Afghan Modern: The History of a Global Nation* (Cambridge, MA: Harvard University Press).
Docher, Valérie, 2017. "Le retour d'Hekmatyâr," *Les Nouvelles d'Afghanistan* 157, June: 3–6.
Dorronsoro, Gilles, 1995. "Afghanistan's Civil War," *Current History* 94, no. 588: 37–40.
Englehart, Neil, and Patrick Grant, 2015. "Governors, Governance, and Insurgency in Karzai's Afghanistan: The Limits of Professionalism," *Asian Survey* 55, no. 2: 299–324.
Fein, Helen, 1993. "Discriminating Genocide from War Crimes: Vietnam and Afghanistan Reexamined," *Denver Journal of International Law and Policy* 22, no. 1: 29–62.
Fergusson, James, 1997. "The Peace Brought by the Taliban," *The Independent*, February 19.
Filkins, Dexter, 2010. "With U.S. Aid, Warlord Builds Afghan Empire," *New York Times*, June 5.
Girardet, Edward, 1985. *Afghanistan: The Soviet War* (London: Croom Helm).
Goldsmith, Ben R., 1997. "A Victory to Fear or a Source of Hope?" *The World Today* 53, no. 7: 182–4.
Goodin, Robert E., 2006. *What's Wrong with Terrorism?* (Cambridge: Polity Press).
Grossman, A. S., 1993. "Sekretnye dokumenty iz osobykh papok: Afganistan," *Voprosy istorii* 3: 3–33.
Hanifi, Shah Mahmoud, 2008. *Connecting Histories in Afghanistan: Market Relations and State Formation on a Colonial Frontier* (Stanford, CA: Stanford University Press).
Hopkins, B. D., 2008. *The Making of Modern Afghanistan* (Basingstoke: Palgrave Macmillan).
Human Rights Watch, 2005. *Blood-Stained Hands: Past Atrocities in Kabul and Afghanistan's Legacy of Impunity* (New York: Human Rights Watch).
Ibrahim, Azeem, 2018. *The Rohingyas: Inside Myanmar's Genocide* (London: Hurst & Co.).
Ibrahimi, Niamatullah, 2017. *The Hazaras and the Afghan State: Rebellion, Exclusion and the Struggle for Recognition* (London: Hurst & Co.).
ICISS (International Commission on Intervention and State Sovereignty), 2001. *The Responsibility to Protect: Report of the International Commission on Intervention and State Sovereignty* (Ottawa: International Development Research Centre).
Khalidi, Noor Ahmad, 1991. "Afghanistan: Demographic Consequences of War, 1978–1987," *Central Asian Survey* 10, no. 3: 101–26.

Khosa, Raspal, 2015. "Playing Three Dimensional Chess: Australia's Civil–Military Commitment in Afghanistan," in William Maley and Susanne Schmeidl, eds, *Reconstructing Afghanistan: Civil–Military Experiences in Comparative Perspective* (Abingdon: Routledge), 80–97.

Kiernan, Ben, 2008. *The Pol Pot Regime: Race, Power, and Genocide in Cambodia Under the Khmer Rouge, 1975–79*, 3rd edn (New Haven, CT: Yale University Press).

Malejacq, Romain, 2016. "Warlords, Intervention, and State Consolidation: A Typology of Political Orders in Weak and Failed States," *Security Studies* 25, no. 1: 85–110.

Maley, William, 1998. "Introduction: Interpreting the Taliban," in William Maley, ed., *Fundamentalism Reborn? Afghanistan and the Taliban* (London: Hurst & Co.), 1–28.

Maley, William, 2002. *The Afghanistan Wars* (New York: Palgrave Macmillan).

Maley, William, 2006. *Rescuing Afghanistan* (London: Hurst & Co.).

Maley, William, 2011. "PRT Activity in Afghanistan: The Australian Experience," in Nik Hynek and Péter Marton, eds, *Statebuilding in Afghanistan: Multinational Contributions to Reconstruction* (Abingdon: Routledge), 124–38.

Maley, William, 2015. "Australian Approaches to Afghanistan," in Jack Cunningham and William Maley, eds, *Australia and Canada in Afghanistan: Perspectives on a Mission* (Toronto: Dundurn), 28–49.

Maley, William, 2018. *Transition in Afghanistan: Hope, Despair and the Limits of Statebuilding* (London: Routledge).

Maley, William, and Susanne Schmeidl, eds, 2015. *Reconstructing Afghanistan: Civil–Military Experiences in Comparative Perspective* (Abingdon: Routledge).

Maley, William, Charles Sampford, and Ramesh Thakur, eds, 2003. *From Civil Strife to Civil Society: Civil and Military Responsibilities in Disrupted States* (Tokyo: United Nations University Press).

Martin, Mike, 2014. *An Intimate War: An Oral History of the Helmand Conflict* (London: Hurst & Co.).

Mashal, Mujib, 2017. "Back in Kabul, This Time Not to Destroy," *New York Times*, May 5.

Mashal, Mujib, and Zahra Nader, 2016. "ISIS Claims Suicide Bombing of Protest in Kabul, Killing at Least 80," *New York Times*, July 24.

Mashal, Mujib, and Jawad Sukhanyar, 2018. "'It's a Massacre': Blast in Kabul Deepens Toll of a Long War," *New York Times*, January 27.

Mason, Whit, ed., 2011. *The Rule of Law in Afghanistan: Missing in Inaction* (Cambridge: Cambridge University Press).

Mohammadi, Hayatullah, 2014. *Tasir-e jahanishodan bar farhang dar Afghanistan* (Kabul: Entesharat-e Farhang).

Mukhopadhyay, Dipali, 2014. *Warlords, Strongman Governors, and the State in Afghanistan* (New York: Cambridge University Press).

Nordland, Rod, 2014. "Warlords with Dark Pasts Battle in Afghan Election," *New York Times*, February 26.

Oakes, Dan, 2010. "It's a War Zone Out There," *Sydney Morning Herald*, December 7.

Osman, Borhan, 2017. *Charismatic, Absolutist, Divisive: Hekmatyar and the Impact of His Return* (Kabul: Afghanistan Analysts Network, May 3).

Partlow, Joshua, 2016. *A Kingdom of Their Own: The Family Karzai and the Afghan Disaster* (New York: Alfred A. Knopf).

Pravda, 1989. "Postanovlenie Verkhovnogo Soveta SSSR Ob Amnistii Sovershivshikh Prestupleniia Byvshikh Voennosluzhashchikh Kontingenta Sovetskikh Voisk v Afganistane," November 30.

Pye, Lucien W., 1971. *Warlord Politics: Conflict and Coalition in the Modernization of Republican China* (New York: Praeger).

Rahimi, Mujib Rahman, 2017. *State Formation in Afghanistan: A Theoretical and Political History* (London: I. B. Tauris).

Rashid, Ahmed, 2000. *Taliban: Militant Islam, Oil and Fundamentalism in Central Asia* (New Haven, CT: Yale University Press).

Rubin, Barnett R., 2002a. *Blood on the Doorstep: The Politics of Preventive Action* (New York: The Century Foundation).

Rubin, Barnett R., 2002b. *The Fragmentation of Afghanistan: State Formation and Collapse in the International System* (New Haven, CT: Yale University Press).

Schmeidl, Susanne, 2010. *The Man Who Would Be King: The Challenges to Strengthening Governance in Uruzgan* (The Hague: Netherlands Institute of International Relations Clingendael).

Schmeidl, Susanne, and William Maley, 2008. "The Case of the Afghan Refugee Population: Finding Durable Solutions in Contested Transitions," in Howard Adelman, ed., *Protracted Displacement in Asia: No Place to Call Home* (Aldershot: Ashgate), 131–79.

Sexton, Renard, 2016. "Aid as a Tool against Insurgency: Evidence from Contested and Controlled Territory in Afghanistan," *American Political Science Review* 110, no. 4: 731–49.

Sharan, Timor, 2011. "The Dynamics of Elite Networks and Patron–Client Relations in Afghanistan," *Europe–Asia Studies* 63, no. 6: 1109–27.

Sharan, Timor, 2013. "The Dynamics of Informal Political Networks and Statehood in Post-2001 Afghanistan: A Case Study of the 2010–2011 Special Election Court Crisis," *Central Asian Survey* 32, no. 3: 336–52.

Sharan, Timor, 2017. *Dawlat-e shabakahi: Rabeteh-i qodrat wa sarwat dar Afghanistan pas az sal-e 2001* (Kabul: Vazhah Publications).

Sharan, Timor, and Srinjoy Bose, 2016. "Political Networks and the 2014 Afghan Presidential Election: Power Restructuring, Ethnicity and State Stability," *Conflict, Security and Development* 16, no. 6: 613–33.

Suhrke, Astri, and Arne Strand, 2005. "The Logic of Conflictual Peacebuilding," in Sultan Barakat, ed., *After the Conflict: Reconstruction and Development in the Aftermath of War* (London: I. B. Tauris), 141–54.

Swenson, Geoffrey, 2017. "Why US Efforts to Promote the Rule of Law in Afghanistan Failed," *International Security* 42, no. 1: 114–51.

Thakur, Ramesh, 2004. "Dealing with Guilt beyond Crime: The Strained Quality of Universal Justice," in Ramesh Thakur and Peter Malcontent, eds, *From Sovereign Impunity to International Accountability: The Search for Justice in a World of States* (Tokyo: United Nations University Press), 272–92.

Thakur, Ramesh, 2017. *The United Nations, Peace and Security: From Collective Security to the Responsibility to Protect*, 2nd edn (Cambridge: Cambridge University Press).

United Nations, 1993. "Situation of Human Rights in Afghanistan: Note by the Secretary-General," A/48/584, November 16.

CONCLUSION

R2P at a crossroads: implementation or marginalization

Ivan Šimonović

Introduction

The central proposition in this chapter is that the value of the Responsibility to Protect (R2P) depends on how far it serves its aim to prevent atrocity crimes – namely, genocide, war crimes, ethnic cleansing, and crimes against humanity. Analyzing the impact of R2P to date, this chapter argues that R2P is at a crossroads: its future lies in implementation or marginalization. The states and institutions that have committed themselves to R2P will lose their credibility unless they take steps to ensure its effective implementation.

It is not just the aim of R2P that makes it distinct. It is the way in which it should be achieved through individual and collective action and by avoiding the costs of inaction and inadequate action. The adoption of R2P, as articulated in paragraphs 138–140 of the 2005 World Summit Outcome, was a landmark achievement: a concept championed by academics, humanitarian activists, and visionary political leaders was transformed into a program of action, adopted by consensus by all member states (United Nations General Assembly 2005). This was an important development, because political commitments imply political accountability. Therefore, political accountability mechanisms can be used to ensure that commitments are met.

I argue in this chapter that it is not viable to consider replacing R2P with another concept; this would permit states to backtrack on vital normative and political commitments expressed in the World Summit Outcome. To direct the trajectory of R2P away from marginalization and toward implementation, this chapter sets out a new agenda that has four core ingredients. First, the reinvigoration of multilateralism is needed to better manage key global trends that shape the current context, including globalization, geopolitical changes, technological advances, and migration. These trends should be harnessed to generate opportunities for

R2P's implementation. Second, effective early-action mechanisms need to be established to respond to early-warning analysis from international to local levels. Third, strengthened accountability of the United Nations (UN) Security Council is needed to improve atrocity-prevention capacity across the UN system. This includes the mobilization of existing human rights mechanisms, and an additional reform track within the UN Secretary-General's current reform agenda to permit better coordination of the currently fragmented sectors of human rights, rule of law, and the various protection mandates, including R2P. Fourth, priority must be given to providing the proper mandate and authority for a UN coordinating body to oversee this vital agenda.

The chapter proceeds in four parts. First, it assesses the progress of R2P in responding to atrocity situations, arguing that the rhetoric on R2P has not been matched by effective implementation. Second, the chapter considers the value that R2P provides to the international community, concluding that despite shortcomings in the track-record of R2P implementation, the concept should not be abandoned given the need for international consensus on the values that R2P represents. It argues that the international community would be unable to reach consensus on a better framework for protecting vulnerable populations in the current political climate. Third, it advances recommendations for making R2P prevention effective, and fourth and finally, it identifies challenges to be navigated in order to realize this agenda.

R2P and atrocity crimes trends

Since 2005, R2P has attracted a lot of attention. The articulation of paragraphs 138 and 139 in the 2005 World Summit Outcome have been reaffirmed by UN General Assembly and UN Security Council resolutions that repeat the same language. References to R2P in UN documents have been numerous, with over fifty Security Council and over twenty UN Human Rights Council resolutions at the time of writing. The post of Special Adviser on R2P was established in 2008 (although on a part-time basis and at an Assistant Secretary-General level) to support the conceptual development and implementation of R2P, and since 2009, the Secretary-General has submitted yearly thematic reports on R2P (prepared by the Special Adviser), informing General Assembly debates and informal interactive dialogues (with one formal debate and eight informal interactive dialogues so far at the time of writing). These reports and dialogues have helped to clarify the concept and provided a general vision of its implementation.[1]

Although there are some disagreements among states on certain aspects of R2P's implementation (especially relating to the use of coercive measures under Pillar Three), the interactive dialogues have demonstrated that most states support R2P, prioritize prevention, and welcome the Secretary-General's strategy for implementation. Furthermore, some states have introduced national mechanisms for atrocity crimes risk assessment and prevention, or formed cross-regional or regional groups, which explicitly or implicitly serve to promote and mainstream R2P, and provide fora for exchanges of experiences and for mutual support in closing atrocity crimes prevention gaps.[2]

Civil society has embraced R2P; some R2P-focused non-governmental organizations (NGOs) have been established, such as the Global Centre for R2P, and the International Coalition for the R2P. Civil society actors have an important role to play in global or regional networks as members and/or by providing secretariat services.[3] R2P has also attracted a lot of academic attention. Various existing atrocity crimes-related institutions have incorporated R2P in their work, and new institutions that focus specifically on R2P have been established, including the Asia Pacific Centre for the Responsibility to Protect and the European Centre for the Responsibility to Protect. The number of academic courses that include or focus on R2P, as well as dedicated books and articles, has been rapidly increasing.

Despite these achievements, ultimately, R2P's value depends on how successful it is in preventing mass atrocities in practice. Its added value should not be presumed, but demonstrated. In assessing R2P's impact, an atrocity-prevention reality check based on available numbers and trends indicates quite disappointing results. Despite an increase in the number of states expressing commitment to and institutionalization of R2P, in recent years, atrocity crimes have been on the rise. Lack of respect for some previously established norms of customary humanitarian law has been so widespread and flagrant that we are facing a threat of their potential "de-customizing." In response to some of the major crises of our times – including in Myanmar, Yemen, and Syria – there has been little concerted effort to prevent atrocity crimes, as other concerns were prioritized.

How did we get to this point? Starting in the mid-1990s, after decisive action was taken in reaction to protection failures in Rwanda and Bosnia, there was a period when atrocity crimes decreased, along with the number of conflicts and civilian casualties. Humanitarian law and international criminal law were finally getting teeth through the establishment of ad hoc tribunals and the International Criminal Court. By the end of the first decade of the twenty-first century, however, we had moved to a period marked by negative trends. These negative trends include an increase in the number of conflicts and resulting casualties,[4] including casualties due to unselective or deliberate attacks against civilians that may have constituted war crimes and – if widespread or systematic (which has increasingly been the case) – crimes against humanity.[5] These trends have contributed to the forced displacement of civilians on a massive scale – the numbers of refugees and internally displaced persons are the highest they have been since the end of the Second World War.[6]

If the true measure of the worth of R2P is its contribution to the prevention of atrocity crimes, has R2P failed? Should we turn to some other concept that would prevent atrocity crimes better?

What is R2P's current value?

Before deciding whether to abandon R2P, it is necessary to at least briefly examine some elements relevant to its objective assessment. What are the reasons for the increase in atrocity crimes? Why did R2P not produce better results by preventing them? Would the international community have performed better in the absence of R2P? Does it have the potential to do so in the future? Would switching to some other concept promise better results?

To answer these crucial questions, it is important to consider social, economic, cultural, and political factors that may have contributed to the increase in atrocity crimes. Some relevant negative developments include tensions and anxieties caused by unregulated globalization, changes in global power relations, the social impact of technological development, climate change,[7] demographic trends, and an increase in migration. These trends have had a negative impact on the overall social and political climate, affecting international cooperation and the willingness and ability of member states to take action individually and collectively to prevent atrocity crimes.

The post-Cold War romance is over. Divisions between key global and regional actors are the deepest they have been since the end of the Cold War. The global financial crisis has cast a long shadow, reducing economic growth in many parts of the world, leading to greater unemployment and disillusionment. Youth unemployment in regions such as the Middle East are catastrophic. For the first time in living memory, future generations cannot expect a better standard of living than the current generation. Populations have grown disenchanted with established elites and turn to populism and more extreme ideologies for answers. The income gap within and among countries is widening, and social cohesion and solidarity are in decline.[8]

In times of uncertainty and stress, we are seeing a tendency toward authoritarianism in an increasing number of states. Democratic space is shrinking. Civil society and the media are under increasing pressure. The commitment to liberal values, human rights, atrocity prevention, multilateralism, and a positive-sum world order based on agreed rules and institutions is weakening. Universal human rights values-based policies are being replaced by unrestricted national interests-based policies.

The UN Security Council is often paralyzed. Compromises in the interests of the common good are being replaced by a zero-sum-game approach.[9] The leverage of the UN as a major forum for global dialogue and coordination is decreasing.[10] In our increasingly interdependent world, a lack of global coordination and weakening capacity to prevent negative global trends is dangerous. With governments confronting situations where they have fewer resources but greater demands are placed on them, commitment to internationalism is in decline. The only solidarity that is strengthening is "negative solidarity": solidarity with one's own group in confronting other groups.

Even some otherwise positive trends may contribute to negative outcomes. The aspirations of more educated and better-informed populations in developing countries are increasing. Young people want a better life now, yet high levels of youth unemployment plague many societies. Demands for more civil, political, social, economic, and cultural rights are becoming stronger.

Under this pressure, regimes are facing a dilemma as to whether to introduce reforms (which may undermine power and privileges of the ruling elites), or to increase repression. Unfortunately, they often resort to the latter. But they are mistaken if they believe that they can prosper without legitimacy. A suppressed uprising merely provides the raw materials for the next uprising: "another spring." The underlying tumult will remain until either governments make the necessary reforms or find themselves unable to resist the popular will any more. Frustrations at lack of opportunity for peaceful change are strong incentives to either resort to violent means or look for a better life elsewhere. As we saw with the Arab Spring, peaceful protests can turn into violent conflicts. In such situations, radical elements of the opposition can take over a leading role, putting pro-democracy and human rights activists between a rock and a hard place.

In a number of countries, frustrated populations are looking for solutions to actual problems by trying to turn back the clock of history and return to conditions of an idealized past (from Salafism in the Islamic world, to isolationism, xenophobia, and extreme nationalism in the West). Instead of solutions, this creates new problems. Frustrations at corruption and lack of the rule of law, increased repression, a shortage of regular channels for political change, and structural discrimination against identity-based groups all provide a fertile breeding ground for violent extremism. In this context, non-state armed groups have increasingly been involved in the commission of atrocity crimes. Lack of perspective, repression, instability, and conflict contribute to increasing waves of migration and forced displacement.

In developed countries, we are facing the ascendance of populist leaders who are cynically manipulating concerns about the effects of globalization, technological change, and migration on the quality of life and job opportunities, as well as cultural identity and security threats. These leaders offer quick fixes, proposing policies favoring unrestricted national interests, closing of national borders, and rejection of diversity. A vicious circle has emerged between rising xenophobia in host countries and radicalization of immigrants.

These developments and trends have contributed to the increase in atrocity crimes and have negatively affected R2P's implementation. In addition, the perceived shortcomings of the intervention in Libya in 2011 – the first in which the Security Council explicitly authorized the use of force to protect populations from atrocity crimes committed by a government against its own people – undermined the credibility of R2P in the eyes of some states, and provided ammunition to its hard-core opponents.[11]

In this context, the approach to R2P has, in recent years, been marked by a widening of the gap between commitments and reality. Expressions of commitment have continued, but there has not been a conducive climate or sufficient political will for its implementation. Although most states still support R2P,[12] there are some signs that the intensity of their support may have begun to stagnate.[13] Unless support is reinvigorated, R2P will lose its political relevance – and hence, its capacity to shape action on atrocities prevention.

There is often a tension between norms/principles (be they legal, political, or moral) and reality. Indeed, the very purpose of a norm is to change behavior. If states already prevented atrocity crimes, we would have no need for a principle telling them to do so. This critical tension between principle and practice is the engine of positive change in world politics. However, the gap between expressed commitments to R2P and the reality of atrocity crimes has become so wide that the very credibility of the institutions responsible for its implementation is at stake. If R2P appears to be nothing but hollow rhetoric, and if those institutions that people look to for protection fail to deliver, they will lose credibility and support. People will turn to other, more radical and dangerous, solutions. In my view, R2P is currently at a crossroads – and the future is either its implementation or its marginalization.

As for the question of whether R2P should or could be replaced with some other concept, this is not a viable option. It is clear from past practice that a deliberate, conscious, and concerted focus on atrocity prevention tends to produce the best effects in practice. When the international community views a situation through the prism of R2P and elects to prioritize atrocity prevention in its response, the results tend to be much better. Atrocity prevention falters when no dedicated approach is adopted or, worse, when other considerations are prioritized (one of the concluding lessons advanced by Bellamy and Luck 2018).

Given global divisions and reduced support for multilateralism today, it would not be possible to obtain the consensus of global leaders (or state representatives in the General Assembly and Security Council) on any new tool nearly as powerful as R2P.[14] By staying with R2P, we are preventing states from backtracking on their important, politically binding commitments.

Also, despite shortcomings in implementation, R2P has demonstrated some important advantages:

- It fits well within overall prevention and protection agendas.[15] It has led to greater attention being paid to the prevention of atrocity crimes.
- It has provided a useful framework for how the international community considers and should respond to atrocity crimes, helping to provoke and shape the debate in and around the UN and other organizations, and involve member states and non-governmental actors.
- It provides a good balance between respect for state sovereignty and the need to protect populations when states are unable or unwilling to do so.
- It respects the UN Charter while expanding the scope of protection through the interpretation that in our increasingly interconnected world, atrocity crimes committed within borders of one state can be qualified as a threat to international peace and security, opening the possibility for coercive measures to be used under Chapter VII of the UN Charter to prevent atrocity crimes.
- It has commanded the consensus of the General Assembly and been reaffirmed by the Security Council and Human Rights Council.

The current impediments to fulfilling the central aims of R2P lie not in the principle itself, but in its inadequate implementation. There is no reason to think that rejecting the principle would help the practice; there is every reason to think, however, that redoubling support for its implementation will help close the gap between principle and reality.

The future of R2P: making prevention effective

Globalization, geopolitical changes, technological advances, climate change, and migration cannot be stopped, but they can and should be better managed. Better management of global developments requires a return to multilateralism and a strengthening of global solidarity. There are already some early signs that these changes are taking place. The successful adoption of the Sustainable Development Goals (SDGs) and the United Nations Framework Convention on Climate Change provide excellent examples of how we should move in other areas, including atrocity crimes prevention.

The mitigation of negative global trends, and the strengthening of multilateralism, human rights, the rule of law, and prevention of atrocity crimes will be an interlinked process. In a future, more favorable context that is shaped by these processes, R2P has an important role to play. The commission of atrocity crimes leads to an escalation of armed conflict, prolongs it, and makes it more difficult to end. Atrocity crimes also have extremely negative effects on development and on post-conflict reconciliation and recovery. Atrocity prevention should, therefore, be of common interest in the interdependent world. Preventing atrocity crimes is not only the right thing to do – it is also a rational choice. It requires investments, but provides huge benefits.

The first case in which the Security Council used R2P when authorizing the use of force to protect populations from their government (Libya) has been controversial in some respects. However, just as events in Srebrenica, Rwanda, and Kosovo helped to shape the development of R2P,[16] its future should be shaped by the lessons learned not only from Libya, but also from the international community's response – or lack of it – to events in Myanmar, Sri Lanka, and Syria.[17] Both action – whether authorized by the Security Council or not – and inaction come at a price. If Libya teaches us the cost of precipitate action, Myanmar, Sri Lanka, and Syria teach us of the huge and unacceptable cost of inaction. However, based on lessons learned from all the examples mentioned, there is no doubt that the cost is lowest if preventive action is taken early.

Libya should not be perceived as a nail in R2P's coffin, but as a painful learning experience. The lessons to be drawn from Libya are, first, do not wait to act until the situation deteriorates to the point at which the use of force becomes necessary for the protection of populations. Second, when force is used, the mandate should be precisely defined and its implementation closely monitored (see in this regard Columbia Global Policy Initiative 2015). Third, before considering the use of force, there is a responsibility to have a clear picture of how to restore sovereignty, including the sovereign responsibility of a state to protect populations on its territory from atrocity crimes, after the intervention. It is also imperative that the international community is responsible to rebuild, in partnership with national authorities and civil society.

Will R2P work in the future? This will depend on political will. Like every other political principle, R2P is not self-executing, but relies on the decisions of states, societies, and individuals. Peer pressure from member states, as well as from civil society – including academia, the media, and NGOs – can influence political will.

The informal interactive dialogue in 2017, as well as its preparatory events, indicated that most states support a shift from conceptual debate about R2P toward practical operationalization. However, some states insist that as long as there is no consensus on all elements of the concept, there should be no implementation. This position seems to overlook the fact that some elements of the concept already constitute a legal obligation, as they are based on an existing framework of international law. Furthermore, consensus has been reached on many aspects of its implementation, especially related to Pillars One and Two. The 2005 commitment to R2P has been noted in subsequent resolutions of the General Assembly, the Security Council, and the Human Rights Council. The Security Council, when deciding to use coercive measures under Chapter VII (including when it concludes that atrocity crimes represent a threat to international peace and security),[18] has the authority to take decisions that do not have the consensus of all member states.

Therefore, the conceptual debate should continue to focus on contentious issues, but a major shift toward R2P's implementation should not be delayed.[19] This shift has already begun with the Secretary-General's 2017 R2P report (Guterres 2017).[20] The report rightly points out that accountability is key for R2P's implementation. To overcome resistance and inertia, it is important to better use existing accountability mechanisms at all levels. In addition, some new specific mechanisms (such as parliamentary atrocity-prevention committees or subcommittees) may be introduced.

Challenges and opportunities in implementing R2P

At the global level, we have recently witnessed an important move to implement one of the key recommendations of the 2017 report: R2P was put on the agenda of the General Assembly's 72nd session (for the first time since 2009).[21] To further strengthen atrocity prevention, it should become a standing item on the General Assembly's agenda, and reporting by the Secretary-General should be mandated. Furthermore, in addition to thematic reporting, the Secretary-General could provide annual reports on trends, challenges, and opportunities in atrocity prevention. In this context, he/she could also report on the implementation of recommendations of previous reports.

Despite the challenges in doing so, there is also scope for advancing R2P within the Security Council. Through the UN Charter, member states have conferred on the Security Council the primary responsibility for the maintenance of international peace and security (Article 24, 1). The 2017 informal interactive dialogue, as well as its preparatory events, have demonstrated that member states expect that the Security Council will be held accountable to those in whose name it acts: the overall UN membership.

Strengthening the accountability of the Security Council for its actions and inactions is fundamental, but difficult. The UN Charter conferred on the Council peace and security powers without clear mechanisms to hold it accountable to other member states. This applies especially to the actions of its permanent members, whose special privileges continue, including the right to use their veto power no matter how other member states assess their performance.

The Charter's requirement that two-thirds of member states and all permanent members must support any change in its provisions limits the possibility of introducing any new accountability mechanism. Fruitless debates on reform of the Security Council have been dragging on for decades. This "evolutionary defect" of the UN Charter is difficult to overcome,[22] but calls by the cross-regional Accountability, Coherence and Transparency Group for the Security Council to adopt a voluntary code of conduct, and the French/Mexican proposal for suspension of the right to use the veto in situations where there is a risk of atrocity crimes, are both supported by most member states and are useful in exercising pressure.

A further important development that would provide for more accountability would be to organize regular and open Security Council debates on atrocity crimes threats and the Council's role in their prevention. When the composition of the Security Council is favorable, it would be possible to get the necessary nine votes for the procedural decision to include in its agenda such an open debate.[23] The success of such a debate could pave the way to put the item on the agenda on a regular basis. Such debates would also create an opportunity to exert pressure for some criteria to be established (along the lines of those proposed by the International Commission on Intervention and State Sovereignty and the UN High-Level Panel on Threats, Challenges and Change) for the authorization of the use of force and consistency in decision-making.

Also, as the Libyan case clearly demonstrated, every instance in which the Council authorizes the use of force must be preceded by a clear assessment of how, after intervention, a country will be supported and sovereignty restored. This "responsibility to rebuild" should also be discussed with the broader membership.

Human rights mechanisms, including the treaty bodies and special procedures mandate holders of the Human Rights Council, can also contribute more to atrocity crimes prevention. The Human Rights Council's Universal Periodic Review process has special potential for identifying atrocity-prevention risks and mobilizing resources for atrocity crimes prevention, and should urgently be put to better use.[24] An assessment of atrocity crimes risks and the measures and support required to close prevention gaps should be included in the reports preceding review, discussed during review, and included in the Periodic Review's recommendations. National R2P Focal Points could play a role in this process. In implementing relevant recommendations, member states under stress should be supported by other member states, facilitated by UN country teams and field operations.

At the level of the UN as an organization, atrocity-prevention efforts need to be integrated in the work of entities dealing with all three pillars, and better coordinated. The inspirational Human Rights up Front initiative, set in motion by Ban Ki-moon,[25] if combined with pragmatic and operationally oriented reforms of António Guterres aimed at strengthening the capacity of the organization to deliver in areas of peace, security, and development and focusing on prevention,[26] could help to bring about the necessary moral and operational strengthening of the UN. In addition to the current reform processes, there seems to be a need for an additional UN reform track that would bring together the fields of human rights, the rule of law, and the various protection mandates, including R2P.

Whoever oversees coordination of operational activities aimed at the prevention of atrocity crimes must have an adequate rank (for example, Under-Secretary-General) and full access to the Secretary-General and operational decision-making fora. Having a part-time Assistant Secretary-General-level Special Adviser on R2P without systematic access to relevant information and key operational decision-making mechanisms (such as the Executive and Deputies' Committees), is a politically and historically conditioned anomaly, especially considering the current need to shift R2P toward its implementation.

It will be necessary to improve mechanisms of early warning and their links to early action. In recent years, both quantitative methods of early warning (mostly based on correlation with certain indicators) and qualitative (mostly based on causality) have advanced. However, problems related to cooperation and information sharing persist. For early action, we need lessons learned on what works best and in what kinds of situations, which should enable formulation of clear, down-to-earth, and user-friendly guidelines for atrocity-prevention practitioners. Once developed and after successful testing in real life situations, the Secretary-General can make implementation of these guidelines obligatory for the UN system. They should also be published, disseminated, and discussed with member states, regional organizations, and civil society. When there is more confidence that early responses will be effective in preventing atrocity crimes, there will be more willingness to invest in them. For example, for countries concerned about the impact of an influx of refugees, it makes sense to invest in the measures that will serve to prevent what most often triggers them: the occurrence or fear of atrocity crimes.[27]

A system of atrocity prevention should rely on a process of continued monitoring, risk assessment, and timely response that is appropriate to threats. Threats can only be eliminated by addressing root causes and strengthening the resilience of societies to periods of stress. Monitoring of human rights, atrocity risks, and SDG implementation can all help to provide early indications of when societies may be on a wrong track. Such monitoring can also be helpful in identifying what remedial action should be taken.

Structural prevention takes time, resources, and a systematic approach (see Ban 2014). Meanwhile, even if the explosive has not yet been removed, we can at least try to defuse detonators. We should closely monitor potential triggers that can serve as catalysts for atrocity crimes, and act quickly and decisively. This will require the close collaboration of various actors: the UN, regional organizations, member states, local community networks, and civil society actors, including NGOs, academia, religious leaders, elders, youth, and women.

The UN should improve its capacity for early action. The timely deployment of light footprint missions that consist of a handful of political and human rights officers can sometimes reduce the need for heavy UN operations that are both expensive and sensitive for national sovereignty. Their timely deployment requires not only a proactive UN Secretariat, but also a supportive Security Council.[28] Member states need to understand that if they do not accept light footprint missions, heavy UN operations may be deployed, including under Chapter VII if necessary.

If all these measures are successfully implemented, will early prevention always be successful? Perhaps not always, but we would hopefully need to deploy peacekeeping operations to protect civilians less often. When we do need to deploy them, strengthening their capacity to protect civilians in line with the Kigali Principles on the Protection of Civilians would contribute significantly to atrocity prevention (for details, see "Kigali Principles on the Protection of Civilians and the Responsibility to Protect" 2016).[29] It is also important that developed countries, in addition to financial resources, contribute more to peacekeeping operations through training, equipment, and troops.

Accountability mechanisms should also be activated at the regional level. Because of their proximity, regional organizations can play a significant role – they have a better understanding of risks and appropriate measures that need to be taken to mitigate them. In addition, they are also less affected by concerns and suspicions related to the negative aspects of globalization.

At the national level, states have a responsibility to prevent atrocity crimes that derives from legal obligations and political commitments. Support should be provided to states in need to help them close atrocity-prevention gaps. Parliaments have an important role to play in improving atrocity prevention in the following ways: they should use their legislative, budgetary, and oversight powers in this regard; relevant international treaties should be ratified, and national legislation should criminalize atrocity crimes as well as their incitement; and sufficient resources should be allocated to structural – as well as operational – prevention, and early-warning and early-action mechanisms set in place. Parliaments can better use existing opportunities, such as annual reports of national human rights institutions and Ombudspersons, to discuss atrocity crimes threats and the prevention measures that are necessary. They can also establish special atrocity crimes prevention committees or subcommittees, and insist that governments provide effective national atrocity-prevention mechanisms.[30]

Some atrocity threats can be first identified and responded to at a local level, and more resources should be allocated for that purpose. This should be done nationally, as well as with international support.

Successful R2P operationalization requires mobilization of a broad coalition, including supportive member states, multinational and regional organizations, and civil society. It also requires a clear strategy and patience in taking sometimes small, but concrete and practical steps in the right direction. As Dag Hammarskjold stated, "the future is the horizon, but it is also the first step we take tomorrow" (Broderick 2015).

Members of the Group of Friends of R2P in New York and Geneva should lead these efforts by example. They should be frank in their assessments of atrocity crimes risks and vulnerabilities in their own and other countries, and provide sufficient resources to close them. Whether in the General Assembly, the Human Rights Council, or the Security Council, they should provide for atrocity-prevention approaches in their analyses and promote early preventive action. For example, they should lead initiatives to place R2P permanently on the General Assembly agenda; use the Universal Periodic Review to identify national atrocity-prevention gaps and help to close them; establish a genocide and other atrocity crimes prevention treaty body, reporting on prevention activities of the state parties;[31] introduce regular Security Council open debates to discuss its role in atrocity crimes prevention and provide for its improved accountability; and establish the Security Council's Atrocity Crimes Prevention Committee.

The Secretary-General should closely cooperate with them, and place atrocity prevention at the heart of the overall prevention agenda. This would require improvement of UN early-warning and early-action mechanisms (see Guterres 2018a).

The R2P mandate holder should have a much more operational role and should be tasked to set up an early-warning information management system, given access to all relevant information gathered by various parts of the UN system, and present at all key policy and operational decision-making fora, especially the Executive Committee, to provide for atrocity-prevention lenses and advocacy.

Conclusion

R2P is a powerful concept. Its application is universal, it is not time bound, and world leaders at their greatest gathering consensually endorsed it. Since 2005, the commitment to R2P has been repeatedly expressed, in numerous ways. R2P has also to a certain degree been institutionalized, moving from an abstract concept toward actionable principle. However, in recent years, relevant global conditions for its implementation have considerably worsened, and we have seen an increase in atrocity crimes.

There are strong grounds to argue that R2P remains both relevant and useful. A range of factors have contributed to an environment in which all human rights and protection mandates, not just R2P, are facing greater challenges. The increase in atrocity crimes is not the result of having the wrong tools for their prevention. R2P did not fail – we did. In deteriorating conditions, we too often failed to implement it. R2P was, to a certain extent, compromised by the shortcomings of the intervention in Libya. Lessons should be learned, but we must move on. Both action and inaction (in Sri Lanka, Syria, and Myanmar) come at a price. However, there is no doubt that the price is the lowest if preventive action is taken before a situation deteriorates to the point when there is a need for use of force.

R2P should be preserved not only because of investments in its institutionalization, but because of its unparalleled potential as an atrocity-prevention tool. Most significantly, member states adopted R2P unanimously and have repeatedly reaffirmed their commitment to it. They have also voiced support for the Secretary-General's strategy for its implementation, as set out in annual reports since 2009. Despite the current lack of consensus about some aspects of its implementation, it is unlikely that a suitable alternative could be negotiated (especially in current, more difficult circumstances).

In addition to existing legal atrocity-prevention obligations, paragraphs 138 and 139 of the consensually adopted World Summit Outcome document (United Nations General Assembly 2005) transform additional moral duties into politically binding commitments that provide for political accountability to deliver on them. Therefore, letting R2P go would mean letting member states renege on their commitments, and further negatively affect efforts to prevent atrocity crimes.

Atrocity crimes prevention is also a litmus test of the credibility of the UN and its member states, as well as the prevention platform of the Secretary-General. The UN is judged on how it prevents/responds to atrocity crimes. If we cannot even muster support for ending atrocity crimes, there is no hope of achieving wider prevention agendas.

The experiences of practitioners and the results of research, including preliminary results of empirical research that I am leading,[32] clearly indicate that articulation of R2P and the subsequent actions that were undertaken by states at different stages in potential or ongoing conflict cycles have contributed to fewer atrocity crimes being committed than expected (Ban 2015 mentions Côte d'Ivoire, Guinea, Kenya, and Kyrgyzstan).

Unfortunately, R2P has not led so far to an overall numerical decrease in atrocity crimes, due to an increase in atrocity crimes risks and lack of implementation in practice. However, there are reasons to believe that it has the potential to do so in the future, when current unfavorable conditions change. Yet waiting for circumstances to change before intensifying implementation of R2P would be a mistake for the following reasons:

- We would miss the opportunity to immediately prevent some atrocity crimes.
- Intensifying implementation of R2P can positively contribute to changing unfavorable circumstances.
- If R2P remains stuck in conceptual debates, it may lose credibility.

Support for R2P should be continued. However, the approach to it should change. To date, R2P has been more conceptually debated than practically implemented. We need to shift the focus to implementation. We should act as persons of thought, and think as persons of action. Discussion of some controversial issues, especially on the use of coercive measures under Pillar Three, should continue, but this should not affect R2P's implementation.[33]

For R2P, therefore, the future is either its implementation, or its marginalization. The Secretary-General's 2017 report on R2P represents a major step in this direction. It focuses on prevention, addressing accountability for R2P's implementation.

It also provides clear, straightforward, and practical recommendations. It is important for subsequent reports to follow the same direction (Guterres 2017).

Successful R2P implementation requires mobilization of a broad coalition, including supportive member states, global and regional organizations, and civil society. It also requires a clear strategy and patience in taking sometimes small – but concrete and practical – steps in the right direction. Members of the Group of Friends of R2P in New York and Geneva should lead these efforts by example. They should be frank in their assessments of the risk of atrocity crimes in their own and other countries, and provide sufficient resources to address them. Whether at the General Assembly, the Human Rights Council, or the Security Council, they should include atrocity-prevention approaches in their analyses and promote early preventive action.

The Secretary-General should put atrocity prevention at the heart of the overall prevention agenda. The mandate holder responsible for atrocity crimes prevention should have direct access to the Secretary-General, as well as access to all relevant information and fora where crucial policy is decided and operational decisions are taken.

Notes

1 Especially important for articulation of the concept through the interpretation of paragraphs 138 and 139 of the World Summit Outcome was Ban (2009), which introduced the three pillars structure of R2P. Pillar One is the enduring responsibility of the state to protect its populations from atrocity crimes. Pillar Two is the commitment of the international community to assist states in meeting these obligations. Pillar Three is the responsibility of member states to respond collectively in a timely and decisive manner when a state is manifestly failing to provide such protection. These would include peaceful and coercive measures if necessary (in accordance with the UN Charter, measures under Chapter VII must be authorized by the Security Council).
2 These include the Group of Friends on the Responsibility to Protect (New York and Geneva); the Global Network of R2P Focal Points; the Global Action Against Mass Atrocity Crimes initiative; the International Conference on the Great Lakes Region's Regional Committee on the Prevention and Punishment of Genocide, War Crimes and Crimes against Humanity and all forms of Discrimination, and national committees of its member states; and the Latin American Network for Genocide and Mass Atrocity Prevention.
3 The Global Centre for the Responsibility to Protect provides secretariat services to the Group of Friends on R2P, and the Auschwitz Institute for Peace and Reconciliation serves as the technical secretariat to the Latin American Network for Genocide and Mass Atrocity Prevention.
4 Between 2005 and 2015, civil wars have almost tripled. Between 2011 and 2015, fatalities increased 600 percent (von Einsiedel et al. 2017, 2). Between 2010 and 2016, the number of major violent conflicts tripled. From a post-Cold War low in 2005 to 2014, conflict-related deaths have increased tenfold. Between 2010 and 2016 alone, civilian deaths in violent conflicts doubled. See Uppsala Conflict Data Program (n.d.).
5 Peacekeepers are also increasingly targeted. From 2016–2017, the number of peacekeeping casualties doubled (Guterres 2018b).
6 According to the United Nations High Commissioner for Refugees (2018, 2), by the end of 2017, there were 68.5 million people forcefully displaced, 25.4 million of them refugees.

7 This is especially true of the links to drought and food insecurity, which trigger confrontations over scarce resources and migration.
8 Together with an increase in armed conflicts and climate change, this has contributed to a dramatic change in trends: after a period of prolonged decline, world hunger is on the rise.
9 That does not apply only to the Security Council. In 2017, because of an inability to reach consensus, the highest number of resolutions in the Human Rights Council's history had to be adopted by vote – thirty-six (32 percent of all adopted texts).
10 This perception can be supported by objective, quantitative indicators. After decades of expansion and budget growth, in recent years, the UN budget has been steadily shrinking.
11 At first, intervention in Libya was perceived by many as a success in that it prevented the population of Benghazi from experiencing the regime's retaliation. However, the perception that NATO overstepped its Security Council protection of civilians' mandate and pushed for regime change, leaving the country in chaos in the aftermath of intervention, dramatically changed prevailing views.
12 The General Assembly vote on inclusion of R2P on the agenda of the General Assembly's 72nd session is a good indicator. Out of 151 member states, 75 percent voted for its inclusion, 14 percent voted against it, and 11 percent abstained (United Nations General Assembly 2017, paragraph 93).
13 Although the number of R2P Group of Friends members, states that have appointed Focal Points, and countries that have introduced specific atrocity prevention mechanisms are still growing, the pace has slowed down.
14 There is some overlap with other existing concepts/principles (the protection of civilians in armed conflict, for example), but they are different in scope and there is no expressed, universal political commitment to them, which is R2P's great comparative advantage.
15 This seems to be particularly relevant in the context of the Secretary-General's overall prevention platform and R2P's potential contribution to it.
16 Srebrenica and Rwanda by lack of action to prevent genocide, and Kosovo by intervention that was initially not endorsed by the Security Council and which was, in the words of the Independent International Commission on Kosovo (2000, 4), "illegal but legitimate." Shaped by these experiences, R2P is, in Michael Doyle's words, a "*licence for* and a *leash against* forcible intervention" through setting up relevant standards (Doyle 2016, 674, emphasis in original).
17 It is interesting to note that in the cases of Rwanda, Srebrenica, and Sri Lanka, major UN inquiries into the response of the international community were initiated; in the cases of Myanmar and Syria, no inquiries have been initiated. The results of the first two inquiries paved the way for R2P, and the third for the Human Rights up Front initiative. An inquiry into the international responses to the situations in Myanmar and Syria, as well as regular inquiries into other similar cases, would help to improve atrocity prevention.
18 In an increasingly interdependent world, it is hard to imagine a situation when atrocity crimes would not threaten international peace and security.
19 Indeed, productive conceptual debate relies on constant input derived from practical experiences. Critical evaluation contributes much more to fine-tuning of the concept and its operationalization than just an entirely academic debate.
20 To confirm such a trend, it is crucial that future reports continue in the same direction.
21 Yearly interactive dialogues have meanwhile been informal, with no official record.
22 The "evolutionary defect" is a much broader problem, negatively affecting the UN's overall ability to adapt to changes in its operating environment.
23 The President of the Security Council plays a significant role in shaping its thematic discussions. It is not uncommon for a member of the Group of Friends of R2P to hold the presidency; such a state should show leadership by calling for a thematic discussion on atrocity prevention.

24 In 2017, the United Nations Office on Genocide Prevention and the Responsibility to Protect circulated a paper to all permanent missions in Geneva, with practical proposals on how this could be done.
25 This initiative is aimed at mobilizing cultural, organizational, and political change and bringing all three UN pillars closer together to stand firmly for human rights and recommit to core values of the UN.
26 It will not be easy. Even this rather dry and common-sense-based reform package has been met with resistance by some member states.
27 The first reactions of the EU Commission when these ideas were presented to them have been very encouraging.
28 The support of regional organizations, as well as neighboring and other states that are influential, is of utmost importance.
29 Studies have shown that robust mandates and larger missions, in terms of budget and troop strength, have greater impact in terms of minimizing civilian deaths.
30 Reactions of parliamentarians to these proposals at the annual meeting of the Parliamentarians for Global Action network in Milan in November 2017 were very encouraging. The network's secretariat circulated to its members a practical guidance note for parliamentarians, prepared by the Office on Genocide Prevention and the Responsibility to Protect.
31 This may require negotiating, adopting, and ratifying an optional protocol to the Convention.
32 During the first phase of the research, eight country situations have been studied to identify which measures work best to prevent atrocity crimes.
33 To be productive, conceptual and operational debates should be based on critical evaluation of practical experiences.

References

Ban Ki-moon, 2009. "Implementing the Responsibility to Protect: Report of the Secretary-General," A/63/677, January 12.

Ban Ki-moon, 2014. "Fulfilling Our Collective Responsibility: International Assistance and the Responsibility to Protect: Report of the Secretary-General," A/68/947–S/2014/449, July 11.

Ban Ki-moon, 2015. "A Vital and Enduring Commitment: Implementing the Responsibility to Protect," A/69/981–S/2015/500, July 13.

Bellamy, Alex J., and Edward C. Luck, 2018. *The Responsibility to Protect: From Promise to Practice* (Cambridge: Polity Press).

Broderick, Elizabeth, 2015. "Creating a More Gender Equal World: Reflecting on 8 Years as the Sex Discrimination Commissioner," Speech, National Press Club, Canberra, September 2, https://www.humanrights.gov.au/about/news/speeches/creating-more-gender-equal-world-reflecting-8-years-sex-discrimination.

Columbia Global Policy Initiative, 2015. *Responsibility While Protecting: Implementation and Future of the Responsibility to Protect*, Conference Report (New York: Columbia Global Policy Initiative, April).

Doyle, Michael W., 2016. "The Politics of Global Humanitarianism: R2P Before and After Libya," in Alex J. Bellamy and Tim Dunn, eds, *The Oxford Handbook of the Responsibility to Protect* (Oxford: Oxford University Press), 673–90.

Guterres, António, 2017. "Implementing the Responsibility to Protect: Accountability for Prevention: Report of the Secretary-General," A/71/1016–S/2017/556, August 10.

Guterres, António, 2018a. "Responsibility to Protect: From Early Warning to Early Action: Report of the Secretary-General," A/72/884–S/2018/525, June 1.

Guterres, António, 2018b. "Secretary-General's Address to the Opening Ceremony of the 30th Ordinary Session of the Assembly of the African Union [As Delivered]," Addis Ababa, January 28, https://www.un.org/sg/en/content/sg/statement/2018-01-28/secretary-generals-address-opening-ceremony-30th-ordinary-session.

Independent International Commission on Kosovo, 2000. *The Kosovo Report: Conflict, International Response, Lessons Learned* (Oxford: Oxford University Press).

"Kigali Principles on the Protection of Civilians and the Responsibility to Protect," 2016. September 21, https://reliefweb.int/report/world/kigali-principles-protection-civilians-and-responsibility-protect.

United Nations General Assembly, 2005. "2005 World Summit Outcome," A/60/L.1, September 20.

United Nations General Assembly, 2017. "Organization of the Seventy-Second Regular Session of the General Assembly, Adoption of the Agenda and Allocation of Items," A/72/250, September 13.

United Nations High Commissioner for Refugees, 2018. *Global Trends: Forced Displacement in 2017* (Geneva: United Nations High Commissioner for Refugees).

Uppsala Conflict Data Program, n.d. http://ucdp.uu.se/.

Von Einsiedel, Sebastian, with Louise Bosetti, James Cockayne, Cale Salih, and Wilfred Wan, 2017. *Civil War Trends and the Changing Nature of Armed Conflict*, Occasional Paper 10 (Tokyo: United Nations University Centre for Policy Research).

INDEX

Note: Page numbers in **bold** indicate tables.

accountability: human rights, defined 186; R2P implementation and 7–8
Action Plan for Africa 119
ACWC *see* ASEAN Commission on the Promotion and Protection of the Rights of Women and Children (ACWC)
affinity variable 148
Afghanistan, civil-military relations in: from 1978–2001 238–41; overview of 236–8; post-2001 developments 241–4; rebuilding responsibility and 244–6; warlords/strongman governors and 242
African R2P implementation: capacity and 116; challenges, regional level 114–16; effective, argument for 110–12; introduction to 109–10; legitimacy and 116; nation-states experiences in 116–18; non-state local actors and 118–20; political will and 116–17; at regional level 112–16; state weakness and 117–18
African Union-United Nations Mission in Darfur (UNAMID) 215
Ahmadzai, Najibullah 239–40
AHRD *see* ASEAN Human Rights Declaration (AHRD)
AICHR *see* ASEAN Inter-Governmental Commission on Human Rights (AICHR)
AIPR *see* ASEAN Institute for Peace and Reconciliation (AIPR)
Akhromeev, Marshal Sergei 239

al-Assad, Bashar 182
Albar, Syed Hamid 99
Albright, Madeleine K. 20, 78
al Hussein, Zeid Ra'ad 42, 66–7
amnesties, as transitional justice mechanism 201, 202, 206, **207**
Aning, Kwesi 115
Annan, Kofi 100, 109, 143, 144, 190
APB *see* Atrocities Prevention Board (APB)
ASEAN *see* Association of Southeast Asian Nations (ASEAN)
ASEAN Commission on the Promotion and Protection of the Rights of Women and Children (ACWC) 90, 158, 161
ASEAN-Emergency Rapid Assessment Team (ASEAN-ERAT) 97
ASEAN Human Rights Declaration (AHRD) 92–4, **93–4**
ASEAN Institute for Peace and Reconciliation (AIPR) 90, 158
ASEAN Inter-Governmental Commission on Human Rights (AICHR) 90, **91**, 158
Asia Foundation 241
Asia Pacific Centre for the Responsibility to Protect (APCR2P), University of Queensland 158
Association of Southeast Asian Nations (ASEAN) 10; achievements/challenges to implementing R2P by 102–5; ACWC creation, joint statements/declarations through 161; advancing WPS and

165–66; as champion of R2P and WPS engagement 161–63; Commission on the Promotion and Protection of the Rights of Women and Children 90; Committee on Disaster Management 97; human protection principles, overview of 90–5; Human Rights Declaration 92–4, **93–4**; Institute for Peace and Reconciliation 90; Inter-Governmental Commission on Human Rights 90, **91**; introduction to 89–90; Myanmar events and 95–102; women's human rights advocates within (see Women, Peace and Security (WPS))
Atrocities Prevention Board (APB) 20, 62; establishment of 63–5
atrocity crime: crimes against humanity as 16, 17; genocide as 16, 17; R2P response to 252–53; war crimes as 16, 17
atrocity prevention: ASEAN (see Association of Southeast Asian Nations (ASEAN)); crimes-based approach to 21–2; development cooperation and 46; direct prevention frameworks 19; human rights-based approach to 22–3; Human Rights Council and 259; local non-state actors in 118–20; national resilience and (see national resilience strengthening, atrocity prevention and); nation-states effectiveness in 116–18; under Obama, Barack (see Obama administration, atrocity prevention under); operational prevention frameworks 19; prioritizing 23–5; Southeast Asian women in (see Women, Peace and Security (WPS)); structural prevention frameworks 19
atrocity prevention, R2P as framework for: crimes-based approach 21–2; General Assembly and 29–30; human rights-based approach 22–3; institutionalizing 25–30; mass atrocities, defining 17–19; overview of 16–17; prioritizing, in institutional context 23–5; Secretariat and 29; Security Council and 27–8; strategic thinking about 19–21; United Nations conceptualization of 21–3; violence types associated with 16
Atuobi, Samuel 115
Aung San Suu Kyi 66, 92

Banholzer, Lilli 202
Ban Ki-moon 24, 29, 111, 117, 152, 157, 260; "Implementing the Responsibility to Protect" report 145; "Responsibility to Protect: State Responsibility and Prevention, The" report 145–47; on strengthening national resilience 141
Barmaki, Hamida 243
Barrow, Adama 115
Bashir, Omar 79
Baylouny, Anne Marie 119
Bellamy, Alex 27, 114, 151
Bensouda, Fatou 164
Biden, Joe 73
Bin Laden, Osama 241
Blinken, Tony 69, 70
Boutros-Ghali, Boutros 25; "An Agenda for Peace" report 142
Bozize, Francois 69
BRICS (Brazil, Russia, India, China, and South Africa) 182
Brunnée, Jutta 26
Buddhist-led protests in Myanmar, ASEAN and 95–7
Burundi, atrocity prevention in 67–9

capacity, as feature of effective atrocity prevention 116
capacity-building to prevent violence against women 166–69
Carnegie Commission on Preventing Deadly Conflict 143
Center for Global Development 79
Central African Republic, atrocity prevention in 69–71
Centre for the Prevention of Genocide 40
civil-military relations, R2P and see Afghanistan, civil-military relations in
Clinton, Hillary 63
Code of Conduct Regarding Security Council Action Against Genocide, Crimes Against Humanity or War Crimes 28
Cohen, William S. 20
Colville, Rupert 240–41
Committee on Economic, Social and Cultural Rights 188
Comprehensive Strategy for Atrocity Prevention 64
conflict prevention, institutionalizing 25–30; General Assembly and 29–30; High-Level Independent Panel on UN Peace Operations assessment 25–6; Secretariat and 29; Security Council and 27–8
Convention against Torture 188
Convention on the Elimination of All Forms of Discrimination against Women 188

270 Index

Convention on the Elimination of All Forms of Discrimination Against Women 160; Resolution 1325 170
Convention on the Rights of the Child 188
Coomaraswamy, Radhika 171
Côte d'Ivoire, application of R2P to 181, 215
crimes against humanity 74–5; as atrocity crime 16, 17
crimes-based approach to atrocity prevention 21–2
Cyclone Nargis, ASEAN and 92, 97–8

Dancy, Geoff 201, 208
DDR programs, as transitional justice mechanism 198, 201–2, 203, 208
Democratic Republic of the Congo, protection of civilians in 224–25
Deng, Francis 109
Denmark, implementation of R2P in: approach used for 38–40; civil society and 40; development cooperation and 46–52; future recommendations for 53–6; Global Network of R2P Focal Points 9; human rights and 40–6; Human Rights Council and 42–6; lessons learned from 52–3; mainstreaming outside Denmark and 55–6; outreach programs for 55; overview of 37–8; R2P Focal Points, international network of 39, 54
Department of Peace Operations 24
Department of Political and Peacebuilding Affairs (DPPA) 24, 29
Desti Murdijana 166–67
development cooperation: added value of R2P and 46–8; atrocity prevention needs, addressing 50; atrocity risks, timely/flexible responses to 50–1; dialogue/peaceful settlement of disputes, support 51; future atrocity crimes, focus on 50; human rights mechanisms/documentation processes for 51; integrating R2P into 48–52; international/local cooperation 52; localize development programming 51–2; programming assessments, atrocity-prevention risk factors for 51; R2P in Denmark and 46–52
direct conflict-related battle deaths, as violence type 201
direct prevention frameworks 19, 22
disarmament, demobilization, and reintegration (DDR) 198, 201–2, 203, 208

Dorronsoro, Gilles 240
Dostam, Abdul Rashid 240
DPPA *see* Department of Political and Peacebuilding Affairs (DPPA)
Duterte, Rodrigo 164

Economic Community of Central African States (ECCAS) 69, 112
Economic Community of West African States (ECOWAS) 112–13, 114–15
ethnic cleansing: as atrocity crime 16; in 1990s 18
EU Programme for the Prevention of Violent Conflicts 126
European Centre for the Responsibility to Protect's Women Network 160
European Consensus on Development 126
European Consensus on Humanitarian Aid 126
European External Action Service 124, 127
European Genocide Network 132
European normative leadership, R2P and 127–29
European Union (EU), R2P in: European Council endorsement of 126; Focal Point on 126; internal contestation, challenges with 131–33; introduction to 124–25; meaningful R2P leadership roles, prospects for 133–35; normative leadership and 127–29; normative power Europe and 129–31; World Summit Outcome document and role of 125–27
Experts Group on Darfur 187

factors, defined 186
Freedom's Concept Note on Integrating Gender Perspectives 159

GAAMAC *see* Global Action Against Mass Atrocity Crimes (GAAMAC)
Gaddafi, Muammar 28, 179
Gambari, Ibrahim 96
Gates, Robert 63
Gbagbo, Laurent 71, 115, 181
Gender Equality Network (GEN) 167–68
General Assembly: conflict prevention and 29–30; R2P dialogues 30; Uniting for Peace procedure 29–30
genocide: Albright and Cohen definition of 20; as atrocity crime 16, 17; concept *vs.* mass atrocity concept 17–18; definition of 3; in 1990s 18; studies, negative cases in comparative 147–50
Genocide Prevention Task Force 20, 61
Gerlach, Christian 197

Ghani, Ashraf 242
Global Action Against Mass Atrocity Crimes (GAAMAC) 9, 40, 43
Global Action to Prevent War 159
Global Centre for the Responsibility to Protect 39, 40
Global Magnitsky Human Rights Accountability Act 74
Global Network of R2P Focal Points 9
Group of Friends for R2P 42–3, 262
Guterres, António 4, 24, 29, 157, 260

Haines, Avril 77
Hammarskjold, Dag 261
harmony and non-racialism principle 149
Hekmatyar, Gulbuddin 240
"Helping Prevent Mass Atrocities" (USAID) 46
Hezb-e Wahdat 240
horizontal violence 201
host-state consent, managing challenge of 227–28
humanism 149
humanitarian intervention 2, 3, 27, 75, 78, 131, 199
human rights accountability, defined 186
human rights accountability, R2P implementation and: concept of 186–87; Côte d'Ivoire application 181; introduction to 179; legal obligation of 184–86; Libya application 179–81; mechanisms for 187–90; status of discussion on states' 183–84; Syria application 181–83; UNSC action on 190–92
human rights approach to atrocity prevention 22–3; ASEAN 90–5; in Denmark 40–6; R2P and 41–2
Human Rights Council (HRC) 4, 7, 23, 24–5; Côte d'Ivoire and 181; fact-finding reports 189; integrating R2P into Danish work at 42–6; Libya and 180; resolutions of, lack of clarity in 183; special procedures mandate holders of 188, 259; Sri Lanka and 188; Syria and 182; Universal Periodic Review (UPR) 42, 94, 161, 186, 188–89, 259, 262
Human Rights up Front (HRuF) initiative 3–4, 24, 25, 52, 190, 260
Human Rights Watch 240

ICC *see* International Criminal Court (ICC)
ICGLR *see* International Conference on the Great Lakes Region (ICGLR)
ICISS *see* International Commission on Intervention and State Sovereignty (ICISS)
IGAD *see* Intergovernmental Authority on Development (IGAD)
implementing R2P, challenges of: accountability and 7–8; decision-making processes/institutional architectures 7; international implementation 6; introduction to 1–2; mass atrocities, social/political contexts of 6–7; normative concept to preventive policy 3–4
"Implementing the Responsibility to Protect" (Ban report) 145
Intergovernmental Authority on Development (IGAD) 112
Internal Review Panel on United Nations Action in Sri Lanka 24
International Atrocity Prevention Working Group 38–9
International Coalition for the Responsibility to Protect 40, 48
International Commission on Intervention and State Sovereignty (ICISS) 16, 110, 128
International Conference on the Great Lakes Region (ICGLR) 112
International Convention on the Elimination of All Forms of Racial Discrimination 188, 189
International Covenant on Civil and Political Rights 188, 189
International Criminal Court (ICC): atrocity prevention and 72–3; Rome Statute 17, 74–5; transitional justice and 199–200
International Security Assistance Force (ISAF) 242
Islamic State of Iraq and Syria (ISIS) 236

Jammeh, Yahya 115

Kagame, Paul 68
Karmal, Babrak 239
Karzai, Hamid 242
Kaunda, Kenneth 149
Khama, Seretse 149
Khan, Ismail 242
Khan, Matiullah 246
Kigali Principles on the Protection of Civilians 227, 261
Kofi Annan International Peacekeeping Training Centre 39
Koh, Harold 78
Komnas Perempuan 166–67
Konaré, Alpha Oumar 147

Kony, Joseph 73
Kouchner, Bernard 97

Latif, Haji Abdul 242
Latin American Network for Genocide and Mass Atrocity Prevention 43
legitimacy, as feature of effective atrocity prevention 116
Liberi, Dawn 68
Libya: application of R2P to 179–81; R2P intervention in 3
Lisbon Treaty 126, 127

Macapagal-Arroyo, Gloria 96
Magna Carta of Women, Republic Act 9710 163
manifest failure 187
Manners, Ian 129, 134
mass atrocities: crisis events as triggers of 19; defining 17–19; social/political contexts and R2P implementation 6–7; strategic thinking about, prevention 19–21; studies of 18
Massoud, Ahmad Shah 240
Mayersen, Deborah 147–48
Medvedev, Dmitry 78
Midlarsky, Manus 148–49
Mitchell, Derek 65–6
multilateral peacekeeping and reform 73
Myanmar: ASEAN atrocities prevention and 95–102; Buddhist-led protests and 95–7; Cyclone Nargis and 97–8, 167; Gender Equality Network 167–68; Rakhine communal conflict and 98–102; Rakhine State crisis 65–7

National Action Plans (NAPs), WPS 163–64; Philippines 163–64
National Intelligence Estimate atrocity prevention tool 72
National Peace Council Act of 2011 120
national R2P implementation mechanisms: in Denmark (see Denmark, implementation of R2P in); Obama administration (see Obama administration, atrocity prevention under)
national resilience strengthening, atrocity prevention and: Ban's 2013 report and 145–47; genocide studies, negative cases in 147–50; implementation, Pillar One and 150–52; overview of 141–42; Pillar One and 141, 142–45
National Strategic Plan for the Advancement of Women 167–68

nature of state, as feature of effective atrocity prevention 117–18
Nkurunziza, Pierre 67–8
normative leadership in Europe, R2P and 127–29
normative power Europe: concept of 130, 134; contestation within Europe over 131–33; R2P and 129–31
Ntaganda, Bosco 73
Nuremberg Declaration on Peace and Justice 200
Nyerere, Julius 149

Obama, Barack 9, 187; Atrocities Prevention Board 20, 142; atrocity prevention under (see Obama administration, atrocity prevention under); Presidential Study Directive 10 38, 62; United States Holocaust Memorial Museum speech 61
Obama administration, atrocity prevention under: Atrocities Prevention Board, establishment of 63–5; blueprint for 61–3; Burundi and 67–9; capacity surge from 76–7; capacity-tool development by 71–5; Central African Republic and 69–71; communications and 80–1; failed proposed tools 73–5; future recommendations for 81–2; intelligence for options and 77; International Criminal Court support 72–3; introduction to 61; multilateral action and 77–9; multilateral peacekeeping and reform 73; National Intelligence Estimate tool 72; negative responses to 77–81; positive praises for 76–7; pragmatism and 80; Rakhine State crisis and 65–7; suspension of entry tool 71–2
Ong Keng Yong 96
Ongwen, Dominic 73
operational prevention frameworks 19, 143
Opération des Nations Unies au Congo (ONUC) mission 224
Operation Enduring Freedom 237, 244
Operation Resolute Support 237
Ouattara, Alassane 181

Palava Hut system of conflict resolution 120
Parliamentary Monitoring Group 119
Patriota, Antonio 28
peacekeeping: consensus on future of 228–29; expansion and reform 73
peacekeeping operations, implementing R2P through UN: Democratic Republic of the Congo example of 224–25; future of peacekeeping, consensus development

Index **273**

of 228–29; ground realities, developing policy and addressing 220–21; host-state consent, managing challenge of 227–28; introduction to 215–17; politics and principles debate 219–20; protection agenda 225–29; protection of civilians in 217–19; South Sudan example of 222–24; strengthening peacekeeping 226–27
peace-*versus*-justice debate 80
Philippine Development Plan 2011–2016 163
Pillar One of R2P, overview of 5, 157; *see also* Pillars of R2P
Pillars of R2P: atrocity prevention and 52, 118, 141, 142–45; Denmark, development cooperation and 46–52; Denmark, human rights and 40–46; Denmark and implementation of, lessons learned from 52–56; in developing policy and addressing ground realities 220–21; Europe Union and 125–26, 133–34; implementing 39, 45, 115, 150–52, 226; integrating into Danish work at UN Human Rights Council 43–46; oversimplified interpretations of 219; overview of 5, 157; peacekkeping and 226, 228; statebuilding and 222; transitional justice mechanisms 199
Pillar Three of R2P, overview of 5, 157; *see also* Pillars of R2P
Pillar Two of R2P, overview of 5, 157; *see also* Pillars of R2P
Political Terror Scale (PTS) 202
political will, as feature of effective atrocity prevention 116–17
Power, Samantha 62, 68–9
Pressman, David 63
Prevention of Violence Against Women Bill 168
Problem from Hell, A (Power) 62, 78, 82
Prorok, Alyssa 200
protection of civilians (POC) mandates 215, 217–19; strengthening peacekeeping and 226–27
Provincial Reconstruction Teams (PRTs) 237
Putin, Vladimir 78

R2P *see* Responsibility to Protect (R2P)
Rakhine State crisis 65–7
Rashid, Ahmed 240
Resolutions, UNSC *see* United Nations Security Council (UNSC)
Responsibility to Protect (R2P): advantages demonstrated by 256; African experiences of (*see* African R2P implementation); ASEAN (*see* Association of Southeast Asian Nations (ASEAN)); as atrocity prevention framework (*see* atrocity prevention, R2P as framework for); atrocity situations, responding to 252–53; challenges/opportunities in implementing 258–62; civil-military relations and (*see* Afghanistan, civil-military relations in); at a crossroads 251–52; development cooperation and, in Denmark 46–52; effective implementation of 110–12; in Europe (*see* European Union (EU), R2P in); gendered approach to (*see* Women, Peace and Security (WPS)); Group of Friends for 42–3; human rights and 41–2 (*see also* human rights accountability, R2P implementation and); "Human Rights up Front" initiative and 3–4; ICISS version of 128; implementation in Denmark 38–40 (*see also* Denmark, implementation of R2P in); implementing, challenges of (*see* implementing R2P, challenges of); implementing through UN peacekeeping operations (*see* peacekeeping operations, implementing R2P through UN); international, implementation of 6; interventions, successful 2; in Libya 3; literature, overview of 4–5; from normative concept to preventive policy 3–4; normative power Europe and 129–31; operationalization, need for 4; Pillars of 5, 39, 43, 45, 141, 157; practical guidance for, development of 53–4; priority countries, establish internal list of 53; protection of civilians and 216–17; recommendations for improving effectiveness of 257–58; resilience context of (*see* national resilience strengthening, atrocity prevention and); transitional justice role in 198–99, 207–9; value of, to international community 253–56
Responsibility to Protect, The (ICISS) 143
"Responsibility to Protect: State Responsibility and Prevention, The" (Ban report) 145–47
Responsibility While Protecting initiative 28, 229
Rewards for Justice (RFJ) Program 72
Rhodes, Ben 76
Rice, Susan 69
risks, defined 186
root causes, structural prevention and 143–44

Rosenberg, Sheri 182
R2P Focal Points 39; strengthening 54

Sandoval, Maria Cleofe Gettie 163
Sayyaf, Abdul Rab al-Rasoul 240
Secretariat, conflict prevention and 29
Security Council *see* United Nations Security Council (UNSC)
Senghor, Leopold 147
Sherzai, Gul Agha 242
social crime prevention 22
South African Development Community (SADC) 112
Southeast Asian women in atrocity prevention; *see also* Women, Peace and Security (WPS): ASEAN and 161–63; capacity-building, preventing violence against women through 166–69; future alignment/engagement recommendations 170–72; national/regional violence against women prevention 163–66; regional WPS networks, prioritizing 169–70; WPS and R2P agendas, relationship between 157–61
South Sudan, statebuilding and protection of civilians in 222–24
Special Adviser on the Prevention of Genocide 39, 55, 145, 190, 252
state violence, as violence type 201
Strand, Arne 237
Straus, Scott 18, 147
structural prevention frameworks 19, 143–44
Suhrke, Astri 237
Sullivan, Jake 76
suspension of entry atrocity prevention tool 71–2
Suu Kyi 101–2
Syria, application of R2P to 181–83

Taliban 240–41; overthrow of 241–42; Pakistani 243–44
terrorist attacks by non-state groups, as violence type 201
Thakur, Ramesh 243
Thein Sein 66
threats, defined 186
Toope, Stephen 26
Touadera, Faustin 70
Touré, Ahmed Sékou 147
transitional justice: as backward-looking social process 198–200; external factors and 206; introduction to 197–98; mechanisms, described 201; presence of, after conflict 203, **204**; role of, within R2P framework 207–9; start of, timing 205, **205**; state and non-state actors 206, **207**; study, described 200–202; study results 202–7
Transitional Justice Database Project 202
Treaty on European Union 127
trials, as transitional justice mechanism 201, 202
Trump, Donald J. 74, 244
truth (and reconciliation) commissions (TRCs), as transitional justice mechanism 201, 202

Ujamaa 149
UNAMID *see* African Union-United Nations Mission in Darfur (UNAMID)
United Nations: crimes-based approach to atrocity prevention 21–2; Framework of Analysis for Atrocity Crimes 41; General Assembly 1; High Commissioner for Human Rights 188, 190; Human Rights Council 23, 42; Human Rights up Front initiative 24, 25, 52; institutionalization of R2P across 17 (*see also* atrocity prevention, R2P as framework for); Mission in South Sudan (UNMISS) 222–24; Mission in Sudan (UNMIS) 222; Multidimensional Integrated Stabilization Mission in the Central African Republic (MINUSCA) 215; Operation in Côte d'Ivoire (UNOCI) 181, 215; Organization Mission in the Democratic Republic of the Congo (MONUC) 224–25; Organization Stabilization Mission in the Democratic Republic of the Congo (MONUSCO) 224–25; peacekeeping operations (*see* peacekeeping operations, implementing R2P through UN); R2P implementation and 16; Security Council (UNSC) 1, 179; Special Adviser on the Prevention of Genocide 39, 55, 145, 190, 252; Working Party (CONUN) 40; *see also* Human Rights Council (HRC); United Nations Security Council (UNSC)
United Nations Security Council (UNSC): R2P applied to Libya, Côte d'Ivoire, and Syria 179–83; R2P implementation mechanisms 187–90; Resolution 1325 156, 158, 163, 170; Resolution 1366 190; Resolution 1820 156; Resolution 1968 181; Resolution 1970 180, 191, 192; Resolution 1973 28, 179–82, 191, 192; Resolution 1975 181; Resolution 2150 189, 192; Resolution 2282 24; reviewing action on implementation of R2P 190–92

United States: Agency for International Development (USAID) 46, 68; atrocity prevention language of 20; Mission to the United Nations (USUN) 68; Obama administration's mass atrocities prevention 9–10
US Holocaust Memorial Museum 40
Universal Periodic Review (UPR) 42, 94, 161, 186, 188–89, 259, 262

Veneracion-Rallonza, Lourdes 168–69
violence: types of 201; against women, preventing 163–64
Violent Societies Index (VSI) 202

war crimes, as atrocity crime 16, 17
warlord 242
Weinstein, Jeremy 76
Welsh, Jennifer 17, 22, 160

Women, Peace and Security (WPS) 4; advancing, ASEAN architecture and 165–66; ASEAN and 161–63; capacity-building to prevent violence against women 166–69; future alignment/engagement areas for R2P and 170–72; introduction to 156–57; National Action Plans 163–64; Philippines National Steering Committee on 163; R2P and, policy/research alignment between 157–61; regional networks on, prioritizing 169–70
Women Network on the Responsibility to Protect, Peace and Security 159
Women's International League for Peace 159
WPS *see* Women, Peace and Security (WPS)

Yang-hee Lee 101
Yuyun Wahyuningrum 165

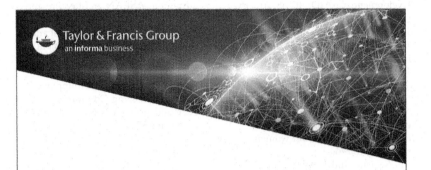